Webster's Concise

WORLD
ATLAS

and ALMANAC

Webster's Concise

WORLD ATLAS
and ALMANAC

CHATHAM RIVER PRESS
New York

Maps, text and index prepared and printed by Kartografie,
Prague, Czechoslovakia

Cartographic Editor:
RNDr. Jiří Novotný
Technical Editor:
Marie Pánková

This edition published in 1987 by Chatham River Press
in association with Macdonald Orbis, a division of
Macdonald & Co (Publishers) Ltd, London & Sydney

Reprinted in 1989
Distributed by Crown Publishers, Inc.

Library of Congress Cataloging in Publication Data
Main entry under title:
Webster's Concise world atlas and almanac.
    "Copyright Kartografie, Prague, 1981" — Verso t.p.
    Previously published as: Orbis pocket encyclopedia
of the world. London: Orbis Publishing, 1981.
    Includes index.
    1. Atlases. I. Kartografie (Firm) II. Title: Concise
world atlas and almanac.
G1021.W38, 1987   912   85-675001
ISBN 0-517-47413-1

hgfedcb

CONTENTS

METRIC CONVERSION TABLE

The metric system is used throughout this encyclopedia. The following guide provides approximate U.S. equivalents for all quantities.

Altitude and *depth* are measured in meters (m). To convert to feet, multiply by 3.28:

$$1 \text{ m} = 3.28 \text{ feet}$$

Mt. Kilimanjaro is 5,895 m, or about 19,336 feet, high.

Distance is generally measured in kilometers (km), or thousands of meters. To convert to miles, multiply by 0.621:

$$1 \text{ km} = 1,000 \text{ m} = 0.621 \text{ mile}.$$

In 1982 Peru had 2,740 km, or 1,702 miles, of railways.
Note: Most maps contain a scale with kilometers and miles.

Rainfall is measured in millimeters (mm), or thousandths of a meter. To convert to inches, multiply by 0.04:

$$1 \text{ mm} = 0.001 \text{ m} = 0.0394 \text{ inch}$$

The annual rainfall in Chicago is 843 mm, or 33.21 inches.

Area is generally measured in square kilometers (sq.km). To convert to square miles, multiply by 0.386:

$$1 \text{ sq.km} = 0.386 \text{ square mile}$$

Cuba occupies 114,524 sq.km, or about 44,206 square miles.
Area is measured in square meters (sq.m) and hectares (ha):

$$1 \text{ sq.m} = 10.76 \text{ square feet}$$
$$1 \text{ ha} = 10,000 \text{ sq.m} = 2.47 \text{ acres}$$

Weight is measured in kilogrammes (kg) and tonnes (= 1,000 kg):

$$1 \text{ kg} = 2.205 \text{ pounds}$$
$$1 \text{ tonne} = 0.984 \text{ long ton, or} = 1.102 \text{ short tons}$$

Volume is measured in cubic meters; 1 cub.m = 35.32 cubic feet

Capacity is measured in liters (l) and hectoliters (hl):

$$1 \text{ l} = 61.02 \text{ cubic inches} = 1.06 \text{ quarts}$$
$$1 \text{ hl} = 3.53 \text{ cubic feet} = 26.4 \text{ gallons}$$

Temperature is measured in degrees centigrade (°C). To convert to Fahrenheit, multiply by 1.8 and add 32:

$$(1.8)°C + 32 = °F$$

The mean July temperature in Manila is 26.9°C, or 80.42°F.

Natural gas is measured in joule (J), $TJ = 10^{12} J$ and $PJ = 10^{15} J$. A terajoule is a measure of energy equivalent to 23.46 tonnes of oil or 34.13 tonnes of coal.

EXPLANATION

CITIES AND TOWNS

British Isles

⊜	**LONDON**	over 1,000,000 inhabitants
◉	**GLASGOW**	500,000 -1,000,000 inhabitants
◎	Belfast	100,000-500,000 inhabitants
⊙	Bath	50,000-100,000 inhabitants
○	Perth	20,000-50,000 inhabitants
○	Douglas	less than 20,000 inhabitants

Other Maps

⊜	**NEW YORK**	over 1,000,000 inhabitants
◉	**CALGARY**	500,000-1,000,000 inhabitants
◎	Utrecht	100,000-500,000 inhabitants
⊙	Calais	50,000-100,000 inhabitants
○	Gibraltar	less than 50,000 inhabitants

Physical and World Maps

○	Ottawa

<u>Canberra</u>	National Capitals

CANADA Ind

Victoria Po
Ot

St. Helena
(U.K.) Ac

BC

— · — · —   Int

— · · — · ·   Bo

· · · · · · · · · ·   Ot

— · · — · ·   Bo
De

— — — —   Dis

— + — + —   Bo

TP

————   Ra

— — — —   Ra

—) - - (—   Tu

· · · · · · · · · · ·   Tra

OF SYMBOLS

...lent States	*Nile*	Streams with Falls (Rapids)
...Units, ...rritories		Seasonal Streams
...tering Country		Principal Canals
	L.Huron	Lakes
...ARIES		Seasonal Lakes
...onal Boundaries		Marshes, Swamps
		Salt Flats
...ies of Federal States		Reefs
		Glaciers
...undaries	**A l p s**	Ranges, Mountains
	Mt. Everest 8848	Peaks, Heights in metres
...ies of International ...ncy Claims	· 5098	Depths in metres
	Sahara	Deserts, Lowlands, Plateaus, Pans
...ll Boundaries		

HEIGHTS ABOVE SEA LEVEL

Map of the World and Polar Regions

Below Sea Level   0   200   500   2000   5000 m

...ies of National Parks

Maps of Continents and Other Maps

Below Sea Level   0   200   500   1000   2000   4000   6000 m

...ORT

British Isles

Below Sea Level   0   100   200   500   1000   2000 m

...under Construction

DEPTHS

0   200   2000   4000   6000   8000 m

...ies

TIME ZONES OF THE WORLD

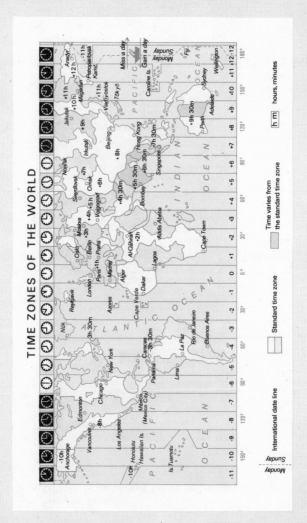

h m hours, minutes

Time varies from the standard time zone

Standard time zone

International date line

map 1

The Orbit of the Earth around the Sun

March 21
Vernal Equinox

Spring

Winter

June 21
Summer
Solstice

147 000 000 km
Sun

Dec. 21
Winter
Solstice

152 000 000 km

Summer

Autumn

Sept 23
Autumnal Equinox

The position of stars on the celestial sphere and the position of places on Earth

The coordinates of stars and the geographical coordinates. The position of places on the Earth is given by the **geographical coordinates** (λ, φ). **The geographical longitude** λ (lambda) is measured from the zero (Greenwich) meridian to the meridian of given point, to the West positively and to the East negatively, always from 0° to 180°. **The geographical latitude** φ (phi) is measured from the equator to the North positively and to the South negatively, always from 0° to 90°.

The position of stars is generally determined by using the equatorial coordinates (α, δ). They are analogous with the geographical ones. On the celestial sphere above the Earth's equator is the celestial equator. The position of Greenwich as a beginning point takes on the sphere **the first point of Aries** (vernal point) – the intersection of the celestial equator and the ecliptic in the place where Sun is going through the vernal equinox (its opposite is the autumnal point). Analogous with the geographical meridians are so-called declination circles; such circles go through both celestial poles and are perpendicular to the celestial equator. The equatorial coordinates are illustrated on the picture above.

The right ascension α (alpha) is an angle on the celestial equator measured from the vernal point to the declination circle of a given point. The right ascension is measured to the East from 0 to 24 hours (or from 0° to 360°).
The declination δ (delta) is an angle measured from the celestial equator to a given star, from 0° to 90° to the North positively and to the South negatively.

THE NORTHERN SKY

map 2

THE MOON

Distance from the Earth:	perigee	364 000 km
	mean	384 400 km
	apogee	406 700 km
Orbital velocity		3 680 km/h (1.02 km/s)
Diameter		3 476 km (0.27 Earth's diameter)
Mass		0.0123 Earth's mass
Mean density		3 340 kg/m³ (0.60 mean Earth's density)
Surface temperature:	daytime +130°C	
	nightime −150°C	
Surface gravity		1.62 m/s² (0.165 Earth's gravity)
circular velocity (at the surface) 1.7 km/s		
parabolic velocity (at the surface) 2.4 km/s		
Sidereal month 27.321 661 days		
Synodic month 29.530 588 days		
Extreme libration: in latitude 6°50′, in longitude 7°54′		

*Almost 59 % of the Moon's surface can be observed from the Earth; 18 %
is visible only at certain times and 41 % can never be seen from the Earth.
Nevertheless, the whole of the Moon has been mapped (except for 1% of its
surface) by means of space probes*

THE MOON'S PHASES

The Moon does not shine by its own light; one of its hemispheres is illuminated by the
Sun / a day /, the opposite is in a shadow / a night /. We can see only the part of the
illuminated hemisphere which belongs to the Near Side. All Moon's phases change
through 1 synodic month.

THE ROTATION OF THE MOON

The Moon's period of rotation on its axis is equal to its period of revolution around the
Earth. Therefore the Moon always presents the same face to an observer on the Earth.

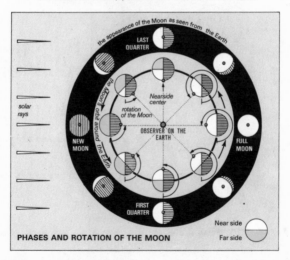

PHASES AND ROTATION OF THE MOON

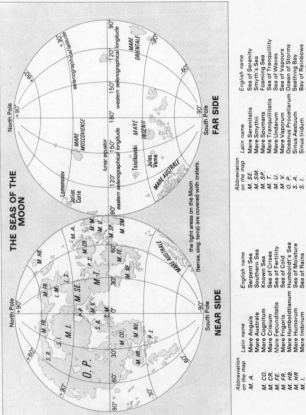

THE SEAS OF THE MOON

the light areas on the Moon (terrae, sing. terra) are covered with craters.

NEAR SIDE

FAR SIDE

Abbreviation on the map	Latin name	English name
M. A.	Mare Anguis	Serpent Sea
	Mare Australe	Southern Sea
M. CO.	Mare Cognitum	Known Sea
M. CR.	Mare Crisium	Sea of Crises
M. FE.	Mare Fecunditatis	Sea of Fertility
M. FR.	Mare Frigoris	Sea of Cold
M. HB.	Mare Humboldtianum	Humboldt's Sea
M. HR.	Mare Humorum	Sea of Moisture
M. HR.	Mare Imbrium	Sea of Rains
M. I.	Mare Ingenii	Sea of Ingenuity
M. M.	Mare Marginis	Border Sea
	Mare Moscoviense	Moscow Sea
M. NE.	Mare Nectaris	Sea of Nectar
M. NU.	Mare Nubium	Sea of Clouds
	Mare Orientale	Eastern Sea

■ on the Far Side of the Moon

Abbreviation on the map	Latin name	English name
M. SE.	Mare Serenitatis	Sea of Serenity
M. SM.	Mare Smythii	Smyth's Sea
M. SP.	Mare Spumans	Foaming Sea
M. T.	Mare Tranquillitatis	Sea of Tranquillity
M. U.	Mare Undarum	Sea of Waves
M. V.	Mare Vaporum	Sea of Vapours
O. P.	Oceanus Procellarum	Ocean of Storms
S. A.	Sinus Aestuum	Seething Bay
S. I.	Sinus Iridum	Bay of Rainbows
S. M.	Sinus Medii	Central Bay
S. R.	Sinus Roris	Bay of Dew
P. E.	Palus Epidemiarum	Marsh of Diseases
P. P.	Palus Putredinis	Marsh of Decay
P. S.	Palus Somni	Marsh of Sleep
L. M.	Lacus Mortis	Lake of Death
L. S.	Lacus Somniorum	Lake of Dreams

WEST

SOLAR

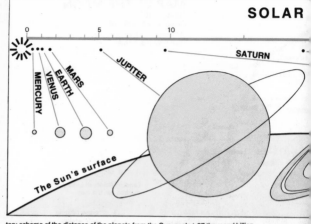

top: scheme of the distance of the planets from the Sun; scale 1:37 thousand billion
botton: relative size of the planets and the Sun; scale 1 : 4.2 billion

PLAN

Planet	Mean distance from the Sun		Sidereal period (years)
	in million km	in astronomical units	
Mercury	57.9	0.387	0.24
Venus	108.2	0.723	0.62
Earth	149.6	1.000	1.00
Mars	227.9	1.524	1.88
Jupiter	778.3	5.205	11.86
Saturn	1432	9.576	29.46
Uranus	2884	19.281	84.01
Neptune	4509	30.142	164.79
Pluto	5966	39.880	247.7

△ Day side   ▲ Night side

SYSTEM

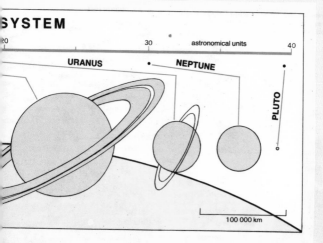

astronomical units

URANUS   NEPTUNE   PLUTO

20   30   40

100 000 km

ETS

Equatorial diameter in km	Mean density (in g/cm³)	Sidereal rotation period	Surface temperature in °C
4,878	5.4	58.6 days	+430 △ −170 ▲
12,102	5.3	243 days	+480
12,756	5.5	23hrs 56mins.	+ 15 ●
6,794	3.9	24hrs 37mins.	− 50 ●
142,800	1.3	9hrs 50mins.	−130 ■
120,000	0.7	10hrs 14mins.	−185 ■
51,200	1.2	17hrs 18mins.	−220 ■
49,500	1.7	15hrs 45mins.?	−200 ■
3,000	1.0?	6.4 days	−230

Mean temperature   ■ Cloud's top

map 3

DIMENSIONS OF THE EARTH

	According to F. N. Krasovskij's ellipsoid	International Ellipsoid (year 1967)
Radius of the Equator (a)	6,378,245 m	6,378,160 m
Radius of the axis (b)	6,356,863 m	6,356,755 m
Flattening of the Earth $\left(\frac{a-b}{b}\right)$	$\frac{1}{298.3}$	$\frac{1}{298.25}$
Circumference of the Equator	40,075,704 m	40,076,600 m
Circumference of one of the meridians	40,008,548 m	40,009,150 m
Total surface area of the Earth	510,083,000 sq.km	510,100,933.5 sq.km
Area of dry land (29.2%)	148,628,000 sq.km	149,408,563 sq.km
Area of sea (70.8%)	361,455,000 sq.km	360,692,370 sq.km
Volume of Earth	1,083,319,780,000 cub.km	1,083,319,780,000 cub.km
Weight of Earth	5.978×10^{24} kg	5.970×10^{24} kg
Area of tropical zone (39.7%)	202,505,000 sq.km	
Area of temperate zones (52%)	265,418,000 sq.km	
Area of polar zones (8.3%)	42,160,000 sq.km	

Chemical composition of the Earth's surface: oxygen 49.13%, silicon 26%, aluminium 7.45%, iron 4.2%, calcium 3.25%, sodium 2.4%, potassium 2.35%, hydrogen 1%, titanium 0.61%, carbon 0.35%, chlorine 0.20%, phosphorus 0.12%, manganese 0.10%, sulphur 0.10%, fluorine 0.08%, barium 0.05%, nitrogen 0.04%, etc.

WATER

Chemical composition of sea water: oxygen 85.82%, hydrogen 10.72%, chlorine 1.89%, sodium 1.056%, magnesium 0.14%, sulphur 0.088%, calcium 0.041%, potassium 0.038%, bromine 0.0065%, carbon 0.002% etc.

Oceans and Seas

Name	Area in 1,000 sq.km	Volume in 1,000 cub.km	Greatest depth in m	Average depth in m
PACIFIC OCEAN	179,680	723,699	10,924	3,780
Philippine Sea	5,726	23,522	10,830	4,188
Coral Sea	4,791	11,470	9,174	2,243
South China Sea	3,537	3,622	5,559	1,024
Tasman Sea	3,336	10,960	5,944	3,285
Bering Sea	2,270	3,796	4,298	1,640
Sea of Okhotsk	1,580	1,316	3,916	821
Sea of Japan	1,062	1,630	3,699	1,535
ATLANTIC OCEAN	91,655	329,700	8,648	3,597
Weddell Sea	2,910	8,375	6,820	2,878
Caribbean Sea	2,776	6,745	7,535	2,429
Mediterranean Sea	2,556	3,603	5,121	1,438
Gulf of Mexico	1,554	2,366	4,376	1,522
Labrador Sea	840	1,596	4,316	1,898
North Sea	565	49	725	87
Baltic Sea	422	215	470	51
Black Sea	413	555	2,245	1,315
INDIAN OCEAN	76,170	282,600	7,725	3,710
Arabian Sea	4,592	14,514	5,803	3,160
Bay of Bengal	2,191	5,664	3,835	2,585
Arafura Sea	1,037	157	3,680	154
Andaman Sea	605	586	4,507	969
Red Sea	460	182	3,039	396
ARCTIC OCEAN	13,950	18,100	5,527	1,328
Barents Sea	1,424	316	610	222
Norwegian Sea	1,383	2,408	3,970	1,735
Greenland Sea	1,205	1,740	5,527	1,641
East Siberian Sea (Vostočno-Sibirskoje More)	913	49	915	54
Hudson Bay	848	92	258	128
Baffin Sea	780	593	2,414	861

Greatest ocean depth: in the Pacific Ocean – Mariana Trench 10,924 m (11°21′ N.Lat., 142°12′ E.Long.); in the Atlantic Ocean – Puerto Rico Trench 8,648 m (19°35′ N.Lat., 68°17′ W.Long.); in the Indian Ocean – Java Trench 7,725 m (10°15′ S.Lat., 109° E.Long. – approx.); in the Arctic Ocean – Eurasia Basin 5,527 m (82°23′ N.Lat., 19°31′ E. Long.).

ARCTIC OCEAN

North Pole

ASIA

BERING SEA

M. Dežneva
C.P. of Wales
Bering
ALASKA
•6194
Mt. Mc Kinley
(Denali)
Alaska Ra.
Aleutian Is.

•3750

Queen Elizabeth Is.

N. Magnetic P.
Victoria

Baffin I.

Arctic Circle

Hudson
Bay

Labrador
Pen.

Ummannaq

Greenland

•3764

Iceland

Rocky Mountains

Vancouver I.

NORTH

AMERICA

Laurentian Plateau

Great
Lakes

Appalachian Mts.

•2037
Mt. Mitchell

Midway Is.

Hawaiian Is.

Tropic of Cancer

6584

4205
Mauna Kea

4418•
Mt. Whitney

•4398
•86

Gulf of
Mexico

Cuba

Florida
Bahamas

Gr. Antilles

CARIBBEAN

•5775

P   A   C   I   F   I   C

Marshall Is.

POLYNESIA

Line Is.

•Kiritimati

170°   180°   170°   160°   150°   140°   130°   120°   110°

5699
V. Citlaltépetl

6488

•4220

Clipperton

100°   90°   80°

Andes

Nauru   Kiribati

Phoenix Is.

Tokelau Is.

Equator

Is. Marquises

Galápagos Is.   Chimborazo
Pta. Paniñas

•6297

5851

6768•

Tuvalu Is.

Sta. Cruz
Is.
Fiji Is.

Samoa Is.

MELANESIA

Vanuatu

Tahiti

Is. Tuamotu

Tropic of Capricorn

Cook Is.

Tonga

Is. Touboual

Pitcairn I.

.I. Sala y Gómez

8064

New
Caledonia

Norfolk I.

Kermadec Is.

10 882

10 047

L de Pascua
(Easter I.)

O   5422   C   E   A   N

Is. Juan
Fernández

•6872•
Co. Bonete
6959•Acc...

S. Valentín
4058

Falklan
Is.

New Zealand

Mt. Cook
3764

Chatham Is.

Bounty Is.

Auckland I.

Campbell I.

5756

5385

Tierra
C. Horn   del Fuego

Antarctic Circle

Alexander I.

Antarctic Pen.

South
Orkney Is.

•463   ROSS SEA

Vinson M.
South Pole
2912

ANTARCTICA

WEDDELL SEA

Longest Rivers of the World

Name	Length in km	River basin in sq.km
1. Amazonas (-Ucayali, -Apurímac)	7,025	7,050,000
2. Nile-Kagera	6,671	2,881,000
3. Mississippi-Missouri	6,212	3,250,000
4. Changjiang/Yangtze/	5,520	1,942,000
5. Ob' (-Irtyš)	5,410	2,975,000
6. Huanghe/Yellow/	4,845	772,000
7. Congo /Zaire/ -Lualaba	4,835	3,822,000
8. Mekong (Lancangjiang/	4,500	810,000
9. Amur (-Silka, -Onon)	4,416	1,855,000
10. Lena	4,400	2,490,000

Largest Islands of the World

Name (Continent)	Area in sq.km
1. Greenland (N.America)	2,175,600
2. New Guinea (Oceania)	785,000
3. Borneo/Kalimantan (Asia)	746,546
4. Madagascar (Africa)	587,040
5. Baffin I. (N.America)	507,414
6. Sumatera (Asia)	433,800
7. Honshū (Asia)	227,414
8. Victoria I. (N.America)	217,274
9. Great Britain (Europe)	216,325
10. Ellesmere I. (N.America)	196,221

Highest Waterfalls of the World

Name (Country)	Height in m
1. Salto Angel (Venezuela)	979
2. Tugela (Natal, South Africa)	948
3. Yosemite (Cal., U.S.A.)	739
4. Cuquenán (Venezuela)	610
5. Sutherland (New Zealand)	579
6. Takakkaw (B.C., Canada)	503
7. Glétroz (Switzerland)	498
8. Ribbon (Cal., U.S.A.)	491
9. King George VI (Guyana)	488
10. Della (B.C., Canada)	440

Largest Lakes of the World

Name (Continent)	Area in sq.km	Greatest depth in m
1. Caspian Sea (Asia)	371,000	1,025
2. L. Superior (N.America)	82,414	393
3. L. Victoria (Africa)	68,800	125
4. Aralskoje More (Asia)	64,115	67
5. L. Huron (N.America)	59,596	226
6. L. Michigan (N. America)	58,016	281
7. L. Tanganyika (Africa)	32,880	1,470
8. O. Bajkal (Asia)	31,500	1,620
9. Great Bear Lake (N.America)	31,328	137
10. Great Slave Lake (N.America)	28,570	140

add page 26

map 3

LAND SURFACE

Continent	Area in 1,000 sq.km	% of Land surface	Altitude in metres			Population in millions (1985)	% of World Popul.
			highest	aver.	lowest		
Europe	10,382	7.0	4,810	340	−28	693	14.3
Asia	44,410	29.7	8,848	960	−400	2,893	59.8
Africa	30,329	20.3	5,895	750	−173	555	11.5
North America	24,360	16.3	6,194	720	−86	401	8.3
South America	17,843	11.9	6,959	580	−40	269	5.6
Australia and Oceania	8,910	6.0	5,030	350	−16	26	0.5
Antarctica	13,175	8.8	5,140	2,020	(−2,536)		
WORLD	149,409	100.0	8,848	840	−400	4,837	100.0

Highest point on the Earth surface: Mount Everest 8,848m.
Lowest point on the Earth surface: The Dead Sea −400m below sea-level.
Highest active volcano: Volcan Guallatiri (in Chile) 6,060m (eruption in 1960).
Largest island: Greenland 2,175,600 sq.km.
Largest peninsula: Arabian Peninsula 2,780,000 sq.km.
Longest mountain chain: Rocky Mountains Range – Andes (Cordilleras), length 15,000km.
Largest lowlands: Amazonian Lowlands (S.America) approx. 5,000,000 sq.km.
Largest desert: Sahara (Africa) 7,820,000 sq.km.
Largest glacier (excl. Antarctica) Greenland, area 1,830,000 sq.km, volume 2,700,000 cub.km.
Largest lake: Caspian Sea 371,000 sq.km.
Deepest lake: O. Bajkal 1,620m.
Longest river: Amazonas (-Ucayali, -Apurímac) 7,025km.
Largest river basin: Amazonas (Amazon) 7,050,000 sq.km.
Highest average flow: Amazonas 120,000 cub.m per sec.
Highest waterfalls: Salto Angel (in Venezuela) 979m.
Deepest cave system: Réseau de la Pierre-Saint-Martin (in French Pyrenees) depth 1,332m.
Longest cave system: Flint Ridge-Mammoth Cave (Kentucky, U.S.A.) 297,080m.
Highest absolute temperature: Al-Azíziyah (in Libya) +58°C.
Highest average annual temperature: Dalol (in Ethiopia) +34.4°C.
Lowest absolute temperature: Vostok (3,488m high, Soviet base in Antarctica) −89.2°C (1983).
Lowest average annual temperature: Pole of Cold (in Antarctica) −57.8°C.
Highest average annual precipitation: Waialeale (Kauai – Hawaii, U.S.A.) 11,684mm.
Lowest average annual precipitation: Arica (in Chile) 0.8mm.
Largest national park: Wood Buffalo National Park, area 44,807 sq.km.

Countries of the World according to area

Name	Area in sq.km
1. U.S.S.R.	22,274,900
2. Canada	9,976,139
3. China	9,560,980
4. U.S.A.	9,363,166
5. Brazil	8,511,965
6. Australia	7,686,848
7. India	3,287,590
8. Argentina	2,780,092
9. Sudan	2,505,813
10. Algeria	2,381,740
11. Zaïre	2,345,409
12. Greenland (Den.)	2,175,600
13. Saudi Arabia	2,149,690
14. Mexico	1,972,546
15. Indonesia	1,919,270
16. Libya	1,759,540
17. Iran	1,648,100
18. Mongolia	1,565,000
19. Peru	1,285,216
20. Chad	1,284,000
21. Niger	1,266,995
22. Angola	1,246,700
23. Mali	1,239,710
24. Ethiopia	1,221,900
25. South Africa	1,221,037

Countries of the World according to population
(Mid-year estimates 1985)

Name	Population
1. China	1,059,525,000[+]
2. India	750,980,000
3. U.S.S.R.	277,505,000
4. U.S.A.	239,575,000
5. Indonesia	165,155,000
6. Brazil	135,564,000
7. Japan	120,754,335
8. Bangladesh	98,657,070
9. Pakistan	96,179,592
10. Nigeria	95,198,000
11. Mexico	78,524,158
12. Vietnam	59,713,000
13. Federal Rep. of Germany	59,165,000[*]
14. Italy	57,127,536
15. United Kingdom	56,518,000
16. France	55,282,000
17. Philippines	54,377,990
18. Thailand	51,301,000
19. Turkey	49,272,000
20. Egypt	48,503,000
21. Iran	44,632,000
22. Ethiopia	43,349,900
23. Republic of Korea	41,258,000
24. Spain	38,601,795
25. Burma	37,614,000
[+] including Taiwan, [*] excluding West Berlin	

map 4

THE UNITED NATIONS (UN)

The most important international organization in the world. The Charter of the United Nations was signed by 50 states at the San Francisco Conference held from 25 April to 26 June 1945, and it came into force on 24 October 1945 (United Nations Day). The Preamble to the Charter lays down the purposes and principles of the UN: to maintain international peace and security; to develop friendly relations among nations; to cooperate internationally in solving international economic, social, cultural and humanitarian problems and in promoting respect for human rights and fundamental freedoms; to support social progress and improve standards of living and to coordinate the fundamental principles of the member nations so as to attain these common ends.

Members of the UN are the sovereign states that established the organization and those admitted by the General Assembly upon recommendation of the Security Council. The UN had 159 members on 21 September 1984. Original member states (since 1945): Argentina, Australia, Belgium, Bolivia, Brazil, Byelorussian S.S.R., Canada, Chile, China, Colombia, Costa Rica, Cuba, Czechoslovakia, Denmark, Dominican Republic, Ecuador, Egypt, El Salvador, Ethiopia, France, Greece, Guatemala, Haiti, Honduras, India, Iran, Iraq, Lebanon, Liberia, Luxembourg, Mexico, the Netherlands, New Zealand, Nicaragua, Norway, Panama, Paraguay, Peru, Philippines, Poland, Saudi Arabia, South Africa, Syria, Turkey, Ukrainian S.S.R., United Kingdom, Uruguay, Union of Soviet Socialist Republics, United States of America, Venezuela and Yugoslavia. Other states admitted as members: in 1946 – Afghanistan, Iceland, Sweden, Thailand; 1947 – Pakistan, Yemen; 1948 – Burma; 1949 – Israel; 1950 – Indonesia; 1955 – Albania, Austria, Bulgaria, Finland, Hungary, Ireland, Italy, Jordan, Kampuchea, Laos, Libya, Nepal, Portugal, Romania, Spain, Sri Lanka; 1956 – Japan, Morocco, Sudan, Tunisia; 1957 – Ghana, Malaysia; 1958 – Guinea; 1960 – Benin, Burkina Faso (formerly Upper Volta), Cameroon, Central African Republic, Chad, Congo, Cyprus, Gabon, Ivory Coast, Madagascar, Mali, Niger, Nigeria, Senegal, Somalia, Togo, Zaïre; 1961 – Mauritania, Mongolia, Sierra Leone, Tanzania; 1962 – Algeria, Burundi, Jamaica, Rwanda, Trinidad and Tobago, Uganda; 1963 – Kenya, Kuwait; 1964 – Malawi, Malta, Zambia; 1965 – Gambia, Maldives, Singapore; 1966 – Barbados, Botswana, Guyana, Lesotho; 1967 – Democratic Yemen; 1968 – Equatorial Guinea, Mauritius, Swaziland; 1970 – Fiji; 1971 – Bahrain, Bhutan, Oman, Qatar, United Arab Emirates; 1973 – Bahamas, German Democratic Republic, Federal Republic of Germany, 1974 – Bangladesh, Grenada, Guinea-Bissau; 1975 – Cape Verde, Comoros, Mozambique, Papua New Guinea, Surinam, São Tomé and Principe; 1976 – Angola, Samoa, Seychelles; 1977 – Djibouti, Vietnam; 1978 – Dominica, Solomon Islands; 1979 – Saint Lucia; 1980 – Zimbabwe, Saint Vincent and the Grenadines; 1981 – Antigua, Belize, Vanuatu; 1983 – Saint Kitts and Nevis; 1984 – Brunei.

The principal organs of the UN: 1. The General Assembly – consists of all member states; each of them has juridically an equal position irrespective of size, power or importance; 2. The Security Council – bears the primary responsibility for the maintenance of peace and security (it has 5 permanent and 10 elected members); 3. The Economic and Social Council (54 elected members); 4. The Trusteeship Council (5 members); 5. The International Court of Justice (with its seat at 's-Gravenhage); 6. The Secretariat – carries out all administrative functions in the UN. It is headed by the Secretary-General, who is appointed by the General Assembly on the recommendation of the Security Council. **Secretary-General:** Javier Pérez de Cuéllar (since 1 Jan. 1982). **Headquarters of the UN:** New York. **Official languages:** Arabic, Chinese, English, French, Spanish and Russian.

The Economic and Social Council have **5 regional economic commissions:** the Economic Commission for Europe (ECE; H.Q.: Genève), the Economic Commission for Asia and the Pacific (ECAP; H.Q.: Krung Thep), the Economic Commission for Latin America (ECLA; H.Q.: Santiago), the Economic Commission for Africa (ECA; H.Q.: Addis Abeba), and the Economic Commission for Western Asia (ECWA; H.Q.: Bayrût); functional commissions (Statistical Commission, Population Commission, Social Development Commission, Commission on Human Rights, Commission on the Status of Women, Commission on Narcotic Drugs, Commission on International Raw Materials Trade). **Special related agencies:** United Nations Children's Fund (UNICEF), Office of the United Nations High Commissioner for Refugees (UNHCR; H.Q.: Genève), United Nations Conference on Trade and Development (UNCTAD; H.Q.: Genève), United Nations Development Programme (UNDP), United Nations Industrial Development Organization (UNIDO; H.Q.: Wien), United Nations Institute for Training and Research (UNITAR), World Food Council (WFC; H.Q.: Rome), United Nations University (UNU, H.Q.: Tōkyō), as well as other commissions and agencies.

International specialized organizations in relationship with the UN (14): International Atomic Energy Agency (IAEA; H.Q.: Wien), International Labour Organization (ILO; H.Q.: Genève), Food and Agriculture Organization (FAO; H.Q.: Rome), United Nations Educational, Scientific and Cultural Organization (UNESCO; H.Q.: Paris), World Health Organization (WHO; H.Q.: Genève), International Bank for Reconstruction and Development (IBRD – World Bank; H.Q.: Washington), International Development Association (IDA; H.Q.: Washington), International Finance Corporation (IFC; H.Q.: Washington), International Monetary Fund (IMF; H.Q.: Washington), International Civil Aviation Organization (ICAO; H.Q.: Québec), Universal Postal Union (UPU; H.Q.: Bern), International Telecommunication Union (ITU, H.Q.: Genève), World Meteorological Organization (WMO; H.Q.: Genève), Inter-Governmental Maritime Consultative Organization (IMCO; H.Q.: London), General Agreement on Tariffs and Trade (GATT; H.Q.: Genève).

INTERNATIONAL ORGANIZATIONS

The Council of Europe – established on 5 May 1949 in London (H.Q.: Strasbourg). Membership: 21 European countries; founder members: United Kingdom, France,. Italy, Belgium, the Netherlands, Luxembourg, Ireland, Denmark, Norway, Sweden, Turkey and Greece joined in 1949, Iceland in 1950, Fed. Rep. of Germany in 1951, Austria in 1956, Cyprus in 1961, Switzerland, Liechtenstein in 1963, Malta in 1965, Portugal in 1976, Spain in 1977. Finland and the Vatican City participate in the work of certain bodies. Control organs: the Committee of Ministers (usually 21 Ministers of Foreign Affairs), the Joint Committee (21 members), the Consultative Assembly (consists of 170 parliamentary representatives from 21 member countries) and the Secretariat. The Council's aim is to achieve a greater unity between its members and to co-ordinate policies on economic, social, cultural, legal, scientific and administrative matters. **European Communities** – short name for 3 communities established by 6 countries of Western Europe to integrate economic policies and move towards political unity. The original members are France, Italy, the Fed. Rep. of Germany, Belgium, the Netherlands and Luxembourg. Other members since 1973 are the United

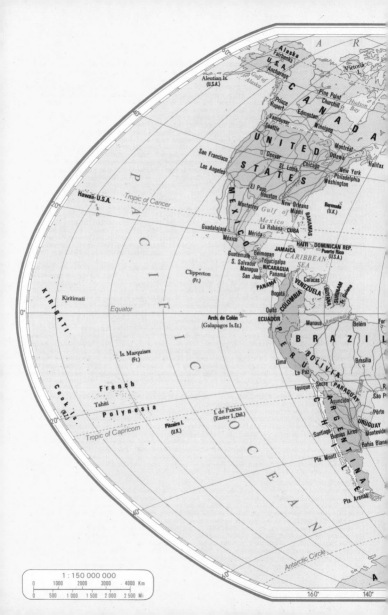

map 4

The **General Agreement on Tariffs and Trade (GATT;** H.Q. Genève) came into force in 1948. It deals with problems of international trade and lays down a code of conduct in international relations. 124 countries were associated in this organization at the beginning of 1986.

The **World Council of Churches** (office: Genève) was formally constituted in Amsterdam on 23 August 1948. In 1984, the Council had 301 members from more than 100 countries and territories.

The **International Olympic Committee** (H.Q.: Lausanne), founded in 1894, unites 159 National Olympic Committees.

MILITARY PACTS

NATO – the North Atlantic Treaty Organization (H.Q.: Bruxelles). The treaty was signed in Washington on 4 April 1949. A military and political grouping of western countries: Belgium, Canada, Denmark, France, Iceland, Italy, Luxembourg, the Netherlands, Norway, Portugal, the United Kingdom and the United States of America; Greece and Turkey since 1952, the Federal Republic of Germany since 1955, Spain since 1982. France withdrew from NATO in 1966.

The Warsaw Pact (H.Q.: Moskva), a military and political union of the European socialist countries for defensive purposes, signed in Warszawa on 14 May 1955. Members: Bulgaria, Czechoslovakia, the German Democratic Republic, Hungary, Poland, Romania and U.S.S.R.; Albania withdrew in 1962.

ANZUS – The Pacific Security Treaty, a military pact signed at San Francisco on 1 Sept. 1951 between Australia, New Zealand and the U.S.A.

SEATO – the South East Asia Treaty Organization (H.Q.: Krung Thep) – a military and political treaty signed in 1954. Members: Australia, France, New Zealand, the Philippines, Thailand, the United Kingdom of Great Britain and Northern Ireland and the United States of America.

Largest Cities of the World
(Population of the city proper)

Name (Country)	Population	(Year)
1. México (Mex.)	10,800,000	(1982)
2. Sôul (Rep. of Korea)	9,501,414	(1984)
3. Moskva (U.S.S.R.)	8,642,000	(1984)
4. São Paulo (Brazil)	8,494,000	(1980)
5. Tôkyô (Japan)	8,361,054	(1983)
6. Bombay (India)	8,243,405	(1981)
7. Jakarta (Indon.)	7,636,000	(1983)
8. New York (U.S.A.)	7,086,096	(1982)
9. Al-Qâhirah (Egypt)	6,780,000	(1980)
10. London (U.K.)	6,756,000	(1984)
11. Shanghai (China)	6,320,872	(1982)
12. Tehrân (Iran)	5,734,199	(1982)
13. Karâchi (Pakistan)	5,180,562	(1981)
14. Delhi (India)	5,157,270	(1981)
15. Tiajin (China)	5,152,180	(1982)

Largest Cities of the World
(Population of the urban agglomeration)

Name (Country)	Population	(Year)
1. New York (U.S.A.)	17,807,000	(1984)
2. México (Mex.)	15,668,800	(1983)
3. São Paulo (Brazil)	12,820,000	(1983)
4. Moskva (U.S.S.R.)	12,600,000	(1984)
5. Los Angeles (U.S.A.)	12,373,000	(1984)
6. Shanghai (China)	11,859,748	(1982)
7. Tôkyô (Japan)	11,746,190	(1983)
8. Sôul (Rep. of Korea)	11,460,000	(1983)
9. Bombay (India)	9,950,000	(1981)
10. Al-Qâhirah (Egypt)	9,750,000	(1982)
11. Buenos Aires (Argen.)	9,710,000	(1980)
12. Paris (France)	9,650,000	(1982)
13. Rio de Janeiro (Brazil)	9,250,000	(1980)
14. Beijing (China)	9,230,687	(1982)
15. Calcutta (India)	9,194,018	(1981)

add page 30

map 4

Kingdom, Denmark, Ireland, Greece since 1981, Portugal and Spain since 1986. **The European Parliament** consists of 434 members who are elected directly within each of the member countries (seat: Strasbourg and Luxembourg). **The European Economic Community (EEC** or "the Common Market"; H.Q.: Bruxelles), established on 25 March 1957 in Rome with the task of achieving a customs union and to co-ordinate the economic policies of member states, 64 independent developing countries of Africa, the Caribbean and the Pacific are affiliated to the Community. – **The European Coal and Steel Community (ECSC**; H.Q.: Luxembourg) established on 18 April 1951 in Paris with a task of contributing to the economic development and rising standard of living in member countries by establishing a common market for coal, coke, iron ore and steel. – **The European Atomic Energy Community (EAEC,** "Euratom"; H.Q.: Bruxelles) founded in Rome on 25 March 1957 to promote the nuclear energy industry and nuclear research.

The European Free Trade Association **(EFTA;** H.Q.: Genève) was set up in Stockholm on 3 May 1960. Its task was to eliminate tariffs and quantitative restrictions on the import and export of goods between member countries. Members: Austria, Iceland, Norway, Portugal, Sweden and Switzerland; Finland since 1985.

The Organization for Economic Co-operation and Development (OECD; H.Q.: Paris) was set up on 30 Sept. 1961 to further economic growth, rises in the standard of living, to contribute to economic co-operation between member and non-member countries and to contribute to the expansion of world trade. Member countries are: Australia, Austria, Belgium, Canada, Denmark, the Federal Republic of Germany, Finland, France, Greece, Iceland, Ireland, Italy, Japan, Luxembourg, the Netherlands, New Zealand, Norway, Portugal, Spain, Sweden, Switzerland, Turkey, the United Kingdom and the U.S.A.; associated member Yugoslavia.

The Council for Mutual Economic Assistance (CMEA; H.Q.: Moskva) was established on 8 Jan. 1949 by the socialist countries to coordinate economic planning, the implementation of joint provisions for the expansion of industry and agriculture on the basis of an international socialist division of labour, specialization and co-operation in production, the construction of fuel and power and transport systems and the exchange of scientific and technological knowledge. This international socialist organization is based on the principle of a voluntary choice of criteria and on mutual collaboration. Member countries: Bulgaria, Czechoslovakia, Hungary, Poland, Romania, the Union of Soviet Socialist Republics; since 1950 – the German Democratic Republic, 1962 – Mongolia, 1972 – Cuba and 1978 – Vietnam (10 members). Albania withdrew in 1961. Observers: Yugoslavia, the Democratic People's Republic of Korea, Laos, Angola; China has not taken part since 1961. Special status of co-operation: Finland, Iraq, Mexico. **The International Bank for Economic Cooperation** (H.Q.: Moskva) came into being in 1963; it is used by member countries of CMEA for accountancy purposes in trade and economic development.

The Organization of American States (OAS; Secretariat: Washington) was formed at a conference in Bogotá on 30 April 1948 to work towards international peace, to promote American solidarity and to coordinate economic, social, scientific, technological and cultural policies. Membership: 32 independent countries (Cuba was expelled in 1962 after U.S. intervention). **The Inter-American Development Bank (IDB**; H.Q.: Washington) was established in 1960 by 25 Latin American countries (excluding Cuba), Canada, the U.S.A., European states and Japan.

The Latin American Integration Association (ALADI = LAIA; H.Q.: Montevideo) was established in August 1980 to replace LAFTA (in 1960). Instead of across-the-board tariff cuts, the treaty envisaged an area of economic preferences, comprising a regional tariff preference for goods originating in member states. Members: Argentina, Bolivia, Brazil, Chile, Colombia, Ecuador, Mexico, Paraguay, Peru, Uruguay, Venezuela. The Andean Group (Grupo Andino) is an association of Bolivia, Chile (withdrew 1977), Colombia, Ecuador, Peru, Venezuela. Its aims are economic control and the regulation of foreign investments. The Latin American Economic System (SELA; secretariat: Caracas) to allow regional co-operation in economic and social progress of 26 Latin American countries, including Cuba.

The Caribbean Community (CARICOM) and the **Central American Common Market (CACM)** – 13 small island countries in the Caribbean (incl. Belize and Guyana) have been associated since 1973 for the purposes of coordinating foreign trade and economic development and restricting the influence of foreign business in the economic life of member countries; observers Dominican Rep., Haiti, Surinam. H.Q.: Georgetown.

The Organization of African Unity (OAU; H.Q. Addis Abeba) was established on 20 May 1963. Its chief aims are the furtherance of African unity and solidarity, the coordination of the political, economic, cultural, health, scientific and defence policies; the elimination of colonialism in Africa, common defence and the independence of the member countries as well as the development of international collaboration according to the Charter of the U.N. There were 50 members in 1984. **The African Bank of Development** (H.Q.: Abidjan) was founded in 1963 to contribute to economic and social development of member countries. **The Arab League** (H.Q.: Tunis) was founded in Cairo on 22 March 1945 with the purpose of promoting collaboration and unity in political, economic, military, financial and cultural matters. Original members: Egypt, Iraq, Jordan, Lebanon, Saudi Arabia, Syria, Yemen. There were 21 Arab member countries, and the Palestine Liberation Organization in 1984.

The Arab Monetary Fund (H.Q.: Abu Zaby) was founded in 1976, 21 members.

The Asian Development Bank (ADB; H.Q.: Manila) was founded 1966; its aims are to raise funds from private and public sources for development purposes in the region. There are 31 member countries within the ESCAP region and 14 others.

The Association of South East Asian Nations (ASEAN; H.Q.: Krung Thep), came into being in 1967 to stimulate the economic growth, social progress and cultural development of this region. Members: Brunei, Indonesia, Malaysia, the Philippines, Singapore and Thailand.

The Organization of Petroleum Exporting Countries (OPEC; H.Q.: Wien), was established in 1960 as an association of the developing countries that extract and export petroleum to protect their interests particularly against the international oil monopolies. Members: Algeria, Ecuador, Gabon, Indonesia, Iran, Iraq, Kuwait, Libya, Nigeria, Qatar, Saudi Arabia, Syria, the United Arab Emirates and Venezuela.

map 5

EUROPE

Europe lies in the temperate belt of the northern hemisphere, and although it is connected to the western side of Asia it is regarded as a separate continent for both historical and cultural reasons. Its name derives from the Accadian word "ereb", meaning "evening twilight or sunset", i.e. "the land where the sun sets", and the ancient Greeks adapted this Semitic word to the form in which it has come down to us.

Europe covers an **area of 10,382,000 sq.km,** which is 7.0% of the world's land surface (including the European part of the U.S.S.R.). It has **693 mn. inhabitants** (1985) and a population density of 65.8 persons per sq.km. **Geographical position:** northernmost point of the mainland: Cape Nordkinn in Norway 71°08' N.Lat. (of the entire continent: Cape Mys Fligeli on O. Rudol'fa island in Zeml'a Franca Iosifa (Fr. Joseph Land) 81°51' N.Lat.); southernmost point: Punta Marroqui in Spain in the Strait of Gibraltar 35°59' N.Lat. (island Gávdhos off the southern coast of Crete 34°48' N.Lat.); westernmost point: Cabo da Roca in Portugal 9°29' W.Long. (Tearaght Island off the west coast of Ireland 10°39' W.Long.); easternmost point: the eastern foothills of the Pol'arnyj Ural in the U.S.S.R. 67°20' E.Long. The eastern continental boundary between Europe and Asia is over 3,500 km long and leads along the· eastern foothills of the Ural Mts. (Ural'skije Gory), further along the river Emba to the Caspian Sea, from there along the Kuma-Manyč Depression (along the rivers Kuma and Manyč) to the mouth of the river Don on the Sea of Azov (Azovskoje More).

Europe's coastline, the longest of all the continents, is extremely varied and measures 37,900 km (excl. the coastlines of all large and small offshore islands). Largest peninsulas: Scandinavia (area 774,000 sq.km), Iberian (581,400 sq.km), Balkan (496,700 sq.km), Appennine (251,000 sq.km). Islands are situated mainly to the North-West, where the largest are Great Britain (area 216,325 sq.km) and Iceland (102,829 sq.km); further to the North Novaja Zeml'a (81,375 sq.km) and Svalbard (62,050 sq.km), and in the South in the Mediterranean Sea there are Sicily (25,426 sq.km), Sardinia (23,813 sq.km), Corsica (8,681 sq.km) and Crete (8,259 sq.km).

The land surface of Europe varies considerably, although it has the lowest average height (340 m) of all the continents. Plains rising no higher than 200 m make up 57% of the total area of the continent. The distribution of lowland and mountain regions is determined by both geological structure and geomorphological evolution. The oldest core of the continent is the lowlands of Eastern Europe ("Fennosarmatia") with the vast East European Plain. The lowest point is the Caspian Sea (−28 m below sea level). To the East rises the longest mountain system, the Ural Mountains (Ural'skije Gory, 1,894 m) stretching over 2,500 km. The Scandinavian mountains (2,472 m) and their numerous glaciers date from the Caledonian age with typical deep fjords. The Central European Plain, which bears the marks of glaciation, and the German-Bohemian ranges (1,602 m) date from the Hercynian age, like the French Massif Central (1,886 m). The highest and most typical European mountains, the Alps (Mt. Blanc, 4,810 m), arose during the Tertiary folding as did the Carpathian Mts. and the Dinara (2,751 m). Most of the Southern European peninsulas are mountainous, the highest ranges (of Tertiary age) are the Pyrenees (3,404 m) and the Appennines (2,914 m). This is a volcanic region (Etna 3,340 m) with earthquakes.

Europe's relatively moist climate has resulted in a dense **network of rivers.** The mean annual discharge is 2,560 cub.km and roughly 80% of its rivers drain into the marginal seas of the Atlantic Ocean. About 20% drain into the Caspian Sea, which has no outlet and is fed by Europe's longest river, the Volga (length 3,531 km, river basin 1,360,000 sq.km, mean annual flow 8,220 cub.m per sec.). The Eastern European rivers are at their fullest in spring and early summer and at their lowest in autumn and winter. The Central and Northern European rivers are at their fullest in spring and their lowest in early autumn. The Western European rivers, however, are at their greatest flow in winter, and at their smallest in the summer. The Southern European rivers are filled mostly by rain water in winter and some of them dry up completely in summer. The rivers of the high mountain regions have their maximum discharge (as much as 85%) in summer. The majority of **European lakes** are of glacial origin and the largest is Lake Ladoga (Ladožskoje Oz., 18,390 sq.km).

Europe spreads across **4 climatic belts** in the Northern hemisphere. In the Far North there is the Arctic and Subarctic zone (Svalbard, Novaja Zeml'a and the northern shores of the U.S.S.R.). The main part of the continent lies in the belt of temperate climate. Western Europe has the oceanic type with prevailing westerly winds (mild winters and summers); Central Europe has a transitional climate (the summer is warm with precipitation, the winter has permanent snow cover) and Eastern Europe has the continental type (long cold winters and hot summers). Highest absolute temperature: Sevilla (Spain) 47.8°C; lowest: Ust'-Cil'ma (U.S.S.R.) −69°C, maximum rainfall Crkvice (Yugoslavia) 4,624 mm a year; minimum Almeria (Spain) 218 mm.

Mean January and July temperatures in °C (annual rainfall in mm) are as follows: Vardø −5.0 and 9.1 (597), Reykjavík −1.2 and 10.9 (870), Bergen 1.7 and 16.3 (2,002), Stockholm −2.9 and 17.8 (555), Perm' −15.1 and 18.1 (570), Aberdeen 3.3 and 13.5 (748), Hamburg −0.3 and 17.0 (734), Warszawa −3.6 and 18.9 (531), Moskva −10.5 and 18.3 (694), London 4.1 and 17.5 (638), Paris 3.6 and 19.3 (645), Davos −7.0 and 12.1 (959), Praha −0.8 and 19.9 (491), Budapest −2.3 and 20.9 (647), Genova 7.5 and 24.4 (1184), Dubrovnik 9.0 and 24.5 (1391), Madrid 4.4 and 23.6 (419), Valletta 12.8 and 25.5 (513), Athinai 8.8 and 26.5 (402).

The soil, **flora and fauna** vary with the climatic conditions. From North to South there are the following soil and vegetation zones: tundra (moss, lichen), taiga with coniferous trees, mixed broad-leaved and coniferous forest, broad-leaved woodland of the temperate belt, tree steppe, (dry grasses), semi-desert (in the Caspian region), evergreen maquis and broad-leaved Mediterranean forest. Alpine flora varies according to the altitude at which it is growing. Europe has widespread cultivated steppe with fertile arable soil. The fauna includes reindeer, wolf, brown bear, lynx, fox, deer, hare, hedgehog, various species of birds, reptiles, amphibious animals, fishes and insects.

BARENTS SEA

Nordkapp Nordkinn
Hammerfest

Pol'Kolskij
Murmansk
Kol'skij pol.

Lappland 1191
Inari
abnekaise 2123
wik
Oz. Imandra

Luleå
Oulu

Vaasa
Finland 417

Oz. Pjaozero
Kem'

BELOJE MORE

Archangel'sk
Sev. Dvina

Pol. Kanin Gusino
Cesskaja Guba
Mezen'
Timanskij kraž 463

Pustozersk
Narodnaja 1894

Ob'
Zapadno-
Sibirskaja Ravnina
Sos'va
Chanty-Mansijsk
70°

Ob'
60°

Ural'skije Gory

Gulf of Bothnia

Paijänne Saimaa
Oz. 225
Oulujärvi

Helsinki
Leningrad

Tallinn

Oz. Vygozero
Sev. Dvina

Onežskoje Oz. 32
Oz. Belanje

293

Suchona
Kotlas

Vyčegda

Kama

Kamskoje Vdchr.
1569

Perm'
Sverdlovsk

B

Stockholm
Riga

Saaremaa
Gotland

Cudskoje Oz.
Lake Peipus

Valdajskaja 343
Vozvyšen.

Moskva 320

Rybinskoje Vdchr.
Volga
Gor'kij

Kazan'

Gor'kovskoje Vdchr.

Kama
Kujbyševskoje Vdchr.

Ufa
G. Jamantau 1640

Ural
405

Orenburg
50°

70

ICE SEA

Neman
Dvina
Minsk 346

Strednerusskaja 293
Vozvyšennost'

274
Char'kov

Oka
Volga
375

Kujbyšev

Privolžskaja Vozvyšen.
358

Volgogradskoje Vdchr.

Volga
Ural

Warszawa
Narew
Polesje
Kijev

Dnepr

Sev. Donec
367

Cimljanskoje Vdchr.

Volgograd
−28

Prikaspijskaja Nizmen.

Gur'jev
Astrachan'

CASPIAN SEA

Kraków
Carpathian Mts.
2655 orlachovský štít
slava

Budapest
Plain of Hungary
Szeged

2305
Moldoveanu 2543
Carpaţii − Mer.
2543

Bucureşti
Wallachia

Beograd

Stara Planina
384

Juž. Bug
Dnestr
Prut

Odessa

Dnepr

Rostov-n.-D.
Don

AZOVSKOJE MORE

Krymskij Pol.
M. Saryč

Kerč

384

Manyč
−132

Kuma
Terek
Bol'šoj Kavkaz
G. El'brus 5642
G. Kazbek 5033
4466
Baku
Tbilisi

Oz. Sevan
4090
40°

2522 mitor
Crkvice 2751
Korab

Botev 2376
Musala 2925

Jalta
1545

İzmail

Danube

Burgas

İstanbul

İnce B.

2565

BLACK SEA
2210

Baba Burnu

Rodhope Mts.

Stara Planina
Snjita

Thessaloníki
Pindhos O.
2917 Olimbos

Athínai

Pelopó-
nnisos

5121
A. Taínaron

Kríti (Crete) 2486

Lésvos

İzmir

SEA OF MARMARA

Ankara

Asia Minor

Toros Dağ

3086

Rhódhos

Cyprus

20°
30°

Kárpathos

5a Gibraltar
1 : 2 500 000

SPAIN
3

Los Barrios
San Roque
Facinas Algeciras
La Línea
832
Gibraltar (U.K.)
36°
Tarifa
 Pta. Marroquí
Strait of Gibraltar

MEDITERRANEAN SEA

1
ATLANTIC OCEAN

R. Šabarij
Ksar-es-Seghir
839 Musa
Ceuta (Sp.)
Benzú

Tanger
Restinga

MOROCCO
Mdiq

Regaia
El-Borj
Ksar-es-Seghir

Aakba
El Fendek
Tétouan
Martil

6°
5°30′

map 5

LONGEST RIVERS

Name	Length in km	River basin in sq.km
Volga	3,531	1,360,000
Danube /Donau, Dunaj, Duna, Dunav, Dunărea/	2,850	817,000
Ural	2,428	231,000
Dnepr	2,201	503,000
Kama	2,032	522,000
Don	1,870	423,000
Pečora	1,809	322,000
Oka	1,480	245,000
Belaja	1,420	142,000
V'atka	1,367	129,000
Dnestr	1,352	72,000
Rhine /Rhein, Rhin, Rijn/	1,326	224,400
Severnaja Dvina (-Suchona)	1,302	367,000
Desna	1,187	89,000
Labe /Elbe/	1,165	144,055
Vyčegda	1,070	123,000
Wisla	1,047	194,424
Loire	1,020	115,000
Zapadnaja Dvina	1,020	88,000
Tisa /Tisza/	997	157,000
Meuse /Maas/	950	49,000

LARGEST LAKES

Name	Area in sq.km	Greatest Depth in m	Altitude in m
Ladožskoje Oz.	18,390	225	4
Onežskoje Oz.	9,616	120	32
Vänern	5,585	93	44
Saimaa	4,400	58	76
Čudskoje Oz. -Pskovskoje Oz.	3,650	14	30
Vättern	1,912	120	88
IJselmeer	1,250	6	0
Oz. Vygozero	1,159	40	29
Mälaren	1,140	64	1
Oz. Beloje	1,125	11	110
Päijänne	1,065	93	78
Inari	1,000	60	114
Oz. Il'men'	982	11	18
Oulujärvi	980	38	124
Oz. Topozero	910	56	109
Kallavesi	900	102	85
Oz. Imandra	880	67	126
Pielinen	850	48	94
Balaton	591	11	106
L. Geneva /Genfer See/	582	310	372

LARGEST ISLANDS

Name	Area in sq.km	Name	Area in sq.km	Name	Area in sq.km
Great Britain	216,325	Novaja Zeml'a (South I.)	33,275	Crete /Kríti/	8,259
Iceland	102,820	Sicily /Sicilia/	25,426	Sjælland	7,019
Ireland	83,849	Sardinia /Sardegna/	23,813	O. Kolgujev	5,250
Novaja Zeml'a (North I.)	48,100	Nordaustlandet	14,530	Évvoia	3,654
Vestspitzbergen	39,044	Corsica /Corse/	8,681	Mallorca	3,411

HIGHEST MOUNTAINS

Name (Country)	Height in m	Name (Country)	Height in m
Mont Blanc /Mte. Bianco/ (Fr.-It.)	4,810	La Meije (Fr.)	3,987
Dufourspitze /Mte. Rosa/ (Switz.-It.)	4,634	Eiger (Switz.)	3,970
Dom (Switz.)	4,545	Mt. Pelvoux (Fr.)	3,946
Weisshorn (Switz.)	4,506	Ortles (It.)	3,899
Matterhorn /Mte. Cervino/ (Switz.-It.)	4,478	Monte Viso (It.)	3,841
Dent Blanche (Switz.)	4,357	Grossglockner (Aust.)	3,797
Grand Combin (Switz.)	4,314	Wildspitze (Aust.)	3,774
Finsteraarhorn (Switz.)	4,274	Grossvenediger (Aust.)	3,674
Aletschhorn (Switz.)	4,195	Tödi (Switz.)	3,614
Jungfrau (Switz.)	4,158	Adamello (It.)	3,554
Les Ecrins (Fr.)	4,103	Mulhacén (Sp.)	3,478
Gran Paradiso (It.)	4,061	Pico de Aneto (Sp.)	3,404
Piz Bernina (Switz.)	4,049	Monte Perdido (Sp.)	3,355

ACTIVE VOLCANOES

Name (Country)	Altitude in m	Latest eruption
Etna (Sicilia, It.)	3,340	1986
Beerenberg (Jan Mayen, Nor.)	2,278	1971
Askja (Iceland)	1,510	1961
Hekla (Iceland)	1,491	1981
Vesuvio (It.)	1,277	1949
Pico Gorda (Azores, Port.)	1,021	1968
Stromboli (Ie. Eolie, It.)	926	1975

FAMOUS NATIONAL PARKS

Name (Country)	Area in sq.km
Hohe Tauern (Austria)	10,000
Pečoro-Ilyčskij Zap. (U.S.S.R.)	7,213
Hardangervidda (Nor.)	3,430
Lake District N.P. (U.K.)	2,251
North Wales (Snowdonia) N.P. (U.K.)	2,188
Šumava-Böhmerwald (Czech.-F.R.Ger.)	1,860
Białowieski P.N. (Pol.-U.S.S.R.)	1,292

map 6

EUROPE

Country	Area in sq.km	Population year 1985	Density per sq.km	Capital
Albania	28,748	2,962,500	103	Tiranë
Andorra	453	42,000	93	Andorra
Austria	83,853	7,555,340	90	Wien
Belgium	30,521	9,853,000[1]	323	Bruxelles/ Brussel
Bulgaria	110,912	8,942,976	81	Sofija
Czechoslovakia	127,896	15,520,000	121	Praha
Denmark	43,075	5,113,691	119	København
Faeroe Islands (Den.)	1,399	45,850	33	Thorshavn
Finland	338,145	4,908,215	14	Helsinki
France	543,998	55,282,000	102	Paris
German Democratic Republic	108,333	16,644,308	154	Berlin
Germany, Federal Republic of	248,198	59,165,000	238	Bonn
Gibraltar (U.K.)	6	29,073[1]	4,846	Gibraltar
Greece	131,957	9,950,000	75	Athínai
Hungary	93,036	10,643,000	114	Budapest
Iceland	102,829	241,000	2.3	Reykjavík
Ireland	70,283	3,552,000	51	Dublin
Italy	301,268	57,127,536	190	Roma
Liechtenstein	160	27,600	173	Vaduz
Luxembourg	2,586	365,900	142	Luxembourg
Malta	316	383,000	1,212	Valletta
Monaco	1.95	27,500	14,103	Monaco
Netherlands	41,548	14,483,985	349	Amsterdam
Norway	323,920	4,152,437	13	Oslo
Poland	312,683	37,202,980	119	Warszawa
Portugal (incl. Azores, Madeira)	91,985	10,229,200	111	Lisboa
Romania	237,500	22,795,000	96	Bucureşti
San Marino	60.6	22,100[1]	365	San Marino
Spain (incl. Canary Is.)	504,783	38,601,795	77	Madrid
Svalbard (Nor.)	62,422	3,458[1]	0.06	Longyearbyen
Sweden	449,964	8,350,366	19	Stockholm
Switzerland	41,293	6,455,600	156	Bern
Turkey – European part	23,764	5,010,000[1]	211	Ankara
Union of Soviet Socialist Republics	22,274,900	277,505,000	12.5	Moskva
U.S.S.R. – European part	5,433,900	199,780,000[1]	37	Moskva
United Kingdom[*]	244,872	56,518,000	231	London
Vatican City, State of	0.44	1,000[2]	2,273	Città del Vaticano
West Berlin	480	1,857,165	3,869	Berlin (West)
Yugoslavia	255,804	23,224,000	91	Beograd

[1] year 1984, [2] year 1983, [*] incl. I. of Man and Channel Is.

14.3% of the world's population live in Europe, **693 million people,** with a population density of 67 persons per sq.km (1985), which makes it the most densely inhabited continent. The most densely populated countries (leaving aside small countries like Monaco, Gibraltar, West Berlin and the Vatican City) are the Netherlands, Belgium, the Federal Republic of Germany, the United Kingdom and Italy. The Scandinavian countries, however, have a low population density. Europe has a low rate of **population growth** – 0.35% in the years 1980–85, birth rate 18.9 per 1,000, death rate 9.8 per 1,000. In 1980–85 the average life expectancy was 70 years (men) and 76.6 (women).

European languages are of three main Indo-European types: Slavonic, Germanic, and Romance. But there are other language groups: Celtic, Semitic, Finno-Ugric, etc. The main European nationalities are Russians, Germans, Italians, English, French, Ukrainians, Spanish and Poles.

Conurbations are typical features of all industrial areas, in particular in Central England, the Netherlands, the Rhine and Ruhr regions of the Federal Republic of Germany. Saxony in the German Democratic Republic, Upper Silesia in Poland, the Donbas region of the U.S.S.R. and the Po Valley in Italy. Europe has 33 cities with a population over one million and 71.5% of all inhabitants live in towns.

Economically Europe is the world's most advanced continent. It looks back on a tradition of industrial development and intensive plant and livestock farming. The extraction of coal, oil, natural gas, iron ore, bauxite, nickel, mercury, magnesite, phosphates and potassium salts is of world-wide importance. But Europe's main and most important industry is engineering. Europe has a highly developed transport network and is the continent with the greatest volume of foreign trade.

map 6

UNITED KINGDOM

The United Kingdom of Great Britain and Northern Ireland, 244,103 sq.km (with the Channel Islands and the Isle of Man 244,872 sq.km), **population** 56,518,000 (mid-year 1985), **constitutional monarchy** (Queen Elizabeth II since 6 February 1952). – **Currency:** £1 = = 100 pence.

Geographical position. The United Kingdom occupies the major part of the British Isles off the north-west coast of Europe. It is separated from the continent by the North Sea and the English Channel, which, at its narrowest point, the Strait of Dover, is only 34 km wide. The largest island is Great Britain, 216,325 sq.km; it is separated by the Irish Sea from Ireland, the northern part of which belongs to the United Kingdom. The islands of the Outer and Inner Hebrides stretch along the indented west coast of Scotland. The Orkney Islands and the Shetland Islands form the northernmost part of the British Isles. The Isle of Wight, the Isles of Scilly, and the Channel Islands are to be found off the south coast of England, the Isle of Man and Anglesey in the Irish Sea.

Geology. Up to the Pleistocene Era the British Isles formed part of the European continental plate. Its geological structure and topography developed in the same way as that of the continent. Caledonian and Hercynian foldings affected the islands in the Paleozoic Era. The Caledonian folding left its mark upon Scotland, the northern part of Ireland, England and Wales; the southern parts of the islands were shaped in the Hercynian movements with the hills running predominantly in a north-south direction. The old rocks have since been gradually eroded into rolling plains with hills of rounded shapes. The newer Alpine folding caused numerous faults, along which rift valleys and horsts have formed. The south-eastern part of Great Britain is taken up by the London Basin, formed of sediments and fringed by striking ridges of high ground. The Pleistocene ice sheets and ice caps covered the entire British Isles north of the Thames valley. To this day the land bears numerous marks of glacial activity: moraines, corries, glacial lakes, etc. The subsidence of the continent gave rise to many islands and river estuaries forming deep inlets along the coastline.

Hills and mountains. The most mountainous part of the United Kingdom is Scotland. The Scottish Highlands comprise the North West Highlands and the Grampian Mountains with Ben Nevis, 1,343 m, the highest mountain peak in the United Kingdom. The fertile Central Lowlands extend southward and are enclosed by the hilly Southern Uplands. The border between England and Scotland runs along the Cheviot Hills and the lower reaches of the River Tweed. The main ranges in England – the Pennines (Cross Fell, 893 m) and the Cumbrian Mountains with Scafell Pike, 978 m, England's highest peak – run in a north-south direction. The Cotswolds rise in the south-west and two rolling uplands, Dartmoor and Exmoor, are in the far south-west. The remaining land consists, for the most part, of either hilly or low-lying country, as in the Midlands. In Wales the highest mountain, at 1,085 m above sea-level, is Snowdon in the Cambrian Mountains. The highest point of Northern Ireland is Slieve Donard, 852 m.

Rivers. The British rivers are short with a strong flow of water throughout the year. The estuaries serve as natural harbours, and some ships have direct access to the hinterland on those rivers with reliable high tides. The sources of the rivers are divided by low watersheds, which facilitated the construction of a wide network of canals. The longest rivers are the Severn (354 km) and the Thames (338 km) with the Thames Barrier below London. Most of the **lakes** are of glacial origin and are to be found in large numbers in Scotland, the Lake District, and in Northern Ireland. Best known are Lough Neagh (396 sq.km), Lough Erne, Loch Lomond and Loch Ness.

Climate. The climate is oceanic with moderate temperatures and abundant precipitation. The temperature is modified in summer and in winter by the Gulf Stream flowing in a north-easterly direction along the west coast. The mean annual temperature in the period 1951–80 in England and Wales was 9.4°C (January 3.6°C, July 15.6°C), Scotland 8.0°C (3.0°C, 13.4°C), Northern Ireland 8.5 (3.5°C, 13.9°C). The prevailing south-westerly winds bring moisture from the Atlantic Ocean. The long-term annual average precipitation (1941–70) was 912 mm in England and Wales, 1,431 mm in Scotland and 1,095 mm in Northern Ireland. Rainfall is at its highest in November and December and at its lowest in April.

Administrative units. The United Kingdom is composed of four countries, England, Scotland, Wales and Northern Ireland. The main pattern of local government is the division into counties – Scotland has had regions since 1975 – within which there are district authorities. The Channel Islands and the Isle of Man enjoy a degree of autonomy.

System of Government. The monarch (King or Queen) is the head of state, succession following the hereditary principle. The Sovereign is the head of the judiciary, the commander-in-chief of all the armed forces and the temporal 'governor' of the established Church of England. The United Kingdom is governed, in the name of the Queen, by Her Majesty's Government, headed by the Prime Minister. The Government exercises executive power and is responsible to Parliament for its activities.

The supreme organ of state is Parliament composed of the House of Commons and the House of Lords, a law-making body which controls the activities of the Government. All British citizens aged 18 and over have the franchise. General elections are held a minimum of every five years. One Member is returned to the House of Commons for each of the 650 constituencies on the principle of a simple majority.

The **political system** is based on two major parties, one forming the Government and the other the Opposition. The majority party, at present, is the Conservative Party (with Mrs M. Thatcher as Prime Minister) and the Opposition is formed by the Labour Party.

Population (1984). The estimated population on 30 June 1984 was 56,488,100 persons, of which: 48.7% were male and 51.3% female. England had a population of 46,956,400, Wales 2,807,200, Scotland 5,146,000 and Northern Ireland 1,578,500. The United Kingdom has a high population density, 231 persons per sq.km, but they are distributed unevenly: England 360 persons per sq.km, Scotland 66, Wales 135 and Northern Ireland 117. 78.4% are English, 8.9% Scots, 4.0% Irish, 1.3% Welsh. In 1985 92.5% of the population lived in towns. London, **the capital,** is the main administrative, economic, cultural and political centre of country. The City of London had 5,400 inhab., Greater London 6.76 mn. London comprises 32 boroughs.

There has been a steady decline in the birth rate from 18.8 per 1,000 in 1964 to 12.9 per 1,000 in 1984. Despite the decline in mortality (11.4 per 1,000) the natural population increase of 1.5 per thousand is very low and a further decline is expected in coming years. The United Kingdom is a country with a very low rate of infant

map 7

mortality, 9.6 per thousand (England and Wales 9.5 per thousand, Scotland 10.3 per thousand, Northern Ireland 10.5 per thousand) and a high average life expectancy. In the period 1980–82 men reached an average age of 70.8 years, women 76.9 years. Those aged 0–14 years make up 19.5% of the population, the age group 15–64 years makes up 59.9% and those aged 65 years and over make up 20.6%. There is a considerable migration to and from the United Kingdom. Since the first half of the 20th century the immigration from Commonwealth countries has been rising but is now regulated by several Immigration Acts. In 1984 172,000 people came to the U.K. from outside Europe and 136,000 persons emigrated mainly to Commonwealth countries.

County districts in the United Kingdom
(estimate, 30 June 1984)

London	6,756,000	Coventry	313,700	Kingston upon Hull	265,600
Birmingham	1,009,400	Wakefield	310,700	Walsall	264,400
Glasgow	744,000	Wigan	307,300	Bolton	261,300
Leeds	712,200	Sandwell	304,900	Plymouth	255,300
Sheffield	540,500	Dudley	300,600	Wolverhampton	254,000
Liverpool	497,200	Sunderland	299,400	Rotherham	252,500
Bradford	464,400	Sefton	298,700	Stoke-on-Trent	249,400
Manchester	454,700	Stockport	289,100	Salford	242,500
Edinburgh	440,000	Doncaster	288,200	Barnsley	224,200
Bristol	396,600	Leicester	281,700	Oldham	220,400
Kirklees	377,700	Cardiff	281,200	Trafford	217,700
Wirral	337,500	Newcastle upon Tyne	281,100	Thameside	215,300
Belfast	319,000	Nottingham	279,700	Derby	214,700

The **official language** is English, together with Welsh in Wales. The Scottish form of Gaelic survives in Scotland, while in Northern Ireland a few people still speak Irish Gaelic.

English is the official language in the Channel Is., with the exception of Jersey, where Norman French (patois) is widely spoken. Manx, the language used on official occasions on the Isle of Man, belongs to the Celtic languages.

Education (1983/84). School attendance is compulsory from the age of 5 to 16 and is free of charge. Primary schools are coeducational but secondary and independent schools are often single sex. The great majority of schools, attended by over 95% of school children, are publicly maintained. Children between the age of 2 and 5 attend 1,260 nurseries or play groups. There are 25,326 primary and 5,328 secondary schools attended by 9.7 mn. pupils with a teaching staff of 552,500. There were 300,593 full-time and 36,319 part-time students at universities, of which 39.6% were women students and 9.6% overseas students. Among the 46 universities (including the Open University) are some of the oldest in the world (Oxford, Cambridge, St. Andrews, Aberdeen, Edinburgh and Glasgow). The universities are autonomous institutions with their own forms of government, but receive grants from the University Grants Committee.

Health Services (1983). Medical care is provided free of charge under the National Health Service. In the United Kingdom there were 28,663 physicians, i.e. 1 to 1,967 inhabitants. Total health service staff and practitioners were 1,057,154. There were 430,915 hospital beds (1984). It is also possible to obtain private medical care.

Religion (1980). 87.8% were Christians (57.0% Anglicans, 13.0% Roman Catholics). The majority of the population are nominally members of the established Church of England or the Church of Scotland or of the Free Churches.

The economy (data for 1985). The United Kingdom is one of the most highly developed countries in the world. It holds an important position in the fields of international trade, seafaring, banking, and insurance. Apart from industry and trade,. important sources of revenue derive from foreign investments, air and sea transport, financial insurance and banking transactions and tourism. Important industries such as steel and the energy industries (coal, gas, electricity, oil), rail, road haulage and air transport, the post office and the majority of ports are in public ownership. The economically active population numbers 27,325,000 persons, i.e. 48.4% of all inhabitants (female 40.0%, unemployed 12.0%). In 1984 total employees 21,155,000, 1.6% of these were engaged in agriculture, forestry and fishery, 33.7% were in industry and construction, 64.7% were in services. **Industry** (1984). The United Kingdom was the first country to develop factory production, and industry is the most important sector of the British economy. Together with the construction and fuel and power industries it produces 33.7% of the gross national product and employs 32.2% of the economically active population. The most important industry is manufacturing, which contributes 24.4% to the GNP (27.6% of the labour force). In recent years the most successful industries have been engineering, chemical, coal and oil processing.

Mining (1984). The United Kingdom suffers a shortage of mineral raw materials with the exception of coal. The main coal mining regions are in Central and North-west England (Lancashire, South and West Yorkshire, Derbyshire, Nottinghamshire, Durham, Northumberland), Central Scotland (Clydeside) and South Wales (Bristol Channel). The run-down of the coal mining industry – 49.5 mn. tonnes – is being reversed with heavy investments. As a consequence of the world energy crisis there has been increasing local production of crude petroleum, 125.9 mn. tonnes and natural gas 1,492,539 TJ, chiefly in the North Sea oil fields (oil: Argyll, Forties, Piper; natural gas: Frigg Leman Bank, West Sole, Hewett, Indefatigable, Viking). Total crude petroleum – tested reserves in the UK Continental Shelf are 2,033 mn. tonnes and natural gas tested reserves 739,000 mn. cub.m. Ore mining, once of considerable importance, is steadily decreasing. Mining (1982) of: iron ore produces 134,160 tonnes (Fe metal content) in Cumbria, Lancashire and Staffordshire, tin ore 4,176 tonnes (Sn metal content) in Cornwall and lead ore 3,240 tonnes (Pb metal content) in Clwyd, Durham and Derbyshire. Salt is mined in Cheshire, potash in Cleveland, as well as china and potter's clay.

Industrial production. Metallurgy (1985, in tonnes). The United Kingdom is one of the world's largest steel producing nations. Output of crude steel totalled 15.7 mn., pig iron 10.5 mn., coke 3.2 mn. The biggest steel works are run by the British Steel Corporation; the main centres of steel production are Sheffield, Swansea, Port Talbot, Teesside, the counties of Lincolnshire, Lancashire, Cheshire and the Greater Glasgow region. The British non-ferrous metal processing and fabricating industry is also very important (1984, in tonnes): virgin aluminium 287,900 and 143,900 of secondary metal (refineries at Kinlochleven, Foyers, Fort William, Dolgarrog, Resolven); refined virgin copper 69,400, secondary metal 67,400; refined lead 331,300 (Northfleet); zinc 85,600 (Avonmouth), refined nickel 22,300.

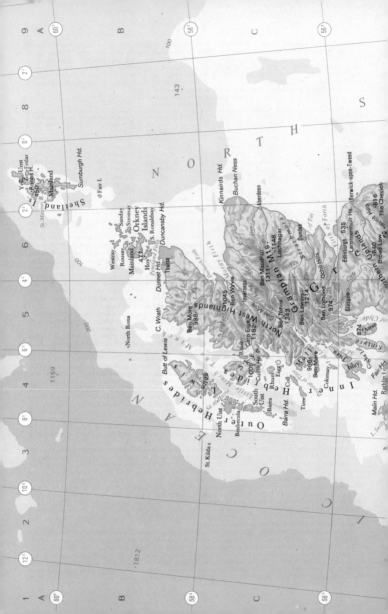

map 7

7a London
1:160 000

map 8

Engineering (1984): The United Kingdom is an important producer of transport equipment (London, Birmingham, Coventry, Manchester, Nottingham, Wolverhampton, Glasgow, Newcastle upon Tyne) 908,906 passenger cars, 224,825 commercial vehicles, of which 157,963 light commercial vehicles; 16,499 buses and coaches (of which 1,688 were double-deckers), 56 ships over 100 GRT (shipyards on Clydeside, Tyneside, Wearside, Merseyside, Teesside and at Barrow-in-Furness), civil and military aircraft (Yeovil, Bristol, Gloucester, Coventry, Luton, Derby, Manchester, Bedford). Engineering industries include the production of textile machinery (Bradford, Halifax, Keighley), industrial plants and electrical and electronic engineering (Manchester, Rugby, Newcastle upon Tyne, Stafford). In the **chemicals industry** (1984) (Birmingham, Glasgow, Newcastle upon Tyne, Wilton, Aberdeen) fast growth has been recorded in organic chemicals, the production of all synthetic resins 1.44 mn. tonnes, pharmaceutical chemicals. The production of sulphuric acid amounted to 2.65 mn. tonnes, phosphates 0.41 mn. tonnes (1983), mixed fertilizers 3.08 mn. tonnes, synthetic rubber 240,400 tonnes (Hythe).

The **textile industry** (1984) produced traditional wool 37,000 tonnes, woollen fabrics 90.7 mn. sq.m (London, Huddersfield, Halifax, Bradford), cotton (single yarn) 38,000 tonnes and 265 mn. m cotton (woven cloth, Lancashire) and new man-made fibres 383 mn. m and fabrics (Wilton, Drighlington, Little Heath, Coventry). The linen industry is centred on Northern Ireland and along the east coast of Scotland (Dundee, Abroath, Montrose). Jute products (Dundee). Macclesfield is the centre of the silk industry and Nottingham and Leicester produce hosiery and knitwear. Footwear production is centred on the Rossendale Valley, Leicester and Norwich 128 mn. pairs. The principal manufacturing centres of the clothing industry are London, Leeds and Manchester. The glass industry is centred in Glasgow, London, Birmingham and Sunderland. Cement production 13.48 mn. tonnes occurs along the Medway and the Humber. The paper industry produced 3.59 mn. tonnes of paper and board, of which 235,700 tonnes newsprint.

The **food, drink and tobacco industries** have, in recent years, been subject to mergers amongst leading firms. Production (1984): 60,105,000 hl beer (London, Burton-upon-Trent, Birmingham, Edinburgh) and alcoholic spirits 2,986,000 hl mainly of Scotch whisky and gin. The tobacco industry (93.4 billion cigarettes) is centred in Bristol, Nottingham, Liverpool, London and Manchester. The cocoa, chocolate and sugar confectionary industry is located in Yorkshire, Bristol and Nottingham.

Energy (1984). The output capacity of electric power stations was 66,431,000 kW (1983). Electric energy output 266.65 billion kWh; 79.4% in thermal power stations, 18.6% in nuclear power stations, 2% in hydro-electric power stations. Of the total power output (1980) petroleum accounted for 37.7%, coal 36.9%, natural gas 21.4%, nuclear power 4.1% and hydro-electric power 0.6%. Thermal power stations are situated on the coalfields, in the vicinity of the big cities and along the lower reaches of the Trent, Aire, Calder, Thames. The largest nuclear power stations are Hunterston B, Hartlepool, Heysham, Torness (each of 1,320 MW capacity), Dungeness B (1,200 MW), Wylfa (840 MW), Hinkley Point B (800 MW). The largest refineries are situated at Shell Haven, Stanlow, the Isle of Grain, Coryton, Fawley, Llandarcy, Grangemouth, Milford Haven.

Agriculture (1984). Agriculture, forestry and fisheries provided about 2.1% of the GNP and occupy a mere 1.6% of the economically active population. The United Kingdom continues to be dependent on imported food, although home agriculture output is gradually increasing. 75.7% of the land was used for agricultural purposes (arable and under permanent culture 28.9%, meadows and pastures 46.8%). Forests 8.9%. Agriculture specializes in **animal husbandry**: cattle breeding 13,213,000 head (of this 3,281,000 dairy cows), sheep 34,802,000 head, pigs 7,689,000 head, poultry 129,436,000. The United Kingdom is one of the world's leading milk producers (15,900 mn. l with an average of 4,846 l per dairy cow per year). Nearly all the eggs consumed in the United Kingdom are home produced, a total of 12,288 mn. Livestock is raised in Scotland, Northern Ireland, in the South and South-west of England. The main corn growing region is the eastern half of England and the east coast of Scotland. **Crops (yields)**: barley 11.03 mn. tonnes (5.39 tonnes per hectare), wheat 14.98 mn. tonnes (7.58 tonnes per hectare), oats 0.55 mn. tonnes (4.67 tonnes per hectare); other crops: potatoes 7.40 mn. tonnes (36.18 tonnes per hectare); vegetables: cabbages, carrots, onions, green peas, etc.; sugar beet 9.02 mn. tonnes (44.0 tonnes per hectare). British agriculture is highly mechanized. The fish catch is relatively small 713,800 tonnes and the high demand is covered by imports. The main fishing ports are Grimsby, Kingston upon Hull, Fleetwood, North Shields, Milford Haven, Lowestoft, Great Yarmouth, Aberdeen, Stornoway.

Transport (1984). Transport is an important modern sector which together with communications contributes 7.1% to the GNP and employs 6.2% of the economically active population. Freight traffic (173,200 mn. tonnes/km) is carried mainly by road 61.7%, railway 7.3% and coastal shipping 24.7%. Pipeline transport is growing at 6.0%. There are 346,872km of roads, of which 2,794km are motorways, 12,422km are trunk roads and 34,717km are principal roads. There were 16.06 mn. licensed private cars in the United Kingdom, 116,000 public road passenger vehicles, and 1.23 mn. motorcycles. Road transport carried 92.4% of passenger transport. The railway network measures 16,816km, of which 3,735km were electrified. Only 7.0% of travellers used rail transport. Britain's railways link up with the European railway system via the cross-Channel ferries and in future a railway tunnel (Eurotunnel) under the Channel. Inland transport uses 1,023km of navigable waterways and canals. The British merchant fleet is one of the largest in the world (3.2% of the world fleet). It has 777 vessels over 500 GRT with a total tonnage of 14.31 mn. GRT of this 276 tankers are of 7.46 mn. GRT). The British merchant fleet transported 24% of the U.K.'s exports and re-exports and 22% of imports. The biggest port is the Port of London handling roughly 46.9 mn. tonnes of goods a year. Other ports include Liverpool, Manchester, the oil port of Milford Haven (30.7 mn. tonnes of crude petroleum), Southampton and Grangemouth; there is also a transoceanic passenger terminal at Southampton; most Channel traffic is handled at Dover; there is a coal port at Newcastle upon Tyne, iron ore is handled at Teesside and the main fishing port is at Kingston upon Hull. 51.2 mn. passengers used air transport on domestic and overseas routes. The biggest of the 40 civil airports with scheduled flights (1985) are London-Heathrow and Gatwick, then Manchester, Glasgow, Aberdeen, Luton. British Airways is the largest U.K. air transport operator.

Foreign trade (1985). Foreign trade continues to be an important factor in the British economy, even if the importance of the United Kingdom as an economic power has declined. London remains one of the most important centres of international trade and finance. The pattern of foreign trade is such that imports usually exceed exports; exports were valued at £ 78,331 million, imports £ 84,790 million. The main items of export (1984) consists of over 66.2% of manufactured goods (mainly machinery, transport equipment and chemical products) and 21.8% of mineral fuels. Other items include food, beverages and tobacco (6.7%), crude materials (2.7%). Manufactured goods form 67.2% of imports and crude materials

map 8

ADMINISTRATIVE UNITS

Local authority areas	Area in sq.km	Population in thousands 30. 6. 1984	Density of population inh. per sq.km
ENGLAND AND WALES	151,124	49,763.6	329
ENGLAND	130,363	46,956.4	360
Metropolitan counties (admin. centre):			
1 Greater London	1,580	6,756.0	4,276
2 Greater Manchester (Manchester)	1,286	2,588.3	2,011
3 Merseyside (Liverpool)	652	1,490,7	2,286
4 South Yorkshire (Barnsley)	1,560	1,305.4	837
5 Tyne and Wear (Newcastle upon Tyne)	540	1,142.4	2,116
6 West Midlands (Birmingham)	899	2,647.0	2,944
7 West Yorkshire (Wakefield)	2,039	2,056.2	1,008
Non-metropolitan counties (admin. centre):			
8 Avon (Bristol)	1,338	939.8	702
9 Bedfordshire (Bedford)	1,235	515.7	418
10 Berkshire (Reading)	1,256	715.3	570
11 Buckinghamshire (Aylesbury)	1,883	594.6	316
12 Cambridgeshire (Cambridge)	3,409	609.2	179
13 Cheshire (Chester)	2,322	937.4	404
14 Cleveland (Middlesbrough)	583	562.7	965
15 Cornwall and Isles of Scilly (Truro)	3,546	439.0	124
16 Cumbria (Carlisle)	6,809	483.6	71
17 Derbyshire (Matlock)	2,631	911.7	347
18 Devon (Exeter)	6,715	978.3	146
19 Dorset (Dorchester)	2,654	617.8	233
20 Durham (Durham)	2,436	603.7	248
21 East Sussex (Lewes)	1,795	678.9	378
22 Essex (Chelmsford)	3,674	1,496.7	407
23 Gloucestershire (Gloucester)	2,638	509.2	193
24 Hampshire (Winchester)	3,772	1,509.5	400
25 Hereford and Worcester (Worcester)	3,927	645.3	164
26 Hertfordshire (Hertford)	1,634	980.3	600
27 Humberside (Kingston upon Hull)	3,512	851.6	243
28 Isle of Wight (Newport)	381	120.9	317
29 Kent (Maidstone)	3,732	1,491.7	400
30 Lancashire (Preston)	3,043	1,379.1	453
31 Leicestershire (Leicester)	2,553	866.1	339
32 Lincolnshire (Lincoln)	5,885	556.6	95
33 Norfolk (Norwich)	5,355	714.5	133
34 Northamptonshire (Northampton)	2,367	539.8	228
35 Northumberland (South Shields)	5,033	300.7	60
36 North Yorkshire (Northallerton)	8,317	691.1	83
37 Nottinghamshire (Nottingham)	2,164	1,000.1	462
38 Oxfordshire (Oxford)	2,611	555.7	213
39 Shropshire (Shrewsbury)	3,490	386.6	111
40 Somerset (Taunton)	3,458	440.9	128
41 Staffordshire (Stafford)	2,716	1,019.4	375
42 Suffolk (Ipswich)	3,800	615.9	162
43 Surrey (Kingston)	1,655	1,014.4	613
44 Warwickshire (Warwick)	1,981	477.7	241
45 West Sussex (Chichester)	2,016	682.7	339
46 Wiltshire (Trowbridge)	3,481	536.2	154
WALES	20,761	2,807.2	135
47 Clwyd (Mold)	2,425	396.3	163
48 Dyfed (Carmarthen)	5,765	335.0	58
49 Gwent (Cwmbran)	1,376	439.7	320
50 Gwynedd (Caernarvon)	3,868	232.7	60
51 Mid Glamorgan (Cardiff)	1,019	533.9	524
52 Powys (Llandrindod Wells)	5,077	110.6	22
53 South Glamorgan (Cardiff)	416	394.4	948
54 West Glamorgan (Swansea)	815	364.6	447
SCOTLAND – regions (admin. centre):	78,303[+]	5,146.0	66
55 Borders (Newtown St. Boswells)	1,662	101.3	22
56 Central (Stirling)	2,590	272.8	105
57 Dumfries and Galloway (Dumfries)	6,475	146.2	23
58 Fife (Glenrothes)	1,308	344.5	263

map 9

59	Grampian (Aberdeen)	8,550	497.3	58
60	Highland (Inverness)	26,136	197.2	8
61	Lothian (Edinburgh)	1,756	744.6	424
62	Strathclyde (Glasgow)	13,856	2,373.5	171
63	Tayside (Dundee)	7,668	394.4	51
64	Orkney (Kirkwall)	974	19.3	20
65	Shetland (Lerwick)	1,427	23.4	16
66	Western Isles (Stornoway)	2,901	31.5	11
NORTHERN IRELAND – districts (admin. centre)		13,483	1,578.5	117
1	Antrim (Antrim)	405	45.8	113
2	Ards (Newtownards)	368	60.4	164
3	Armagh (Armagh)	667	51.0	76
4	Ballymena (Ballymena)	634	55.4	87
5	Ballymoney (Ballymoney)	417	23.5	56
6	Banbridge (Banbridge)	441	30.8	70
7	Belfast (Belfast)	130	318.6	2,451
8	Carrickfergus (Carrickfergus)	85	28.8	339
9	Castlereagh (Castlereagh)	84	59.4	707
10	Coleraine (Coleraine)	478	47.3	99
11	Cookstown (Cookstown)	512	29.4	57
12	Craigavon (Portadown)	280	74.4	266
13	Down (Downpatrick)	638	54.5	85
14	Dungannon (Dungannon)	763	45.8	60
15	Fermanagh (Enniskillen)	1,700	51.4	30
16	Larne (Larne)	337	29.6	88
17	Limavady (Limavady)	585	28.5	49
18	Lisburn (Hillsborough)	436	89.1	204
19	Londonderry (Londonderry)	373	97.2	261
20	Magherafelt (Magherafelt)	562	34.3	61
21	Moyle (Ballycastle)	494	14.6	30
22	Newry and Mourne (Newry)	886	84.6	95
23	Newtownabbey (Newtownabbey)	151	72.4	479
24	North Down (Bangor)	72	67.6	939
25	Omagh (Omagh)	1,124	47.0	42
26	Strabane (Strabane)	861	37.1	43
	+ including water area			

for industry 6.2% of imports. The United Kingdom is now less dependent on food imports, which have dropped to 9.9%. Fuels 13.0% form a big portion of imports. British trade with Commonwealth countries has greatly declined in recent years. In the last decade the main trading partners of the United Kingdom have been the EEC countries taking 44.8% of exports, and providing 44.7% of imports, while other countries in Western Europe handled 12.4% of exports and 16.8% of imports. The United States (exports 14.4%, imports 11.9%) and Canada (1.7%, 2.1%) continue to play an important role as do other developed countries 5.2% and 7.1%. Trade with the developing countries represents 10.7% of exports and 10.9% of imports, and to oil exporting countries exports 8.2% and imports 3.6%.

Membership of international organizations. The United Kingdom stands at the head of the Commonwealth, which is a free association of sovereign independent countries. The original dominions and most of the former colonies in the British Empire have retained membership in the Commonwealth after declaring independence. Individual member countries are linked by treaties and agreements on mutual cooperation in political life, economic affairs, finance, education, science, and culture. The British Queen stands at the head of the Commonwealth. The following were 49 member states of the Commonwealth in 1986: America: Antigua and Barbuda, the Bahamas, Barbados, Belize, Canada, Dominica, Grenada, Guyana, Jamaica, Saint Kitts and Nevis, Saint Lucia, Saint Vincent and Grenadine Is., Trinidad and Tobago; Europe: United Kingdom, Malta; Africa: Botswana, Gambia, Ghana, Kenya, Lesotho, Malawi, Mauritius, Nigeria, Seychelles, Sierra Leone, Swaziland, Tanzania, Uganda, Zambia, Zimbabwe; Asia: Bangladesh, Brunei, Cyprus, India, Malaysia, Maldives, Singapore, Sri Lanka; Australia and Oceania: Australia, Fiji, Kiribati, Nauru, New Zealand, Papua New Guinea, Samoa, Solomon Islands, Tonga, Tuvalu, Vanuatu.

The United Kingdom is a founder-member of the United Nations and a permanent member of the Security Council with the right of veto. It takes an active part in NATO. It is a member of the following international organizations: The International Monetary Fund (IMF), the International Bank for Reconstruction and Development (IBRD), the General Agreement on Tariffs and Trade (GATT), the Organization for Economic Co-operation and Development (OECD), the United Nations Conference on Trade and Development (UNCTAD), the European Atomic Energy Community (EAEC or Euratom), the European Coal and Steel Community (ECSC), and others. Since 1973 the United Kingdom has been a member of the European Economic Community (EEC).

THE ISLE OF MAN
572 sq.km, 64,300 inhabitants (1986), **crown dependency of the United Kingdom.** Currency: £ 1 = 100 pence. **Position:** Island in the Irish Sea. **Capital:** Douglas 19,944 inhabitants (1981); other towns: Onchan 7,478, Ramsey 5,818 (1981). **Official language:** English; Manx sometimes used.
Economy: Agriculture: barley, oats, wheat, potatoes. Fish catch (1982): 6,297 tonnes; **animal husbandry** (1984): sheep 135,688 head, cattle 34,062 head, pigs 7,174 head, poultry 75,614. Petroleum refinery; fish processing. Tourism 0.5 mn. visitors annually; airport; railway. The island is the setting of the annual Tourist Trophy motorcycle race.

map 9

THE CHANNEL ISLANDS
197 sq.km, 130,000 inhabitants (1983), **crown dependency of the United Kingdom. Currency:** £1 = 100 pence.
Position: Islands in the English Channel off the coast of France. **Jersey** 116 sq.km, 76,050 inhabitants (1981), administrative centre Saint Helier (28,135 inhab., 1976) and **Guernsey** 63 sq.km, 53,268 inhabitants (1981), administrative centre Saint Peter Port; dependencies of Guernsey: Alderney 8 sq.km, 2,000 inhabitants (1980); Sark 5 sq.km, 420 inhabitants (1984); Brechou 0.3 sq.km; Herm 2 sq.km.; Jethou 0.18 sq.km; Lihou 0.15 sq.km. **Capital:** Saint Peter Port 16,303 inhabitants (1976). **Official language:** English, French on the island of Jersey; Norman French is spoken on the smaller islands.
Economy: Agriculture: potatoes, tomatoes, spring vegetables, flowers; cattle breeding, pigs, poultry. Fish catch (1982): 2,241 tonnes, lobster and crab fishing. Wool and milk processing. Tourism. 3 airports.

ALBANIA

Republika Popullore Socialiste e Shqipërisë, area 28,748 sq.km, population 2,962,500 (1985), **socialist republic** (Chairman of the Presidium of the People's Assembly Ramiz Alia since 1982).
Administrative units: 26 districts (Rrethët). **Capital:** Tiranë 206,100 inhab. (1983); **other towns** (1981, in 1,000 inhab.): Shkodër 65, Durrës 62, Vlorë 61, Elbasan 53, Korçë 53, Berat 33, Fier 29. **Population:** Albanians. **Density** 103 persons per sq.km; average annual rate of population increase 2.4% (1975–82); urban population 35.3% (1980). 60% of inhabitants employed in agriculture (1981). – **Currency:** lek = 100 quindarkas.
Economy: agricultural and industrial country. **Mining** (1983, in 1,000 tonnes, metal content): brown coal 1,700, crude petroleum 3,500 (Qytet Stalin, Patos), chromium 258 (Kam, Bulqizë), copper 15, nickel 9, asphalt. Electricity 2.9 billion kWh (1983). **Industries:** textiles and foodstuffs. **Agriculture** (1983, in 1,000 tonnes): maize (corn) 366, wheat 583, rice, potatoes, sugar beet, cotton, olives, grapes, tobacco; livestock (1983, in 1,000 head): cattle 600, sheep 1,200, goats 700; fish catch 4,000 tonnes; roundwood 2.3 mn. cub.m (1983). – **Communications:** railways 380km, roads 4,827km. Merchant shipping 56,000 GRT (1984). – **Exports:** petroleum and petroleum products, ores and metals, cigarettes, fresh and canned fruit and vegetables. **Imports:** machines and equipment, transport equipment.

ANDORRA

Principat d'Andorra – Principauté d'Andorre, area 453 sq.km, population 42,000 (1985), **republic under the joint suzerainty of France and the Bishop of Seo de Urgel** (Spain), headed by two Syndics (Prime Minister Oscar Ribas de Reig).
Administrative units: 7 villages. **Capital:** Andorra la Vella 15,698 inhab. (1984). **Official languages:** Catalan, Spanish, French. – **Currency:** French franc, Spanish peseta. – **Economy:** mountain agriculture and grazing, cultivation of cereals, vines, tobacco in the valleys; raising of sheep and goats. Tourism is the chief source of inhabitants' incomes.

AUSTRIA

Republik Österreich, area 83,853 sq.km, population 7,555,340 (1985), **neutral federal republic** (President Kurt Waldheim since 1986).

Administrative units: 9 federal countries (Wien, Niederösterreich, Burgenland, Oberösterreich, Salzburg, Steiermark, Kärnten, Tirol, Vorarlberg). **Capital:** Wien (Vienna) 1,501,700 inhab. (1984); **other towns** (1981, in 1,000 inhab.): Graz 243, Linz 200, Salzburg 140, Innsbruck 117, Klagenfurt 87. **Population:** German speaking Austrians 98%, small Croatian, Czech and Slovenian minorities. **Density** 90 persons per sq.km; average annual rate of population increase –0.4‰; urban population 55% (1983). 33.2% of inhabitants employed in industry. – **Currency:** schilling = 100 groschen.
Economy: highly developed industrial country with considerable mineral resources. **Principal industries:** metallurgy (Steiermark, Linz), engineering (Steiermark, Wien, W. Neustadt), petroleum refining, energy production, chemicals and electronics. **Mining** (1983, in 1,000 tonnes, metal content): brown coal 3,041, crude petroleum 1,269 (Marchfeld – Matzen, Weinviertel – Mühlberg etc.), natural gas 49,021 TJ, iron ore 1,107 (Steiermark: Erzberg, Radmer), lead 5.7, zinc 22,7, tungsten 1,117 tonnes, antimony 705 tonnes, magnesite 1,006 (Tirol – Hochfilzen, Kärnten – Radenthein, Steiermark – Trieben, Breitenau), salt 530 (Salzkammergut), graphite 40.4. Electricity 42.1 billion kWh (1983), of which 72% hydro-electric power stations. **Production** (1983, in 1,000 tonnes): pig iron 3,333, crude steel 4,410, lead 11, zinc 18.8, refined copper 34, aluminium 482, nitrogenous fertilizers 209, plastics 550, rayon and acetate fibres 11.5, rayon and acetate staple fibres 110, cotton yarn 16, woven cotton fabrics 77 mn. m, cement 4,907, chemical wood pulp 850, paper 1,613, musical instruments (Wien), sugar 464, meat 691, milk 3,650, butter 43, cheese 82, eggs 89, wine 3.7 mn. hl, beer 8.4 mn. hl; 15 billion cigarettes.
Agriculture: principal branch is livestock raising. Land use: arable land 18.3%, meadows and pastures 24.3%, forests 39% (with important hunting grounds in the Alps). **Crops** (1983, in 1,000 tonnes): wheat 1,415, rye 348, barley 1,442, oats, maize (corn) 1,454, potatoes 1,012, sugar beet 1,975, grapes 518, fruit 1,179, vegetables 679; **livestock** (1983, in 1,000 head): cattle 2,546, pigs 3,981, sheep 199, goats, horses, poultry; roundwood 13.6 mn. cub.m. – **Communications:** railways 5,756km (1984), of which 3,105km electrified, roads 11,393km, motorways 1,137km (1981), passenger cars 2,468,500 (1984). Navigable waterways 358km. Civil aviation (1984): 25.6 mn. km flown, 1,514,000 passengers carried. Important tourism 14.5 mn. visitors (1983) – **Exports:** finished products, especially machines, steel, chemicals, textiles, metals, wood, paper, salt, electricity. **Imports:** coal, metals, chemicals, transport equipment, machines, finished electronic products, textile raw materials, foodstuffs. Chief trading partners: Fed. Rep. of Germany, Italy, Switzerland, United Kingdom, France, U.S.S.R.

map 10

BELGIUM

Royaume de Belgique – Koninkrijk België, area 30,521 sq.km, population 9,853,000 (1984), **kingdom** (King Baudouin I since 1951).

Administrative units: 9 provinces: **Capital:** Bruxelles – Brussel 138,900 inhab. (1982); with agglomeration 989,877 (1983); **other towns** (1983, in 1,000 inhab.): Antwerpen 491 (with agglom.), Gent 237, Charleroi 216, Liège 207, Brugge 118, Namur 102, Mons 92, Leuven 85, Alost 78, Mechelen 77, Kortrijk 76, Oostende 69. **Population:** Walloons, Flemings. **Density** 323 persons per sq.km; average annual rate of population increase 0.1% (1975–82): urban population 73%. 27.5% of inhabitants employed in industry (1982). – **Currency:** Belgian franc = 100 centimes.
Economy: highly developed industrial country with large concentration of industry and intensive agriculture. **Principal industries:** metallurgy, engineering, chemicals, textiles. **Mining:** coal 6,096,000 tonnes (1983, reg. Borinage, Liège, reg. Campine, Charleroi-Namur), natural gas. Electricity 52.7 billion kWh (1983), of which 40% are nuclear power stations (Mol). **Production** (1983, in 1,000 tonnes): pig iron 8,033, crude steel 10,266 (prov. Liège, Hainaut, Brabant), coke oven coke 5,106, lead 134, zinc 276 (Flône, Balen), refined copper 431, tin 2,214 tonnes (Hoboken), merchant vessels 194,000 GRT (Hoboken, Temse), assembly of passenger cars 972,000 units (Antwerpen, Bruxelles), radio receivers 1,006,000 units, television receivers 766,000, sulphuric acid 1,902, nitric acid 1,445, synthetic nitrogen 495, nitrogenous fertilizers 706[+], phosphorus fertilizers 515[+], plastics 2,246, pharmaceuticals (Bruxelles), capacity of petroleum refineries 28 mn. tonnes (1984, Antwerpen, Gent, Bruxelles), motor spirit 3,943, mineral oils 12,176, cement 5,724, paper products 778[+], woven cotton fabrics 51 (Gent and surroundings), woollen – yarn 87, woven fabrics 36 (Verviers), flax industry (Vlaanderen) – sugar 860[+] (Tienen), meat 1,163[+], butter 115[+], milk 4,170[+], cheese 47.5[+], eggs 185[+], beer 14.2 mn. hl (1983); 29.7 billion cigarettes (1983). ([+]Figures for Belgium and Luxembourg combined.)
Agriculture: highly productive with animal production predominating. Land use: arable land 26%, meadows and pastures 21.1%, forests 23%. **Crops** (1983, in 1,000 tonnes): wheat 1,084[+], barley 745, oats 136, potatoes 1,245, sugar beet 5,070[+], fruit; **livestock** (1983, in 1,000 head): cattle 3,115, pigs 5,210; fish catch 48,600 tonnes (1983); roundwood 3[+] mn. cub. m (1983).
Communications (1984): railways 3,741km, of which 1,907km electrified, roads 15,305km, motorways 1,488km, passenger cars 3,258,000. Navigable rivers and canals 1,956km. Merchant shipping 2,407,000 GRT. Largest ports: Antwerpen and Gent. Civil aviation 49.6 mn. km flown, 2,032,000 passengers carried. Tourism 6.6 mn. visitors.
Exports: metals, machines and equipment, cars, chemical and pharmaceutical products, textiles etc. **Imports:** raw materials, especially for the power industry, foodstuffs, machines and equipment. Chief trading partners: Fed. Rep. of Germany, France, Netherlands, United Kingdom, Italy.

BULGARIA

Narodna Republika Bălgarija, area 110,912 sq.km, population 8,942,976 (1985), **socialist republic** (Chairman of the State Council Todor Zhivkov since 1972).

Administrative units: 27 regions (okrăg) and the capital. **Capital:** Sofija (Sofia) 1,093,752 inhab. (1984); **other towns** (1982, in 1,000 inhab.): Plovdiv 367, Varna 295, Ruse 178, Burgas 178, Stara Zagora 142, Pleven 136, Sliven 101, Šumen 100, Tolbuhin 99, Pernik 95, Haskovo 88, Jambol 86, Gabrovo 81, Pazardžik 78. **Population:** Bulgarians 92%, Gipsies, Macedonians etc. **Density** 81 persons per sq.km; average annual rate of population increase 0.6% (1975–82); urban population 62.8% (1981). 29.6% of inhabitants employed in agriculture, 28% in industry. – **Currency:** lev = = 100 stotinki.
Economy: industrial and agricultural country. **Principal industries:** metallurgy (Kremikovci, Pernik), engineering (Sofija, Plovdiv, Ruse), chemicals (Sofija, Burgas, Dimitrovgrad, Stara Zagora, Devnja), textiles (Gabrovo, Sofija), foodstuffs.
Mining (1983, in 1,000 tonnes, metal content): brown coal 32,124 (Marica-East, Dimitrovgrad, Pernik, Bobovdol), crude petroleum 300, natural gas, iron ore 554 (Kremikovci), lead 95, zinc 68, copper 80 (Sredna Gora Mts.), manganese 13.1, molybdenum 150 tonnes, silver 25 tonnes, uranium, pyrites 680, salt 87. Electricity 42.9 billion kWh (1983), of which 11% are hydro-electric and 25% nuclear power stations (near Kozoduj). **Production** (1983, in 1,000 tonnes): pig iron 1,632, crude steel 2,820, copper smelted 60, lead 116, zinc 93, vessels 159,000 GRT (1984, Varna, Ruse), sulphuric acid 861, nitric acid 977, nitrogenous fertilizers 813, phosphorus fertilizers 204, soda ash 1,245, plastics and resins 270, capacity of petroleum refineries 15 mn. tonnes (1984), motor spirit 1,800, oils 9,430, cement 5,644, cotton yarn 85, woven fabrics – cotton 367 mn. m, woollen 49 mn. m, rayon and acetate 37 mn. m – synthetic staple fibre 42, leather shoes 18 mn. pairs, meat 717, milk 2,080, cheese 176, eggs 146, wine 464, canned vegetables 300, beer 5.5 mn. hl (1983); 91.3 billion cigarettes (1983).
Agriculture: vegetable production predominates. Land use: arable land 34.4%, meadows and pastures 18.3%, forests 34.7%. **Crops** (1983, in 1,000 tonnes): wheat 3,600, barley 1,046, maize (corn) 3,101, rice, potatoes 428, cotton -seed 12, sugar beet 749, sunflower seeds 448, soya beans 84, fruit 2,030, grapes 1,034, strawberries 14, vegetables 1,690, tomatoes 658, legumes, roses (Kazanlák), tobacco 118, walnuts 24: **livestock** (1983, in 1,000 head): cattle 1,783, buffaloes 40, horses 119, asses 347, pigs 3,810, sheep 10,761, goats 502; poultry 41,000, silkworms 200 tonnes, wool 17,700 tonnes, honey 8,638 tonnes; fish catch 121,100 tonnes (1983); roundwood 4.8 mn. cub.m (1983).
Communications: railways 4,278km, of which 2,053km electrified (1984), roads 33,253km (1984), passenger cars 500,000 (1980). Navigable waterways 471km. Merchant shipping 1,283,000 GRT (1984). Chief ports: Varna and Burgas. Civil aviation: 12.7 mn. km flown, 1,800,000 passengers carried. Tourism 5,771,000 visitors (1983).
Exports: machines and equipment, foodstuffs (fresh and canned fruit and vegetables), rose oil, wine, cigarettes, tobacco, chemical products and textiles, furs. **Imports:** petroleum, fuels and raw materials, machines, consumer goods. Chief trading partners: (1984): the socialist countries 76%, of which the U.S.S.R. 57.5%, German Dem. Rep., Poland, Czechoslovakia and Fed. Rep. of Germany.

map 10

CZECHOSLOVAKIA

Československá socialistická republika, area 127,896 sq.km, population 15,520,000 (1985), **socialist federal republic** (President Dr Gustáv Husák since 1975).

Administrative units: 2 socialist federal republics – the Czech Socialist Republic (7 regions, the capital of the ČSSR Praha with the status of a region), the Slovak Socialist Republic (3 regions, the capital of SSR Bratislava with the status of a region). **Capital:** Praha (Prague) 1,193,513 inhab. (1986); **other towns** (1986, in 1,000 inhab.): Bratislava 417, Brno 386, Ostrava 328, Košice 222, Plzeň 175, Olomouc 106, Ústí n. Labem 104, Liberec 101, Hradec Králové 100, České Budějovice 94, Pardubice 94, Havířov 92, Žilina 92, Gottwaldov 86, Nitra 85, Prešov 83, Banská Bystrica 78, Karviná 75, Kladno 73, Trnava 70, Most 65, Frýdek-Místek 63, Martin 62. **Population:** Czechs 63.4%, Slovaks 31.3%, Hungarians 4%, Poles, Germans. **Density** 121 persons per sq.km; average annual rate of population increase 0.34% (1980–84); urban population 64% (1981). 37.4% of inhabitants employed in industry, 12.4% in agriculture (1985). –**Currency:** koruna (Kčs) = = 100 halers.
Economy: advanced industrial and agricultural country. **Principal industries:** mineral mining, machinery, metallurgy, foodstuffs, textiles and wood-working . **Mining** (1983, in 1,000 tonnes, metal content): coal 26,437 (Ostrava – Karviná), brown coal 102,416 (Chomutov, Most, Sokolov), crude petroleum 93. natural gas 20,100 TJ, iron ore 507, copper 10, lead 2.7, tin 226 tonnes, mercury 144 tonnes, antimony 0.8 tonne, silver 40 tonnes, magnesite (Slovenské rudohorie), uranium (Českomoravská vrchovina, Příbram), salt 77, graphite 27, kaolin and glass sands. Electricity 80.6 billion kWh (1985), of which 5% are hydro-electric and 14.6% nuclear power stations (Jaslovské Bohunice, Dukovany).
Production (1983, in 1,000 tonnes): pig iron 9,466, crude steel 15,024, coke oven coke 10,340 (Ostrava, Třinec, Kladno, Košice), aluminium 36.1 (Žiar nad Hronom), smelted copper 25.7 (Krompachy), lead 21; engineering – Praha, Plzeň ("Škoda" Works), Brno, north-western Slovakia (1983, in 1,000 units): metal cutting machines 35.4, passenger cars 177.5 (Mladá Boleslav), lorries 43.2 (Kopřivnice), motorcycles 136, tractors 34, electric locomotives 148 units, television receivers 415; chemical industry – Záluží, Ostrava vicinity, Elbeland, Bratislava, south-western Slovakia (1983, in 1,000 tonnes): sulphuric acid 1,244, nitrogenous fertilizers 591, phosphorus fertilizers 326, plastics and resins 1,006, synthetic rubber 67.2 (Kralupy nad Vltavou), capacity of petroleum refineries 23 mn. tonnes (1984) – pipeline for the import of Soviet petroleum; motor spirit 1,500, oils 11,470, cement 10,498, paper 934 (Štětí, Větřní, Ružomberok); textile industry uses mainly imported raw materials (northern and north-eastern Bohemia, northern Moravia, Žilina, Ružomberok), cotton yarn 140, woven fabrics – cotton 585 mn. m, linen 105 mn. m, woollen 61.7 mn. m, silk 140,000m, rayon 50.7 mn. m – synthetic fibres 112, shoes 128 mn. pairs (Gottwaldov), glass (northern Bohemia), porcelain (Karlovy Vary), ceramics (Horní Bříza near Plzeň), costume jewellery (Jablonec n. N.), musical instruments (Kraslice, Hradec Králové, Krnov); food industry: sugar 836 (Elbeland), meat 1,382, milk 6,496, condensed milk 147, butter 149, cheese 188, eggs 275, malt, beer 24.9 mn. hl (Plzeň, České Budějovice), wine 127; 25 billion cigarettes.
Agriculture: arable land 37.4%, meadows and pastures 12.8%, forests 35.8%. **Crops** (1983, in 1,000 tonnes): wheat 5,820, rye 751, barley 3,276, maize (corn) 722, oats 410, potatoes 3,177, flax 99, hemp, rapeseed 300, sunflower 40, sugar beet 6,041, hops 12 (Žatec region), fruit 939, grapes 317 (Malé Karpaty, southern Moravia), vegetables 1,194; **livestock** (1983, in 1,000 head): 5,190, pigs 7,070, sheep 1,041, goats, horses; poultry 50,977; fish catch 19,525 tonnes (1983); roundwood 18.9 mn. cub.m (1983).
Communications (1985): railways 13,130km, of which 3,507km electrified, roads 73,809km, passenger cars 2,639,600 (1984). Navigable waterways 483km. Merchant shipping 184,000 GRT (1984). Civil aviation (1984): 21.6mn. km flown, 911,000 passengers carried. Tourism 4.6 mn. visitors (1983).
Exports: machines, equipment, machine tools and transport equipment (cutting machines, cars, power stations and other plant equipment, electromotors), fuels (coal, coke), raw materials, hops, malt, beer, glass, porcelain, wood, shoes, textiles.
Imports: fuels (petroleum, natural gas, coal) and raw materials (iron ores, non-ferrous metals, machines and equipment, consumer goods, foodstuffs (cereals, fruit, vegetables), textile raw materials. Chief trading partners: U.S.S.R., German Dem. Rep., Poland, Hungary, Fed. Rep. of Germany, Yugoslavia, Bulgaria, Austria, Romania.

DENMARK

Kongeriget Danmark, area 43,075 sq.km, population 5,113,691 (1985), **kingdom** (Queen Margrethe II since 1972).

Administrative units: 15 districts (Ämter) and 2 cities (Kóbenhavn and Frederiksberg). The autonomous Faeroe Islands (Faeröerne) and Greenland belong to Denmark. **Capital:** Kóbenhavn (Copenhagen) 638,163 inhab. (1984), with Frederiksberg and agglom. 1,372,019 inhab. (1983); **other towns** (1983, in 1,000 inhab.): Århus 249, Odense 171, Ålborg 155, Esbjerg 80, Randers 62, Helsingör 56, Herning 56, Kolding 56, Vejle 56. **Population:** Danes. **Density** 119 persons per sq.km; average annual rate of population increase 0.2% (1975–82); urban population 85% (1983). 18.6% of inhabitants employed in industry (1983). – **Currency:** Danish krone = 100 öre.
Economy: advanced industrial and agricultural country. **Principal industries:** metal-working and engineering (especially shipbuilding, electrical and radio engineering), foodstuffs, chemicals, paper and textiles. Kóbenhavn is the chief industrial centre. **Mining:** petroleum mining under the sea near the west coast 2.1 mn. tonnes (1983), lignite, salt 452,000 tonnes (1983), sulphur. Electricity 22.2 billion kWh (1983), 100% thermal power stations. **Production** (1983, in 1,000 tonnes): crude steel 492, vessels 525,000 GRT (Kóbenhavn and others), cement 1,556, nitrogenous fertilizers 202.5, meat 1,408, milk 5,427, butter 131, cheese 251, eggs 81, fish flour 430, sugar 376, beer 11 mn. hl, 9.8 billion cigarettes. **Agriculture** is highly developed with intensive animal production. Arable land 61.6%, meadows and pastures 5.7%, forests 11.4%. **Crops** (1983, in 1,000 tonnes): barley 4,450, wheat 1,577, oats 83, rye 321, potatoes 870, sugar beet 2,632; **livestock** (1983, in 1,000 head): cattle 2,900, pigs 9,289, poultry 15,000; fish catch 1,862,100 tonnes (1983); roundwood 3 mn. cub.m (1983).

map 11

Communications (1984); railways 2,448km, roads 70,170km, motorways 549km, passenger cars 1,450,400 (1984). Merchant shipping: 5,211,000 GRT (1984). Chief port København. Civil aviation (1984): 41.3 mn. km flown, 4,126,000 passengers carried.
Exports: industrial products 70% (machinery, transport equipment, vessels, chemical products), agricultural products 30% (meat, live animals, butter, milk products, eggs, fish products). **Imports** fuels and raw materials, machines, equipment and transport equipment. Chief trading partners: Fed. Rep. of Germany, United Kingdom, Sweden, U.S.A.

FAEROE ISLANDS

Færøerne, area 1,399 sq.km, population 45,850 (1985), **autonomous region of Denmark. Capital:** Thorshavn 13,951 inhab. (1984). **Economy:** potatoes, sheep, fish 330,000 tonnes (1983), whaling.

FINLAND

Suomen Tasavalta – Republiken Finland, area 338,145 sq.km, population 4,908,215 (1985), **republic** (President Mauno Henrik Koivisto since 1982).

Administrative units: 12 regions (Lääni), of which islands Ahvenanmaa (Åland) are an autonomous province. **Capital:** Helsinki 484,471 inhab. (1984); **other towns** (1983), in 1,000 inhab.): Tampere 168, Turku 163, Espoo 149, Vantaa 139, Oulu 96, Lahti 95, Pori 79, Kuopio 78, Jyväskylä 65, Kotka 60. **Population:** Finns 93.2%, Swedes 6.6%. **Density** 14 persons per sq.km; average annual rate of population increase 0.5% (1975–82); urban population 63% (1982). 25% of inhabitants employed in industry (1980) – **Currency:** markka = 100 penni.
Economy: developed industrial and agricultural country with modern industry, intensive agriculture and forestry. Large resources of water power. **Chief industries:** wood working, chemical wood pulp and paper manufacturing (Lahti, Kuopio, Kotka, Kemi, Oulu and others), metallurgy, shipbuilding, engineering (Helsinki, Turku, Tampere), foodstuffs and textiles. **Mining** (1983, in 1,000 tonnes, metal content): iron ore 555, chromium 91, copper 37.7 (Ylöjärvi), lead 2.1, zinc 56.3 (Kisko), nickel 5.3 (Leppävirta), cobalt 930 tonnes, vanadium 3,359 tonnes, mercury 65 tonnes, gold 784 kg (Haveri), silver 30 tonnes, pyrites 449. Electricity 40.2 billion kWh (1983), of which hydro-electric power stations 26%, nuclear 17%. **Production** (1983, in 1,000 tonnes): pig iron 1,957, crude steel 2,416 (Tampere, Imatra, Raahe), copper -smelted 70.1, -refined 55.4 (Harjavalta), zinc 128, vessels 317,000 GRT (Raahe, Vaasa, Pori), sulphuric acid 1,145 (Harjavalta), nitrogenous fertilizers 293, phosphorus fertilizers 191.7, capacity of petroleum refineries 12 mn. tonnes (1984, Naantali), motor spirit 2.4 mn. tonnes, oils 6.2 mn. tonnes, cement 1,979; wood-working and paper industry – Lahti, Kuopio, Kemi, Kotka, Oulu and others (1983, in 1,000 tonnes): chemical wood pulp 4,195, paper products 4,775, plywood 580,000 cub.m, sawnwood 7,995,000 cub.m; textile industry (Tampere, Turku, Pori): rayon and acetate staple fibre 57.6, glass industry (Riihimäki, Lahti), porcelain (Helsinki); food industry: meat 331, milk 3,173, cheese 78, butter 70, eggs 83; 8.4 billion cigarettes.
Agriculture: arable land 7.6%, meadows and pastures 0.5%, forests 69.2% – the chief natural wealth of the country. **Crops** (1983, in 1,000 tonnes): cereals 3,865 (barley 1,764, oats 1,407, wheat), hay 2,057, potatoes 804, sugar beet 955; **livestock** (1983, in 1,000 head): cattle 1,800, pigs 1,500, sheep; poultry 8,000, raising of reindeer 205 and fur animals; fish catch 157,100 tonnes (1983); roundwood 38 mn. cub.m (1983). – **Communications** (1984): railways 5,998 km, roads 63,909km, motorways 205km, passenger cars 1,474,000. Navigable waterways 6,057km. Merchant shipping 2,168,000 GRT (1984). Chief port Helsinki. Civil aviation (1984): 37 mn. km flown, 2,991,000 passengers carried. Tourism 451,000 visitors (1983).
Exports: wood-working and paper industry products, machines and equipment, iron and steel, chemical and food products. **Imports:** raw materials, semi-finished products, fuels. Chief trading partners: U.S.S.R., Sweden, United Kingdom, Fed. Rep. of Germany.

FRANCE

République Française, area 543,998 sq.km, population 55,282,000 (1985),**republic** (President François Maurice Mitterrand) since 1981).
Administrative units: The Republic of France comprises 96 metropolitan departments which make up 22 administrative regions. **Overseas departments:** Guadeloupe, Martinique, Guiana, Réunion, St. Pierre et Miquelon, Mayotte; overseas territories New Caledonia, the Wallis and Futuna islands, and French Polynesia. **Capital:** Paris 2,166,449 inhab. (1982, with agglom. 9,650,000 inhab.); **other towns** (in 1,000 inhab.): Marseille 879, Lyon 418, Toulouse 354, Nice 338, Strasbourg 252, Nantes 247, Bordeaux 211, Saint-Étienne 206, Montpellier 201, Le Havre 199, Rennes 192, Reims 182, Toulon 181, Lille 174, Brest 160, Grenoble 159, Clermont-Ferrand 151, Le Mans 150, Dijon 146, Limoges 144. **Population:** French 90%, Italians, Spaniards, Algerians, Portuguese and others. **Density** 102 persons per sq.km; average annual rate of population increase 0.4% (1975–82); urban population 78% (1982). 33.9% of inhabitants employed in industry, 7.5% in agriculture (1983). – **Currency:** French franc = 100 centimes.
Economy: highly developed industrial and agricultural country. With its high concentration of industrial plants France belongs to the leading group of industrial countries in the world. Industry has an insufficient fuel and power base and has to import coal, coke and petroleum. **Chief industries:** mineral mining, metallurgy, engineering, energy production, chemicals, electrical and radio engineering, ship and aircraft building, textile and food industries.
Mining (1983, in 1,000 tonnes, metal content): coal 18,649 (Nord, Pas-de-Calais, reg. Lorraine), lignite 2,606, crude petroleum 1,660 (reg. Aquitaine, Paris Basin, reg. Alsace), natural gas 379,000 TJ (Lacq, Saint Marcet), iron ore 5,174 (Metz-Thionville and Briey-Longwy areas), bauxite 1,660 (Brignoles, Bédarieux, Les Baux), lead 1.5, zinc 34, tungsten 1,243 tonnes, antimony, gold 2,040kg, silver 1,107 tonnes, uranium 3,529 tonnes (Mts. du Forez-Bois Noirs), salt 5,686, potassium salt 1,651 (at Mulhouse), phosphates. Electricity 283.4 billion kWh (1983), of which 27% hydro-electric power stations (Alps, Massif Central and Pyrenees) and 34.3% nuclear power stations (Chinon, Marcoule, Fessenheim, Blayais).

map 11

Production (1983, in 1,000 tonnes): pig iron 2,207, crude steel 7,219, aluminium 59, copper – smelted 17, refined 50 – vessels 362,000 GRT (Rostock, Wismar), passenger cars 188,000 units (Eisenach, Zwickau), radio receivers 975,000 units, television receivers 667,000 units, sulphuric acid 926, soda ash 887, caustic soda 687, fertilizers: nitrogenous 968, phosphorus 315; synthetic rubber 161 (Schkopau), plastics and resins 1,045, photographic materials (Wolfen), electrochemistry (Bitterfeld): capacity of petroleum refineries 26.6 mn. tonnes (1984), pipeline for the import of Soviet petroleum, motor spirit 4 mn. tonnes, oils 15 mn. tonnes, cement 11.8 mn. tonnes, chemical wood pulp 170 (Premnitz), paper 1,154. Textile industry mainly in Saxony, Thuringia (1983, in 1,000 tonnes): yarn – cotton 134.7, woollen 76.4 – woven fabrics – cotton 298 mn. sq.m, woollen 39 mn. sq.m, rayon and acetate 48.6 mn. sq.m – fibres – rayon and acetate 35, synthetic 82 – staple fibre – rayon and acetate 131, synthetic 150 – shoes 87 mn. pairs. Food industry (1983, in 1,000 tonnes): meat 1,746, milk 8,208, butter 266, cheese 225, eggs 350, sugar 750, beer 25.3 mn. hl (1983); 27.4 billion cigarettes (1983). Glass industry (Jena), porcelain (Meissen), printing (Leipzig, Gotha).
Agriculture: mainly cultivation of cereals and potatoes. Land use: arable land 46.5%, meadows and pastures 11.4%, forests 27.3%. **Crops** (1983, in 1,000 tonnes): wheat 3,470, barley 3,990, rye 2,064, oats 500, potatoes 7,500, flax, sugar beet 6,400, rapeseed 303, vegetables 1,278, tobacco; **livestock** (1983, in 1,000 head): cattle 5,690, pigs 12,107, sheep 2,198; poultry 51,000, honey 39,000 tonnes; fish catch 239,900 tonnes (1983); roundwood 10.9 mn. cub.m (1983). – **Communications** (1984): railways 14,226km, of which 2,321km are electrified, roads 47,261km, passenger cars 3,157,100. Navigable waterways 2,319km. Merchant shipping 1,422,000 GRT (1984). Chief ports: Rostock, Wismar, Stralsund. Civil aviation: 1,359,000 passengers carried. Tourism 1.5 mn. visitors (1983).
Exports: machines and equipment, transport equipment, precision instruments, optics and electronics, chemical products, dyes, photo materials, brown coal, potassium salts and consumer goods. **Imports:** petroleum, ores and other raw materials, foodstuffs. Chief trading partners: U.S.S.R., Czechoslovakia, Fed. Rep. of Germany, Hungary, Poland, Bulgaria, Romania, West Berlin.

GERMANY, FEDERAL REPUBLIC OF

Bundesrepublik Deutschland, area 248,198 sq.km, population 59,165,000 (1985), **federal republic** (President Dr. Richard von Weizsäcker since 1984).

Administrative units: 10 federal countries (Schleswig-Holstein, Hamburg, Niedersachsen, Bremen, Nordrhein-Westfalen, Hessen, Rheinland-Pfalz, Baden-Württemberg, Bayern /Bavaria/, Saarland). **Capital:** Bonn 289,688 inhab. (1985); **other towns** (1984, in 1,000 inhab.: Hamburg 1,606, München (Munich) 1,283, Köln (Cologne) 997, Essen 635, Frankfurt am Main 614, Dortmund 600, Düsseldorf 576, Stuttgart 562, Duisburg 578, Hannover 544, Bremen 540, Nürnberg 473, Bochum 414, Wuppertal 393, Bielefeld 307, Mannheim 302, Gelsenkirchen 296, Münster 273, Karlsruhe 271, Wiesbaden 268, Mönchengladbach 260, Braunschweig 255, Kiel 248, Augsburg 246, Aachen 245, Oberhausen 228, Krefeld 227. **Population:** Germans. **Density** 238 persons per sq.km, average annual rate of population increase –0.2% (1983); urban population 85%. 42% of inhabitants employed in industry. There were 4.5 mn. foreign workers in 1983. – **Currency:** Deutsche mark = 100 pfennigs.
Economy: highly developed industrial country with advanced agriculture. The Fed. Rep. of Germany belongs economically among the most advanced countries of the world, ranking fourth in value of production, after the U.S.A., the U.S.S.R. and Japan, and it holds a decisive position in the EEC. **Industry:** the 50 largest firms produce more than 50% of the total industrial output. **Principal industries:** mining, metallurgy, engineering (shipbuilding, manufacture of motor vehicles, electrotechnical), chemicals, building, textiles and food processing. The production of optical instruments, watches, toys, musical instruments and jewellery is important, too. The principal economic region is the Ruhr agglomeration with more than one third of total industrial production in the country, followed by the Saarland, Siegerland, Peine-Salzgitter and metropolitan agglomerations. **Mining** (1983, in 1,000 tonnes, metal content): coal 89,620 (the Ruhr Basin, Aachen, Saarland), brown coal 124,335 (reg. Ville near Köln), crude petroleum 4,116 (Emsland, Hannover region, smaller resources near Hamburg and in Bayern, extensive pipeline network from abroad; Ingolstadt is a major centre of petroleum industry, natural gas 634,733 TJ (Emsland, Niedersachsen, Rehden, Hengstlage; gas pipeline from Netherlands resources in Groningen to Hamburg), iron ore 280 (Peine, Salzgitter, Siegen and Amberg), lead 23, zinc 92.6 (Harz, Sauerland), copper 1.2, gold 9,296kg (1980), silver 40 tonnes, uranium 40 tonnes (Schwarzwald), kaolin 1,969, salt 6,862 (Schwäbisch Hall, Berchtesgaden), potassium salt 2,985 (valleys of the Leine and Werra rivers), pyrites 480, sulphur. Electricity 372 billion kWh (1983), of which 4% are hydro-electric and 12% nuclear power stations (Biblis, Neckarwestheim, Brunsbüttel, Würgassen, Stade.
Production: metallurgy (1983, in 1,000 tonnes): pig iron 26,633, crude steel 35,728 (most plants in the Ruhr Basin – Duisburg, Oberhausen, Bochum, Gelsenkirchen, in Niedersachsen – Peine, Salzgitter, in the Saarland and elsewhere), lead 365 (Braubach, Nordenham), zinc – primary 247, secondary 314 (Datteln, Harlingerode), aluminium – primary 743.4, secondary 48 (Töging, Rheinfelden), copper – smelted 159, refined 420 (Hamburg, Lünen), magnesium 638 tonnes, tin 562 tonnes (1981, Essen), coke oven coke 23 mn. tonnes.
Engineering: the Ruhr Basin (Düsseldorf, Wuppertal, Köln), Hamburg, Bremen, Solingen, Stuttgart and others (1983, in 1,000 units): motor vehicles – passenger 3,875 (Wolfsburg – "Volkswagen", Rüsselsheim, Bochum – "Opel", Köln – "Ford", Stuttgart – "Mercedes", München – "BMW"), commercial 260 – locomotives (München, Essen, Düsseldorf), carriages (Köln, Braunschweig), tractors 119 (Hannover, Kassel), vessels 528,000 GRT (Hamburg, Bremen, Emden, Kiel), printing

map 11

Industry: manufacturing is concentrated in the Paris Basin and the territory of the lower Seine, the North, East, Lyon district, Atlantic ports and Marseille. A major part of metallurgy is situated near the resources: reg. Lorraine (from Longwy to Nancy), Nord (Dunkerque, Valenciennes and others), centre (Le Creusot, Saint-Étienne). The main concentration of engineering is to be found around Paris, Lille and its surroundings and Lyon. Chemical industry: in the coal and metallurgical regions, Paris region, petroleum processing in the ports. Textile industry: reg. Alsace, Lille and vicinity, Lyon.

Production (1983, in 1,000 tonnes): pig iron 14,304, crude steel 17,612, coke oven coke 8,458, aluminium 523 (Saint-Jean-de-Maurienne, Noguères), zinc 286, lead 174, refined copper 62.4, magnesium 11,075 tonnes, synthetic nitrogen 2,016 (1980), nitric acid, sulphuric acid 4,243, hydrochloric acid 242.5, nitrogenous fertilizers 1,600, caustic soda 1,393, soda ash 1,560 (1980), phosphorus fertilizers 1,230, synthetic rubber 512, plastics and resins 2,877; capacity of petroleum refineries 109.6 mn. tonnes (1984), oil pipelines network 102,540 km (1978), naphtha 3,127, motor spirit 16,046, oils 44,946, cosmetics and pharmaceuticals (Paris, Lyon), tyres 47.3 mn. units, motor vehicles – pasenger 3,359,000 (Paris, Le Mans, Rennes, Flins, Sochaux), – commercial 457,000 (Lyon-Vénissieux) – ships 229,000 GRT (shipyards Saint-Nazaire, La Ciotat, Dunkerque), aircraft (Paris, Toulouse, Bordeaux), locomotives, carriages, railway equipment (Le Creusot, Lille, Belfort), agricultural machines (Vierzon, Beauvais, Saint-Dizier), radio receivers 2,498,000 units, television receivers 1,956,000, cement 24,504, chemical wood pulp 1,361, paper 5,041, yarn – cotton 199, woollen 107.9, jute 3.3 – woven fabrics -cotton 128, -woollen 76, -silk 606 tonnes – jute 2.8 – rayon and acetate – fibres 8.4, staple fibre 29.6 – synthetic – fibres 63.6, staple fibre 144 – sugar 3,875, meat 5,568, milk 35,150, condensed milk 125, butter 645, cheese 1,200, eggs 900, canned fish 98, wine 6,000 (second world producer, reg. Languedoc, Bordeaux, reg. Bourgogne, reg. Champagne), alcoholic spirits (Cognac, Fécamp, reg. Armagnac, Isère), beer 22.1 mn. hl (1983); 62.1 billion cigarettes (1983).

Agriculture: France has many large agricultural establishments, although small and medium-sized farms predominate. Animal production exceeds vegetable production. Land use: arable land 31.5%, meadows and pastures 23.3%, forests 26.7%; tractors 1,535,000 (1983), combine harvesters 148,000 (1983). **Crops** (1983, in 1,000 tonnes): wheat 24,781 (Paris Basin, reg. Picardie), barley 8,865, oats 1,469, rye, maize (corn) 10,143 (reg. Aquitaine, Paris Basin), rice (Camargue), sorghum, potatoes 5,325, flax 31, sugar beet 23,955 (second world producer, Nord, Paris Basin), rapeseed 969, olives, sunflower seed 837, hops, fruit 11,914, apples 1,950, grapes 8,550 (second world producer, principal vine-growing region from the lower Rhône to the Pyrenees and Gironde), strawberries 90, vegetables 7,104, tomatoes 870, tobacco 37; **livestock** (1983, in 1,000 head): cattle 23,656, sheep 12,103, goats 1,243, pigs 11,709, horses 312, asses, mules; poultry 187,000, wool 11,000 tonnes, honey 19,000 tonnes; fish catch 784,000 tonnes (1983), roundwood 39.8 cub.m (1983).

Communications (1984): railways 34,688 km, of which 11,335 km are electrified, roads 781,869 km, of which 32,869 km are national and 345,000 km departmental roads; motorways 4,514 km, canals 19.3 mn. (1982). Navigable waterways 8,500 km, of which canals take up 4,575 km. Merchant shipping 8,945,000 GRT (1984). Chief ports: Marseille (second largest European port, 92 mn. tonnes of freight in 1982), Le Havre, Dunkerque, Rouen, Nantes, Bordeaux. Civil aviation (1984): 270.4 mn. km flown, 23,646,000 passengers carried. Tourism 33.6 mn. visitors (1983).

Exports: machines, cars, aircraft, raw materials and semi-finished products (iron, ores), textile and chemical products, agricultural products, wine and others. **Imports:** fuels (petroleum, coal), finished products and equipment, agricultural products (fruit, early vegetables), raw materials and semi-finished products (cotton, wool, rubber), consumer goods. Chief trading partners: Fed. Rep. of Germany, Italy, Belgium-Luxembourg, United Kingdom, U.S.A., Netherlands.

GERMAN DEMOCRATIC REPUBLIC

Deutsche Demokratische Republik, area 108,333 sq.km, population 16,644,308 (1985), **socialist republic** (Chairman of the Council of State Erich Honecker since 1976).

Administrative units: 15 regions (Bezirke), **the capital** Berlin 1,185,533 inhab. (1984) also has the status of a region; **other towns** (1983, in 1,000 inhab.): Leipzig 559, Dresden 523, Karl-Marx-Stadt 319, Magdeburg 289, Rostock 241, Halle 236, Erfurt 214, Potsdam 136, Gera 130, Schwerin 123, Cottbus 121, Zwickau 120, Jena 107, Dessau 104, Stralsund 75, Weimar 63, Gotha 58. **Population:** Germans (over 99%). **Density** 154 persons per sq.km; average annual rate of population increase only 0.7‰; urban population 76.5%. 38% of inhabitants employed in industry. – **Currency:** Mark of the DDR = 100 pfennigs.

Economy: highly developed industrial country with intensive agriculture. **Principal industries:** engineering (Saxony, Thuringia, Magdeburg, Berlin with surroundings), electrotechnical (Berlin), chemicals (region of brown coal deposits, Leuna), electronics, precision mechanics and optics (Jena), textiles. **Mining** (1983, in 1,000 tonnes, metal content): brown coal 277,968 (leading world producer, Thuringian-Saxon Basin – Leipzig, Halle, Merseburg; Lower-Lusatian Basin – Senftenberg, Spremberg), natural gas 145,028 TJ, copper 12 (Harz), nickel 2.2, tin 1,800 tonnes, silver 45 tonnes, uranium (Aue), potassium salt 3,430 and salt 2,907 (Stassfurt, Halberstadt, Bleicherode, valleys of the Werra and Unstrut). Limited mining of coal, iron ore, lead, zinc, tungsten. Electricity 105 billion kWh (1983), of which 88% are thermal and 10% nuclear power stations (at Rheinsberg, Lubmin).

machines (Augsburg, Offenbach), textile machines (Mönchengladbach, Esslingen), agricultural machines (Mannheim, Hannover), precision engineering (München, Kassel, Göttingen), watches (Schwarzwald), radio receivers 3,292 (1983), television receivers 4,705 (1983).
Chemical industry in the lower Rhine zone (Köln–Leverkusen–Ruhr Basin), southern zone (from Mannheim-Ludwigshafen to Frankfurt am Main). Production (1983, in 1,000 tonnes): acids: sulphuric 4,340, hydrochloric 900, nitrogenous 2,626; soda ash 1,218, caustic soda 3,350 (second world producer), synthetic nitrogen 1,703, chlorine 2,848, fertilizers: nitrogenous 746, phosphorus 552, potash 2,275, plastics and resins 7,031, synthetic rubber 432, dyes (Frankfurt am Main), pharmaceuticals and photo materials (Leverkusen), synthetic fibres 332; capacity of petroleum refineries 105 mn. tonnes (1984, Ruhr Basin, Karlsruhe, Ingolstadt, Hamburg, Bremen, Emden, Missburg/Hannover), naphtha 6,825, motor spirit 19,913, fuel oils 50,849, tyres 37.9 mn. units. Production of cement 30.5 mn. tonnes (1983). **Chemical wood pulp and paper industry** (1983, 1,000 tonnes): chemical wood pulp 576, newsprint 654, paper and paper products 7,619.
Textile industry in the Rhineland (from Aachen, Krefeld to Bielefeld, Bonn), Münster, Osnabrück, south-west zone (Esslingen, Reutlingen), Augsburg, Kempten, Hof (1983, in 1,000 tonnes): yarn – cotton 181.4, woollen 46.4, flax and hemp 3.4, jute 3.4, woven fabrics (in mn. sq.m) – cotton 881, woollen 79.2, rayon and acetate 320.9, footwear (Pirmasens, Stuttgart), sale of furs (Frankfurt am Main). Glass industry (Ruhr Basin, Saarland), optics, photographic apparatus (München, Stuttgart), ceramics (München), musical instruments (Trossingen, Mittenwald), jewellery (Pforzheim), toys, **Food industry:** mainly in large cities and surroundings (1983, in 1,000 tonnes): meat 4,694, milk 26,141, condensed milk 538, butter 627, cheese 848, margarine 606, eggs 800, honey 14, wheat flour 2,280, sugar 3,150 (Braunschweig), wine, beer 91.4 mn. hl (second world producer), Bayern – München, Nürnberg): 156 billion cigarettes, 1.6 billion cigars.
Agriculture: is very intensive. 80% of the food supply derives from domestic agricultural resources. Animal production predominates (³/₄ of agricultural production). Land use: arable land 31%, meadows and pastures 19.1%, forests 29.5%. High average hectare yields, extensive use of synthetic fertilizers. Tractors 1,471,681 (1983), combine harvesters 165,500 (1983). **Crops** (1983, in 1,000 tonnes): wheat 8,998 (Rhineland and Danubeland), barley 8,914, rye 1,599 (North German Lowlands), oats 2,068, maize (corn) 934, potatoes 6,088, sugar beet 16,500 (surroundings of Braunschweig and Köln), rapeseed 580, fruit 4,386, grapes 1,739 (cultivation of fruit and viniculture – middle Rhineland, valleys of the Mosel, Main, Neckar and others), vegetables 6,088, hops 37 (leading world producer, Danubeland), flax, tobacco; **livestock** (1983, in 1,000 head): cattle 15,098, pigs 22,478, horses 369, sheep 1,172, goats; poultry 80,000, fish catch 305,600 tonnes; roundwood 29.5 mn. cub.m.
Communications (1984): railways 30,808 km, of which 11,571 km are electrified, roads 267,050 km, motorways 8,080 km, passenger cars 25,217,800. Navigable waterways 4,354 km (river transport – the Rhein and the Ruhr and North German canal system), the largest river port Duisburg. Merchant shipping 6,242,000 GRT (1984). Chief ports: Hamburg (turnover 58.9 mn. tonnes in 1981), Bremen, Wilhelmshaven, Emden, Lübeck. Civil aviation (1984): 215.3 mn. km flown, 14,052,000 passengers carried. Tourism 11.3 mn. visitors (1983).
Foreign trade: the Fed. Rep. of Germany is the second most important trading country in the world. – **Exports:** machines of all kinds, cars, chemical and electrotechnical products, iron and steel, textiles, products of precision mechanics, coal, metals. **Imports:** finished products (machines, motor vehicles, electrotechnical products, textile and clothes, paper and paper products, semi-finished products (non-ferrous metals, fuel and lubricating oils), raw materials (petroleum, iron ore, cotton, wool), foodstuffs (fruit, vegetables, meat, coffee, tobacco). Chief trading partners: France, Netherlands, Italy, Belgium-Luxembourg, United Kingdom, U.S.A., Switzerland, Austria.

GIBRALTAR

Dominion of Gibraltar, area 6 sq.km, population 29,073 (1984), **British territory** since 1704, **with extended internal autonomy** according to the 1969 Constitution. Security, foreign affairs and defence fall within the competence of the British Governor (Sir William Jackson). – **Currency:** Gibraltar pound = 100 pence. **Importance:** British naval and air base of great strategic importance, also a merchant port. Transit trade, fishing, food processing. Tourism 66,000 visitors (1983).

GREECE

Eliniki Dimokratia, area 131,957 sq.km, population 9,950,000 (1985), republic (President Dr. Christos Sartzetakis since 1985).

Administrative units: 12 provinces, 52 prefectures (Nomói). One of these is the monastic state of Mount Áthos (Áyion Óros), area 336 sq.km, 1,472 inhab. in 1981 on the Khalkidhiki Peninsula. **Capital:** Athínai (Athens) 885,737 inhab. (1981), Greater Athínai with agglomeration 3,027,331 inhab.; **other towns** (census 1981, in 1,000 inhab.): Thessaloníki (Salonica) 406, Pátrai 142, Lárisa 103, Iráklion 102, Vólos 71, Kavála 56, Khaniá 48, Khalkís 45, Ioánnina 44. **Population:** Greeks 95%, Turks, Albanians. **Density** 75 persons per sq.km; average annual rate of population increase 1.1% (1975–82); urban population 63% (1981). 35% of inhabitants employed in agriculture (1983), 15% in industry. – **Currency:** drachma = 100 lepta. **Economy:** industrial and agricultural country with heavy foreign investments (Philips, Pirelli, Benz, Péchiney and others). **Principal industries:** textiles, food processing, chemicals and mining. Heavy industry is only developing. **Mining** (1983, in 1,000 tonnes, metal content): brown coal 30,336 (Ptolemaís, Alivérion, Megalópolis), crude petroleum 1,332, iron ore 572 (Khalkidhiki), manganese 2.6, chromium 15 (reg. Thessaalía, Kozáni), lead 19.4, zinc 21.4, nickel 15.0 (Larimna), silver 50 tonnes, bauxite 2,387 (Elevsis, Distomon), magnesite 937.7 (island Évvoia), salt 133, pyrites 144, emery (island Náxos), marble. Electricity 22 billion kWh (1983). **Production** (1983, in 1,000 tonnes): crude steel 755, aluminium 157.9 (Distomon); capacity of petroleum refineries 18 mn. tonnes (1984 – Thessaloníki, Athínai), petroleum products 11.7 mn. tonnes; sulphuric acid 988, phosphorus fertilizers 194, cement 14,124, cotton yarn 118, woollen yarn 14, carpets (Thessaloníki, Athínai), sugar 326, meat 530, milk 690, cheese 196, eggs 125, canned food, raisins 145, wine 530, olive oil 259; 26.2 billion cigarettes (1983).

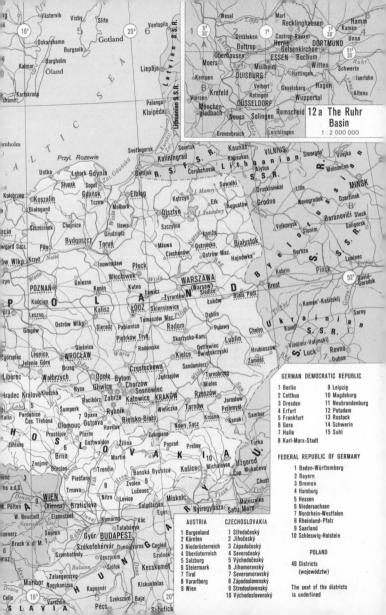

12 a The Ruhr Basin
1 : 2 000 000

GERMAN DEMOCRATIC REPUBLIC

1 Berlin	9 Leipzig
2 Cottbus	10 Magdeburg
3 Dresden	11 Neubrandenburg
4 Erfurt	12 Potsdam
5 Frankfurt	13 Rostock
6 Gera	14 Schwerin
7 Halle	15 Suhl
8 Karl-Marx-Stadt	

FEDERAL REPUBLIC OF GERMANY

1 Baden-Württemberg
2 Bayern
3 Bremen
4 Hamburg
5 Hessen
6 Niedersachsen
7 Nordrhein-Westfalen
8 Rheinland-Pfalz
9 Saarland
10 Schleswig-Holstein

POLAND

49 Districts
(wojewodztw)

The seat of the districts
is underlined

AUSTRIA

1 Burgenland
2 Kärnten
3 Niederösterreich
4 Oberösterreich
5 Salzburg
6 Steiermark
7 Tirol
8 Vorarlberg
9 Wien

CZECHOSLOVAKIA

1 Středočeský
2 Jihočeský
3 Západočeský
4 Severočeský
5 Východočeský
6 Jihomoravský
7 Severomoravský
8 Západoslovenský
9 Stredoslovenský
10 Východoslovenský

map 12

Agriculture: arable land 22%, meadows and pastures 39.8%, forests 19.8%. **Crops** (1983, in 1, 000 tonnes): wheat 2,026, barley 572, maize (corn) 1,622, rice, potatoes 809, cotton -seed 275, -lint 140, sugar beet 2,560, olives 1,052, groundnuts, sesame, fruit 3,636 – watermelons 660, oranges 550, lemons 165, grapes 1,600, figs, vegetables 3,849, tomatoes 1,970, tobacco 115, walnuts 21; **livestock** (1983, in 1,000 head): cattle 850, sheep 8,400, goats 4,630, pigs 1,400 horses 97, asses 220, mules, buffaloes; poultry 36,000; silkworms, honey 12,500 tonnes, wool 5,100 tonnes; fish catch 100,000 tonnes (1983); roundwood 2.8 mn. cub.m (1983).

Communications (1984): railways 2,479km, roads 61,613km, passenger cars 1,151,000. Merchant shipping 35,059,000 GRT. Chief port is Athínai-Piraiévs. Corinth canal: length 6,345m, depth 7m, width at level 24.6m, at bottom 21m, opened in 1893. Civil aviation: 47.5 mn. km flown, 6,878,000 passengers carried. Tourism 4.8 mn. visitors. **Exports:** iron and steel, fresh and dried fruit, aluminium, chemical products, tobacco, cotton. **Imports:** industrial and consumer goods, raw materials, foodstuffs, fuels and oils. Chief trading partners: Fed. Rep. of Germany, Italy, U.S.A., France, United Kingdom.

HUNGARY

Magyar Népköztársaság, area 93,036 sq.km, population 10,643,000 (1985), **socialist republic** (Chairman of the Presidential Council Pál Losonczi since 1967).

Administrative units: 19 counties (megye) and the **capital** – Budapest 2,064,374 inhab. (1984); **other towns** (1984, in 1,000 inhab.): Miskolc 211, Debrecen 206, Szeged 176, Pécs 174, Győr 128, Nyíregyháza 114, Székesfehérvár 109, Kecskemét 101, Szombathely 86, Szolnok 79, Tatabánya 78, Kaposvár 74, Békéscsaba 70, Eger 64, Veszprém 62, Zalaegerszeg 60, Salgótarján 50. **Population:** Hungarians 98%, Serbs, Croats, Slovenians, Germans, Slovaks. **Density** 114 persons per sq.km; average annual rate of population increase 0.2% (1975–81); urban population 54% (1981). 13.5% of inhabitants employed in agriculture, 50.6% in industry. – **Currency:** forint = 100 fillers.

Economy: industrial and agricultural country. **Principal industries:** engineering, metallurgy, chemicals, textiles and food processing. Half the industrial production occurs in Budapest. Shortage of energy resources. **Mining** (1983, in 1,000 tonnes, metal content): coal 2,832 (Pécs, Komló), brown coal 22,392 (Salgótarján, Tatabánya, Gyöngyös), crude petroleum 2,004 (Nagylengyel, Algyő, Demjén, Szolnok), natural gas 248,517 TJ (Karcag, Szolnok), bauxite 2,917 (Iszkaszentgyörgy, Gánt, Halimba), iron ore 96, manganese 23.3, uranium (Pécs), copper, lead, zinc. Electricity 25.7 billion kWh (1983), 14% nuclear power stations. **Production** (1983, in 1,000 tonnes): pig iron 2,047 and crude steel 3,617 (Dunaújváros, Miskolc-Diósgyőr, Ózd), aluminium 74.4 (Ajka, Várpalota, Tatabánya), refined copper 12, engineering (Győr, Eger, Debrecen, Pécs, Miskolc) – lorries 13,200 units, buses 11,800 units (Budapest), railway carriages (Győr), – television receivers 363,000 units, cutting machines, sulphuric acid 606, nitric acid 1,076, nitrogenous fertilizers 700 (Leninváros); capacity of petroleum refineries 11 mn. tonnes (1984), oil pipeline for the import of Soviet petroleum, photochemical (Vác) and pharmaceutical products (Debrecen, Tiszavasvári), cement 4,248, textile industry (Szeged, Vác, Sopron) – woven fabrics – cotton 280 mn. sq.m, – woollen 23 mn. sq.m, – rayon and acetate 36 mn. sq.m, yarn – cotton 56.4, – woollen 10.8, synthetic fibres 9.6, artificial fibres 6.1, leather shoes 43.5 mn. pairs, food industry (Debrecen, Szeged) – meat 1,664, milk 2,800, butter 32.7, cheese 80, eggs 215, Hungarian salami for export, sugar 478, wine 640 (Tokaj), beer 7.8 mn. hl (1983); 25.7 billion cigarettes.

Agriculture: vegetable production and cereals predominate; important viniculture, cultivation of fruit and vegetables. Land use: arable land 54.3%, meadows and pastures 13.9%, forests 17.6%. **Crops** (1983, in 1,000 tonnes): wheat 5,985, maize (corn) 7,600, barley 1,000, rye, rice, potatoes 1,506, flax 10, hemp 11, sugar beet 4,800, sunflower seed 638, soya beans, hops, fruit 2,581, grapes 1,000, vegetables 1,766, walnuts 12; **livestock** (1983, in 1,000 head): cattle 1,922, pigs 9,035, sheep 3,180, horses 112; poultry 63,000, honey 15,000 tonnes; fish catch 43,900 tonnes (1983); roundwood 6.4 mn. cub.m (1983).

Communications (1984): railways 7,830km, of which 1,903km electrified, roads 29,633km, passenger cars 1,344,000. Navigable waterways 1,373km (1984). Civil aviation (1984): 17.6 mn. km flown, 1,039,000 passengers carried. Tourism 6.8 mn. visitors (1983).

Exports: machines and industrial equipment, transport equipment, chemical products, bauxite, aluminium, foodstuffs (meat, smoked meat products, canned products, wine, fruit, vegetables). **Imports:** fuels (petroleum, natural gas), raw materials, semi-finished products, machines and equipment, cars, industrial consumer goods. Chief trading partners: U.S.S.R. 30%, socialist countries 21% (mainly German Dem. Rep., Czechoslovakia, Yugoslavia), Fed. Rep. of Germany, Austria.

ICELAND

Lyðveldið Ísland, area 102,829 sq.km, population 241,000 (1985), **republic** (President Mrs Vigdis Finnbogadottir since 1980).

Administrative units: 7 districts. **Capital:** Reykjavík 86,092 inhab. (1982); **other towns** (in 1,000 inhab.): Akureyri 14, Kópavogur 14, Hafnarfjördur 12. **Population:** Icelandic. **Density** 2 persons per sq.km; average annual rate of population increase 1.1% (1975–82); urban population 87% (1981). – **Currency:** Icelandic króna = 100 aurars.

Economy: agricultural country without raw material resources. The economy is based on fishing – catch 839,200 tonnes (1983) – whaling, raising of sheep 748,000 head (1983), cattle 64,000 (1983). Electricity 3.8 billion kWh (1983), of which 97% are hydro-electric power stations; hot springs. **Industry:** fish processing, canning, freezing plants, production of aluminium and textiles. – **Communications:** roads 11,619km (1984). Merchant shipping 179,000 GRT (1984). – **Exports:** fresh and canned fish 68%, aluminium, diatomite, woollen products. **Imports:** industrial products, fuels and foodstuffs. Chief trading partners: U.S.A., United Kingdom, Fed. Rep. of Germany, U.S.S.R.

map 13

IRELAND

Éire, area 70,283 sq.km, population 3,552,000 (1985), **republic** (President Dr Padraig Ohlrighile/ Dr Patrick J. Hillery since 1976).

Administrative units: 4 provinces (27 counties). **Capital:** Dublin (Baile Átha Cliath) 525,882 inhab. (census 1981); **other towns** (1981, in 1,000 inhab.): Cork 136, Limerick 61, Dún Laoghaire 54. **Population:** Irish. **Density** 51 persons per sq.km; average annual rate of population increase 1.3% (1975–1982); urban population 58% (1981). 19.3% of inhabitants employed in agriculture, 31% in industry. – **Currency:** Irish pound = 100 pence.

Economy: industrial and agricultural country. **Principal industries:** mining of minerals, metallurgy, engineering, chemicals, textiles and food processing. Centres of industry: Dublin, Cork, Cobh. **Mining** (1983, in 1,000 tonnes, metal content): coal, peat (Timahoe), natural gas 87,000 TJ, zinc 186, lead 33.6 (Tynagh), silver 20 tonnes. Electricity 11.2 billion kWh (1983). **Production** (1983, in 1,000 tonnes): cement 1,486, woven fabrics – cotton 36 mn. sq.m , woollen 2.7 mn. sq.m, rayon and acetate 48.3 mn. sq.m, sugar 203, meat 601, milk 5,490, butter 150, cheese 53, eggs 34, beer 4 mn. hl ("Guinness"), alcoholic spirits; 7.5 billion cigarettes (1983). **Agriculture** – animal production predominates. Land use: arable land 13.8%, meadows and pastures 69%, forests 4.6%. **Crops** (1983, in 1,000 tonnes): wheat 350, oats 103, barley 1,437, potatoes 800, sugar beet 1,520; **livestock** (1983, in 1,000 head): cattle 6,771, sheep 3,480, pigs 1,145; poultry 8,000; fish catch 203,400 tonnes (1983).

Communications: railways 1,944 km (1984), roads 89,579 km, passenger cars 716,800 (1984). Navigable waterways 1,040 km. Merchant shipping 221,000 GRT (1984). Chief ports: Dublin, Cobh. Civil aviation (1984): 20.5 mn. km flown, 1,838,000 passengers carried. Tourism 2.3 mn. visitors (1983).

Exports: meat, live cattle, machines, textiles, chemicals, pharmaceuticals, beverages. Chief trading partners: United Kingdom (34% of export and 43% of import in 1984), Fed. Rep. of Germany, U.S.A., France, Netherlands.

ITALY

Repubblica Italiana, area 301,268 sq.km, population 57,127,536 (1985), **republic** (President Dr Francesco Cossiga since 1985).

Administrative units: 20 regions (95 provinces). **Capital:** Roma (Rome) 2,826,733 inhab. (1984); **other towns** (1984, in 1,000 inhab.): Milano, 1,536, Napoli (Naples) 1,207, Torino (Turin) 1,050, Genova 738, Palermo 716, Bologna 442, Firenze (Florence) 436, Catania 378, Bari 368, Venezia (Venice) 338, Messina 266, Verona 261, Taranto 244, Trieste 244, Padova 229, Cagliari 224, Brescia 202, Modena 178, Parma 177, Reggio di Calabria 177, Livorno 176, Prato 160, Foggia 158, Salerno 156, Ferrara 146, Ravenna 137, Pescara 132, Reggio n.Emilia 130. **Population:** Italians 98%. **Density** 190 persons per sq.km; average annual rate of population increase 0.4% (1975–81); urban population 70% (1981). 9.5% of inhabitants employed in agriculture, 36.3% in industry (1983). – **Currency:** Italian lira.

Economy: highly developed industrial and agricultural country, economically the most advanced in southern Europe. There is considerable difference between the advanced industrial North with its large modern plants and the under-developed agricultural South. **Principal industries:** engineering, hydroenergetics, electrometallurgy, electrotechnics, electronics, chemistry, textiles and food processing. **Mining** (1983, in 1,000 tonnes, metal content): lignite 1,908, crude petroleum 2,196 (Gela, Ragusa), natural gas 500,835 TJ (The Po plain and others), manganese 2,200 tonnes, lead 12.5, zinc 21 (Iglesias), mercury 159 tonnes (1982, Monte Amiata, Grosseto), copper, bauxite 14, silver 73 tonnes, uranium (Pie-monte Alps, Novazza), salt 3,454 (Sicilia), potassium salts 140 (Sicilia), pyrites 646 (Grosseto), sulphur 8 (Sicilia), marble, magnesite, asbestos 139, fluorite 173, barytes 180, graphite, kaolin. Electricity 182.9 billion kWh (1983), of which 27% are hydro-electric, nuclear power stations 4% (Caorso, Trino, Garigliano, Latina). **Production** (1983, in 1,000 tonnes): metallurgy: pig iron 10,519 (Trieste, Napoli, Piombino, Aosta), crude steel 21,810 (reg. Lombardia – Milano, reg. Liguria – Genova, reg. Piemonte – Torino; Taranto and others), lead 40 (Sardegna, La Spezia), zinc 156 (Monteponi), cadmium 500 tonnes, aluminium 473.7 (Marghera near Venezia), magnesium 9,799 tonnes. **Engineering** (1983, in 1,000 units): vessels 241,000 GRT (1984, Genova, La Spezia, Livorno, Napoli, Palermo), electric locomotives 209 units, railway carriages 2,940 units (Torino, Pinerolo, Vado Ligure), aircraft (Torino, Varese), passenger cars 1,395 ("Fiat" – Torino, 71% of production, "Alfa Romeo" – Milano, "Lancia" – Torino, "Ferrari" – Maranello), bicycles 1,978 (Milano), motorcycles 780, tractors 84 (Torino), precision mechanics (microtechnics, photo and cinema apparatus – Milano, Torino), spectacles, electrotechnical apparatus (Milano, Roma, Torino), radio receivers, television receivers 1,615, calculating machines, typewriters 439 ("Olivetti" – Ivrea).

Chemical industry (Lombardia, 1983, in 1,000 tonnes): acid – sulphuric 2,339, hydrochloric, nitric 1,021 – caustic soda 1,009, synthetic nitrogen 1,134, nitrogenous fertilizers 1,081 (Novara, Merano), phosphorus fertilizers 434, potash fertilizers 125, coke oven coke 6,450, pharmaceuticals, dyes (Milano and surroundings), plastics and resins 2,436 (Ferrara, Castellanza), synthetic fibres 536, synthetic rubber 233, capacity of petroleum refineries 145.3 mn. tonnes, oil pipeline network 3,266 km, gas pipelines 14,270 km, motor spirit 14.5 mn. tonnes, oils 49.6 mn. tonnes; production of cement 39.8 mn. tonnes, sheet and crystal glass (Marghera near Venezia, Milano), chandeliers (Murano), chemical wood pulp 148, paper and paper products 4,065, furniture (Cantù, Lissone), musical instruments (Emilia-Romagna, Marche, Milano).

Textile industry – cotton processing (The Po Plain, Lombardia), wool processing (reg. Piemonte - Biella), silk processing (reg. Lombardia - Como), flax processing (Lombardia and Piemonte). Production (1983, in 1,000 tonnes): cotton yarn 217, woven fabrics -cotton 206, -woollen 154 (1982), -silk 16, -jute 11, rayon and acetate fibres 4.2 (1981), non-cellulosic staple fibre 313, shoes 500 mn. pairs (Vigevano).

Food industry (1983, in 1,000 tonnes): sugar 1,360, meat 3,606, milk 10,650, butter 76, cheese 636, eggs 640, production of spaghetti etc., sweets, canned fish and foodstuffs, olive oil 874 (leading world producer), wine 8,000 (leading world producer, "Chianti", "Barbero", "Cinzano", "Martini" etc.); beer 10 mn. hl; 73.6 billion cigarettes.

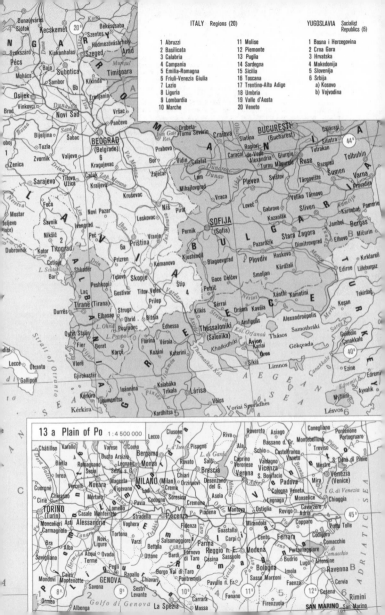

ITALY Regions (20)

1 Abruzzi
2 Basilicata
3 Calabria
4 Campania
5 Emilia-Romagna
6 Friuli-Venezia Giulia
7 Lazio
8 Liguria
9 Lombardia
10 Marche
11 Molise
12 Piemonte
13 Puglia
14 Sardegna
15 Sicilia
16 Toscana
17 Trentino-Alto Adige
18 Umbria
19 Valle d'Aosta
20 Veneto

YUGOSLAVIA Socialist Republics (6)

1 Bosna i Hercegovina
2 Crna Gora
3 Hrvatska
4 Makedonija
5 Slovenija
6 Srbija
   a) Kosovo
   b) Vojvodina

13 a Plain of Po   1 : 4 500 000

map 13

Agriculture: arable land 31,4%, meadows and pastures 17%, forests 21%. Number of tractors 1,169,513 (1983).
Crops (1983, in 1,000 tonnes): wheat 8,514 (The Po Plain), barley 1,174, oats 307, rye, maize (corn) 6,900 (Veneto and Lombardia), rice 1,060 (Piemonte and Lombardia), potatoes 2,828, flax, hemp, cotton, sugar beet 10,000 (Po delta, Emilia-Romagna), sunflower seed 140, olives 4,212 (leading world producer, Puglia, Calabria), fruit 21,277 – oranges 1,945 (Sicilia), tangerines 400, lemons 770 (second world producer), almonds 175, figs 71, apples 1,990, pears 1,235 (leading world producer), peaches 1,700 (second world producer), apricots 157 (second world producer), grapes 12,255 (leading world producer, Veneto, Puglia, Piemonte, Sicilia), sweet chestnuts 70, walnuts 49 – vegetables 13,503, water-melons 780, tomatoes 4,550, strawberries 150, tobacco 141. **Livestock** (1983, in 1,000 head): cattle 9,127, horses 271, asses 123, mules, buffaloes 110, sheep 9,256, goats 1,031, pigs 9,132; poultry 110,000; wool 7,370 tonnes, raising of silkworms (20 tonnes of cocoons); fish catch 478,000 tonnes (1983); roundwood 8.7 mn. cub.m (1983).
Communications (1984): railways 19,793km, of which 10,175km are electrified (1983), roads 299,849km, motorways 5,901km, passenger cars 20,388,600 (1983). Navigable waterways 1,366km, of which 322km are canals. Merchant shipping 9,158,000 GRT (1984). Chief ports: Genova, Trieste, Augusta, Taranto, Venezia. Civil aviation (1984): 132.6 mn. km flown, 12,594,000 passengers carried. Important tourism, 22.1 mn. visitors (1983).
Exports: machines and equipment, cars, tractors, chemical products (plastics, pharmaceuticals, fertilizers), metals, products of precision mechanics (calculating machines and typewriters), metallurgical products, textiles, shoes, rubber products, wine, fresh fruit, vegetables.
Imports: raw materials and semi-finished products, fuels, machines and equipment, metals, cars, agricultural products (cereals; meat, wool, cotton, rubber, cattle, sugar, coffee etc.). Chief trading partners: Fed. Rep. of Germany, France, U.S.A., United Kingdom, Switzerland, Saudi Arabia, Libya, Belgium-Luxembourg.

LIECHTENSTEIN

Fürstentum Liechtenstein, area 160 sq.km, population 27,600 (1985), **principality** (titular Prince Franciz Joseph II since 1938, Head of the State Prince Hans Adam since 1984).
Administrative units: 11 villages. **Capital:** Vaduz 4,896 inhab. (1984). – **Currency:** Swiss franc, customs union with Switzerland. – **Economy:** agriculture (cereals, potatoes), livestock raising. Textiles and other industries. Tourism. Chief sources of revenue are the numerous registered foreign firms and postage stamps.

LUXEMBOURG

Grand-Duché de Luxembourg – Grousherzogdem Lezeburg, area 2,586 sq.km, population 365,000 (1985), **grand duchy** (Grand Duke Jean since 1964).

Administrative units: 12 cantons. **Capital:** Luxembourg (Lezeburg) 78,924 inhab. (census 1981). **Density** 142 persons per sq.km; average annual rate of population increase –0.1% (1975–82); urban population 67% (1981). 41% of inhabitants employed in industry (1982). **The official language** is French, but the inhabitants speak mainly Luxemburgish (German dialect). – **Currency:** Luxembourg franc = 100 centimes.
Economy: advanced industrial country. Metallurgy is the principal industry. Financial centre of Western Europe. Electricity 437 mn. kWh (1983). **Production** (1983, in 1,000 tonnes): pig iron 2,316, crude steel 3,294. **Agriculture:** cultivation of cereals. **Crops** (1983, in 1,000 tonnes): wheat 19, barley 35, potatoes 17, fruit and vines 18; raising of cattle 224,645 head and pigs 71,957 head, poultry. – **Communications** (1984): railways 270km, roads 2,885km, passenger cars 145,800. – **Exports:** steel, plastics, textiles and others. Chief trading partners: Fed. Rep. of Germany, Belgium, France. Customs union with Belgium.

MALTA

Republika Ta Malta, Republic of Malta, area 316 sq.km, population 383,000 (1985), **republic, member of the Commonwealth** (President Agatha Barbara since 1982).

Administrative units: 6 regions. **Capital:** Valletta 14,096 inhab. (1983). **Population:** Maltese of Italian-Arabic descent. **Density** 1,212 persons per sq.km; average annual rate of population increase 1.8% (1975–81); urban population over 94%. – **Currency:** Maltese pound = 100 pence.
Economy: cultivation of wheat, potatoes, vines, tomatoes, fruit, citrus fruit; livestock (1983, in 1,000 head): cattle 15, sheep 5, goats 7, pigs 5; poultry 1 mn. Electricity 675 mn. kWh (1983). Manual production of lace on Gozo I. (Ghawdex). Naval base. – **Communications** (1984): roads 1,324km, passenger cars 80,300. Merchant shipping 1,366,000 GRT. Civil aviation: 5.1 mn. km flown, 364,000 passengers carried. Tourism 491,000 visitors (1983). – **Exports:** domestic manufactures. Chief trading partners: Fed. Rep. of Germany, United Kingdom, Italy.

MONACO

Principauté de Monaco, area 1.95 sq.km, population 27,500 (1985), **principality** (Prince Rainier III since 1949).
The state consists of 3 joint urban districts: Monaco, Monte Carlo and La Condamine. **Capital:** Monaco 1,649 inhab. (1982). Tourist centre on the French Riviera. – **Currency:** French franc. Customs union with France. Chief sources of revenue are tourism and gambling.

map 14

NETHERLANDS

Koninkrijk der Nederlanden, area 41,548 sq.km, population 14,483,985 (1985), **kingdom** Queen Beatrix Wilhelmina Armgard since 1980).

Administrative units: 13 provinces; autonomous state Netherlands Antilles. **Capital:** Amsterdam 676,439 inhab. (1984, with agglomeration 994,062 inhab.); **other towns** (1984, in 1,000 inhab.): Rotterdam 555 (with agglom. 1,025), 's-Gravenhage 445 (the seat of the Royal Court and Government), Utrecht 230, Eindhoven 193, Groningen 168, Tilburg 154, Haarlem 153, Nijmegen 147, Enschede 145, Arnhem 128, Breda 119, Maastricht 113, Dordrecht 107. **Population:** Dutch, small number of Frisians in the North. **Density** 349 persons per sq.km is the highest in Europe (excluding miniature countries); average annual rate of population increase 0.7% (1975–82); urban population 76% (1981). 28% of inhabitants employed in industry, in agriculture 4.7% (1983). – **Currency:** gulden = 100 cents.
Economy: highly developed industrial and agricultural country. **Principal industries:** engineering (especially shipbuilding), electrotechnics, metallurgy, chemistry, textiles and food processing. **Mining** (1983, in 1,000 tonnes): crude petroleum 2,592 (Coevorden-Schoonebeek, Rijswijk), natural gas 2,690,966 TJ (Groningen surroundings – Slochteren, Delfzijl, North Sea shelf, Ameland I., Zuidwal), salt 3,084 (Hengelo, Delfzijl). Electricity 59.7 billion kWh (1983), of which 96% are thermal and 4% nuclear power stations. **Production** (1983, in 1,000 tonnes): pig iron 3,744, crude steel 4,488 (IJmuiden), coke oven coke 2,126, zinc 188 (Budel), aluminium 294 (Delfzijl), lead 9.6, vessels 190,000 GRT (shipyards Amsterdam, Rotterdam), passenger cars 105,600 units (Eindhoven, Born), electrotechnics ("Philips" in Eindhoven, vacuum tubes, radio receivers, telephones), nitrogenous fertilizers 1,659 (IJmuiden), phosphorus fertilizers 403, sulphuric acid 1,436, synthetic rubber 196, soda ash 417, plastics and resins 2,777; capacity of petroleum refineries 78.6 mn. tonnes (1984, near Rotterdam, Amsterdam), naphtha 8 mn. tonnes, motor spirit 9.2 mn. tonnes, fuel oils 30.5 mn. tonnes, cement 3,108, paper and paperboard 1,567, production of porcelain and ceramics (Delft, Maastricht), yarn – cotton 9.1, woollen 6.5 – woven fabrics – cotton 14.8 (reg. Twente), woollen 2.7 mn. sq.m (Tilburg) – synthetic fibres 33.6, sugar 815, meat 2,085, milk 13,200, condensed milk 537, cheese 488 (Edam, Gouda, Hoorn), butter 271, margarine 235, eggs 650, canned fish 19, chocolate and cocoa (Amsterdam, Bussum, Weesp, Zaandam), beer 17.3 mn. hl (1983), alcoholic spirits (curaçao – Amsterdam, gin); 46.3 billion cigarettes (1983), production of quinine (Amsterdam), diamond cutting and polishing (Amsterdam).
Agriculture is highly productive. There is a shortage of land which is partly overcome by the reclamation of polders from the sea. Cereal yields are among the highest in the world. Land use: arable land 22.3%, meadows and pastures 30.6%, forests 7.9%. **Crops** (1983, in 1,000 tonnes): wheat 1,043 (leading world yield per ha 7,037kg), barley 197 (world 6.5 – woven flax, sugar beet 5,600, fruit 523, vegetables 2,835, tomatoes 463, important cultivation of flowers (hyacinths, tulips etc); **livestock** (1983, in 1,000 head): cattle 5,390, pigs 10,590, sheep 750, poultry 90,000; fish catch 503,300 tonnes (1983); roundwood 900,000 cub.m.
Communications (1984): railways 2,852km, of which 1,796km electrified, roads 53,848km, motorways 1,889km, passenger cars 4,772,000. Navigable waterways and canals 4,384km. Highly developed sea transport and trade. Chief ports: Rotterdam (the world's largest port, turnover of cargo 246 mn. tonnes, 1982), Amsterdam. Merchant shipping 4,586,000 GRT (1984). Civil aviation (1984): 118.4 mn. km flown, 5,655,000 passengers carried. Tourism 2,992,000 visitors (1983).
Exports: foodstuffs (dairy products, eggs, meat), machines and transport equipment, petroleum products, chemicals, electrotechnical goods, manufactured products, flowers. **Imports:** raw materials (petroleum, metals, tropical fruit), machines and equipment, cars, and others. Chief trading partners: Fed. Rep. of Germany, Belgium and Luxembourg, France, United Kingdom, Italy.

NORWAY

Kongeriket Norge, area 323,920 sq.km, population 4,152,437 (1985), **kingdom** (King Olav V since 1957).

Administrative units: 19 counties (fylker), overseas territories in Europe: Svalbard, Bjørnøya and Jan Mayen; in the Antarctica: island Bouvetøya. **Capital:** Oslo 447,257 inhab. (1984); **other towns** (1984, in 1,000 inhab.): Bergen 207, Trondheim 134, Stavanger 93, Bærum 82, Kristiansand 62, Drammen 51, Tromsø 46. **Population:** Norwegians 97.5%, Lapps, Finns. **Density** 13 persons per sq.km; average annual rate of population increase 0.4% (1975–82); urban population 53% (1981). 28% of inhabitants employed in industry (1983). – **Currency:** Norwegian krone = 100 øre.
Economy: developed industrial and agricultural country. Large resources of hydro-electricity and timber. **Principal industries:** mining of minerals, shipbuilding, electrometallurgy, electrochemistry, radioelectronics, wood and paper processing, fishery. **Mining** (1983, in 1,000 tonnes, metal content): coal 480 (Svalbard), crude petroleum 30.6 mn. tonnes (North Sea shelf – Ekofisk, Statfjord), natural gas 1,031,867 TJ (Frigg, Cod, Heimdal, Odin, Troll, Statfjord), iron ore 2,307 (Fossdalen, Rana), copper 22.6, lead 4,100 tonnes, zinc 32.3, titanium, pyrites 357 (Løkken, Sulitjelma). Electricity 106.2 billion kWh (1983), almost 100% from hydro-electric power stations. **Production** (1983, in 1,000 tonnes): pig iron 1,620, crude steel 903 (Stavanger, Arendal, Rana), copper – smelted 26, refined 28.6, zinc 90.7, nickel 28, aluminium – primary 713 (Kristiansand, Tyssedal, Odda, Sunndalsøra, Årdal, Eydehamn) – magnesium 29.8, vessels 97,000 GRT (shipyards in Oslo, Bergen, Frederikstad), sulphuric acid 440 (chemical industry – Rjukan, Notodden, Odda), capacity of petroleum refineries 12.8 mn. tonnes (1984), petroleum products 7.1 mn. tonnes, cement 1,666, chemical wood pulp 645, paper and paper products 1,390, rayon and acetate staple fibre 20 (textile industry in Bergen, Oslo, Sandnes), meat 204, milk 2,017, butter 26, cheese 66, eggs 51.
Agriculture: intensive animal production predominates. Land use: arable land 2.6%, meadows and pastures 0.3%, forests 25.7%. **Crops** (1983, in 1,000 tonnes): cereals 1,081 (barley 569, oats), potatoes 470; **livestock** (1983, in 1,000 head): cattle 975, sheep 2,272, pigs 705; raising of fur animals (foxes and minks), reindeer in the North (174,300 head in 1980); fish catch 2,822,300 tonnes (1983); whaling: roundwood 9.6 mn. cub.m (1983).
Communications (1984): railways 4,242km, of which 2,443km electrified, roads 71,842km, passenger cars 1,428,700.

HUNGARY:
19 counties and capital district

1 Bács-Kiskun
2 Baranya
3 Békés
4 Borsod-Abaúj-Zemplén
5 Csongrád
6 Fejér
7 Győr-Sopron
8 Hajdú-Bihar
9 Heves
10 Komárom
11 Nógrád
12 Pest
13 Somogy
14 Szabolcs-Szatmár
15 Szolnok
16 Tolna
17 Vas
18 Veszprém
19 Zala

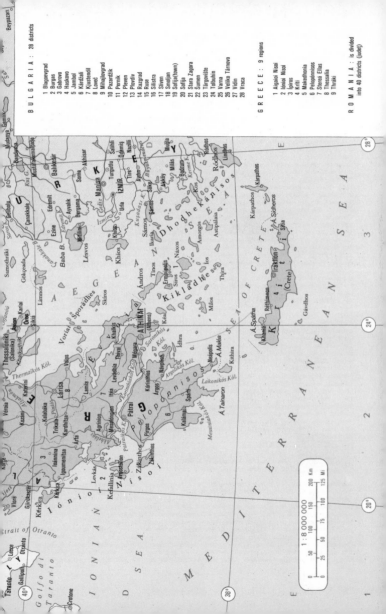

B U L G A R I A : 28 districts

1 Blagoevgrad
2 Burgas
3 Gabrovo
4 Haskovo
5 Jambol
6 Kärdžali
7 Kjustendil
8 Loveč
9 Mihajlovgrad
10 Pazardžik
11 Pernik
12 Pleven
13 Plovdiv
14 Razgrad
15 Ruse
16 Silistra
17 Sliven
18 Smoljan
19 Sofija(town)
20 Sofija
21 Stara Zagora
22 Šumen
23 Tärgovište
24 Tolbuhin
25 Varna
26 Veliko Tarnovo
27 Vidin
28 Vraca

G R E E C E : 9 regions

1 Aigaíoí Nísoi
2 Iónioi Nísoi
3 Ípiros
4 Kríti
5 Makedhonía
6 Pelopónnisos
7 Stereá Ellás
8 Thessalía
9 Thráki

R O M A N I A : is divided into 40 districts (județ)

Scale 1 : 8 000 000
0   50   100   150   200 Km
0   25   50   75   100   125 Mi

map 14

Merchant shipping 17,663,000 GRT (1984). Chief ports: Narvik, Oslo, Bergen. Civil aviation (1984): 59 mn. km flown, 6,114,000 passengers carried. Tourism 1.3 mn. visitors (1983). – **Exports:** petroleum and products, machines and equipment, vessels, non-ferrous metals, fish and fish products, iron, paper. **Imports:** fuels, ores, machines, cars and others. Chief trading partners: United Kingdom, Fed. Rep. of Germany, Sweden, Netherlands, U.S.A., Denmark.

POLAND

Polska Rzeczpospolita Ludowa, area 312,683 sq.km, population 37,202,980 (1985), socialist republic (Chairman of the Council of State Gen. Wojciech Jaruzelski since 1985).

Administrative units: 49 provinces (województwo). **Capital:** Warszawa (Warsaw) 1,649,000 inhab. (1985); **other towns** (1983, in 1,000 inhab.): Łódź 848, Kraków 735, Wrocław 631, Poznań 571, Gdańsk 465, Szczecin 389, Katowice 361, Bydgoszcz 358, Lublin 320, Sosnowiec 252, Bytom 238, Częstochowa 244, Gdynia 240, Białystok 240, Gliwice 211, Radom 201. **Population:** Poles 98.5%, Ukrainians, Byelorussians, Germans. **Density** 119 persons per sq.km; average annual rate of population increase 0.9% (1975–82); urban population 59.8% (1983). 28% of inhabitants employed in agriculture, 25% in industry (1983). – **Currency:** złoty = 100 groszy.

Economy: advanced industrial and agricultural country with important mining industry. Industry is concentrated chiefly in the south-west part of the country and the Kraków region. **Principal industries:** mineral mining, engineering (Poznań, Wrocław, Katowice, Kraków, Kielce), chemical (Upper Silesian region, Łódź, Poznań), textile (cotton processing – Łódź, wool processing – the South), food processing. Metallurgy plays an important role. **Mining** (1983, in 1,000 tonnes, metal content): coal 191,092 (Upper and Lower Silesian Basins in the vicinity of Katowice, Bytom, Zabrże, Lublin Basin), brown coal 42,532 (Turoszów Basin – Bogatynia, Konin, Bełchatów), crude petroleum 252 (Krosno), natural gas 166,151 TJ (Lubaczów, Przemyśl), iron ore, copper 393 (Bolesławiec, Polkowice, Lubin), lead 47 and zinc 189 (Olkusz, Bytom, Chrzanów), nickel 2.1, silver 678 tonnes, cadmium, magnesite 16, salt 4,326 (Wapno, Inowrocław, Kłodawa), sulphur 4,999 (leading world producer, Tarnobrzeg/Machów, Jeziórko, Grzybów), kaolin. Electricity 125.8 billion kWh (1983), of which 93% are thermal power stations. **Production** (1983, in 1,000 tonnes): pig iron 9,372 and crude steel 16,236 (Silesia, Kraków-Nowa Huta, Częstochowa, Katowice, Warszawa), zinc 170 and lead 81 (Silesia), copper – smelted 320, – refined 348 (Katowice), aluminium 44 (Skawina, Konin), locomotives, railway carriages, agricultural machines, tractors 55,500 units, passenger cars 270,200 units (Warszawa), vessels 320,000 GRT (Gdańsk, Szczecin, Gdynia), radio 2.1 mn. and television receivers 566,500 units, suphuric acid 2,786, nitric acid 2,065, soda ash 808, nitrogenous fertilizers 1,342, phosphorus fertilizers 872, plastics and resins 525, synthetic rubber 120 (Oświęcim), coke oven coke 17,580; capacity of petroleum refineries 19.5 mn. tonnes (1984, Płock, Gdańsk), pipeline for the import of Soviet petroleum, motor spirit 2.4 mn. tonnes, fuel oils 7.5 mn. tonnes, pharmaceuticals (Warszawa), cement 16,200, chemical wood pulp 664, paper 1,026, yarn – cotton 177, woollen 81 – woven fabrics – cotton 744 mn. m, woollen 148 mn. m, linen 80 mn. m, silk 1 mn. m – rayon and acetate – fibres 15.9, staple fibre 51.9, woven fabrics 58.3 mn. m – synthetic – fibres 80.3, staple fibre 49.1; meat 2,281, milk 16,496, butter 280, cheese 401, eggs 423, sugar 2,141, beer 10.3 mn. hl; 82.8 billion cigarettes (1983).

Agriculture: private holdings predominate, vegetable production concentrates on cereals and potatoes. Land use: arable land 46.5%, meadows and pastures 13.0%, forests 27.8%. Tractors 757,000 (1983). **Crops** (1983, in 1,000 tonnes): rye 8,781 (second world producer), wheat 5,165, barley 3,262, oats 2,377, maize (corn), potatoes 34,473 (third world producer), flax 20 (second world producer), hemp 10, sugar beet 16,358, rapeseed 505, hops, fruit 2,572, tomatoes 513, strawberries 191, vegetables 4,373, tobacco 85; **livestock** (1983, in 1,000 head): cattle 11,269, pigs 15,587, sheep 4,103, horses 1,600, poultry 61,000; wool 6,900 tonnes, honey 20,873 tonnes; fish catch 735,100 tonnes (1983); roundwood 24.7 mn. cub.m (1983).

Communications (1984): railways 24,353 km, of which 8,307 km electrified, roads 253,976 km, passenger cars 3,425,800. Navigable waterways 2,977 km, important river port Koźle on the Odra. Merchant shipping 3,267,000 GRT (1984). Chief ports: Szczecin, Gdańsk, Gdynia. Civil aviation (1984): 23 mn. km flown, 1,596,000 passengers carried. Tourism 1.9 mn. visitors (1983).

Exports: coal, coke oven coke, iron and steel, copper, sulphur, cars, vessels, engineering, chemicals, textiles and food products. **Imports:** petroleum, natural gas, raw materials (iron ore, cotton), foodstuffs, machines and transport equipment, industrial consumer goods. Chief trading partners: socialist countries 50%, of turnover (chiefly U.S.S.R., German Dem. Rep., Czechoslovakia), Fed. Rep. of Germany, United Kingdom, France.

PORTUGAL

República Portuguesa, area 91,985 sq.km, population 10,229,200 (1985), republic (President Dr Mário Alberto Nobre Lopes Soares since 1986).

Administrative units: 22 districts (distrito), of which 3 on Azores and 1 on Madeira (both autonomous territories). **Capital:** Lisboa (Lisbon) 807,200 inhab. (1981); **other towns** (1981, in 1,000 inhab.): Porto 327, Amadora 96, Setúbal 78, Coimbra 75, Vila Nova de Gaia 63, Braga 63, Barreiro 51, Funchal 44. **Population:** Portuguese. **Density** 111 persons per sq.km; average annual rate of population increase 0.9% (1975–82); urban population 29.7% (1981), 24% of inhabitants employed in agriculture, 36.8% in industry (1983). – **Currency:** escudo = 100 centavos.

Economy: agricultural and industrial country, having good raw material resources. **Mining** (1983, in 1,000 tonnes metal content): tungsten 1.4 (Panasqueira), tin 347 tonnes, uranium 100 tonnes, gold 211 kg, silver, iron ore, manganese, pyrites 262, sulphur, copper, salt 508, marble 370, tantalum and niobium. Electricity 18.2 billion kWh (1983). **Production** (1983, in 1,000 tonnes): pig iron 432, crude steel 384, vessels 36,000 GRT, cement 5,988, chemical wood pulp 950, woven cotton fabrics 70.4, traditional textile industry – embroidery, lace – canned fish 43.3, wine 795 (Porto), beer 4 mn. hl; 15.6 billion cigarettes; further data for 1983: meat 481, milk 800, butter 3.7, cheese 33, eggs 70.

map 15

Agriculture: arable land 38.6%, meadows and pastures 5.8%, forests 39.5%. **Crops** (1983, in 1,000 tonnes): cereals 1,087 (chiefly wheat and maize), rice 100, potatoes 954, sugar beet, olives 110, fruit 1,615 – grapes 1,150, oranges 80, lemons 20, bananas – vegetables 1,551, tomatoes 500, sweet chestnuts 19; **livestock** (1983, in 1,000 head): cattle 990, sheep 5,220, goats 750, pigs 3,480, asses 180, mules; poultry 18,000; fish catch 246,500 tonnes (1983); roundwood 8.3 mn. cub.m, cork 125,100 tonnes (1982, leading world producer).

Communications: railways 3,614 km (1983), of which 458 km are electrified, roads 18,849 km (1984), passenger cars 1,517,600 (1983). Navigable waterways 124 km (1984). Merchant shipping 1,571,000 GRT (1984). Chief port: Lisboa. Civil aviation (1984): 37.3 mn. flown, 2,330,000 passengers carried. Tourism 3,714,000 visitors (1983).

Exports: woven cotton fabrics and textile products, wine, canned fish and tomatoes, cork. **Imports:** industrial products, transport equipment, metals, petroleum, chemicals and foodstuffs. Chief trading partners: United Kingdom, Fed. Rep. of Germany, France, U.S.A., Netherlands, Italy.

Azores

Area 2,247 **sq.km, population** 243,400 (1981), mountainous volcanic islands in the Atlantic Ocean (the largest São Miguel 747 sq.km). **Capital:** Ponta Delgada 54,600 inhab. **Economy:** cultivation of maize, wheat, bananas and vines; raising of cattle and pigs, fish catch and whaling. Roads 1,657 km (1980), sea and air transport.

ROMANIA

Republica Socialistă România, area 237,500 **sq.km, population** 22,795,000 (1985), **socialist republic** (President and Chairman of the State Council since 1974 Nicolae Ceaușescu).

Administrative units: 40 districts including capital district București. **Capital:** București (Bucharest) 1,961,189 inhab. (1984): **other towns** (1000 in 1,000 inhab.): Brașov 331, Constanța 316, Iași 306, Timișoara 303, Cluj-Napoca 301, Galați 285, Craiova 260, Ploiești 230, Brăila 225, Oradea 206, Arad 184, Sibiu 172, Bacău 166, Tîrgu Mureș 155, Pitești 150, Baia Mare 130, Buzău 127, Satu Mare 125, Piatra Neamț 103, Reșița 102, Drobeta-Turnu Severin 92, Hunedoara 87.

Population: Romanians 88%, Hungarians 7.9%, Germans 1.6%, Gipsies 1.1%. **Density** 96 persons per sq.km, average annual rate of population increase 0.8% (1971–83); urban population 49.6% (1980). 44.6% of inhabitants employed in agriculture, 28% in industry (1983). **Currency:** leu = 100 bani.

Economy: industrial and agricultural country. **Principal industries:** engineering, mining, metallurgy, chemical, textiles and food processing. Industry is concentrated in the south of the country. 50% of Romanian industry is located at București and in the petroleum extraction region near Ploiești. **Mining** (1983, in 1,000 tonnes, metal content): crude petroleum 11,600 (Ploiești, Pitești, Ticleni, Moinești), oil pipelines to București and ports, natural gas 1.6 mn. TJ (Transylvanian Depression, Bacău Region), brown coal 35,998 (Rovinari), coal 7,793 (Petroșani, Reșița), iron ore 510 (Munții Poiana Ruscăi, Ocna de Fier), manganese 78, lead 28.5, bauxite 420 (Roșia), gold (Munții Apuseni), silver 28 tonnes, salt 4,596, pyrites 930, graphite 12.5. Electricity 70.3 billion kWh (1983), of which 14% are hydro-electric power stations. **Production** (1983, in 1,000 tonnes): pig iron 8,190, crude steel 12,593 (Galați, Hunedoara, Reșița, Roman), coke oven coke 4,268, aluminium 244 (Oradea, Slatina), lead 49 (Baia-Mare), zinc 42, tractors 82,700 units (Brașov), motor vehicles – commercial 40,800 (Brașov), passenger 90,000 units (Pitești) – locomotives and carriages (Craiova), agricultural machines, petroleum mining and processing equipment (Ploiești, București), vessels 263,000 GRT (Galați, Constanța), radio 542,000 and television receivers 390,000 units, sulphuric acid 1,941, nitrogenous – 2,091 and phosphorus fertilizers 733, soda ash 788, synthetic rubber 147, plastics and resins 633; capacity of petroleum refineries 30.9 mn. tonnes (1984), motor spirit 5,102, oils 14,400, cement 13,027, chemical wood pulp 565. Textile industry (București, Arad, Timișoara, Brașov and others – 1983, in 1,000 tonnes): yarn – cotton 171, woollen 79 – woven fabrics – cotton 709 mn. sq.m, woollen 144 mn. sq.m, silk 1 mn. sq.m – rayon and acetate staple fibre 64, synthetic fibres 171, shoes 114 mn. pairs; food industry (1983, in 1,000 tonnes): meat 1,612, milk 3,134, butter 47, cheese 125, eggs 347, sugar 556, canned fruit and vegetables 447, vegetable oil 371, wine 1,000, beer 9.9 mn. hl (1983); 36 billion cigarettes (1983).

Agriculture: vegetable production is predominant. Land use: arable land 41.6%, meadows and pastures 18.7%, forests 26.7%. **Crops** (1983, in 1,000 tonnes): wheat 5,250, barley 2,192, maize (corn) 11,982, rice 50, potatoes 6,100, linseed 41, hemp 20, sugar beet 4,819, sunflower seed 705, soya beans 280, castor beans 5, fruit 3,677 (apples 755, peaches 85, plums 665, grapes 1,710), vegetables 5,130 (tomatoes 2,000, onions 356, chillies 279), walnuts 40, tobacco 37; **livestock** (1983, in 1,000 head): cattle 6,010, horses 600, buffaloes 220, sheep 16,921, goats 513, pigs 12,000; poultry 111,000; wool 23,000 tonnes, raising of silkworms (120 tonnes of cocoons), honey 15,000 tonnes; fish catch 242,500 tonnes (1983); roundwood 23 mn. cub.m (1983).

Communications (1984): railways 11,106 km, of which 2,868 km are electrified , roads 73,369 km. Navigable waterways – primarily the Danube – 1,659 km. Merchant shipping 2,667,000 GRT (1984). Chief port Constanța. Civil aviation (1984): 19.5 mn. flown, 1,163,000 passengers carried. Tourism 5.8 mn. visitors (1983).

Exports: machines, chemical products, minerals and metals, foodstuffs. **Imports:** machines and industrial equipment, raw materials, electrotechnical and chemical products, consumer goods. Chief trading partners: U.S.S.R., Fed. Rep. of Germany, German Dem. Rep., Poland, Iran, Italy, China, U.S.A., Czechoslovakia.

SAN MARINO

Repubblica di San Marino, area 60.6 **sq.km, population** 22,100 (1984), **republic,** (headed by two Captains-Regents, appointed every 6 months).

Capital: San Marino 4,516 inhab. (1983); Italian **currency,** customs union with Italy. **The official language** is Italian. **Economy:** agriculture (wheat, maize, vines, fruit); tourism (3 mn. visitors yearly) and postage stamps are the chief sources of revenue.

15a Iceland 1 : 10 000 000

map 15

SPAIN

Estado Español, area 504,783 sq.km, population 38,601,795 (1985), including Balearic and Canary Is., **kingdom** (King Juan Carlos I since 1975).

Administrative units: 17 regions (50 provinces – continental Spain, Balearic Is., Canary Is., North African settlements – towns Ceuta and Melilla, islands Islas Chafarinas, Peñón de Vélez de la Gomera, Peñón de Alhucemas). **Capital:** Madrid 3,272,000 inhab. (1982); **other towns** (census 1981, in 1,000 inhab.): Barcelona 1,755, Valencia 752, Sevilla 654, Zaragoza 591, Málaga 503, Bilbao 433, Las Palmas de G. Can. 366, Valladolid 330, Palma de Mallorca 304, Hospitalet 294, Murcia 289, Córdoba 285, Granada 262, Vigo 259, Gijon 256, Alicante 251, La Coruña 232, Badalona 228, Santa Cruz de Tenerife 191, Oviedo 190, Sabadell 185, Pamplona 183, Santander 180, Jerez de la Frontera 176, San Sebastian 176, Cartagena 173, Salamanca 167, Elche 165, Cádiz 158, Tarrasa 156, Burgos 153, Almería 141, Huelva 128, León 127.

Population: Spaniards 75%, Catalans, Basques, Galicians. **Density** 77 persons per sq.km; average annual rate of population increase 0.9% (1975–82); urban population 75% (1981). 15.1% of inhabitants employed in agriculture, 18% in industry (1980). – **Currency:** peseta = 100 centimos.

Economy: industrial and agricultural country with considerable raw material resources. Heavy foreign investments have encouraged the rapid development of industry in the last few years. Developed industries: mineral mining, metallurgy, engineering, production of motor vehicles, electrotechnics, the chemical and textile industries. **Mining** (1983, in 1,000 tonnes, metal content): coal 15,800 (Asturia, Castilla-León), brown coal 23,850 (Teruel), crude petroleum 2,977 (Ayoluengo), iron ore 3,652 (prov. Vizcaya, Santander, Oviedo), copper 54.8 (Minas de Ríotinto, Cangas de Onís), lead 82 (Sierra Morena), zinc 175.8 (Reocín), tungsten 352 tonnes, mercury 1,619 tonnes (second world producer, Almadén, Mieres), tin 444 tonnes, antimony 489 tonnes, titanium, gold 5,434 kg, silver 177 tonnes, magnesite 597, bauxite 5, uranium 150 tonnes (Ciudad Rodrigo), tantalum and niobium 59 tonnes – 1982), salt 3,158, potassium salt 773 (Suria), pyrites 2,306 (prov. Huelva), kaolin 698. Electricity 115.4 billion kWh (1983), of which 28% are hydro-electric and 21.5% nuclear power stations (Zorita, Santa Maria de Garoña, Vandellós).

Production: Metallurgy (1983, in 1,000 tonnes): pig iron 5,681, crude steel 13,262 (San Vicente de Baracaldo, Avilés, Mieres, Santander, Sagunto), coke oven coke 4,150, aluminium 395 (Valladolid), copper – smelted 118, refined 159 (Minas de Ríotinto, Córdoba) – lead 130 (Cartagena), zinc 190 (Avilés), tin 3,762 tonnes (Villagarcía de Arosa). **Engineering** predominantly in large cities: locomotives (Barcelona), passenger cars 1,136,000 units (1983, Madrid, Barcelona, Zaragoza), aircraft (Madrid and vicinity, Sevilla), tractors 17,484 (1983), vessels 669,000 GRT (1983, El Ferrol del Caudillo, Cartagena), weapons (Reinosa, Toledo), television receivers 818,000 (1981). **Chemical industry** (Cataluña, Barcelona and vicinity, Asturia, Madrid, Valladolid, Zaragoza – 1983, in 1,000 tonnes): acid -sulphuric 2,995, -nitric 1,055, -hydrochloric 135, caustic soda 458, soda ash 500, fertilizers -nitrogenous 858, -phosphorus 410, potash 656; synthetic rubber 51, plastics and resins 1,175; capacity of petroleum refineries 76 mn. tonnes (1984, Tarragona, Bilbao, Cartagena, Puertollano), motor spirit 5.7 mn. tonnes, fuel oils 30 mn. tonnes; cement 31 mn. tonnes, chemical wood pulp 1,093, paper 2,639. **Textile industry** (chiefly Barcelona and vicinity, 1983, in 1,000 tonnes): yarn (1981) – cotton 102, woollen 31.8 – woven fabrics (1981) – cotton 101, woollen 15.5 – artificial fibres 10.5, synthetic fibres 65. **Food industry** (1983, in 1,000 tonnes): sugar 1,318, meat 2,785, milk 6,250, cheese 141, butter 13, eggs 719, olive oil 268 (second world producer), wine 3,157 (Jerez, Málaga, Sherry), beer 19.3 mn. hl (1981), canned fish 92.3; 44 billion cigarettes, 1 billion cigars (1983). Glass industry (Bilbao, Santander), ceramics.

Agriculture is extensive, not very productive. Vegetable production predominates; large output of cereals, fruit and viniculture are of importance. Irrigation in dry areas. Land use: arable land 30.8%, meadows and pastures 21.2%, forests 30.8%. **Crops** (1983, in 1,000 tonnes): wheat 4,330 (Castilla, Andalucía), barley 6,571, maize (corn) 1,788 (Galicia), rye 247, rice 223, oats 470, rice 223, potatoes 5,098, sweet potatoes, cotton – seed 58, -lint 35; sugar beet 9,132 (provinces Valladolid, Burgos, León), sugarcane 302, pulses 314, sunflower seed 674, olives 1,297 (second world producer), soya beans, hops, fruit 11,998; oranges 1,895 (Valencia), tangerines 1,113 (second world producer), lemons 522, almonds 160, dates 12, figs, bananas 461 (Canary Is.), grapes 5,046 (Mediterranean coast, Castilla-La Mancha and Andalucía), peaches, apricots 161, sweet chestnuts 19; vegetables 8,566: tomatoes 2,258, watermelons 554, melons 668, onions 957, garlic 203; tobacco 42, alfalfa 20. **Animal production** is extensive (1983, in 1,000 head): cattle 5,070, horses 250, asses 177, mules 169, sheep 17,000, goats 2,500, pigs 11,700, poultry 54,000; wool (merinos) 11,360 tonnes, honey 9,500 tonnes, raising of silkworms; fish catch 1,250,000 tonnes (1983); roundwood 14.8 mn. cub.m (1983), cork 110,715 tonnes (1980).

Communications (1984): railways 15,083 km, of which 6,394 km are electrified, roads 149,553 km, motorways 2,018 km, passenger cars 8,874,400. Navigable waterways – only the Guadalquivir 103 km. Merchant shipping 7,005,000 GRT (1984). Chief ports: Barcelona, Bilbao, Cartagena, Valencia. Civil aviation (1984): 156.5 mn. km flown, 14,284,000 passengers carried. Tourism 25.6 mn. visitors (1983).

Exports: transport equipment, petroleum products, metals, food products (citrus fruit, wine, olive oil, canned fish), engineering products, chemicals, textiles, shoes and hides. **Imports:** petroleum, chemical products, machines and equipment, iron and steel, foodstuffs (cereals, sugar and others). Chief trading partners: France, Fed. Rep. of Germany, United Kingdom, U.S.A., Italy, Netherlands, Saudi Arabia.

SVALBARD

Area 62,422 sq.km, population 3,458 (1984), **autonomous territory of Norway,** including the islands of Jan Mayen and Bjørnøya. **Capital:** Longyearbyen.

Economy: mining of coal 480,000 tonnes (1983), exported to Norway and the U.S.S.R.; petroleum prospecting is in progress. Fishing station. **Jan Mayen, area 372 sq.km,** inhabited by radio and meteorological staff.

map 16

SWEDEN

Konungariket Sverige, area 449,964 sq.km, population 8,350,366 (1985), **kingdom** (King Carl XVI Gustaf since 1973).

Administrative units: 24 provinces (län). **Capital:** Stockholm 647,121 inhab. (1982, with agglomeration 1,383,481); **other towns** (1982, in 1,000 inhab.): Göteborg 428, Malmö 232, Uppsala 148, Norrköping 119, Västerås 118, Örebro 117, Linköping 113, Jönköping 107, Borås 102, Helsingborg 102, Sundsvall 95, Eskilstuna 90, Gävle 87, Umeå 82, Lund 79, Karlstad 74, Skellefteå 74, Kristianstad 69. **Population:** Swedes 95%, in the North Finns, nomadic Lapps. **Density** 19 persons per sq.km; average annual rate of population increase 0.2% (1975–82); urban population 88% (1981). 30% of inhabitants employed in industry (1983). – **Currency:** Swedish krona = 100 öre.
Economy: highly developed industrial country with intensive, mechanized agriculture. Sweden is one of the economically most advanced countries in the world. Basic natural resources: forests, iron ore, hydro-electric energy. **Chief industries:** engineering (electrotechnics, shipbuilding), wood processing and paper industry, mineral mining, energy production. Metallurgy, the chemical industry and food processing are also highly developed. **Mining** (1983, in 1,000 tonnes, metal content): iron ore 8,442 (Kiruna, Gällivare), copper 64 (Boliden, Aitik), lead 78 (Laisvall), zinc 203 (Åmmeberg), tungsten 301 tonnes, silver 171 tonnes, gold 3,199 kg (Boliden), uranium, pyrites 430. Electricity 109.6 billion kWh (1983), of which 59% hydro-electric and 37% nuclear power stations (Ringhals, Oskarshamn).
Production (1983, in 1,000 tonnes): pig iron 2,016, crude steel 4,212 (Borlänge, Luleå, Oxelösund, Sandviken), aluminium, primary 81.6 (Kubikenborg), copper – smelted 101.8, refined 63 (Rönnskär, Helsingborg), lead 30 (Landskrona), electro-technics (Västerås), motor vehicles – passenger 280,800 units ("Volvo"), commercial 45,600 (Göteborg, Trollhättan, Södertälje) – weapons (Bofors), aircraft (Malmö, Linköping), vessels 292,000 GRT (Göteborg, Malmö, Landskrona), sulphuric acid 884, nitric acid 407, plastics and resins 520, explosives; capacity of petroleum refineries 20.6 mn. tonnes (1984), motor spirit 2,500, fuel oils 10,250, cement 2,232, sawnwood 11.5 mn. cub.m, chemical wood pulp 6,444 (Husum, Örnsköldsvik, Karlsborg), paper and paper products 5,000, matches (Jönköping), leather industry (Örebro, Kumla), ornamental glass (prov. Kronoberg), woven cotton fabrics 8.4 (Borås), rayon and acetate staple fibre 39.3, meat 556, milk 3,766, butter 73, eggs 115, cheese 179; 10.4 billion cigarettes (1983).
Agriculture: predominantly animal production. Land use: arable land 6.6%, meadows and pastures 1.8%, forests 58.7%. **Crops** (1983, in 1,000 tonnes): wheat 1,721, barley 2,026, oats 1,268, rye, potatoes 958, sugar beet 1,922, rapeseed 365; **livestock** (1983, in 1,000 head): cattle 1,932, sheep 435, pigs 2,620; poultry 13,000; fish catch 265,500 tonnes (1983); roundwood 53.3 mn. cub.m (1983).
Communications (1984): railways 12,101 km, of which 7,595 km are electrified, roads 98,418 km, motorways 1,352 km, passenger cars 3,081,000 (1983). Navigable waterways 1,165 km. Merchant shipping 3,520,000 GRT (1984). Chief ports: Göteborg, Luleå, Stockholm, Helsingborg. Civil aviation (1984): 78.8 mn. km flown, 7,335,000 passengers carried. Tourism 3.4 mn. visitors (1983).
Exports: engineering and metal products, cars, paper, chemical wood pulp, wood and wood products, iron and steel. **Imports:** petroleum, fuels, machines and transport equipment, metals, foodstuffs, chemicals. Chief trading partners: Fed. Rep. of Germany, United Kingdom, Norway, Denmark, U.S.A., Finland.

SWITZERLAND

Schweizerische Eidgenossenschaft – Confédération Suisse – Confederazione Svizzera – Confederaziun Svizra, area 41,293 sq.km, population 6,455,600 (1985), **federal republic** (President Pierre Aubert in 1987).

Administrative units: 26 cantons. **Capital:** Bern 143,070 inhab. (1983); **other towns** (1983, in 1,000 inhab.): Zürich 363, Basel 180, Genève (Geneva) 158, Lausanne 127, Winterthur 86, St. Gallen 74, Luzern 62. **Official languages:** German (65% of inhabitants), French (18%), Italian (10%), Romansch (1%). **Density** 156 persons per sq.km; average annual rate of population increase –0.1% (1975–80); urban population 59% (1981). 38% of inhabitants employed in industry. – **Currency:** franc = 100 rappen.
Economy: highly developed industrial country and a leading financial and banking centre. **Principal industries:** precision engineering (watches, electrical and optical apparatus), the chemical and textile industries, food processing. Chief industrial centres: Zürich, Basel. **Mining:** salt 317,000 tonnes (1983). Electricity 51.8 billion kWh (1983), of which 70% are hydro-electric and 28% nuclear power stations (Beznau, Mühleberg). **Production** (1983, in 1,000 tonnes): crude steel 835, aluminium 76 (canton Valais), watches 52 mn. pieces (cantons: Neuchâtel, Bern and Solothurn; Genève, Schaffhausen), geodetic apparatus (Genève), electrical apparatus (Basel, Baden), electrochemical products (canton Valais), dyes and pharmaceuticals (Basel), cement 4,138, paper and paper products 705 (Jura, Alp region), cotton yarn 53, woven cotton fabrics 109 mn. m (eastern Switzerland), wool processing (Solothurn, canton Thurgau), woven silk fabrics 16.3 mn. m (Zürich, Basel), synthetic fibres 30.5, shoes 7.5 mn. pairs, meat 447, milk 3,733, cheese 130, butter 39, eggs 44.7, chocolate, wine 161, beer 4.2 mn. hl (1983); 25.7 billion cigarettes (1983).
Agriculture: predominantly livestock, chiefly cattle raising. Land use: arable land 9.6%, meadows and pastures 39.3%, forests 25.5%. **Crops** (1983, in 1,000 tonnes): cereals 888, potatoes 711, sugar beet 832, fruit 751, grapes 209, vegetables; **livestock** (1983, in 1,000 head): cattle 1,919, pigs 2,166, sheep 349; poultry 6,000; roundwood 4.3 mn. cub.m (1983).
Communications (1984): railways 5,064 km (all electrified), roads 69,775 km, motorways 1,258 km (1981) passenger cars 2,552,100. Navigable waterways 21 km, river port Basel. Merchant shipping 319,000 GRT (1984). Civil aviation (1984): 103.6 mn. km flown, 6,254,000 passengers carried. Tourism 9.2 mn. visitors (1983).

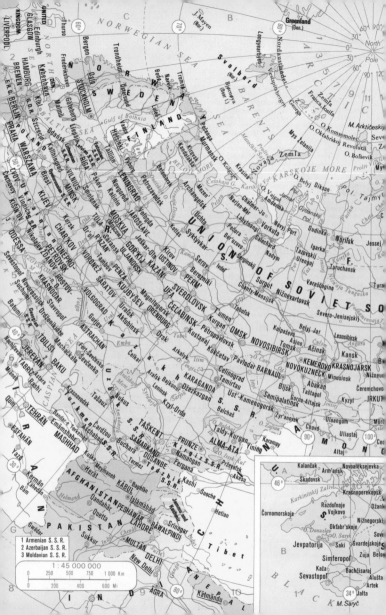

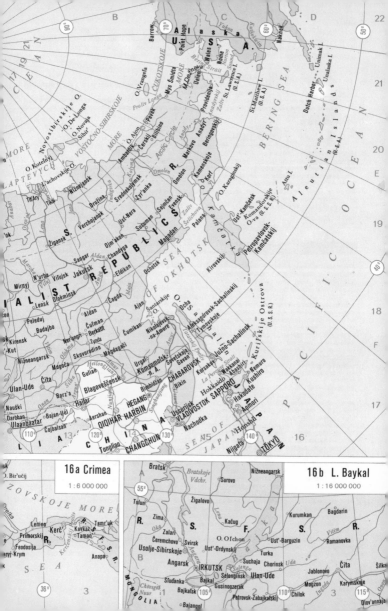

map 16

Exports: machines and apparatus, watches, chemical products (dyes, pharmaceuticals), textiles, foodstuffs (dried and condensed milk, cheese, chocolate). **Imports:** machines, transport equipment, fuels (petroleum), raw materials for the textile and food industries. Chief trading partners: Fed. Rep. of Germany, France, U.S.A., Italy, United Kingdom.

VATICAN CITY, STATE OF

Stato della Città del Vaticano, area 0.44 sq.km, population 1,000 (1983), papal state (Pope John Paul II [Karol Wojtyla] since 1978).

The smallest state in the world as to the area; religious and political centre of the Roman Catholic Church, seat of the Pope, Cardinals and the highest ecclesiastical officials. **Official languages** are Latin and Italian. – **Currency:** Italian lira. Revenue from tourism and postage stamps.

WEST BERLIN

Berlin (West), area 480 sq.km, population 1,857,165 (1985), administered by the Senate, headed by the Ruling Burgomaster (Eberhard Diepgen since 1984).

Density 3,862 persons per sq.km. After the Second World War Berlin was divided into 4 sectors on the basis of the Potsdam Agreement (1945). West Berlin consisted of 3 sectors under the control of the U.S.A., the United Kingdom and France. West Berlin contains the **administrative districts** of Kreuzberg, Neukölln, Schöneberg, Steglitz, Tempelhof, Zehlendorf, Charlottenburg, Spandau, Tiergarten, Wilmersdorf, Wedding, Reinickendorf.

Economy: highly developed industries, dependent on imported raw materials. Leading industries: electrotechnical, engineering and textiles. The extensive exchange of goods between West Berlin and Fed. Rep. of Germany is dependent upon specific autobahns and air corridors for transport across the territory of the German Dem. Rep.

YUGOSLAVIA

Socialistička Federativna Republika Jugoslavija, area 255,804 sq.km, population 23,224,000 (1985), socialist federal republic (President of the Presidency Sinan Hasani in 1986).

Administrative units: 6 socialist republics – Bosna i Hercegovina, Crna Gora, Hrvatska, Makedonija, Slovenija, Srbija (2 autonomous regions of Vojvodina and Kosovo). **Capital:** Beograd (Belgrade) 1,145,000 inhab. (1981 with agglomeration 1,455,046 inhab.); **other towns** (1981, in 1,000 inhab.): Zagreb 763, Sarajevo 448, Skopje 406, Ljubljana 303, Novi Sad 170, Split 169, Niš 161, Rijeka 158, Banja Luka 124, Maribor 105, Osijek 104, Subotica 100, Titograd 96, Kragujevac 87, Bitola 81, Zrenjanin 81, Pančevo 70, Priština 70. **Population:** Serbs, Croats, Slovenians, Montenegrians. **Density** 91 persons per sq.km; average annual rate of population increase 0.9% (1975–82); urban population 46% (1981). 33.8% of inhabitants employed in agriculture, 38% in industry (1983). **Currency:** dinar.

Economy: developed industrial and agricultural country. Rich resources of raw materials, forests and hydro-electric energy. **Principal industries:** mining of minerals, engineering, metallurgy, textiles, wood-working and food processing. Manufacturing of motor vehicles, shipbuilding, electrotechnics, radioelectronics and the chemical industry are under development. **Mining** (1983, in 1,000 tonnes, metal content): coal 392, lignite 58,188 (Slovenija – Trbovlje, Zagorje; Srbija), crude petroleum 4,128 (Lendava, Gojilo, Kloštar), natural gas 104,569 TJ, iron ore 1,756 (Ljubija, Vareš), manganese 9.6 (Drača), copper 128.6 (Bor, Majdanpek, Raška), lead 114.6 and zinc 87.8 (Mežica, Crna), antimony 1,360 tonnes, gold 3,732kg, silver 124 tonnes, bauxite 3,501 (Rovinj, Mostar, Titograd), magnesite 308 (Štip), pyrites 810, salt 425, asbestos 11. Electricity 71.6 billion kWh (1983), of which 44% are hydro-electric power stations and 5% nuclear power stations.

Production (1983, in 1,000 tonnes): pig iron 3,096, crude steel 4,135 (Zenica), coke oven coke 3,440, copper -smelted 153, -refined 122 (Bor), lead 98 (Mežica), zinc 87 (Celje), aluminium 284 (Lozovac, Kidričevo), motor vehicles – commercial 16,400 units, passenger 220,000 (Maribor, Kragujevac) – tractors 55,900 (Kruševac), agricultural machines (Subotica, Novi Sad), railway carriages (Kraljevo), locomotives (Slavonski Brod), vessels 243,000 GRT (Rijeka, Split, Trogir), electrotechnics (Beograd), sulphuric acid 1,300 (Bor), nitric acid 741, nitrogenous fertilizers 410, phosphorus fertilizers 383 (Kosovska Mitrovica); capacity of petroleum refineries 15.5 mn. tonnes (1984, Rijeka, Beograd, Sisak), motor spirit 2,497, fuel oils 8,902, cement 9,588, yarn – cotton 120, woollen 51 – woven fabrics – cotton 379 mn. sq.m, woollen 96.7 mn. sq.m, silk 34.9 mn. sq.m – rayon and acetate staple fibre 58, woven rayon and acetate fabrics 34.9 mn. sq.m, leather shoes 80.1 mn. pairs, chemical wood pulp 531, paper and paper products 1,116, sugar 722, meat 1,433, milk 4,550, butter 14, cheese 156, eggs 239, wine 720, beer 12.4 mn. hl (1983), alcoholic spirits; 58.5 billion cigarettes (1983).

Agriculture: arable land 27.8%, meadows and pastures 24.9%, forests 36.5%. **Crops** (1983, in 1,000 tonnes): maize (corn) 10,688, wheat 5,519, barley 670, oats 248, rice, potatoes 2,580, hemp, sugar beet 5,700, sunflower seed 135, sesame, olives, soya beans 220, hops, fruit 3,797; apples 589, plums 1,508 (second world producer), grapes 1,629 (Dalmacija, Danubeland); pulses 217, vegetables 2,935, tomatoes 475, watermelons 622, tobacco 77 (Bosna i Hercegovina, Makedonija), walnuts 37; **livestock** (1983, in 1,000 head): cattle 5,351, buffaloes 60, horses 505, asses, sheep 7,452, pigs 8,370, poultry 68,000; wool 6,004 tonnes, honey 5,540 tonnes; fish catch 79,800 tonnes; roundwood 15.4 mn. cub.m (1983).

Communications (1984): railways 9,279km, of which 3,462km are electrified, roads 116,602km, motorways 714km, passenger cars 2,874,000. Navigable waterways 2,001km. Merchant shipping 2,682,000 GRT (1984). Chief ports: Rijeka, Split, Dubrovnik. Civil aviation (1984): 29.8 mn. km flown, 2,944,000 passengers carried. Important tourism 5.9 mn. visitors (1983).

Exports: ores and non-ferrous metals, machines and equipment, transport equipment (vessels, cars, railway carriages), foodstuffs (meat, canned fish, fruit, wine), electrotechnical products, furniture, textiles and leather goods. **Imports:** machinery, transport and industrial equipment, fuels (petroleum), chemicals, raw materials and semi-finished products, foodstuffs. Chief trading partners: U.S.S.R., Italy, Fed. Rep. of Germany, Czechoslovakia, U.S.A.

map 17

UNION OF SOVIET SOCIALIST REPUBLICS

Soyuz Sovyetskikh Sotsialisticheskikh Respublik, area 22,274,900 sq.km (22,402,200 sq.km incl. Beloje More 90,000 sq.km and Azovskoje More 37,300 sq.km); of this, the European part has approx. 5,443,900 sq.km and the Asiatic part about 16,831,000 sq.km; population 277,505,000 (1985); Union of Soviet Socialist Republics (Chairman of the Presidium of the Supreme Soviet of the U.S.S.R. Andrei Andreievich Gromyko since 1985. General Secretary of the Central Committee of the Communist Party of the Soviet Union Mikhail Sergeievich Gorbachev since 1985).

Administrative units: 15 federal Soviet Socialist Republics (S.S.R.) divided into 3,201 districts and 630 urban districts (1983). In addition to this, some of the republics include Autonomous Soviet Socialist Republics (A.S.S.R., 20), Autonomous Regions (8), Autonomous Areas (only in the Russian Soviet Federal Socialist Republics, 10,) Territories and Regions. Capital: Moskva (Moscow) 8,642,000 inhab. (1984); other towns (1984, in 1,000 inhab.): Leningrad 4,832, Kijev 2,411, Taškent 1,985, Char'kov 1,536, Minsk 1,442, Gor'kij 1,392, Novosibirsk 1,386, Sverdlovsk 1,288, Kujbyšev 1,251, Baku 1,116, Dnepropetrovsk 1,140, Tbilisi 1,140, Jerevan 1,114, Odessa 1,113, Omsk 1,094, Čeľabinsk 1,086, Doneck 1,064, Perm' 1,049, Ufa 1,048, Alma-Ata 1,046, Kazan' 1,039, Rostov-na-Donu 983, Volgograd 969, Saratov 894, Riga 875, Krasnojarsk 860, Zaporožje 844, Voroněž 841, Ľvov 728, Krivoj Rog 680, Jaroslavľ 623, Karaganda 608, Kišin'ov 605, Ustinov 603, Krasnodar 603, Vladivostok 591, Irkutsk 590, Frunze, 590, Toljatti 576, Novokuzneck 572, Chabarovsk 569, Barnaul 567, Dušanbe 539, Vilnius 535, Tula 529, Uljanovsk 524, Penza 521, Ždanov 520, Samarkand 515, Orenburg 513, Kemerovo 495, Vorošilovgrad 485, R'azan' 483, Astrachan' 481, Ivanovo 474, Nikolajev 474, Tomsk 459, Tallinn 454, Makejevka 446, Kalinin 433, Gomeľ 432, Lipeck 432, Magnitogorsk 419.

Population: the most numerous nationalities at the 1979 census were 197.4 mn. Russians, 42.3 mn. Ukrainians, 12.5 Uzbeks, 9.5 mn. Byelorussians, 6.9 mn. Tatars, 6.6 mn. Kazakhs, 5.5 mn. Azerbaijanians, 4.2 mn. Armenians, 3.6 mn. Georgians, 2,9 mn. Lithuanians. 3 mn. Moldavians, 1.8 mn. Jews, 2.9 mn. Tadzhiks, 1.9 mn. Germans, 1.7 mn. Chuvashes. 1.9 mn. Kirghizians, 2 mn. Turkmenians, 1.4 mn. Latvians, 1.2 mn. Mordovians, 1.4 mn. Bashkirs, 1.2 mn. Poles. Density 12.4 persons per sq.km; average annual rate of population increase 0.98%; urban population 65% (1984). 14.5% of the economically active inhabitants employed in agriculture. — Currency: rouble = 100 kopeks.

Economy: well-developed industrial and agricultural country. It produces about 20% of the total world industrial output and holds the leading position in many branches of mining and processing: mining of crude petroleum, natural gas, peat, iron ore, manganese, nickel, chromium, mercury, asbestos, potash, magnesite; in the production of pig iron and crude steel, coke oven coke, cement, bricks, cotton and woollen yarn, woven woollen and linen fabrics, milk, butter, flour etc. The U.S.S.R. is the second greatest producer in the world of lignite and brown coal, copper, zinc, tungsten, vanadium, diamonds and phosphates. The size of the cultivated area is the largest in the world, and the U.S.S.R. is the world's leading producer of wheat, barley, rye, oats, potatoes, sunflower seed, flax fibre, sugar beet, roundwood and it has the largest sheep population. The U.S.S.R. is the second greatest producer in the world of hemp, cotton lint, cattle and pigs, fish catch and honey. Arable land constitutes 10%, meadows and pastures 17% and forests 41% of the total land area.

Agriculture: (1983, in 1,000 tonnes) — crops: wheat 82,000 (Ukraine, Plain of Kuban', a district called the Black Earth Central Zone – Tambov, Voroněž, Kursk; North Kazakhstan), barley 54,000 (southern European Russia), maize (corn) 14,000 (Ukraine, North Caucasia, Moldavia), rye 13,500 (central European Russia), oats 16,000 (western Siberia, central European Russia), rice 2,500 (Central Asian republics), millet 2,200, sorghum 180, potatoes 83,060 (European Russia, Byelorussia), sunflower seed 5,040 (southern European Russia), linseed 220, flax fibre 469 (Byelorussia, Baltic shore, central European Russia), hemp 30, cotton-seed 5,694, -lint 2,716 (Uzbekistan); sugar beet 81,813 (Ukraine), tomatoes 7,250, grapes 6,443 (Moldavia, Transcaucasia, Central Asia), oranges 345 (Georgia), tea 150 (Georgia), tobacco 377. Livestock (1983, in 1,000 head): horses 5,601, asses 344, cattle 117,186, buffaloes 320, camels 240, pigs 73,671, sheep 142,182, goats 6,340, poultry 1,044,000. Production (1983): eggs 4,116,000 tonnes, cowhides 752,000 tonnes, sheepskins 126,000 tonnes, wool-grease 454,000 tonnes, honey 190,000 tonnes. Fish catch 9,756,800 tonnes (second world catch). Roundwood 356 mn. cub.m (leading world producer).

Mining (1983, in 1,000 tonnes, metal content): coal 486,812 – Donbas Basin (Doneck and Vorošilovgrad region), Kuzbas Basin (Kemerovo region), Karaganda (Ekibastuz), lignite and brown coal 154,774 peat, combustible shale, crude petroleum 616,343 (the Ural-Volga area – Tatar A.S.S.R., Bashkir A.S.S.R., Kujbyšev region; T'umen' region in western Siberia, Baku etc.), international oil pipelines supply Czechoslovakia, Hungary, German Dem. Republic and Poland; natural gas 18,637.8 PJ (T'umen' region, Doneck-Dnepr district, North Caucasia, Volga Basin, an extensive gas pipeline system supplies industrial regions in the U.S.S.R. and in a number of European countries (Czechoslovakia, German Dem. Republic, Fed. Rep. of Germany, Austria, Italy, France, Yugoslavia), uranium, iron ore 133,563 (Fe content – Krivoj Rog, Kursk, the Ural Mts.), manganese 2,957 (Nikopoľ, Čiatura), copper 1,180 (Kazakhstan, the Ural Mts.), bauxite 4,600 (the Ural Mts., Kazakhstan, eastern Siberia), zinc 805 (Kazakhstan, Kuzbas Basin, North Caucasia), lead 435 (Kazakhstan, North Caucasia, the Ural Mts.), nickel 170 (northern Siberia, the Ural Mts., Koľskij Pol. – Kola Peninsula), chromium 977 (the Ural Mts., Kazakhstan), tin 17, antimony 9,200 tonnes (Kazakhstan, Central Asia), molybdenum 11,100 tonnes (Transcaucasia, Central Asia, eastern Siberia), tungsten 9,100 tonnes (Kazakhstan, Central Asia, eastern Siberia), vanadium 9,500 tonnes (the Ural Mts., Kazakhstan), mercury 2,206 tonnes (Central Asia), asbestos 2,250 (the Ural Mts., mica (eastern Siberia), gold 267,500 kg (eastern Siberia, the Ural Mts.), silver 1,465 tonnes (Kuzbas Basin, Central Asia), platinum (the Ural Mts., northern Siberia), diamonds 11 mn. carats (Yakut A.S.S.R., the Ural Mts.), magnesite 2,500 (the Ural Mts.), cobalt, phosphates 27,000 (Kola Pen., Kazakhstan), sulphur 1,800 (the Ural Mts., Ukraine), potash 9,300 (the Ural Mts., Byelorussia, Turkmenistan), salt 16,178.

Electricity 1,418 billion kWh, of which 180 billion kWh hydro-electric power stations. Largest power station (in mn. kWh): Reftinsk 3.8, Kostroma 3.6, Krivoj Rog 3 (thermal), Krasnojarsk 6, Bratsk 4.6, Sajano-Šušenskaja 6.4 (hydro-electric), Sosnovyj Bor 4, Novovoronežskaja 2.5 (nuclear).

Metallurgy: iron – Doneck-Dnepr district (Krivoj Rog), the Ural Mts.; non-ferrous metals – the Ural Mts., Kazakhstan, North Caucasia, Kola Peninsula. Production (1983, in 1,000 tonnes): pig iron 110,000, crude steel 153,000, aluminium 1,790, copper 1,450, lead 525, zinc 785, coke oven coke 86,000.

map 17

17 b Moscow
(Moskva)
1:350 000

Engineering (1983, in 1,000 units): metal-working machines 190 (Moskva, Leningrad), motor vehicles – passenger 1,315 (Toljatti, Ustinov, Moskva, Gor'kij), commercial 1,307 (Moskva, Brežnev), buses 85.1 (L'vov) – locomotives 1.8 (Vorošilovgrad, Char'kov, Kolomna), railway carriages 60.3 (Nižnij Tagil, Ždanov), tractors 564.0 (Volgograd, Char'kov, Minsk), grain combines 118 (Rostov-na-Donu), shipbuilding (Leningrad, Nikolajev, Cherson), radio receivers 9,297, television receivers 8,578, refrigerators 5,700).

Chemical industry – Moskva and surroundings, the Ural Mts., Doneck-Dnepr district, Leningrad, Gor'kij, regions near raw material deposits. Production (1983, in 1,000 tonnes): sulphuric acid 24,700, synthetic resins and plastics 4,419, caustic soda 2,853, nitrogenous fertilizers 11,481, phosphate fertilizers 6,560, chemical wood pulp 7,913.

Building industry – Moskva and surroundings, Leningrad, Char'kov, Krivoj Rog, Volgograd, Kujbyšev, the Ural Mts. Production (1983): cement 128 mn. tonnes, bricks 42 billion pieces. **Wood and paper industry:** production of furniture – Moskva, Ivanovo, Leningrad, Riga, Užgorod, Kijev; paper 5.7 mn. tonnes, of which 1.4 mn. tonnes newsprint.

Textile industry: cotton yarn 1.6 mn. tonnes, woollen yarn 447,100 tonnes; woven fabrics – cotton 8,029 mn. sq.m, woollen 911 mn. sq.m, silk 56.6 mn. sq.m, linen 753 mn. sq.m. Leather footwear 745 mn. pairs. **Food industry** – in cities and agricultural production regions (1983, in 1,000 tonnes): meat 16,196, milk 96,000, butter 1,455, cheese 1,622, flour 43,000, sugar 12,400, margarine 1,483, wine 34.4 mn. hl, beer 63 mn. hl; 364 billion cigarettes.

Communications (1983): railways 143,690 km, roads 973,000 km, of which hard surfaced 773,000 km, motor vehicles – passenger 9.6 mn., commercial 8.3 mn. Navigable waterways 138,931 km. Merchant shipping 24.5 mn. GRT. Chief ports: Novorossijsk, Odessa (with Iljičovsk), Leningrad, Nachodka, Astrachan', Archangel'sk, Murmansk, Baku. Civil aviation 109.5 mn. passengers carried. Length of oil and oil products pipelines 76,225 km, gas pipelines 155,095 km. Tourism 6,777,000 visitors (1983).

Foreign trade: with 120 countries (1983). Total turnover 127.5 billion roubles, of which exports 67,9 billion, imports 59.6 billion roubles. – **Exports:** fuels, raw materials, ores 60.8%; machines, equipment and transport equipment 12,9%; chemical products, building materials and other products 17.9%; agricultural raw materials and their products, consumer goods. **Imports:** machines, industrial and transport equipment 38%, raw materials, rolled iron, food materials, foodstuffs and consumer goods. Chief trading partners: German Dem. Rep., Czechoslovakia, Bulgaria, Poland, Hungary, Fed. Rep. of Germany, Finland, Yugoslavia, Italy, France, Romania, Japan.

map 18

RUSSIAN SOVIET FEDERAL SOCIALIST REPUBLIC (R.S.F.S.R.), Rossiskaya Sovietskaya Federativnaya Sotsialisti-cheskaya Respublika, **area 17,075,400 sq.km, population 143,078,000** (1985); 16 Autonomous Soviet Socialist Republics (A.S.S.R.): Bashkir A.S.S.R., Buryat A.S.S.R., Checheno-Ingush A.S.S.R., Chuvash A.S.S.R., Daghestan A.S.S.R., Kabar-dino-Balkar A.S.S.R., Kalmyk A.S.S.R., Karelian A.S.S.R., Komi A.S.S.R., Mari A.S.S.R., Mordovian A.S.S.R., North Osse-tian A.S.S.R., Tatar A.S.S.R., Tuva A.S.S.R., Udmurt A.S.S.R., Yakut A.S.S.R.; **capital:** Moskva 8,642,000 inhab. (1984). **Population:** more than 100 nationalities live there; the most numerous are (1980): Russians 82.6%, Tatars 3.7%. – **Economy:** the R.S.F.S.R. produces about two thirds of the total industrial and one half of the agricultural output of the Soviet Union. 90% of the total coal and 80% of petroleum reserves are found here as well as 60% of iron ore, 80% of peat, 90% of wood, 70% of hydro-electric resources, the majority of precious ores and gems. About 60% of the total cultivated area of the U.S.S.R. lies here.

UKRAINE, Ukrainska Radyanska Sotsialistichna Respublika (Ukrainian S.S.R.), **area 603,700 sq.km, population 50,843,000** (1985); **capital:** Kijev 2,411,000 inhab. (1984). **Population** (1980): Ukrainians 73.6%, Russians 21.1%. – **Economy:** raw materials, high quality coal, iron and manganese ores, petroleum, chemical raw materials, important metallurgical, en-gineering and chemical production, intensive agriculture (sugar beet, wheat, maize [corn]).

BYELORUSSIA, Belaruskaya Sovietskaya Sotsialistychnaya Respublika, **area 207,600 sq.km, population 9,941,000** (1985); **capital:** Minsk 1,442,000 inhab. (1984). **Population** (1980): Byelorussians 79.4%, Russians 11.9%, Poles 4.2%. – **Economy:** raw materials – forest products, peat, phosphides; engineering and food industry, cultivation of potatoes and flax; cattle breeding.

AZERBAIJAN, Azerbaijchan Soviet Sotsialistik Republikasy, **area 86,000 sq.km, population 6,614,000** (1985), 1 autono-mous republic – Nakhichevan A.S.S.R.; **capital:** Baku 1,166,000 inhab. (1984). **Population** (1980): Azerbaijanis 78.1%, Russians 7.9%, Armenians 7.9%. – **Economy:** important mining of petroleum, chemical, engineering, textile and food industries, cultivation of cotton, subtropical products and sheep breeding.

GEORGIA, Sakartvelos Sabchota Sotsialisturi Respublica, **area 69,700 sq.km, population 5,203,000** (1985), 2 auto-nomous republics – Abkhaz A.S.S.R. and Adzhar A.S.S.R.; **capital:** Tbilisi 1,140,000 inhab. (1984). **Population** (1980): Georgians 68.8%, Armenians 9.0%, Russians 7.4%. – **Economy:** mineral resources – manganese ore and coal, metallur-gical, engineering, textile and food industries. Main crops: tea, tobacco, cotton, citrus fruit, grapes.

ARMENIA, Haikakan Sovetakan Sotsialistakan Respublika, **area 29,800 sq.km, population 3,320,000 inhab.** (1985); **capital:** Jerevan 1,114,000 inhab. (1984). **Population** (1980): Armenians 89.7%, Azerbaijanis 5.3%, Russians 2.3%. **Economy:** mining and processing of copper ore, engineering, chemical and food industries; cultivation of cotton, vines, fruit.

MOLDAVIA, Respublika Sovietike Sochialiste Moldovenyaske, **area 33,700 sq.km, population 4,105,000** (1985); **capital:** Kišin'ov 605,000 inhab. (1984). **Population** (1980): Moldavians 63.9%, Ukrainians 14.2%, Russians 12.8%, Gagauzians 3.5%. – **Economy:** cultivation of vines, fruit, sugar beet, tobacco, cereals. Food industry.

ESTONIA, Eesti Nõukogude Sotsialistik Vabariik, **area 45,100 sq.km, population 1,529,000** (1985); **capital:** Tallinn 454,000 inhab. (1984). **Population** (1980): Estonians 64.9%, Russians 27.4%. – **Economy:** mining of combustible shales and peat; engineering, textile industry, production of cement. Cultivation of potatoes, flax, barley, fodder crops. Cattle breeding.

LATVIA, Latvijas Padomju Socialistiska Republika, **area 63,700 sq.km, population 2,604,000** (1985); **capital:** Riga 875,000 inhab. (1984). **Population** (1980): Latvians 53.7%, Russians 32.8%, Byelorussians 4.5%. – **Economy:** mining of peat; engineering (electrotechnical), food industry. Cultivation of flax, sugar beet, potatoes; livestock breeding.

LITHUANIA, Lietuvos Tarybu Socialistine Respublika, **area 65,200 sq.km, population 3,572,000** (1985); **capital:** Vilnius 535,000 inhab. (1984). **Population** (1980): Lithuanians 80%, Russians 8.9%, Poles 7.3%, Byelorussians 1.7%. – **Econo-my:** mining of peat, engineering and food industry. Cultivation of flax and potatoes; livestock breeding.

KAZAKHSTAN, Kazak Soviettik Sotzialistik Respublikasy, **area 2,717,300 sq.km, population 15,858,000** (1985); **capital:** Alma-Ata 1,046,000 inhab. (1984). **Population** (1980): Kazakhs 36%, Russians 40%. – **Economy:** mining and metallurgy of non-ferrous metals, extraction of coal and petroleum. Cultivation of wheat, fruit, cattle breeding.

TURKMENISTAN, Tiurkmenostan Soviet Sotsialistik Respublikasy, **area 488,100 sq.km, population 3,197,000** (1985); **capital:** Ašchabad 356,000 inhab. (1984). **Population** (1980): Turkmenians 68.4%, Russians 12.6%, Uzbeks 8.5%. – **Economy:** extraction and processing of petroleum, mining of sulphur, textile industry. Deserts and dry steppes cover about 90% of the land area; cultivation of cotton and rice on irrigated land. Karakul sheep breeding.

UZBEKISTAN, Ozbekistan Soviet Sotsialistik Respublikasy, **area 447,400 sq.km, population 17,989,000** (1985); 1 auto-nomous republic – Karakalpak A.S.S.R.; **capital:** Taškent 1,985,000 inhab. (1984). **population:** (1980): Uzbeks 68.7%, Russians 10.8%, Tatars 4.2%, Kazakhs 4%. – **Economy:** mining of petroleum, coal, copper, sulphur; heavy engineering, chemical, textile and food industries. Cultivation of cotton and breeding of Karakul sheep.

TADZHIKISTAN, Respubliksai Sovieth Sotsialistii Tojokiston, **area 143,100 sq.km, population 4,500,000** (1985); **capital:** Dušanbe 539,000 inhab. (1984). **Population** (1980): Tadzhiks 58.8%, Uzbeks 22.9%, Russians 11.9%. – **Economy:** mining of coal, petroleum, polymetallic ores; processing of agricultural products. Cultivation of cotton, rice, fruit and vines; sheep breeding.

KIRGIZIA, Kyrgyz Sovietik Sotsialistik Respublikasy, **area 198,500 sq.km, population 3,976,000** (1985); **capital:** Frunze 590,000 inhab. (1984). **Population** (1980): Kirghizians 47.9%, Russians 25.9%. – **Economy:** mining of petroleum, coal, mercury, non-ferrous metals; engineering. Cultivation of cotton, sugar beet, fruit; cattle and sheep breeding.

map 18

ASIA

The Asian continent lies in the northern hemisphere, although in the south-east some Indonesian islands belong to the southern hemisphere. On its western side Asia is linked to Europe, which is in fact a gigantic peninsula of Asia (Eurasia). In the south-west the boundary with Africa runs along the Isthmus of Suez (120 km long) on the Sinai Peninsula. The name "Asia" derives from the Accadian word "Asu", meaning "Land of the East, the Dawn".

Asia covers an **area of 44,410,000 sq.km** (including the islands) and takes up 29.7% of the world's land surface, making it the largest continent. It has **2,893 mn. inhabitants** (1985, including the Asian part of the U.S.S.R.), i.e. 59.8% of the world's population with a density of 65 persons per sq.km.

Geographical position – northernmost point of the continent: Cape Mys Čeľuskin (U.S.S.R.) 77°43′ N.Lat. (of the entire continent: Cape Mys Arktičeskij /O. Komsomolec island/ in Severnaja Zemľa 81°16′ N.Lat.); southernmost: Cape Tg. Buru on the Malay Peninsula 1°25′ N.Lat. (island Pulau Roti in the Indonesian Lesser Sunda Is. 11° S.Lat.); westernmost: Cape Baba Burnu in Asia Minor 26°03′ E.Long. and easternmost: Cape Mys Dežneva on the peninsula Čukotskij Poluostrov (U.S.S.R.) 169°40′ W.Long. (O. Ratmanova island in the Diomede Is. in the Bering Strait 169°02′ W.Long.).

The coast line of Asia is very varied and is 69,000 km long (excluding the offshore islands). Largest peninsulas: Arabian (area: 2,780,000 sq.km), India (1,850,000 sq.km), Indo-China (1,450,000 sq.km), Asia Minor (580,000 sq.km), Tajmyr (420,000 sq.km), and Kamčatka (275,000 sq.km). There are numerous islands; the largest include: The Greater Sunda Is. (area: 1,548,600 sq.km), the Japanese Is. (377,458 sq.km), the Philippines (297,413 sq.km), the Lesser Sunda Is. (91,860 sq.km) and the Moluccas (Maluku, 74,500 sq.km).

The complex **geological and tectonic structure** of Asia is the main reason for its varied relief. The basic geological structure is formed by Primary continental tables: the Siberian table in the North and the Chinese table in the East, the Indian in the South and the Arabian in the South-West. **The surface.** The vertical features of the Asian continent differ enormously. The average height above sea level is 960 m, i.e. a figure higher than that for any other continent, with the exception of Antarctica. About 26% of Asia is lowland, not higher than 200 m, but 14% of the land is above 2,000 m. Huge mountain ranges cross the continent in two zones which link up in the Pamir in Central Asia (7,719 m). The first zone, a system of folded ranges of the Alpine-Himalayan type, stretches from Asia Minor across Central Asia, and through Indo-China as far as Sumatra and Java. This includes: The Armenian Plateau (5,165 m), the Caucasus (Boľ. Kavkaz, 5,642 m), the Iranian Mountains (5,670 m) and the Hindu Kush (7,708 m) which adjoins the Pamir. The Karakoram Range (Godwin Austen, 8,611 m) runs in a south-easterly direction from the Pamir, as well as the mighty range of the Himalayas (11 summits above 8,000 m), with the highest mountain in the world, Mt. Everest (8,848 m). The Kunlunshan (Ulugh Muztagh, 7,723 m) lies to the east of the Pamir. The second zone of mountains stretches in a north-easterly direction from the Pamir as far as the peninsula of Čukotskij Pol.: Tien Shan (7,439 m), Altai (4,506 m), and the lower Sayan Mts., Stanovoj Chr. and Chr. Čerskogo (3,147 m). The Pacific zone of Tertiary mountains lies in eastern Asia, with high volcanic activity (130 volcanoes) and frequent earthquakes. – Greatest plains: Western Siberian (Zapadno-Sibirskaja Nizm.), Indo-Gangetic, Great Plain of China. The Dead Sea (– 400 m) is the lowest point of Asia. O. Bajkal the deepest crypto-depression (–1,286 m below sea level).

The river system. Over 40% of central and south-west Asia has no outlet to the sea. The Siberian rivers carry most water and flow into the Arctic Ocean (the longest is the Ob'-Irtyš, 5,410 km, which has a drainage basin of 2,975,000 sq.km and a mean annual discharge of 12,600 cub.m per sec.). Monsoon rivers are an important source of water for agriculture. They include Asia's longest river, the Yangtze (Changjiang), 5,520 km, drainage basin 1,942,000 sq.km, and a mean annual discharge of 31,000 cub.m per sec. The rivers in the tropical belt, especially on the islands, have ample water throughout the year. The largest among the many **lakes** is the Caspian Sea covering 371,000 sq.km (depth 1,025 m), –28 m below sea level.

Large parts of Asia have a continental **climate**; the very low winter temperatures and hot inland summers cause oscillations in the atmospheric circulation. The north of Asia is influenced by the cold Arctic air and has heavy frosts. The lowest absolute temperature, –78°C, was measured at Ojm'akon in Siberia. Almost two thirds of Asia lie in the temperate belt and the Asian Plateau is a region of extreme drought. The south of Asia has a tropical climate: the south-west is dry with high temperatures; the highest absolute temperature, 53°C, was measured at Jacobābād in Pakistan; in south-east, in particular on the islands, it is hot and damp with only minor variations in temperature. The monsoon rains are a life-giving force bringing an average precipitation of 2,500 mm per year. Maximum rainfall was recorded at Cherrapunji (India) 11,013 mm a year and the minimum at Al-'Aqabah (Jordan) 24 mm annually.

Mean January and July temperatures in °C (and annual rainfall in mm) are as follows: Verchojansk –48.9 and 15.3 (142), Sapporo –6.2 and 19.4 (1,063), Beijing –4.7 and 25.6 (610), Ulaanbaatar –26.7 and 17.2 (101), Alma-Ata –7.4 and 23.3 (575), İstanbul 5.6 and 23.1 (679), Baghdād 9.4 and 34.7 (156), Tehrān 2.1 and 29.7 (250), Multān 13.5 and 36.1 (161), Bombay 23.8 and 27.4 (1,878), Calcutta 19.6 and 28.9 (1,625), Cherrapunji 11.7 and 20.4 (11,013), Hong Kong 15.6 and 27.9 (2,177), Tōkyō 3.2 and 25.0 (1,575), Manila 24.6 and 26.9 (2,123), Krung Thep 26.1 and 28.6 (1,420), Ar-Riyād 14.4 and 33.8 (82), Aden 25.4 and 32.5 (41), Colombo 26.2 and 27.2 (2,236), Singapore 26.1 and 27.4 (2,413), Jakarta 25.9 and 26.5 (1,784), Kupang 26.8 and 25.3 (1,458).

The vegetation of Asia falls into two zones. First, the extensive Holarctic realm in the north, west and south-west which includes, from north to south, tundra with woodland, typical taiga with coniferous forest, mixed forest, broad-leaved deciduous forest, the Sino-Japanese region of evergreen plants, Central Asian wooded steppe, grassland steppe, semi-desert with scrub, Mediterranean evergreen maquis, and the North-African-Indian desert region with xerophilous scrub. Second, the extensive Paleo-tropical realm in the south and south-east of Asia, which includes semi-desert with sparse thorn forest, dry deciduous tropical forest ånd grassland savanna in India and monsoon tropophilous woodland, subtropical forest, evergreen tropical rain forest and mangrove swamp, etc., in India and Southeastern Asia. – **The fauna** belongs to two zoogeographical realms: the larger is Paleoarctic and poorer in species (e.g. polar bear, ermine, reindeer, wolf, tiger, stag, sheep, forest and water fowl, pheasant, vulture, bustard, numerous rodents, fresh water fish, insects, etc.). The smaller Indo-Malaysian is richer in species and older in evolution (e.g. monkeys, rare orangutans, Indian elephant, rhinoceros, buffalo, leopard, tiger, tapir, pheasant, peacock, python, crocodile, flying gurnard, and large numbers of insects and other fishes).

map 19

LONGEST RIVERS

Name	Length in km	River Basin in sq.km
Changjiang /Yangtze/	5,520	1,942,000
Ob' (-Irtyš)	5,410	2,975,000
Huanghe /Yellow/	4,845	772,000
Mekong /Lancangjiang/	4,500	810,000
Irtyš	4,422	1,595,680
Amur (-Šilka, -Onon)	4,416	1,855,000
Lena	4,400	2,490,000
Jenisej	4,092	2,580,000
Indus /Sindh/	3,190	960,000
Syrdarja (-Naryn)	3,019	219,000
Nižn'aja Tunguska (-Nepa)	2,989	473,000
Brahmaputra /Yaluzangbujiang/	2,960	935,000
Salween /Nujiang/	2,820	325,000
Euphrates /Al-Furāt, Fırat/	2,760	765,000
Talimuhe /Tarim/	2,750	1,210,000
Ganga - Padma /Ganges/	2,700	1,125,000
Vil'uj	2,650	454,000
Amudarja (-P'andž)	2,620	227,000
Kolyma	2,513	647,000

LARGEST LAKES

Name	Area in sq.km	Greatest Depth in m	Altitude in m
Caspian Sea[+]	371,000	1,025	−28
Aral'skoje More[+]	64,115	67	53
O. Bajkal	31,500	1,620	455
O. Balchaš	18,200	26	340
D.-y. Orūmīyeh[+]	7,500	15	1,275
O. Issyk- Kul'[+]	6,280	702	1,609
Tônlé Sab	5,700	10	15
O. Tajmyr	4,560	26	6
Qinghai /Kukunuoer/[+]	4,460	38	3,250
O. Chanka	4,200	10	68
Hongzehu	3,780	.	3
Dongtinghu	3,750	.	25
Van Gölü[+]	3,738	25	1,662
Uvs-Nuur[+]	3,350	.	759
Poyanghu	3,150	.	15
Chövsgöl Nuur	2,620	.	1,645
Luobubo /Lop Nor/[+]	2,600	.	780
Dead Sea[+]	980	399	−400

[+] Salt Lake

LARGEST ISLANDS

Name	Area in sq.km	Name	Area in sq.km	Name	Area in sq.km
Borneo (Kalimantan)	746,546	Mindanao	98,692	Hainandao	33,670
Sumatera	433,800	Hokkaidō	78,073	Timor	33,615
Honshū	227,414	Sachalin	76,400	Seram	18,625
Sulawesi (Celebes)	179,416	Sri Lanka (Ceylon)	65,607	Shikoku	18,256
Jawa (Java)	126,700	Kyūshū	36,554	Halmahera	17,800
Luzon	106,983	Taiwan	35,961	Flores	15,600

HIGHEST MOUNTAINS

Name (Country)	Height in m	Name (Country)	Height in m
Mt. Everest /Sagarmatha, Zhumulangmafeng/ (Nepal, China)	8,848	Himālchūli (Nepal)	7,893
Godwin Austen /Qogir/ /K2/ (China-Pakistan)	8,611	Nuptse (Nepal)	7,855
Kānchenjunga (Nepal-India)	8,586	Masherbrum (Pak.)	7,821
Lhotse (Nepal-China)	8,516	Nandā Devi (India)	7,816
Makālu (Nepal-China)	8,463	Rakaposhi (Pak.)	7,789
Lhotse-Shar (Nepal-China)	8,430	Disteghil Sar (Pak.)	7,785
Cho Oyu (China-Nepal)	8,201	Batura (Pak.)	7,785
Dhaulāgiri (Nepal)	8,167	Kāmēt (India-China)	7,756
Manāslu (Nepal)	8,163	Namuchabawashan (China)	7,755
Nānga Parbat (Pak.)	8,125	Ulugh Muztagh (China)	7,723
Annapūrna (Nepal)	8,091	Gonggeershan (China)	7,719
Gasherbrum (Pak.-China)	8,068	Tirich Mīr (Pak.)	7,708
Phalchan Kangrī /Broad Pk./ (Pak.-China)	8,047	Pik Kommunizma (U.S.S.R.)	7,495
Xixabangma (China)	8,013	Nowshāk (Afghan.)	7,492
		Pik Pobedy (U.S.S.R.)	7,439

ACTIVE VOLCANOES

Name (Country)	Altitude in m	Latest eruption
V. Kľučevskaja Sopka (U.S.S.R.)	4,750	1984
Gunung Kerintji (Indon.)	3,805	1968
Gunung Rinjani (Indon.)	3,726	1966
Gunung Semeru (Indon.)	3,676	1981
Korjakskaja Sopka (U.S.S.R.)	3,456	1957
Gunung Slamet (Indon.)	3,428	1967
Galunggung (Indon.)	2,830	1982

FAMOUS NATIONAL PARKS

Name (Country)	Area in sq.km
Kronockij Zap. (U.S.S.R.)	9,770
Altajskij Zap. (U.S.S.R.)	8,638
Issik-Kulskij Zap. (U.S.S.R.)	7,816
Taman Negara (Malaysia)	4,360
Gunung Leuser (Indon.)	4,165
Sagarmatha (Mt. Everest, Nepal)	1,243
Fuji-Hakone (Jap.)	948

map 19

ASIA

Country	Area in sq.km	Population year 1985	Density per sq.km	Capital
Afghanistan	649,969	18,136,446	28	Kābul
Bahrain	662	417,210	630	Al-Manāmah
Bangladesh	143,998	98,657,070	685	Dacca
Bhutan	47,000	1,417,000	30	Thimbu
Brunei	5,765	224,400	39	Bandar Seri Begawan
Burma	678,033	37,614,000	56	Rangoon
China (incl. Taiwan)	9,596,961	1,059,525,000	110	Beijing
Cyprus	9,251	665,200	72	Levkosia
Democratic Yemen	332,968	2,293,900	7	Adan (Aden)
Egypt-Sinai Peninsula	58,824	175,000[2]	3	Al-Qāhirah
Ghaza Strip (Egypt)	378	490,000	1,296	
Hong Kong (U.K.)	1,067	5,579,000	5,229	Victoria
India	3,287,590	752,900,000	229	New Delhi
Indonesia (incl. East Timor)	2,027,087	165,155,000	82	Jakarta
Iran	1,648,100	44,632,000	27	Tehrän
Iraq	438,446	15,898,000	36	Baghdād
Israel	20,770	4,233,200	204	Yerushalayim
Japan	377,619	120,754,335	320	Tōkyō
Jordan	97,740	3,515,000	36	Ammān
Kampuchea	181,035	7,284,000	40	Phnum Pénh
Korea, Democratic People's Rep. of	120,538	20,385,000	169	P'yöngyang
Korea, Republic of	98,824	41,258,000	418	Sŏul
Kuwait	17,818	1,709,860	96	Al-Kuwayt
Laos	236,800	3,625,803	15	Viangchan
Lebanon	10,400	2,668,000	257	Bayrūt
Macau (Port.)	16	392,000	24,500	Macau
Malaysia	329,749	15,567,000	47	Kuala Lumpur
Maldives	298	180,453	606	Male
Mongolia	1,565,000	1,890,500	1.2	Ulaanbaatar
Nepal	140,797	16,625,312	118	Kätmändu
Oman	212,457	1,242,000	6	Masqat
Pakistan	803,942	96,179,592	120	Islämäbäd
Philippines	297,413	54,377,990	183	Manila
Qatar	11,000	315,000	29	Ad-Dawhah
Saudi Arabia	2,153,168	11,542,000	5	Ar-Riyād
Singapore	597	2,558,000	4,285	Singapore
Sri Lanka	65,610	15,837,000	241	Colombo
Syria	185,180	11,162,585	60	Dimashq
Taiwan (China)	36,174	18,859,000	521	T'aipei
Thailand	514,121	51,410,000	100	Krung Thep
Turkey	779,452	51,428,745	66	Ankara
U.S.S.R. – Asiatic part	16,831,000	75,320,000[1]	4.5	Moskva
United Arab Emirates	83,600	1,327,000	16	Abu Zaby
Vietnam	332,560	59,713,000	180	Ha-Noi
Yemen	195,000	9,274,173	48	San'a

[1] year 1984, [2] year 1981

Asia has a **population of 2,893 mn.** (1985), which is roughly 60% of the total population of the world, with a density of 65 persons per sq.km. Its geographical distribution is very uneven. Large desert regions, tundra and forest zones are almost uninhabited. The fertile agricultural lands of China, India, Bangladesh and elsewhere, and the industrial areas of Japan, are among the most densely populated regions in the world. Extreme density of population is found in the smallest countries: Macau 24,500, Hong Kong 5,334, Singapore 4,285; among other countries: Bangladesh 685, Bahrain 630, Maldives 606, Rep. of Korea 418 and Japan 320 (1985).

The average **population increase** is highest (1980–85) in Qatar 6.8%, United Arab Emirates 6.1% and Kuwait 5.5%. The highest birth rate is in Yemen (48.6 per 1,000), Afghanistan (48.4 per 1,000), the highest death rate in Afghanistan (27.3 per 1,000), Kampuchea (19.7 per 1,000). The average life expectancy in southern Asia is 53 years and 68 years in eastern Asia (1980–85). There are several hundred nations and nationalities in Asia. The country with the highest population is China. Asia has an ancient tradition of urban settlement. The highest percentages of urban dwelling are in Japan (76%) and Israel 90%). There are (incl. the U.S.S.R.) more than 90 **towns** and urban agglomerations with over 1 mn. people. The largest are: Sŏul, Tōkyō, Bombay, Jakarta, Shanghai, Tehrän, Beijing, Tiajin, Karāchi, Delhi.

Economy: Asia is an important source of raw materials, primarily petroleum, ores, textile raw materials, skins and hides, oil-producing crops and fruit. In the majority of Asian countries agriculture remains the most important industry. 55.5% of the working population worked in agriculture, tilling 455 mn. hectares of arable land (1983). Not quite one third of the world total of arable land is in Asia, which is far less than its share of the world's population. Industry is located unevenly on the continent, and in the majority of countries industrial production is in its infancy. Exceptions to this include Japan, a leading industrial world power, Israel and the Republic of Korea.

map 20

AFGHANISTAN

De Afghanistan Democrateek Jamhuriat, area 649,969 sq.km, population 18,136,446 (1985),
republic (Chairman of the Revolutionary Council and Prime Minister Hadji Mohammad Samkanai
since 1986).
Administrative units: 28 provinces. **Capital:** Kābul 913,164 inhab. (1982, with agglom. 1,127,417); **other towns** (1982,
in 1,000 inhab.): Qandahār 198, Herāt 155, Mazār-e Sharīf 115. **Population:** Afghans 60%, Tadzhiks 25–30%, Uzbeks
etc. Average annual rate of population increase 2.6% (1973–83); urban population 17.0% (1983). 77% of the economically
active inhabitants engaged in agriculture (1981). – **Currency:** afghāni = 100 puls.
Economy: predominantly agricultural country. Arable land 12.4% of the land area. **Agriculture** (1983, in 1,000 tonnes):
wheat 3,750, rice 650, barley 450, maize (corn) 1,000, millet, sesame, cotton – seed 30, – lint 15; sugar beet 20,
vegetables, fruit, grapes 510, raisins 88; livestock (1983, in 1,000 head): cattle 3,800, sheep 20,000 (of which more than
one third are karakul sheep, camels 250, goats 3,000; hides and skins, wool; roundwood 6.7 mn. cub.m (1983). **Mining**
(1983): coal, natural gas 99,482 TJ, salt 10,000 tonnes. Textile and food industries. – **Communications:** roads 18,752 km.
Civil aviation: 3.8 mn. km flown, 220,000 passengers carried (1984). – **Exports:** natural gas, karakul skins, sheep, wool,
cotton, carpets, raisins, fruit. Chief trading partners: U.S.S.R., India, Japan, Pakistan, the United Kingdom.

BAHRAIN

Dowlat al-Bahrain, area 662 sq.km, population 417,210 (1985), **emirate** (Amir Shaikh Isa bin
Sulman Al-Khalifa since 1961).
Capital: Al-Manāmah 108,684 inhabitants (1981). – **Currency:** Bahrain dinar = 1,000 fils.
Economy (1983, in 1,000 tonnes): dates 43, pearl fishery, fish catch 6.8; mining of petroleum 2,049, natural gas 125,860
TJ, petroleum refineries, production of aluminium 171.7, motor spirit 653, jet fuel 1,269; electricity 2,026 mn. kWh (1983). –
Communications: roads 700 km, passenger cars 60,100. – **Exports:** petroleum and petroleum products, aluminium,
dates, pearls. Chief trading partners: United Kingdom, Japan, U.S.A., Fed. Rep. of Germany, Saudi Arabia.

BANGLADESH

People's Republic of Bangladesh, area 143,998 sq.km, population 98,657,070 (1985), **republic,**
member of the Commonwealth (President Lieut.-Gen. Hossain Mohammad Ershad since 1983).

Administrative units: 21 districts. **Capital:** Dacca 3,458,602 inhab. (1981); **other towns** (in 1,000 inhab.): Chittagong
1,388, Khulna 623, Nārāyanganj 298, Rājshāhi 171. **Population:** Bengals. **Density** 685 persons per sq.km; average annual
rate of population increase 2.4% (1973–83); urban population 17% (1983). 83% of the economically active inhabitants
engaged in agriculture (1983). – **Currency:** taka = 100 poisha.
Economy (1983): predominantly an agricultural country. Arable land 63.5% of the land area. **Agriculture – crops** (in
1,000 tonnes): rice 21,700, wheat 1,095, sugarcane 7,307, jute 908, bananas 678, tea 45, tobacco 52, vegetables,
pineapples 160; **livestock** (1983, in 1,000 head): cattle 36,000, buffaloes 1,700, sheep 1,090, goats 12,000; fish catch 728,500
tonnes. **Mining:** coal, crude petroleum, natural gas 78,808 TJ, salt 249,000 tonnes. Electricity: 3,758 mn. kWh. **Production**
(1983): fabrics 1,235 mn. sq.m, sugar 178,000 tonnes. Textile and food industries. – **Communications** (1983):
railways 4,473 km, roads 22,471 km. Merchant shipping 367,000 GRT. Civil aviation: 11.5 mn. km flown. **Exports:** jute and
jute products, hides and skins, tea. Chief trading partners: U.S.A., Japan, Singapore, United Kingdom, China.

BHUTAN

Druk-yul, area 47,000 sq.km, population 1,417,000 (1985), **monarchy** (King Jigme Singhye
Wangchuck since 1974).
Capital: Thimbu 20,000 inhab. (1981), winter seat Paro. – **Currency:** ngultrum = 100 chetrums.
Economy: arable land 2%, meadows and permanent crops 4.6%, forests 69.4%. Agriculture in the valleys (1983, in
1,000 tonnes); rice 60, maize (corn) 83, millet, barley; cattle raising in the mountains (1983, in 1,000 head): cattle 312,
sheep 43, horses. Mining of coal, handicrafts. – **Exports:** wood, rice, coal, animal products.

BRUNEI

The Sultanate of Brunei, area 5,765 sq.km, population 224,400 (1985) **sultanate, member of**
the Commonwealth (Sultan Hasan al-Bolkiah Muizzaddin Waddaulah since 1967).
Capital: Bandar Seri Begawan 49,902 inhab. (1981). **Population:** Malays 65%, Chinese, Dayaks and others. Average
annual rate of population increase 5.6% (1973–83). – **Currency:** Brunei dollar = 100 cents.
Economy (1983, in 1,000 tonnes): rice 10, bananas 5, coconuts, natural rubber, rare timber; raising of buffaloes 15,000
head, pigs 15,000 head. Fish catch 3,100 tonnes. **Mining** of petroleum 8.1 mn. tonnes, natural gas 339,499 TJ (1983).
Petrochemical industry. – **Communications:** roads 1,474 km, passenger cars 62,500 (1983). – **Exports:** petroleum and
petroleum products 95%, natural gas, natural rubber, rare timber.

BURMA

Pyidaungsu Socialist Thammada Myanma Naingngandaw, area 678,033 sq.km, population
37,614,000 (1985), **federal socialist republic** (President Gen. U San Yu since 1981).
Administrative units: 7 states and 7 provinces. **Capital:** Rangoon 2,458,712 inhab. (1983); **other towns** (in 1,000

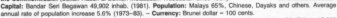

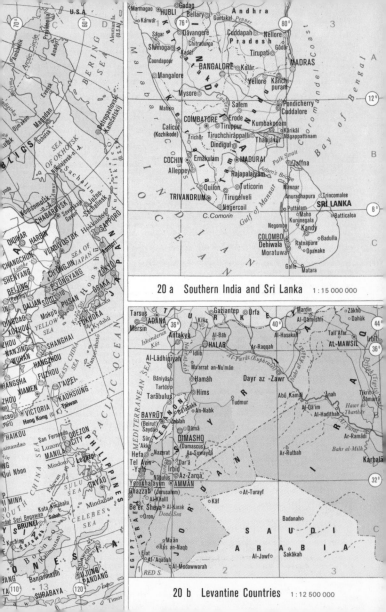

20 a   Southern India and Sri Lanka   1:15 000 000

20 b   Levantine Countries   1:12 500 000

map 20

inh.): Mandalay 533, Bassein 336, Henzada 284, Pegu 260, Myingyan 220, Moulmein 220. **Population:** Burmese, minorities: Karens, Shans, Kachins and others. **Density** 56 persons per sq.km; average annual rate of population increase 2% (1973–83); urban population 29% (1983). 50% of the economically active inhabitants engaged in agriculture (1983). – Currency: kyat = 100 pyas.

Economy: predominantly an agricultural country with extraction industry. Arable land 14.9%, forests 47.5% of the land area. **Agriculture** (1983, in 1,000 tonnes): rice 14,500, millet 119, sugarcane 3,135, groundnuts 691, cotton, jute 45, vegetables, fruit, tobacco 50, teak, natural rubber 16; livestock (1983, in 1,000 head): cattle 9,400, buffaloes 2,150, pigs 2,900, sheep 260, goats 770, fish catch 585,800 tonnes. **Mining** (1983, in 1,000 tonnes): crude petroleum 1,493, natural gas 18,563 TJ, lead, zinc, copper, nickel, silver 16 tonnes, tungsten 738 tonnes, tin 1.6, salt, precious stones. Food and textile industries. Production of woven cotton fabrics 91 mn. m; electricity 1,872 mn. kWh.

Communications (1982): railways 4,473 km, roads 22,471 km, passenger cars 47,800. Civil aviation: 6.7 mn. km flown, 515,000 passengers carried. – **Exports:** rice, teak, ores, vegetable oil, natural rubber, cotton, jute. Chief trading partners: Japan, Singapore, Indonesia, United Kingdom, Fed. Rep. of Germany, China, India.

CHINA

Zhonghua Renmin Gonghe Guo – People's Republic of China, area (including Taiwan) **9,596,961 sq.km, population 1,059,525,000** (1985), **people's republic** (Head of the State and Chairman of the State Council Zhao Ziyang since 1987).

Administrative units: 22 provinces (incl. Taiwan), 5 autonomous regions, 3 self-administrated municipalities. **Capital:** Beijing 5,760,000 mn. inhab. (1984, 9.23 mn. – 1982); **other towns** (1984, in 1,000 inhab.): Shanghai 6,880 (with agglom. 11,860), Tianjin 5,300 (with agglom. 7,790), Shenyang 4,130, Wuhan 3,340, Guangzhou 3,220, Chongqing 2,730, Harbin 2,590, Chengdu 2,540, Xi'an 2,280, Nanjing 2,210, Taiyuan 1,840, Changchun 1,810, Dalian 1,590, Kunming 1,480, Lanzhou 1,460, Jinan 1,390. **Population:** about 93% Chinese (Han), minorities Chuang, Uighur, Hui, Yi, Tibetans, Mongolians and others. **Density** 110 persons per sq.km; average annual rate of population increase 1.5% (1973–83); urban population 21% (1983). 57% of the economically active inhabitants work in agriculture. – **Currency:** renminbi juan = 10 chiao = 100 fen.

Economy: agricultural and industrial country. The main industrial region is eastern China (40% of industrial production – provinces Jiangsu, Anhui, Zhejiang, Fujian and self-administered province of Shanghai). Large raw material resources and heavy industry in north-east China (provinces Liaoning, Jilin, Heilongjiang). **Agriculture** (1983): arable land 11%, meadows and pastures 29.8%, forests 14% of the land area. There are two or three harvests annually in the east and south-east of China. **Crops** (in 1,000 tonnes): rice 172,184 (leading world producer), wheat 81,392 (second world producer), millet 7,004 (second world producer), sorghum 8,369, barley 3,400, maize (corn) 64,135 (second world producer), oats 800, sweet potatoes 95,700 (leading world producer), potatoes 50,033 (second world producer), beans 1,745, peas 2,000, sugarcane 37,941, sugar beet 9,182, cotton – lint 4,637 – seed 9,282 (leading world producer), jute 1,019 (second world producer), flax, hemp, sisal, ramie, soya beans 9,770, sesame 350 (second world producer), coconuts 63, palm kernels 50, palm oil 200, tung oil 62 (leading world producer), rapeseed 4,288 (leading world producer), groundnuts 4,036 (second world producer), tea 429 (second world producer), tobacco 1,523 (leading world producer), oranges 1,203, tangerines 269, grapefruit 157, lemons 99, pineapples 295, mangoes 353, grapes 264, bananas 480, apples 2,740, pears 2,098 (leading world producer), tomatoes 4,559, walnuts 120, chestnuts 230, spices, vegetables 85.9 mn. tonnes. **Livestock** (in 1,000 head): horses 10,981 (leading world population), cattle 57,450, buffaloes 18,750 (second world population), camels 610, pigs 305,580 (highest world population), sheep 106,568, goats 75,397, asses 8,999, mules 4,464, chickens 1,144,000 (highest world population), silkworms. **Production** (in 1,000 tonnes): eggs 3,614, cattle hides 89, goatskins 60, wool 194, raw silk 38 (leading world producer), honey 125 (second world producer); fish catch 5,213,300 tonnes, roundwood 231.7 mn. cub.m, natural rubber 165.

Mining (1983, in 1,000 tonnes): coal 688,000 (leading world producer – provinces Shānxī, Shaanxī, Hebei, Liaoning), crude petroleum 106,068 (Heilongjiang, Shandong, northern China, north-west China), uranium, natural gas 475,162 TJ (provinces Hebei, Hubei), combustible shale (Liaoning), iron ore 56,834, manganese 479, antimony 10, cobalt, bauxite 1,500, copper 200, lead 160, magnesite 2,000, mercury 760, molybdenum 2.0, nickel, gold 59,097 kg, silver 78 tonnes, tin 17, tungsten 12.5 (leading world producer – provinces Jiangxi, Guangdong, Hunan), zinc 160, phosphates 12,500, potash, sulphur 200, asbestos 110, graphite 185 (second world producer), vanadium, salt 15,876. Electricity 351.44 billion kWh. **Production** (1983, in 1,000 tonnes): pig iron 37,385, crude steel 40,136, cement 105,864, fertilizers 13,790, metal-working machines 120,000 units, motor vehicles 240,000 units, locomotives 486, woven cotton fabrics 17,968 sq.m, silk fabrics 1,092 mn. sq.m, newsprint 400, sugar raw 4,100, meat 16,862, cow milk 6,052, buffalo milk 1,500, butter 40.5, cheese 115.3.

Communications (1983): railways 51,100 km, roads 890,000 km, motor vehicles 2.8 mn. (of which 240,000 passenger cars. Merchant shipping 9,300,000 GRT. Civil aviation: 87.6 mn. km flown, 5 mn. passengers carried. Tourism 9.5 mn. visitors (1983). – **Exports:** rice, soya beans, cotton, fruit, tea, meat and meat products, eggs, sugar, edible oils, tung oil, silk; chemical and textile products, raw materials for the power industry, ores – especially tungsten and ore concentrates. Chief trading partners: Japan, Hong Kong, Fed. Rep. of Germany, U.S.A., U.S.S.R.

TAIWAN

Ta Chunghwa Min-Kuo, area 36,174 sq.km, population 18,859,000 (1985), **part of China** under the control of the Kuomintang Nationalist Party (President Chiang Ching-kuo since 1978).

Capital: T'aipei 2,271,000 inhab. (1981); **other towns** (in 1,000 inhab.): Kaohsiung 1,227, T'aichung 607, T'ainan 595, T'aipeihsien 403; urban population 94.2%. – **Currency:** New Taiwan dollar = 100 cents.

Economy: arable land 8.9%, forests 64.5% of the land area. **Agriculture** (1982, in 1,000 tonnes): rice 2,483, sugarcane 8,275, manioc, soya beans, sweet potatoes 741, pineapples 145, bananas 203, tea 24; livestock (1983, in 1,000 head):

cattle 130, pigs 5,888, silkworms; fish catch 930,582 tonnes. **Mining** (in 1,000 tonnes): coal 2,384, crude petroleum, gold 223 kg, silver 2,232 kg, salt 262. Electricity 45,517 mn. kWh (1983). **Industry:** textile and chemical industries, electrical machinery, shipbuilding, engineering. **Production:** woven cotton fabrics 822 mn.m, sugar, cement. **Communications** (1982): railways 3,409 km, roads 17,522 km, passenger cars 619,500; merchant shipping 2,225,000 GRT. – **Exports:** textile products, plastic products, television and radio receivers, synthetic fibres.

CYPRUS

Kypriaki Dimokratia – Kıbrıs Cumhuriyeti, area 9,251 sq.km, population 665,200 (1985), **republic, member of the Commonwealth** (President Dr. Spyros Kyprianou since 1977).

Administrative units: Since 27 July 1976 Cyprus has been divided into two parts: southern with Greek and northern with Turkish speaking population by Attila Line. **Capital:** Levkosia (Nicosia) 180,000 inhab. (1982); **other towns** (in 1,000 inhab.): Lemesós 107.2, Ammókhostos 39.4. **Population:** Cyprian Greeks 80%, Cyprian Turks 18%, Armenians, Englishmen and others. **Density** 72 persons per sq.km; average annual rate of population increase 1.4% (1980–83); urban population 43% (1983). 32.9% of the economically active inhabitants engaged in agriculture. – **Currency:** Cyprus pound = 100 cents.
Economy: Mediterranean agriculture and extraction of raw materials. Arable land and permanent crops 47%. **Agriculture:** crops (1983, in 1,000 tonnes): grapes 200, oranges 140, lemons 47, grapefruit 87, olives 12, wheat 10, vegetables, early potatoes, tobacco; livestock (1983, in 1,000 head): cattle 43, pigs 200, sheep 500, goats 360, fish catch 2,100 tonnes.
Mining (1983, in 1,000 tonnes): pyrites Fe 47, copper 1.1, chromium, asbestos 17, sulphur. **Production:** wine 450,000 hl, olive oil 3,000 tonnes, raisins, cigarettes 3.3 mn.
Communications: roads 10,950 km, passenger cars 110,600. Civil aviation: 10.2 mn. km flown, 536,000 passengers carried (1984). Merchant shipping 6,728,000 GRT (1984). Tourism 621,000 visitors (1983). – **Exports:** citrus fruit, potatoes, tobacco and cigarettes, wine, copper and concentrates, pyrites. Chief trading partners: United Kingdom, Fed. Rep. of Germany, Greece, Italy, U.S.A.

INDIA

Bharat, area 3,287,590 sq.km, population 752,900,000 (1985), **federal republic, member of the Commonwealth** (President Giani Zail Singh since 1982).

Administrative units: 23 federal states and 8 territories. **Capital:** New Delhi 273,036 inhab. (census 1981); **other towns** (in 1,000 inhab., [+]with agglom.): Bombay 8,243 ([+]9,950), Delhi 4,865 ([+]5,228), Calcutta 3,292 ([+]9,194), Madras 3,266 ([+]4,277), Bangalore 2,483 ([+]2,914), Hyderābād 2,142 ([+]2,566), Ahmadābād 2,025 ([+]2,515), Kānpur 1,531 ([+]1,875), Nāgpur 1,215 ([+]1,298), Pune 1,203 ([+]1,685), Jaipur 967 ([+]1,006), Lucknow 896 ([+]1,060), Indore 827, Madurai 818, Surat 776, Patna 774, Howrah 742, Baroda 734, Āgra 724, Vārānasi 705. **Population:** Hindustani, Bihari, Marathi, Bengali, Santhali, Telugu and others. **Density** 229 persons per sq.km; average annual rate of population increase 2.3% (1973–83); urban population 24% (1983). 60.9% of the economically active inhabitants engaged in agriculture (1983). – **Currency:** Indian rupee = 100 paise.
Economy: agricultural and industrial country; arable land 50.2%, meadows and pastures 3.7%, forests 20.5%.
Agriculture. Crops (1983, in 1,000 tonnes): rice 90,000 (second world producer), wheat 42,502, millet 10,050 (leading world producer), sorghum 12,000 (second world producer), maize (corn) 7,300, sugarcane 189,129 (second world producer), potatoes 10,108; important legumes: peas 330, lentils 550, soya beans 730, groundnuts 7,300 (second world producer), chick-peas 5,092 (leading world producer), sesame 590 (leading world producer), coconuts 3,900, copra 350, cotton – seed 2,540, – lint 1,260, linseed 476, jute 1,590 (leading world producer), hemp 60, tea 595 (leading world producer), coffee 130, oranges 1,200, lemons 500, bananas 4,500 (second world producer), pineapples 660, apples 920, cashew nuts 200, tobacco 594, vegetables 43.1 mn. tonnes – tomatoes 780. **Animal production** (1983, in 1,000 head): horses 900, cattle 182,000 (highest world population), buffaloes 63,000 (highest world population), camels 1,050, pigs 8,600, sheep 41,700, goats 78,000 (highest world population), silkworms; cattle hides 810,000 tonnes (second world producer), goatskins 72,900 tonnes (leading world producer), grease wool 37,000 tonnes, raw silk 2,650 tonnes. Fish catch 2,520,000 tonnes (1983). Roundwood 228.3 mn. cub.m. Natural rubber 170,000 tonnes.
Mining (1983, in 1,000 tonnes, metal content): coal 133,349 (West Bengal – Rāniganj and Bihār), brown coal 7,347, crude petroleum 25,148 (Mahārāshtra), natural gas 106,575 TJ, uranium, iron ore 24,359 (Bihār, Orissa, Madhya Pradesh), manganese 488.3, lead 20.7, zinc 40.4, chromium 108, copper 46.9, gold 2,156 kg, mica 16.0 (second world producer – Bihār-Hazāribāgh, Andhra Pradesh, Rājasthān), asbestos 23, bauxite 1,929, magnesite 436, salt 9,979, phosphates 241, diamonds. Electricity 147,952 mn. kWh. **Industry.** Important textile and food industries, metal-working.
Production (1983, in 1,000 tonnes): pig iron 9,087, crude steel 11,030, coke oven coke 11,610, motor vehicles – commercial 106,400, – passenger 45,000 units; merchant vessels 95,000 GRT, radio receivers 1.23 mn. units, cement 25,422, naphtha 3,474, motor spirit 1,880, jet fuel 1,163, sulphuric acid 2,388, soda ash 744, nitrogenous fertilizers 3,358, phosphate fertilizers 373, superphosphates 222, woven fabrics – cotton 8,632 mn. m, – silk, jute 2,916 mn. sq.m – of cellulosic fibres 899 mn. m – of non-cellulosic fibres 683 mn. m, woven woollen fabrics, sugar 6,635, flour 2,475, meat 958, cow milk 14,000, buffalo milk 20,000, butter 740 (second world producer), cheese; cigarettes 86,850 mn.
Communications (1983): railways 61,240 km, roads 1,604,000 km, motor vehicles – passenger 1,351,000, commercial 1,450,800. Merchant shipping 6,415,000 GRT. Civil aviation: 98.3 mn. km flown, 9,165,000 passengers carried. Tourism 1,305,000 visitors (1983). – **Exports:** woven cotton fabrics and products, jute and jute products, tea, hides, skins and furs, spices, fruit, vegetables, tobacco, sugar, iron ore and concentrates, handicraft products. Chief trading partners: U.S.A., United Kingdom, U.S.S.R., Japan, Fed. Rep. of Germany.

map 21

INDONESIA

Republik Indonesia, area 2,027,087 sq.km (incl. East Timor), **population 165,155,000** (1985), **republic** (President Gen. I. Suharto since 1967).

Administrative units: 27 provinces, in 1976 annexed East Timor. **Capital:** Jakarta 7,636,000 inhab. (1983); **other towns** (1980, in 1,000 inhab.): Surabaya 2,028, Bandung 1,463, Medan 1,379, Semarang 1,027, Palembang 787, Ujung Pandang 709, Malang 512, Padang 481, Surakarta 470, Yogyakarta 399, Banjarmasin 381, Pontianak 305, Balikpapan 281. **Population:** Malay Indonesians (over 140 ethnic groups; most numerous are the Javanese and the Chinese among the minorities). **Density** 82 persons per sq. km; average annual rate of population increase 2.3% (1973–83); urban population 24% (1983). 56.5% of the economically active inhabitants engaged in agriculture (1983). – **Currency:** Indonesian rupiah = 100 sen.
Economy: agricultural country, and mining of minerals. Arable land and permanent crops 10.2%, meadows and pastures 6.3%, forests 63.9% of the land area. **Agriculture:** Crops (1983, in 1,000 tonnes): rice 34,300, manioc 19,770, sweet potatoes 2,120 (second world producer), soya beans 590, groundnuts 760, sugarcane 24,531, sisal, cotton, coconuts 11,100 (leading world producer), copra 1,070 (second world producer), palm kernels 154, palm oil 950 (second world producer), sesame, fruit, tea 110, coffee 233, tobacco 122; **livestock** (1983, in 1,000 head): cattle 6,600, buffaloes 2,500, pigs 3,600, sheep 4,300, goats 7,900, horses 660; fish catch 2,112,200 tonnes (1983). Natural rubber 920,000 tonnes (second world producer), roundwood 122.2 mn. cub.m.
Mining (1983, in 1,000 tonnes, metal content): coal 486, crude petroleum 65,971, natural gas 689,582 TJ, tin 26.5 (second greatest producer in the world), nickel 31, manganese, bauxite 778, gold 259 kg, diamonds 27,000 carats, phosphates, salt 698. **Electricity** 15,280 mn. kWh. **Industry:** Important processing of tin, petroleum refineries, food and textile industries. **Production** (1983, in 1,000 tonnes): tin 28 (second world producer), motor spirit 1,597, jet fuel 355, naphthas 865, nitrogenous fertilizers 1,077, phosphate fertilizers 368, sugar 1,759; 91,463 mn. cigarettes; radio 1.1 mn. and television receivers 517,000 units.
Communications (1983): railways 6,877 km, roads 128,900 km, motor vehicles – passenger 791,000, commercial 791,500; merchant shipping 1,857,000 GRT; civil aviation: 117.6 mn. km flown, 6,494,000 passengers carried. Tourism 626,000 visitors (1983). – **Exports:** petroleum and petroleum products, natural gas, wood, natural rubber, palm oil, coffee, tin concentrates, tea, tobacco, spices. Chief trading partners: Japan, U.S.A., Fed. Rep. of Germany, Australia.

IRAN

Jomhori-e-Islami-e-Irân, area 1,648,100 sq.km, population 44,632,000 (1985), **republic** (President Hojatolislam Sayed Ali Khamenei since 1981).
Administrative units: 21 provinces (ostán), 2 governorates (farmándár). **Capital:** Tehrán 5,734,199 inhab. (with agglom., 1982); **other towns** (in 1,000 inhab.): Mashhad 1,120, Esfahán 927, Shíráz 880, Tabríz 852, Bakhtarán 531, Karaj 526, Ahváz 471, Qom 424. **Population:** two thirds are Iranian Persians; Azerbaijanis, Kurds, Arabs. **Density** 27 persons per sq.km; average annual rate of population increase 3.1% (1973–83); urban population 53%. 36.3% of the economically active inhabitants engaged in agriculture (1983). – **Currency:** rial = 100 dinars.
Economy: agricultural and industrial country with important mining of petroleum. Arable land and land under perr anent crops 10%, forests 10.9% of the land area. **Agriculture:** Crops (1983, in 1,000 tonnes): wheat 6,669, barley 1,413, rice 1,400, millet 27, sorghum 10, maize (corn) 55, potatoes 800, beans 100, peas 34, lentils 29, groundnuts, soya beans 96, sunflower, sesame, olives, castor beans, cotton – seed 170, –lint 90; sugar beet 2,340, sugarcane 1,600, vegetables, tea 22, oranges 72, lemons 36, apricots 170, grapes 1,600, raisins 52, almonds 12, dates 302, hazelnuts, pistachios 35 (leading world producer), tomatoes 407, onion 253; **livestock** (1983, in 1,000 head): horses 350, cattle 8,600, sheep 34,500, goats 13,800, asses 1,800, cattle hides 41,139 tonnes, sheepskins 38,886 tonnes, grease wool 16,000 tonnes, eggs 200,000 tonnes.
Mining (1983, in 1,000 tonnes, metal content): coal, crude petroleum 123,119 (chiefly in south-west Iran), natural gas 264,000 TJ, iron ore 340, manganese, copper 48.5, lead 26, zinc 39.9, bauxite, magnesite, sulphur 50, salt 753. Electricity 29,900 mn. kWh, (of which 19% hydro-energy). The most developed **industries** are petrochemical and chemical, textile, leather, and food processing. **Production** (1983, in 1,000 tonnes): naphtha 430, motor spirit 3,400 (of which aviation spirit 60), jet fuel 390, coke oven coke 300, sulphuric acid 100, phosphate fertilizers 3.9, nitrogenous fertilizers 23.6, cement 10,665, woven cotton fabrics 118 mn. m, woven woollen fabrics 16 mn. m, non-cellulosic continuous fibres 18, meat 726, sugar 600, flour 2,517, milk 1,786.
Communications (1983): railways 4,567 km, roads 63,115 km, motor vehicles – passenger 1,079,133, commercial 405,994. Merchant shipping 2,106,000 GRT (1983). Civil aviation: 28.6 mn. km flown, 4,088,000 passengers carried. Tourism 100,000 visitors (1983). – **Exports:** petroleum and petroleum products, cotton and cotton goods, carpets, dates, raisins, skins, pistachios. Chief trading partners: countries of CMEA 60%, Japan, Fed. Rep. of Germany, United Kingdom, U.S.A., Italy, France, Netherlands, India.

IRAQ

al Jumhouriya al'Iraqia, area 438,446 sq.km, population 15,898,000 (1983), **republic** (President Saddam Hussein at-Takriti since 1979).
Administrative units: 15 governorates (liwa), 3 autonomous regions. **Capital:** Baghdád 3,200,000 inhab. (with agglom. 1983); **other towns** (1980, in 1,000 inhab.): Al-Basrah 720, Al-Mawsil (Mosul) 570, Kirkük 570, An-Najaf 190, Al-Hillah 140, Irbíl 110, Karbalá 110. – **Population:** about 80% Arabic speaking Iraqis, 15% Kurds, 2% Turks. Average annual rate of population increase 3.6% (1973–83); urban population 69% (1983). 38% of the economically active inhabitants engaged in agriculture. – **Currency:** Iraqi dinar = 1,000 fils.

map 22

Economy: agricultural country with developing industry. Arable land 12% and forests 3.5% of the land area. **Agriculture** (1983, in 1,000 tonnes): rice 200, wheat 1,000, barley 900, cotton – lint 5, – seed 10, almonds 700, sesame, olives, oranges 140, lemons; livestock (1983, in 1,000 head): cattle 3,000, buffaloes 240, camels 250, sheep 12,000, goats 3,800; grease wool 17,500 tonnes; fish catch 26,200 tonnes. **Mining** (1983, in 1,000 tonnes): crude petroleum 46,819 (Kirkūk, Al-Mawsil), natural gas 17,000 TJ, sulphur 300, salt 72. Electricity 13,700 mn. kWh (1983). Petrochemical, textile and food **Industries. Production** (1983, in 1,000 tonnes): naphtha 460, motor spirit 1,300, jet fuel 360, nitrogenous fertilizers 14, phosphate fertilizers 86, sulphuric acid, woven cotton fabrics; 7,900 mn. cigarettes, sugar, canned fruit and vegetables, vegetable oils.
Communications: railways 1,589 km, roads 15,123 km, motor vehicles – passenger 345,900, commercial 206,300 (1982). Merchant shipping 1,074,000 GRT (1983). Civil aviation: 13.4 mn. km flown, 435,000 passengers carried. Tourism 1,673,000 visitors (1983). – **Exports:** petroleum and petroleum products, dates, skins, wool. Chief trading partners: France, Fed. Rep. of Germany, United Kingdom, Italy, U.S.S.R., Brazil, Japan.

ISRAEL

Medinat Israel, area 20,770 sq.km, population 4,233,200 (1985), **republic** (President Chaim Herzog since 1983).
Administrative units: 6 districts (mechnusa). **Capital:** Yerūshalayim (Jerusalem) 428,668 inhab. (1983); **other towns** (1982, in 1,000 inhab.): Tel Aviv-Yafo 327 (with agglom. 1,555), Hefa (Haifa) 226, Holon 133, Bat Yam 129. **Population:** Jews 83%, Arabs 15%. **Density** 204 persons per sq.km; average annual rate of population increase 2.3% (1973–83); urban population 90% (1983). 6.2% of the economically active inhabitants engaged in agriculture. – **Currency:** shekel.
Economy: industrial and agricultural country. Arable land 16.8%, meadows and pastures 39.4%, forests 5.6% of the land area. **Agriculture** (1983, in 1,000 tonnes): wheat 335, potatoes 210, sugar beet, oranges 857, tangerines, grapefruit 450 (second world producer), bananas 66, peaches, cotton, vegetables, grapes 88; livestock (1983, in 1,000 head): cattle 330, sheep 240, goats 115; eggs 100,800 tonnes. Fish catch 22,400 tonnes. **Mining** (1983, in 1,000 tonnes): crude petroleum, natural gas 2,297 TJ, salt 203, phosphates 1,966, potash salt 1,000. Electricity 14,578 mn. kWh. Engineering and electronics, chemical, textile and food **industries. Production** (1983, in 1,000 tonnes): motor spirit 1,107, jet fuel 520, nitrogenous fertilizers 81.6, phosphate fertilizers 100, potash fertilizers 955.8; meat 210, cheese 62, butter, margarine; 6,373 mn. cigarettes, wine 328,000 hl.
Communications: railways 827 km, roads 11,950 km, motor vehicles – passenger 599,300, commercial 113,100. Merchant shipping 563,000 GRT (1983). Civil aviation: 34.9 mn. km flown, 1,669,000 passengers carried. Tourism 1,093,000 visitors (1983). – **Exports:** polished gems, citrus fruit, products of engineering, chemical and textile industries. Chief trade with U.S.A.

JAPAN

Nippon (or **Nihon**), **area 377,619 sq.km, population 120,754,335** (1985), **empire** (Emperor Hirohito since 1926).

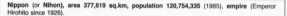

Administrative units: 47 prefectures. **Capital:** Tōkyō 8,361,054 inhab. (with agglom. 11,746,190 – 1983); **other towns** (in 1,000 inhab.): Yokohama 2,899, Ōsaka 2,624, Nagoya 2,100, Sapporo 1,496, Kyōto 1,484, Kōbe 1,384, Fukuoka 1,138, Kawasaki 1,066, Kitakyūshū 1,065, Hiroshima 908, Sakai 810, Chiba 766, Sendai 669, Okayama 555, Kumamoto 527, Kagoshima 519, Amagasaki 509, Hamamatsu 504, Higashiōsaka 502, Funabashi 494, Shizuoka 464, Sagamihara 463, Niigata 461, Nagasaki 449, Himeji 449, Yokosuka 429, Matsuyama 418, Matsudo 416, Kanazawa 415, Kurashiki 412, Gifu 409, Nishinomiya 405, Hachioji 405, Wakayama 404, Toyonaka 399. **Density** 320 persons per sq.km; average annual rate of population increase 0.9% (1973–83); urban population 76% (1983). 9.2% of the economically active inhabitants engaged in agriculture and 34.8% in industry (1983). – **Currency:** yen = 100 sen.
Economy: economically highly developed industrial and agricultural country. Arable land 13%, forests 67% of the land area. **Agriculture: Crops:** (1983, in 1,000 tonnes): rice 12,958, wheat 747, barley 380, oats, maize 3 (corn), soya beans 217, groundnuts 51, beans 93, sugarcane 2,400, sugar beet 3,412, potatoes 3,700, sweet potatoes 1,400, hemp, flax, vegetables 14,925 (tomatoes 900, onions 1,200), fruit – apples 1,001, pears 534, oranges 3,767, tangerines 3,767 (leading world producer), grapes 324, strawberries 196, sweet chestnuts 59, tobacco 138; **livestock** (1983, in 1,000 head): cattle 4,590, pigs 10,273, poultry 297,000, raising of silkworms; eggs 2,085,000 tonnes, raw silk 13,000 tonnes (second world producer); fish catch 11,250,000 tonnes (largest world catch). Roundwood 32.8 mn. cub.m (1983).
Mining (1983, in 1,000 tonnes, metal content): coal 17,062, crude petroleum 418, natural gas 89,685 TJ, uranium, iron ore 185, pyrites 551, copper 46, lead 47, zinc 255.7, chromium 11, tin 600 tonnes, manganese 19.9, tungsten 474 tonnes, gold 3,139 kg, silver 307 tonnes, molybdenum 95 tonnes, mercury, salt 921. Electricity 602,357 mn. kWh, of which hydro-energy 15%, nuclear energy 13.5% (1983).
Industry: one of the chief producers in the world in metallurgy (Kitakyūshū, Muroran), electronic machinery, many branches of the engineering (Ōsaka, Yokohama, Kōbe, Nagasaki, Hiroshima), chemical (Kōbe, Tōkyō, Ōsaka) and textile industries. **Production** (1983, in 1,000 tonnes): coke oven coke 46,675, pig iron 72,900 (second world producer), crude steel 97,200 (second world producer), aluminium 1,096.2, copper 1,075, lead 241, zinc 701 (second world producer), magnesium 19,038 tonnes, radio receivers 13.3 mn., television receivers 13.3 mn. (leading world producer), merchant vessels 9,408,000 GRT (leading world producer), of which tankers 698,000 GRT, motor vehicles – passenger 7,152,000 (leading world producer), – commercial 3,897,000 (leading world producer), cement 80,890, naphtha 8,328, motor spirit 26,428, jet fuel 3,597, tyres 123 mn., sulphuric acid 6,662, hydrochloric acid 560.1, nitric acid 540, caustic soda 2,778, nitrogenous fertilizers 1,076, phosphate fertilizers 467, woven cotton fabrics 2,079 mn. sq.m, woven silk fabrics 121.8 mn. sq.m (second world producer), woven woollen fabrics 301 mn. sq.m, synthetic fabrics

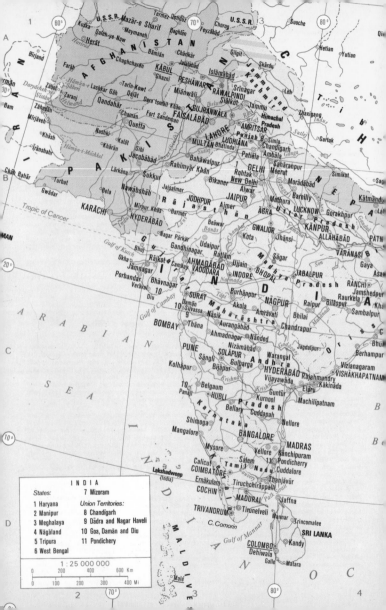

CHINA

Rohtak Meerut Morādābād
DELHI New Delhi Rāmpur Birendranagar
Haryāna Aligarh Bareilly Nepalganj Pokhara Kāthmāndu Namche Bazar
Alwar Mathura Shāhjahānpur Bhaktapur Sikkim Thimbu Punākha
AGRA Farrukhābād Lalitpur Dhankutā Dārjiling Gāngtok BHUTAN
Fīrozābād Etāwah Faizābād Gorakhpur Āmlekhganj Biratnagar Siliguri Koch Bihār Assam
GWALIOR KĀNPUR LUCKNOW Uttar Pradesh Chapra Muzaffarpur Darbhanga Saidpur Rāngpur Brahmaputra Mymensingh Meghālaya
Shivpuri Jhānsi ALLĀHĀBĀD Jaunpur PATNA Katihār
Bārān Banda VĀRĀNASI Arrah Bihār Bhāgalpur RĀJSHĀHI Sirājganj DHAKA (Dacca)
Guna Lalitpur Mirzāpur Sāsarām Munger Deoghar Pābnā Comilla
Bīna-Etāwa Satna Gayā BANGLADESH Faridpur Chāndpur
Sāgar Rewa Baharāmpur Durgāpur Barddhamān Jessore KHULNA Barisal
BHOPĀL Murwāra Dhānbād Asansol Bhātpāra HĀORA
JABALPUR RĀNCHI West CALCUTTA
Jamshedpur Bengal Kharagpur
Raurkela Orissa Bay of Bengal

Madhya Pradesh

Yaluzangbujiang Rikaze Jiangzi
Sikkim Thimbu Arunachal Pradesh Xichang
BHUTAN Gāngtok Murkong-Selek Dāngori Putao N Lijiang Huize GUIYANG Doyun Guilin
jiling Itānagar Dibrugarh DUKOU Dushan
aidpur Guwāhāti Dīspur Kohima Tengchong Dali Chuxiong Qujing Anshun Yishan LIUZHOU Wuzhou
BANGLADESH Shillong Myitkyinā KUNMING NANNING Beihai Maoming
DHAKA Mymensingh Imphal Gejiu Pingxiang Yulin ZHANJIANG
RA KHULNA Agartala Aizawl Mengzhi Lao-Cai Lang-Son Beihai
CALCUTTA CHITTAGONG Lashio Jinghong Phong Saly HA-NOI Hon-Gai Gulf Uizhongbuhaixia HAIKOU
Cox's Bazar Shwebo Chiang Rai Loungphrabang Hoa-Binh HAI-PHONG Hainandao
BURMA MANDALAY Nam-Dinh of
Pakokku Myingyan Chiang Mai Thanh-Hoa Tonkin Yaxian
Sittwe Chauk Meiktila Taunggyi Xiangkhoang Vinh Ha-Tinh
Magwe Pyinmana LAN OISE DA-NANG
Prome Toungoo Viangchan (Vientiane) Nong Khai Paracel Is. (Viet.)
Myanaung Lampang Udon Thani M. Khammouan Hue
Henzada Pegu Phitsanulok Savannakhet Khemmaral
Bassein RANGOON Martaban Khon Kaen Ubon- Pakxé Qui-Nhon
Moulmein Nakhon Sawan Ratchathani
Koko Kyunzu (Burma) THAILAND Nakhon Ratchasima
Tavoy Ye THON BURI Siêm Réap Stoeng Trêng Nha-Trang
ANDAMAN Nam Tok KRUNG THEP (Bangkok) Bāttâmbang KAMPUCHEA Da-Lat Cam-Ranh
Andaman Is. (India) Chanthaburi Loc-Ninh Phan-Rang
Port Blair Myeik Kyunzu PHNOM PÉNH VT-PHŐ HŐ CHI MINH (Saigon)
SEA Tenasserim Kāmpóng Saōm Kāmpót My-Tho Vung-Tau
Gulf Mỹak Rach-Gia
Chumphon of Can-Tho Vinh-Long
Kra Buri Thailand Quan-Long Côn Dao
Surat Thani Mui Bai-Bung
NICOBAR Nakhon Si Thammarat
Nicobar Is. (India) Phuket Trang SOUTH
Ko Phuket Hat Yai Songkhla CHINA
Banda Aceh Lhokseumawe Pinang MALAYSI Kota Baharu SEA
Sumatera Langsa Alor Setar Kuala Terengganu
INDONESIA MEDAN Taiping Kuantan Kep. Bunguran
Pattani

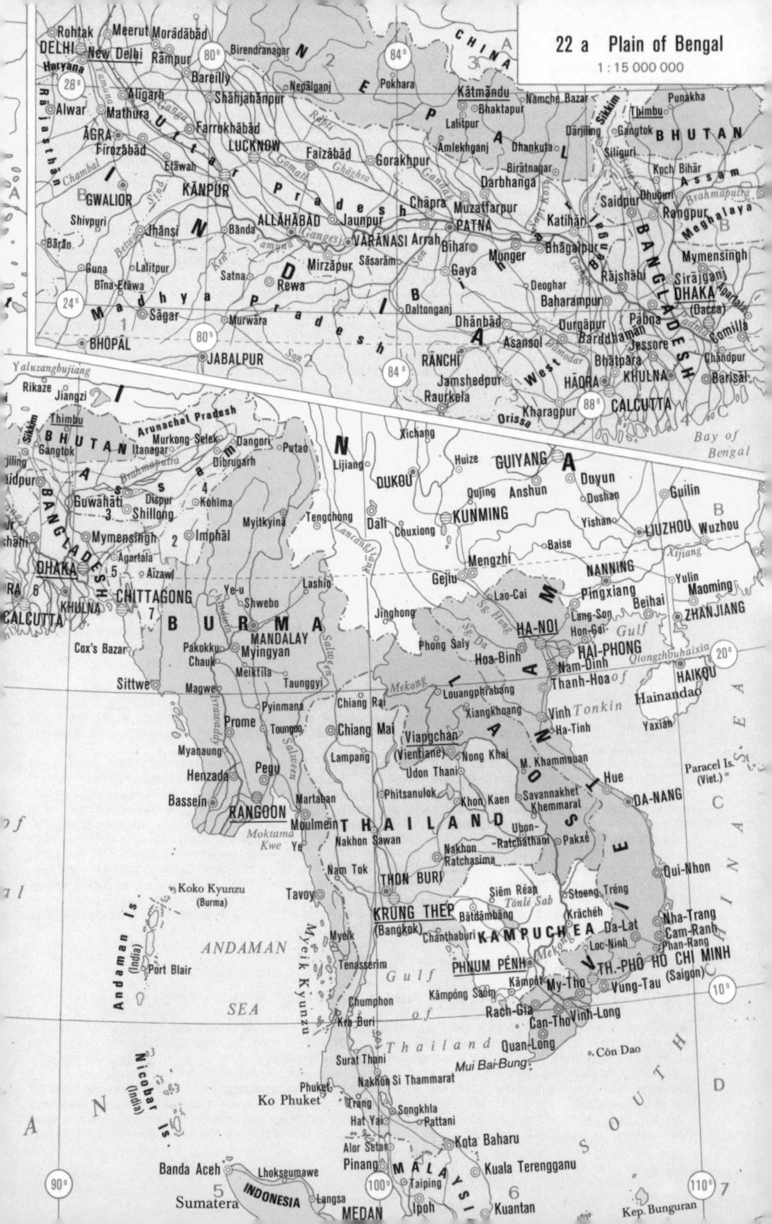

map 22

3,218 mn. sq.m, cotton yarn 438, woollen yarn 110, non-cellulosic staple and tow 750 (second world producer), newsprint 2,562, milk 7,042, butter 75, meat 3,208, beer 50,534,000 hl, wine 402,000 hl, sugar 476, flour 4,356; 306,320 mn. cigarettes. **Communications** (1983): railways 26,889 km, of which about 50% are electrified; roads 1,088,300 km, motor vehicles – passenger 26.4 mn., commercial 15.7 mn. Merchant shipping 40,752,000 GRT (1984 world's second largest fleet). Civil aviation: 377.1 mn. km flown, 46,554,000 passengers carried. Tourism 1.67 mn. visitors.
Exports: 55% machines and equipment – cars, vessels, products of heavy engineering, radio and television receivers, 14% metals and metal products, textile products – cotton and silk fabrics and others, chemical products. Chief trading partners: U.S.A., Saudi Arabia, Australia, Canada, Indonesia, Iran, Fed. Rep. of Germany, Hong Kong, Republic of Korea, China.

JORDAN

Al Mamlaka al Urduniya al Hashemiyah, area 97,740 sq.km (incl. the territory occupied by Israel), **population 3,515,000, kingdom** (King Hussein Ibn Talal since 1952).
Administrative units: 8 districts (liwa) and the Desert Area. **Capital:** Ammãn 744,000 inhab. (1983); **other towns** (in 1,000 inhab.): Az-Zarqã 256, Irbid 131.2. – **Currency:** Jordan dinar = 1,000 fils.
Economy: developing agricultural country with nomadic cattle raising. Arable land and permanent crops 14.1% of the land area. **Agriculture** (1983, in 1,000 tonnes): wheat 120, barley 28, lentils 8.4, olives 30, grapes 28, oranges 26, dates, vegetables 1,260, tomatoes 210; livestock (1983, in 1,000 head): cattle 40, camels 15, sheep 1,000, goats 500. **Mining:** phosphates 4.75 mn. tonnes, potash salt, salt, sulphur. Electricity 1,918 mn. kWh (1983). Processing of fruit and vegetables, chemical and textile industries. – **Communications** (1982): railways 544 km, roads 5,227 km, passenger cars 147,200 (1983). Civil aviation: 25.1 mn. km flown, 1.5 mn. passengers carried. Tourism 1.7 mn. visitors (1983). **Exports:** phosphates, citrus and other fruit, vegetables, olive oil, chemical products. Chief trading partners: Saudi Arabia, U.S.A., Fed. Rep. of Germany and other EEC countries, Iraq.

KAMPUCHEA

Satharanart pracheamanitu Kampuchea, area 181,035 sq.km, population 7,284,000 (1985), **republic** (Chairman of the People's Revolutionary Council Heng Samrin since 1979).
Administrative units: 4 self-administered cities and 17 provinces. **Capital:** Phnum Pénh 650,000 inhab. (1985). – **Currency:** riel = 100 sen.
Economy: agricultural country. Arable land 16.8%, forests 74% of the land area. **Agriculture** (1983, in 1,000 tonnes): rice 1,700, maize (corn) 60, sweet potatoes 25, soya beans, groundnuts 12, sugarcane 181, cotton, sesame, bananas 82, coconuts 33, pineapples 7, oranges 30, spices, tobacco; livestock (1983, in 1,000 head): cattle 1,148, pigs 717; fish catch 63,800 tonnes (1983). Natural rubber 8,000 tonnes (1983), teak and other timber – roundwood 5.1 mn. cub.m. Electricity 129.7 mn. kWh (1983). Developing chemical, textile and food industries. – **Communications:** railways 272 km, roads 15,029 km, passenger cars 38,300. Civil aviation: 800,000 km flown, 113,000 passengers carried. – **Exports:** rice, natural rubber, rare timber, pepper, fruit, vegetables. Chief trading partners: U.S.S.R., Vietnam.

KOREA, DEMOCRATIC PEOPLE'S REPUBLIC OF

Chosun Minchu-chui Inmin Konghwa-guk, area 120,538 sq.km, population 20,385,000 (1985), **people's democratic republic** (Chairman of the Presidium of the Supreme People's Assembly Kim Il Sung since 1972).
Administrative units: 2 statutory cities and 9 provinces. **Capital:** P'yŏngyang 1,283,000 inhab. (1981); **other towns** (in 1,000 inhab.): Hamhŭng 775, Ch'ŏngjin 520, Wŏnsan 500, Sinŭiju 420, Kaesŏng 420. **Population:** Koreans. **Density** 169 persons per sq.km; 44.1% of the economically active inhabitants engaged in agriculture. – **Currency:** won = 100 yun.
Economy: agricultural and industrial country. Arable land 18.6%. **Agriculture** (1983, in 1,000 tonnes): rice 5,200, wheat 500, barley 420, maize (corn) 2,500, millet 475, sorghum 160, potatoes 1,650, sweet potatoes 400, soya beans 380, tobacco 50, fruit, vegetables; livestock (1983, in 1,000 head): cattle 1,000, pigs 2,500, sheep 330, silkworms; fish catch 1.6 mn. tonnes. Raw silk 3,150 tonnes. **Mining** (1983, in 1,000 tonnes, metal content): coal 38,000, iron ore 3,200, tungsten 500 tonnes, graphite 25, magnesite 1,850, lead 95, silver 45 tonnes, gold 5,000 kg, zinc 140, salt 572, phosphates. Electricity 28,200 mn. kWh (1983). – **Production** (1983): pig iron 3.1 mn. tonnes, crude steel 3.6 mn. tonnes, cement 8 mn. tonnes, nitrogenous fertilizers 608,000 tonnes, tractors, textile and food industries. – **Communications:** railways 11,000 km, roads 21,000 km. Merchant shipping 439,000 GRT (1983). – **Exports:** ores, coal, graphite, fish, industrial and agricultural products. Chief trading partners: U.S.S.R., China.

KOREA, REPUBLIC OF

Han Kook, area 98,824 sq.km, population 41,258,000 (1983), **republic** (President Chun Doo Hwan since 1980).
Administrative units: 4 statutory cities and 9 provinces. **Capital:** Sŏul 9,501,414 inhab. (1984, with agglom 11.46 mn.); **other towns** (1983, in 1,000 inhab.): Pusan 3,395, Taegu 1,959, Inch'ŏn 1,220, Kwangju 843, Taejŏn 800, Ulsan 510, Masan 424, Songnam 417, Suwŏn 374. **Population:** Koreans. **Density** 418 persons per sq.km; urban population 62% (1983). 35.6% of the economically active inhabitants engaged in agriculture. – **Currency:** won = 100 chun.
Economy: industrial and agricultural country with advanced consumer industries. Arable land 22.3%, forests 66.7% of the land area. **Agriculture** (1983, in 1,000 tonnes): rice 7,608, wheat 112, barley 815, sweet potatoes 1,012, potatoes 469, soya beans 233, maize (corn) 101, pulses 52, sesame 43, vegetables 8,868, fruit 1,467, tobacco 101; livestock (1983, in 1,000 head): cattle 1,754, pigs 2,183, goats 251, poultry 48 mn., silkworms; fish catch 2,400,400 tonnes. Raw silk 2,500 tonnes.

map 23

Mining (1983, in 1,000 tonnes, metal content): coal 18,945, iron ore 331, tungsten 2.29, graphite 33.3, gold 2,224 kg, lead 10, manganese, molybdenum 142 tonnes, silver 49 tonnes, tin, zinc 57, salt 853. Electricity 53,047 mn. kWh (1983).
Production (1983, in 1,000 tonnes): pig iron 8,024, crude steel 5,062, cement 21,282, shipbuilding 2,515,000 GRT, radio 6,719,000 and television receivers 7,641,000 units, sulphuric acid 1,610, hydrochloric acid 50.9, nitrogenous 580.3 and phosphate fertilizers 457.5, woven fabrics – cotton 442 mn. sq.m – silk 19.6 mn. sq.m, non-cellulosic staple and tow 327, newsprint 232; meat 679, milk 712, eggs 295.
Communications (1983): railways 3,135 km, roads 53,935 km, passenger cars 381,000, commercial vehicles 391,400. Merchant shipping 6,771,000 GRT. Civil aviation: 72.1 mn. km flown, 5,097,000 passengers carried (1983). Tourism 1.2 mn. visitors (1983). – **Exports:** machinery and electronic machinery, ships, chemical products, fish and fish products, textile, ores. Chief trading partners: U.S.A. 30%, Japan almost 30%, Saudi Arabia, United Kingdom, Fed. Rep. of Germany.

KUWAIT

Dowlat al Kuwayt, area 17,818 sq.km, population 1,709,860 (1985), **emirate** (Emir Shaikh Jabir al-Ahmad al-Jabir al-Sabah since 1978).
Capital: Al-Kuwayt 181,800 (1980, with agglom. 1.1 mn.) inhab. – **Currency:** Kuwait dinar = 1,000 fils.
Economy: based on mining and the processing of petroleum and natural gas. **Agriculture.** Arable land only 1,000 ha; livestock (1983, in 1,000 head): cattle 18, camels 5, sheep 550, goats 300, fish catch 4,100 tonnes. **Mining** (1983): crude petroleum 53,545,000 tonnes, natural gas 90,000 TJ (both incl. one half of the former Neutral Zone production). Electricity 12,831 mn. kWh. Petrochemical industry. **Production** (1983, in 1,000 tonnes): naphtha 2,444, motor spirit 1,174, jet fuel 1,016, distillate fuel oils 6,127. – **Communications:** roads 920 km, passenger cars 519,500. Merchant shipping 2,551,000 GRT (1983). Civil aviation: 26.1 mn. km flown, 1,498,000 passengers carried (1983). – **Exports:** petroleum and petroleum products almost 95%. Chief trading partners: Japan, United Kingdom, Fed. Rep. of Germany and other EEC countries, U.S.A.

LAOS

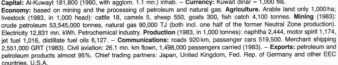

Sa Thalanalath Pasathipatay Pasason Lao; area 236,800 sq.km, population 3,625,803 (1985), **people's democratic republic** (President Phoumi Vongvichit since 1986).
Administrative units: 16 provinces (khueng). **Capital:** Viangchan (Vientiane) 300,000 inhab. (1983); **other towns** (in 1,000 inhab.): Savannakhet 60, Pakxé 50, Louangphrabang 48. – **Currency:** kip = 10 bi = 100 att.
Economy: developing agricultural country. Arable land 3.7%, forests 54.9%. **Agriculture** (1983, in 1,000 tonnes): rice 1,002, maize (corn) 39, sweet potatoes 35, potatoes 44, manioc 74, groundnuts, coffee 4, cotton, tobacco 4, rare timber, roundwood 3.9 mn. cub.m, natural rubber; livestock (1983, in 1,000 head): cattle 490, buffaloes 910, pigs 1,300; fish catch 20,000 tonnes (1983).
Mining: tin 600 tonnes (1983). Electricity 1,250 mn. kWh (1983). Handicraft production. – **Communications:** roads 10,200 km (1981). – **Exports:** coffee, tin, timber, rice, cotton, tobacco.

LEBANON

al-Jumhouriya al-Lubnaniya, area 10,400 sq.km, population 2,668,000 (1985), **republic** (President Amin Gemayel since 1982).
Administrative units: 5 provinces (mohafazat). **Capital:** Bayrūt 750,000 inhab. (1983), **other towns** (in 1,000 inhab): Tarābulus 195, Zahlah 68, Saydā 35. – **Currency:** Lebanese pound = 100 piastres.
Economy: arable land 33.5%. **Agriculture** of Mediterranean type (1983, in 1,000 tonnes): grapes 172, oranges 205, tangerines 30, lemons 56, olives 20, vegetables 418, cereals 31; livestock (1983, in 1,000 head): cattle 50, sheep 140, goats 440; fish catch 1,400 tonnes (1983). Electricity 1,220 mn. kWh (1983). Food **industry**, production of carpets and jewellery. Processing of imported petroleum. – **Communications** (1980): railways 417 km, roads 7,350 km. Merchant shipping 458,000 GRT (1983). Civil aviation: 28.3 mn. km flown, 411,000 passengers carried (1983). – **Exports:** jewellery, textile products, fruit, vegetables, skins, wool, olive oil.

MALAYSIA

Persekutuan Tanah Malaysia, Federation of Malaysia, area 329,749 sq.km, population 15,567,000 (1985), **federation, member of the Commonwealth** (Supreme Head of State Sultan Mahmood Iskandar ibni Al-Marhum Sultan Ismail since 1984).
Administrative units: Peninsular Malaysia: 11 states and 1 capital district, Sabah, Sarawak. **Capital:** Kuala Lumpur 937,875 inhab.; **other towns** (census 1980, in 1,000 inhab): Petaling Jaya 373, Ipoh 301, Pinang (George Town) 251, Johore Baharu 250, Kuala Terengganu 187, Kota Baharu 171, Butterworth 161, Kuantan 137, Seremban 136, Sandakan 118, Kuching 74 (Sarawak), Kota Kinabalu 60 (Sabah). **Population:** mainly Malays (55%) and Chinese (35%). **Density** 47 persons per sq.km; average annual rate of population increase: 2.4%; (1973–83) urban population 31% (1983). 45.4% of the economically active inhabitants engaged in agriculture. – **Currency:** Malaysian ringgit = 100 sen.
Economy: plantational agriculture and mining industry. Arable land 13.2%, forests 66.7%. **Agriculture** (1983, in 1,000 tonnes): rice 2,000, maize (corn), sweet potatoes 69, coconuts 1,200, copra 204, palm kernels 840 (leading world producer), palm oil 3,000 (leading world producer), groundnuts, manioc 375, bananas 475, fruit 880, pineapples 160, sugarcane 1,000, coffee, cocoa beans 55, tea, cashew nuts 735 tonnes, pepper; livestock (1983, in 1,000 head): cattle 600, buffaloes 300, pigs 2,100, goats 350, poultry 55 mn.; fish catch 741,000 tonnes. Natural rubber 1,530,000 tonnes (leading world producer), roundwood 41.9 mn. cub.m, rare timber.

23 a Java

1 : 15 000 000

1 : 25 000 000

23 b Philippines

1 : 15 000 000

map 23

Mining (1983, in 1,000 tonnes metal content): crude petroleum 18,972, natural gas 13,320 TJ, iron ore 64, bauxite 502, copper 29, manganese, tin 41.4 (leading world producer), antimony 180 tonnes, tungsten 25 tonnes, gold 185 kg. Electricity 12,135 mn. kWh. **Industry:** processing of tin, petroleum and agricultural products. **Production** (1983, in 1,000 tonnes): tin 53,338 tonnes (leading world producer), naphtha 110, motor spirit 935, jet fuel 360, woven cotton fabrics 241 mn. sq.m, sugar 75, meat 240.

Communications (1982): railways 2,375 km, roads 38,900 km, motor vehicles – passenger 1,332,000, commercial 350,000. Merchant shipping 1,475,000 GRT (1983). Civil aviation: 44.3 mn. km flown, 5,685,000 passengers carried (1983). Tourism 1,050,000 visitors. – **Exports:** natural rubber, tin, petroleum and petroleum products, wood, palm oil, copra. Chief trading partners: Japan, U.S.A., Singapore, United Kingdom, Fed. Rep. of Germany, Australia.

MALDIVES

Divehi Jumhuriya, area 298 sq.km, population 180,453 (1983), **republic** (President Maumoon Abdul Gayoom since 1978).

Capital: Male 45,000 inhab. (1982). – **Currency:** Maldive rupee = 100 laaris. – **Economy:** coconuts 9,000 tonnes, copra 1,000 tonnes, sweet potatoes, fruit; fish catch 38,500 tonnes. – **Exports:** coconuts, copra, fish.

MONGOLIA

Bügd Nayramdakh Mongol Ard Uls, area 1,565,000 sq.km, population 1,890,500 (1985), **people's democratic republic** (Chairman of the Presidium of the People's Great Khural Dr. Jambyn Batmunkh since 1984).

Administrative units: 18 provinces (aimag) and 3 self-administered cities. **Capital:** Ulaanbaatar 435,400 inhab. (1982); **other towns** (1981, in 1,000 inhab.): Darchan 56, Erdenet 39. **Density** 1.2 person per sq.km. – **Currency:** tugrik = = 100 möngö.

Economy: agricultural and industrial country with nomadic cattle raising and processing of agricultural products. Arable land only 0.8%, meadows and pastures 78.8%. **Agriculture** (1983, in 1,000 tonnes): wheat 650, barley 90; livestock (1983, in 1,000 head): horses 2,028, cattle 2,396, camels 570, sheep 14,955, goats 4,802; hides 11,500 tonnes, sheepskins 15,600 tonnes. Electricity 1,975 mn. kWh (1983). Food industry (1983, in 1,000 tonnes): milk 170, meat 255, butter 8, cheese 3. – **Communications** (1982): railways 1,585 km, roads 29,018 km. Airport Ulaanbaatar. – **Exports:** hides and skins, wool, meat. Chief trading partners: U.S.S.R. (80%), China.

NEPAL

Sri Nepala Sarkar, area 140,797 sq.km, population 16,625,000 (1985), **kingdom** (King Mahárájádhirája Birendra Bir Bikram Sháh Dev since 1972).

Administrative units: 14 zones. **Capital:** Kátmándu 393,494 inhab. (1981); **other towns:** Birátnagar 93,544, Lalitpur 59,000 inhab. – **Currency:** Nepalese rupee = 100 pice.

Economy: agriculture, home crafts and industrial processing of agricultural products in new plants. **Agriculture** (1983, in 1,000 tonnes): rice 2,744, wheat 657, maize (corn) 768, millet 113, jute 40; livestock (1983, in 1,000 head): cattle 6,980, buffaloes 4,460, pigs 365, sheep 2,480, goats 2,650; roundwood 14.4 mn. cub.m. Electricity 257 mn. kWh (1983). – **Communications** (1983): railways 63 km, roads 5,270 km. – **Exports:** rice, jute, wood.

OMAN

Sultanate of Oman, area 212,457 sq.km, population 1,242,000 (1983), **sultanate** (Sultan Qaboos bin Said since 1970).

Capital: Masqat (Muscat) 30,000 inhab. (1983, with agglom. 100,000); **other towns:** Sur 30,000, Naswa 25,000 inhab. – **Currency:** Oman rial = 1,000 baiza.

Economy. Agriculture (1983, in 1,000 tonnes): dates 75, cereals 3, fruit, lemons 13, tobacco; livestock (1983, in 1,000 head): cattle 150, sheep 140, goats 250, camels 6. Fish catch 108,000 tonnes. Electricity 1,402 mn. kWh (1983). **Mining** (1983): crude petroleum 18,685,000 tonnes, natural gas. – **Communications:** roads 1,911 km (1983). – **Exports:** petroleum, dates, citrus fruit, tobacco, fish, pearls. Chief trading partners: Japan, Fed. Rep. of Germany, U.S.A.

PAKISTAN

Islami Jumhouryat-e-Pakistan, area 803,942 sq.km, population 96,179,592 (1985) – excluding the territory of "Free Kashmir" (Azad Kashmir, 79,900 sq.km), **republic** (President Gen. Mohammad Zia ul-Haq since 1978).

Administrative units: 6 provinces. **Capital:** Islâmâbâd 204,364 inhab. (census 1981); **other towns** (in 1,000 inhab.): Karáchi 5,180, Lahore 2,953, Faísalâbâd 1,104, Râwalpindi 794, Hyderábâd 751, Multân 722, Gujránwâla 659, Peshâwar 566, Siâlkot 302, Sargodha 291, Quetta 291. **Population:** Punjabi, Sindhi, Urdu etc. **Density** 120 persons per sq.km. – **Currency:** Pakistani rupee = 100 paisa. – Average annual rate of population increase 3% (1973–83); urban population 29% (1983). 52% of the economically active inhabitants engaged in agriculture. – **Currency:** Pakistani rupee = 100 paisa.

Economy: agricultural and industrial country. Arable land 25% of the land area. **Agriculture. Crops** (1983, in 1,000 tonnes): wheat 12,414, rice 5,210, maize (corn) 1,000, barley 185, millet 270, sorghum 235, chick-peas 491, sugarcane 32,534,

map 24

groundnuts 84, sesame 12, cotton – seed 1,040, – lint 520, dates 218; **livestock** (1983, in 1,000 head): horses 448, cattle 16,157, buffaloes 12,483, sheep 23,531, goats 27,716, asses 2,626; grease wool 42,700 tonnes, cattle hides 83,468 tonnes. Fish catch 343,400 tonnes. Roundwood 19.1 mn. cub.m. **Mining** (1983, in 1,000 tonnes, metal content): coal 1,855, crude petroleum 588, natural gas 318,984 TJ, chromium 2, antimony, magnesite, manganese, sulphur, salt 544, graphite, mica. Electricity 19.6 billion kWh (1983). Food, textile and leather **industries. Production** (1983, in 1,000 tonnes): cow milk 2,353, buffalo milk 6,902, butter 224, meat 949; 38,199 mn. cigarettes, woven cotton fabrics 370 mn. m.
Communications (1982): railways 8,823 km, roads 57,494 km, motor vehicles – passenger 339,800, commercial 140,800 (1983). Merchant shipping 507,000 GRT (1983). Civil aviation: 47.3 mn. km flown, 3,642,000 passengers carried (1983). Tourism 365,000 visitors (1983). – **Exports:** cotton and cotton products 60%, rice 20%, woollen and jute products. Chief trading partners: U.S.A., Japan, Fed. Rep. of Germany, United Kingdom, Saudi Arabia.

PHILIPPINES

Republika ng Pilipinas – Republic of the Philippines – República de Filipinas, area 297,413 sq.km, population 54,377,900 (1985), **republic** (President Corazon Aquino since 1986).

Administrative units: 73 provinces. **Capital:** Manila 1,630,485 inhab. (1980, with agglom. 6.8 mn.); **other towns** (in 1,000 inhab., ⁺with agglom.): Quezon City 1,166, Davao⁺ 611, Cebu⁺ 600, Caloocan 471, Makati 372, Zamboanga⁺ 344, Pasay 286, Pasig 269, Bacolod 267. – **Population:** Filipino; chief tribes: Visay, Tagal, Igorot. **Density** 183 persons per sq.km; average annual rate of population increase 2.7% (1973–83); urban population 39% (1983). 44% of the economically active inhabitants engaged in agriculture. – **Currency:** Philippine peso = 100 centavos.
Economy: plantational agriculture with developing industry. Arable land 26%, forests 41% of the land area. **Agriculture. Crops:** (1983, in 1,000 tonnes): rice 8,150, maize (corn) 3,385, manioc 2,300, sweet potatoes 1,050, sugarcane 21,467, coconuts 9,200 (second world producer), copra 1,930 (leading world producer), palm kernels 2.7, palm oil 13.4, abaca, bananas 4,200, pineapples 1,300 (second world producer), coffee 160, tobacco 45, vegetables 2,114; **livestock** (1983, in 1,000 head): horses 300, cattle 1,938, buffaloes 2,946, pigs 7,980, goats 1,859, poultry 72 mn.; fish catch 1,836,900 tonnes. Roundwood 35.8 mn. cub.m.; natural rubber 80,000 tonnes (1983). **Mining** (1983, in 1,000 tonnes, metal content): coal 1,020, brown coal, crude petroleum 731, uranium, iron ore, manganese, chromium 89, copper 208, nickel 14.4, silver, zinc, gold 25,397 kg, salt 382. Electricity 20,761 mn. kWh (1983). **Production** (1983, in 1,000 tonnes): cement 4,560, television receivers 190,000 units, motor vehicles – passenger 42,996, commercial 26,004 units, merchant vessels 260,000 GRT, woven cotton fabrics 156 mn. m, meat 830, sugar 2,578; 57,812 mn. cigarettes.
Communications: railways 1,069 km, roads 119,220 km, motor vehicles – passenger 367,000, commercial 556,000. Merchant shipping 3,441,000 GRT (1984). Civil aviation: 90.9 mn. km flown, 4,394,000, passengers carried (1983). Tourism 848,000 visitors (1983). – **Exports:** electrotechnical goods, sugar, coconuts, copra, coconut oil, abaca, copper concentrates, pineapples, bananas, wood. Chief trading partners: U.S.A., Japan, Fed. Rep. of Germany, Saudi Arabia.

QATAR

Dawlat Qatar, area 11,000 sq.km, population 315,000 (1985), **monarchy** (Amir Shaikh Khalifa bin Hamad Al-Thani since 1972).
Capital: Ad-Dawhah (Doha) 209,000 inhab. (1982). – **Currency:** Qatar riyal = 100 dirhams.
Economy: agriculture in oases (1983): dates, citrus fruit, extensive cattle raising (cattle 10,000, camels 6,000, sheep 53,000 head), fish catch 2,100 tonnes, pearl fishery. **Mining** (1983, in 1,000 tonnes): crude petroleum 14,540, natural gas 210,400 TJ. Electricity 3,105 mn. kWh (1983). **Production** (1983, in 1,000 tonnes): motor spirit 130, jet fuel 61. – **Communications:** roads 1,700 km, cars 136,800 (1982). Port Ad-Dawhah. – **Exports:** petroleum, dates. Chief trading partners: Japan, United Kingdom, Fed. Rep. of Germany, U.S.A.

SAUDI ARABIA

al-Mamlaka al-'Arabiya as-Sa'udiya, area 2,153,168 sq.km, population 11,542,000 (1985), **kingdom** (King Fahd ibn Abdul-Aziz since 1982).

Administrative units: 5 regions. **Capital:** Ar-Riyāḍ 1,250,000 inhab. (1980); **other towns** (in 1,000 inhab.): Jiddah 1,300, Makkah (Mecca) 550, At-Tā'if 300, Al-Madīnah (Medina) 290. – **Population:** mainly Arabs, minorities: Iranians, Ludas and others. Average annual rate of population increase 4.7% (1973–83); urban population 68% (1981). 58% of the economically active inhabitants engaged in agriculture (1983). – **Currency:** Saudi rial = 100 halala.
Economy: the country with the largest resources of petroleum in the world (about 15,000 mn. tonnes) and large-scale extraction. Arable land 0.5% and pastures 39.5% of the land area. Cultivation of cereals and fruit in the oases, nomadic raising of cattle on pastures. **Agriculture** (1983, in 1,000 tonnes): dates 440, wheat 72, barley 12, maize (corn), millet 7, sorghum 87, oranges 26; **livestock** (1983, in 1,000 head): cattle 500, camels 160, sheep 3,500, goats 2,300. **Mining** (1983, in 1,000 tonnes): crude petroleum 252,707 (along the shore of the Persian Gulf and offshore wells), natural gas 50,000 TJ, Saudi Arabia participates with Kuwait in petroleum and natural gas extraction in the former Neutral Zone. Iron ore, pyrites, gold, phosphates. Electricity 32,000 mn. kWh (1983). **Production** (1983, in 1,000 tonnes): naphtha 1,100, motor spirit 3,300, jet fuel 91, distillate fuel oils 9,500.
Communications: railways 1,248 km, roads 20,134 km, motor vehicles – passenger 1,250,000, commercial 150,000 (1983). Merchant shipping 3,863,000 GRT. Civil aviation: 112.3 mn. km flown, 11.4 mn. passengers carried. – **Exports:** petroleum and petroleum products (one of the largest petroleum ports in the world is Ra's At-Tannūrah), dates, oranges. Chief trading partners: Japan, U.S.A., Fed. Rep. of Germany, Italy, United Kingdom.

CHINA:

Autonomous regions:

1 Guangxi Zhuangzu Z.
2 Nei Mongol Z.
3 Ningxia Huizu Z.
4 Xinjiang Uygur Z.
  (Sinkiang)
5 Xizang Z. (Tibet)

Provinces:

6 Anhui
7 Fujian
8 Gansu

9 Guangdong
10 Guizhou
11 Hebei
12 Heilongjiang
13 Henan
14 Hubei
15 Hunan
16 Jiangsu
17 Jiangxi
18 Jilin
19 Liaoning

20 Qinghai
21 Shaanxi
22 Shandong
23 Shanxi
24 Sichuan
25 Taiwan
26 Yunnan
27 Zhejiang

Municipalities:

28 Beijing
29 Shanghai
30 Tianjin

1 : 25 000 000

| 0 | 200 | 400 | 600 Km |

| 0 | 100 | 200 | 300 | 400 Mi |

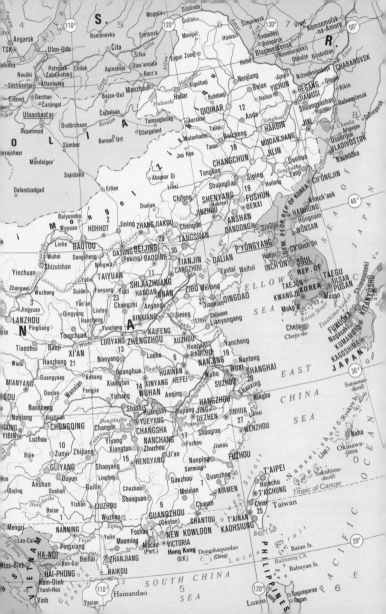

map 24

SINGAPORE

Republik Singapura – Republic of Singapore, area 597 sq.km, population 2,558,000 (1985), republic, member of the Commonwealth (President Wee Kim Wee since 1985).
Capital: Singapore 2,529,100 inhab. (1984). – **Population:** about 77% Chinese, 15% Malays, Indians, Pakistanis. **Density** 4,285 persons per sq.km; average annual rate of population increase 1.3% (1973–83); urban population 100%. 1.9% of the economically active inhabitants engaged in agriculture (1983). – **Currency:** Singapore dollar = = 100 cents.
Economy: important transit port, processing of Malayan tin (the largest tin smelting plant in Asia), shipyards, petrochemical industry, processing of natural rubber, textile industry. Arable land 10.5% of the land area. **Agriculture:** sweet potatoes, manioc, coconuts, natural rubber; raising of pigs 1,300,000 head (1983); fish catch 19,500 tonnes (1983). Electricity 8,626 mn. kWh (1983). **Production** (1983, in 1,000 tonnes): vessels 39,000 GRT, naphtha 3,550, motor spirit 2,325, jet fuel 2,125, distillate fuel oils 7,050.
Communications (1984): railways 25.8 km, roads 2,569 km, passenger cars 223,116. Merchant shipping 6,512,000 GRT (1983). Civil aviation: 75.6 mn. km flown, 4,792,000 passengers carried (1984). Tourism 2,854,000 visitors (1983). – **Exports:** petroleum products, machinery products, textiles, transit from Malaysia (natural rubber, tin, iron ore, copra). Chief trading partners: U.S.A., Malaysia, Japan, Hong Kong, United Kingdom, Australia.

SRI LANKA

Janarajaya Srī Lanka, area 65,610 sq.km, population 15,837,000 (1985), republic, member of the Commonwealth (President Junius Richard Jayawardene since 1978).
Administrative units: 9 provinces. **Capital:** Colombo 623,000 inhab. (1983); **other towns** (in 1,000 inhab.): Dehiwala-Mt. Lavinia 181, Moratuwa 137, Jaffna 128. – **Population:** about 74% Sinhalese, 13% Ceylon and Indian Tamils, 7% Moors etc. **Density** 241 persons per sq.km; average annual rate of population increase 1.7% (1983). 52% of the economically active inhabitants engaged in agriculture. – **Currency:** Srī Lanka rupee = 100 cents.
Economy: tropical fruit growing on plantations and mineral mining. Arable land 15.6%, land under permanent crops 17.1%, forests 36.3% of the land area. **Agriculture** (1983, in 1,000 tonnes): rice 2,200, sweet potatoes 160, tea 175, coconuts 2,300, copra 145, natural rubber 135, cocoa beans 3; **livestock** (1983, in 1,000 head): cattle 1,700, buffaloes 880, pigs 80, sheep 28; fish catch 222,000 tonnes. Roundwood 8.4 mn. cub.m. **Mining:** graphite 5,870 tonnes (1983), gem stones, salt 128. Electricity 2,114 mn. kWh (1983). Chemical, textile and food **industries.**
Communications (1983): railways 1,453 km, roads 31,150 km, motor vehicles – passenger 136,900, commercial 109,600. Merchant shipping 746,000 GRT. Civil aviation: 13.1 mn. km flown, 681,000 passengers carried (1983). Tourism 338,000 visitors (1983). **Exports:** tea (60% of exports), textiles, natural rubber, coconuts, copra, graphite, gem stones, cocoa beans. Chief trading partners: Japan, U.S.A., Iraq, Saudi Arabia, United Kingdom.

SYRIA

al-Jamhouriya al-'Arabiya as Souriya, area 185,180 sq.km, population 11,162,585 (1985), republic (President Gen. Hafez al-Assad since 1971).
Administrative units: 14 districts (mohafaza). **Capital:** Dimashq (Damascus) 1,251,028 inhab. (census 1981); **other towns** (in 1,000 inhab): Halab (Aleppo) 977, Hims 355, Al-Lādhiqiyah 197, Hamāh 177, Dayr az-Zawr 87, Ar-Raqqah 87. – **Population:** Syrian Arabs, minorities: Kurds 5%, Armenians, Cherkese. **Density** 60 persons per sq.km; average annual rate of population increase 3.3% (1973–83); urban population 48%. 46% of the economically active inhabitants engaged in agriculture (1983). – **Currency:** Syrian pound = 100 piastres.
Economy: agricultural and industrial country. Arable land 28.2%, meadows and pastures 45.2% of the land area. **Agriculture** (1983, in 1,000 tonnes): wheat 1,612, barley 1,043, potatoes 300, cotton – seed 335, – lint 18, legumens, vegetables 3,294. Mediterranean products – chiefly olives 235, oranges 55, lemons 12, grapes 389, tobacco 14; **livestock** (1983, in 1,000 head): cattle 800, sheep 11,000, goats 1,100; fish catch 3,800 tonnes (1983). **Mining** (1983, in 1,000 tonnes): crude petroleum 9,359, natural gas 2,960 TJ, natural asphalt, phosphates 1,231, salt 88. Electricity 6,175 mn. kWh (1983). **Industry:** petrochemical, textile and food industries. **Production** (1983, in 1,000 tonnes): woven cotton fabrics 374, motor spirit 474, jet fuel 200, disillate fuel oils 2,095.
Communications (1982): railways 2,086 km, roads 18,850 km, motor vehicles – passenger 127,300, commercial 108,700. Civil aviation: 8.8 mn. km flown, 464,000 passengers carried (1983). – **Exports:** petroleum, cotton, fruit and vegetables, cereals, hides and skins, furs, phosphates. Chief trading partners: U.S.S.R., Italy, United Kingdom, France, Greece.

THAILAND

Prathes Thai (Muang-Thai), area 514,121 sq.km, population 51,410,000 (1985), monarchy (King Bhumibol Adulyadej since 1946).
Administrative units: 72 provinces (changwad). **Capital:** Krung Thep (Bangkok) 5,468,286 inhab. (1983, with Thon Buri); **other towns** (census 1980, in 1,000 inhab.): Chiang Mai 100, Hat Yai 98, Khon Kaen 94, Nakhon Ratchasima 89, Nakhon Sawan 89, Udon Thani 81, Phitsanulok 73. – **Population:** Thais 85% (chiefly Siamese and Lao), Chinese, Malays etc. **Density** 100 persons per sq.km; average annual rate of population increase 2.3% (1973–83); urban population 18% (1983). 74% of the economically active inhabitants engaged in agriculture. – **Currency:** baht = 100 satang.
Economy: agricultural country with few industries. Arable land 31.6%, forests 30.7% of the land area. Rice is cultivated on 65–70% of the arable land. **Agriculture** (1983, in 1,000 tonnes): rice 18,535, maize (corn) 3,552, sorghum 327, sweet potatoes 355, manioc 17,000, sugarcane 24,407, groundnuts 157, sesame 26, jute 234, cotton – seed 87, lint 44, bananas

map 25

2,035, pineapples 1,439 (leading world producer), oranges 57, coconuts 800, palm kernels 12.4, tobacco 92; **livestock** (1983, in 1,000 head): cattle 4,600, buffaloes 6,150, pigs 3,800; fish catch 2,250,000 tonnes (1983); roundwood 40.4 mn. cub.m; natural rubber 570,000 tonnes. **Mining** (1983, in 1,000 tonnes, metal content): brown coal 2,250, crude petroleum, natural gas 56,972 TJ, iron ore 23, tungsten 563 tonnes, tin 19.9, antimony 1,236 tonnes, manganese 2.3, gem stones. Electricity 18,875 mn. kWh. **Industry:** ore processing, textile and food industries. **Production** (1983, in 1,000 tonnes): pig iron 12, crude steel 244, tin 18.6, woven cotton fabrics 800, sugar 2,550, meat 771; 28,941 mn. cigarettes.
Communications (1982): railways 3,735 km, roads 44,200 km, motor vehicles – passenger 511,200, commercial 351,500. Merchant shipping 567,000 GRT (1983). Civil aviation: 57.7 mn. km flown, 3,671,000 passengers carried (1983). Tourism 2,154,000 visitors (1983). – **Exports:** rice 15%, maize (corn), manioc, textiles, natural rubber, tin, jute, wood. Chief trading partners: Japan, U.S.A., Singapore, Fed. Rep. of Germany, United Kingdom, Saudi Arabia.

TURKEY

Türkiye Cumhuriyeti, area 779,452 sq.km, population 51,428,745 (1985), of which the Asiatic part 755,688 sq.km and population 40,804,869, **republic** (President Gen. Kenan Evren since 1980).

Administrative units: 67 provinces (iller). **Capital:** Ankara 1,981,300 inhab. (1983, with agglom. 3.4 mn. 1985); **other towns** (in 1,000 inhab., [+]with agglom. 1985): İstanbul 2,903, İzmir 832 ([+]2,300), Adana 637, Bursa 510, Gaziantep 421, Konya 385, Eskişehir 340, Kayseri 332, Diyarbakır 282, Mersin 262, Erzurum 207. – **Population:** over 90% Turks, about 7% Kurds, Arabs etc. **Density** 66 persons per sq.km, in the Asiatic part 54 persons per sq.km; average annual rate of population increase 2.2% (1973–83); urban population 45% (1983). 50% of the economically active inhabitants engaged in agriculture (1983). – **Currency:** Turkish Lira = 100 kuruş.
Economy: agricultural and industrial country with great regional differences. Arable land 32.5%, meadows and pastures 12.4%, forests 25.9% of the land area. **Agriculture. Crops** (1983, in 1,000 tonnes): wheat 16,400, barley 5,600, maize (corn) 1,375, rye 430, rice 325, oats 330, potatoes 3,080, beans 166, lentils 450, peas, sugar beet 12,000, sunflower 725, groundnuts 65, sesame 12, chick-peas 250, cotton – seed 800, lint 520 – olives 450, figs, raisins 300 (second world producer), oranges 691, tangerines 232, lemons 330, grapes 3,400, apples 1,700, pears 344, almonds 35; hazelnuts 370 (leading world producer), walnuts 121 (second world producer), pistachios 20, chestnuts 60, tomatoes 3,700, dry onions 1,040, tobacco 225. **Livestock** (1983, in 1,000 head): horses 770, cattle 17,100, buffaloes 808, camels 10, sheep 49,636, goats 18,213, asses 1,300; cattlehides 70,000 tonnes, sheepskins 67,000 tonnes, grease wool 64,000 tonnes, mohair; fish catch 567,300 tonnes (1983), roundwood 19.2 mn. cub.m.
Mining (1983, in 1,000 tonnes, metal content): coal 4,110, brown coal 17,000, crude petroleum 2,203, uranium, chromium 135, iron ore 2,207, manganese, lead 6.3, zinc, mercury 127 tonnes, antimony 1,089 tonnes, cobalt, copper 25, magnesite 719, sulphur, bauxite 296, asbestos, marble, salt 1,261, phosphates 50. Electricity 27,321 mn. kWh (1983). **Industry:** food, tobacco and textile industries. **Production** (1983, in 1,000 tonnes): pig iron 2,645, crude steel 2,479, cement 13,595, sulphuric acid 338, nitrogenous fertilizers 783.1, phosphate fertilizers 621.5, motor spirit 1,917, jet fuel 283, naphtha 893, distillate fuel oils 4,582, motor vehicles, merchant vessels 74,000 GRT, radio receivers 188,000, television receivers 603,000, woven cotton fabrics 234 mn. m, woven woollen fabrics 8 mn. m, carpets, meat 943, sugar 1,654, milk 3,700, cheese 133.5, butter 125, olive oil 70, flour 1,582, wine 370,000 hl, beer 3.2 mn. hl; 61,500 mn. cigarettes.
Communications (1983): railways 8,373 km, roads 60,712 km, motor vehicles – passenger 856,400, commercial 342,500. Merchant shipping 3,125,000 GRT (1983). Civil aviation: 25.1 mn. km flown, 2.2 mn. passengers carried (1983). Tourism 1.2 mn. visitors (1983). – **Exports:** fruit and raisins, cotton and textiles, cotton fabrics, tobacco and tobacco products, fruit (hazelnuts, raisins etc.), animal products (cattle, wool, hides), carpets, clothing. Chief trading partners: Iran, Fed. Rep. of Germany, Iraq, U.S.A., Italy, United Kingdom, Switzerland.

UNITED ARAB EMIRATES

Dawlat al-Imārāt al-'Arabīya al Muttahida, area 83,600 sq.km, population 1,327,000 (1985), **federation of emirates** (President Sheikh Zayed bin Sultan al Nahyan since 1971).
Administrative units: 7 emirates. **Capital:** Abu Zaby 242,975 inhab., census 1980); **other towns:** Dubayy 267,702, Ash-Shāriqah 125,149. – **Population:** average annual rate of population increase 11.3% (1973–83); urban population 79%. – **Currency:** dirham = 100 fils.
The economy is based on petroleum and natural gas extraction. Cultivation of vegetables. Arable land covers only 15,000 ha. Fish catch 73,100 tonnes (1983), pearl fishery. **Mining** (1983, in 1,000 tonnes): crude petroleum 53,640 (of which more than two thirds emirate Abu Zaby), natural gas 542,200 TJ. Electricity 7,900 mn. kWh. **Production** (1983, in 1,000 tonnes): motor spirit 370, naphtha 250, distillate fuel oils 280. – **Exports:** petroleum and petroleum products, dry fish, pearls. Chief trading partners: Japan, U.S.A., United Kingdom, Fed. Rep. of Germany, France, Italy, Bahrain.

VIETNAM

Cộng Hòa Xã Hội Chu Nghĩa Việt Nam, area 332,560 sq.km, population 59,713,000 (1985), **socialist republic** (Chairman of the State Council Truong Chinh since 1981).
Administrative units: 3 self-administrated cities, 37 provinces. **Capital:** Ha-Noi 2,570,909 inhab., census 1979); **other towns** (in 1,000 inhab.): Thanh-phô Hô Chi Minh (Saigon) 3,120, Hai-Phong 1,279, Da-Nang 620, Can-Tho 183, Nha-Trang 173, Hue 166, Nam-Dinh 161. – **Population:** Vietnamese 84%, other nationalities Thai, Khmer, Meo etc. **Density** 180 persons per sq.km; average annual rate of population increase 2.7% (1973–83); urban population 20%. 69% of the economically active inhabitants engaged in agriculture. – **Currency:** dông = 10 liao = 100 xu.

map 25

Economy: agricultural country with developing industrial production. Arable land 18%, forests 31% of the land area.
Agriculture. Crops (1983, in 1,000 tonnes): rice 11,500, maize (corn) 420, sweet potatoes 1,700, potatoes 500, manioc 2,700, soya beans 107, groundnuts 87, sugarcane 4,600, jute 38, cotton, vegetables 2,839, fruit 3,107 (oranges 95, pineapples 380), tea 28, coffee 9, tobacco 32; **livestock** (1983, in 1,000 head): cattle 2,000, buffaloes 2,390, pigs 10,787; raw silk 300 tonnes; fish catch 710; roundwood 23.7 mn. cub.m, natural rubber 43,000 tonnes. **Mining** (1983, in 1,000 tonnes): coal 6,000, iron ore, molybdenum, tin, gold, phosphates 200, salt 889. Electricity 4,200 mn. kWh (1983). **Industry:** textile and food industries, processing of phosphates. **Production:** phosphate fertilizers 35,000 tonnes (1983), woven cotton fabrics 287 mn. m, cement 910,000 tonnes.
Communications (1983): railways 3,216km, main roads 60,000km, motor vehicles – passenger 170,000; merchant shipping 358,400 GRT. – **Exports:** natural rubber, fruit, tea, fish, wood, vegetables, minerals. Chief trading partners: U.S.S.R. and CMEA countries, Japan, South-eastern Asia countries.

YEMEN (Y.A.R.)

al Jamhuriya al Arabiya al Yamaniya, area 195,000 sq.km, population 9,274,173 (1985), **republic** (President Ali Abdullah Saleh since 1978).
Administrative units: 8 provinces (liwa). **Capital:** San'â' 440,000 inhab. (1984); **other towns:** Ta'izz 220,000, Al-Hudaydah 140,000. – **Population:** Arabs, minorities of other Asian and African nationals. **Density** 48 persons per sq.km; urban population 18%. 73% of the economically active inhabitants engaged in agriculture. – **Currency:** Yemeni riyal = = 100 fils.
Economy: developing agricultural country. Arable land 14%, meadows and pastures 36%. **Agriculture** (1983, in 1,000 tonnes): wheat 27, barley 10, sorghum 248, maize 32, potatoes 140, coffee 4, cotton 5, grapes 59, dates 84; **livestock** (in 1,000 head): cattle 950, camels 108, sheep 3,150, goats 7,500, fish catch 22,200 tonnes. **Mining** of salt. – **Communications:** main roads 2,170km, chief port Al-Hudaydah. **Exports:** cotton, coffee, hides and skins, fish.

YEMEN, DEMOCRATIC (D.Y.)

Jumhurijah al-Yemen al Dimuqratiyah al Sha'abijah, area 287,683 sq.km, population 2,293,900 (1985), **people's democratic republic** (Chairman of the Presidium of the Supreme People's Council Haidar Abūbaker Al Attâs since 1986).
Administrative units: 6 governorates (muchafaz). **Capital:** Adan (Aden) 343,000 ir:hab. (1980); **other towns:** Al-Mukallà 100,000. – **Population:** Arabs, small number of Indians and Somalis. **Density** 7 persons per sq.km; average annual rate of population increase 2.2% (1973–83): urban population 37% (1983). 57% of the economically active inhabitants engaged in agriculture. – **Currency:** Yemeni dinar (YD) = 1,000 fils.
Economy: nomadic raising of cattle, petrochemical industry, major transit port. Arable land only 0.6% of the land area. **Agriculture** (1983, in 1,000 tonnes): wheat 15, millet 80, cotton, dates 44; livestock (1983, in 1,000 head): cattle 120, sheep 1,000, goats 1,350, camels 140, fish catch 74,000 tonnes. Electricity 280 mn. kWh (1983). **Production** (1983, in 1,000 tonnes): motor spirit 230, jet fuel 160, distillate fuel oils 480. – **Communications:** roads 1,152km, rough tracks 10,270km, motor vehicles – passenger 17,800, commercial 19,400 (1981). Adan is an important naval and air base and a major transit port. – **Exports:** petroleum products, cotton.

BRITISH TERRITORY:

HONG KONG

Crown Colony of Hong Kong, area 1,067 sq.km, population 5,579,000 (1985), **British Dependent Territory** (Governor Sir Edward Youde).
Capital: Victoria 633,138 inhab. (census 1981): **other towns** (in 1,000 inhab.): New Kowloon 1,651, Kowloon 799, Tsuen Wan 720, Sha Tin 625, Tuen Mun 547. **Density** 5,229 persons per sq.km; average annual rate of population increase 2.5% (1973–83); urban population 92%. – **Currency:** Hong Kong dollar = 100 cents.
Economy: important industrial and trading centre, naval and air base. **Agriculture:** arable land and permanent crops 8% of the land area. Crop of rice 4,000 tonnes, raising of pigs and poultry. Fish catch 188,800 tonnes (1983). Textile, clothing and leather **industries**, shipbuilding, electronics, chemical and printing industries. Electricity 16,482 mn. kWh. **Production** (1983): radio receivers 47,986,000 units, television receivers 368,000 units, woven cotton fabrics 642 mn. sq.m, woven silk fabrics 1.6 mn. sq.m, clocks and watches, plastic products, toys.
Communications: railways 73km, roads 1,237km, passenger cars 33,000. Merchant shipping 5,784,000 GRT. Tourism 2,137,000 visitors (1983). – **Exports:** textile products and clothing, electronic products, cameras, watches, fish, metalware. Chief trading partners: U.S.A., China, Japan, Singapore, Fed. Rep. of Germany, United Kingdom.

PORTUGUESE TERRITORY:

MACAU

Provincia de Macau, area 16 sq.km, population 392,000 (1985). **Portuguese territory.** (Gov. Vasco Almeida e Costa). **Capital:** Macau 276,673 inhab. (1980). – **Currency:** pataca = 100 avos. **Economy:** fish catch 7,000 tonnes (1983). **Industry:** clothing, knitwear, porcelain ware. Transit merchant port. Tourism 673,000 visitors. – **Exports:** textiles, clothing, fish.

map 26

AFRICA

Africa lies on both sides of the Equator, with the larger part in the northern hemisphere. The name Africa is derived from a Berber tribe, the Afrigi (or Afridi), who lived in the territory of today's Tunisia. The Latin name "Africa" was applied to a Roman province extending over the area previously under the control of Carthage.

Africa covers an **area of 30,329,000 sq.km**, i.e. 20.3% of the land surface of the Earth and is the second largest continent. It has **555 million inhabitants** (1985), and a population density 18.3 persons per sq.km. **Geographical position:** northernmost point: Cape Rás Ben Sekka (Tunisia) 37°21' N.Lat.; southernmost point: Cape Agulhas (South Africa) 34°52' S. Lat.; westernmost point: Cape Pointe des Almadies 17°38' W.Long. (4 km northwest of Cap Vert); easternmost point: Cape Rás Hafún 51°23' E.Long. Africa is joined to Asia by the Isthmus of Suez (120 km long), and it is separated from Europe by the Strait of Gibraltar (14 km wide). The coast of Africa, 30,500 km in length, has little articulation. The largest peninsula is the Somali Pen. (area 850,000 sq.km). The principal islands are Madagascar (area 587,041 sq.km) and the small Mascarene Is. (4,555 sq.km) in the Indian Ocean; off the northwest coast in the Atlantic Ocean lie the Canary Is. (7,273 sq.km) and the Cape Verde Is. (4,033 sq.km).

Orographically, Africa is divided into 3 main regions: the Atlas Mts., the African Tableland and the East African Highlands. The Atlas Mts. stretch over 2,000 km in north-west Africa (highest peak: Jbel Tubqál, 4,165 m) adjoined by the Plateau of the Shotts and its salt lakes. To the south of the Atlas Mts. lie the extensive Sahara-Sudanese plains and plateau (average height 200–500 m). The Sahara is the world's largest desert (7,820,000 sq.km); it is a rock (hamada), gravel (reg, serir) and sand desert with dunes (ergs), with the barren Mountains of Ahaggar (3,005 m), Tibesti (Emi Koussi, 3,415 m), Aïr (2,310 m) and Dárfür (3,088 m) in its centre. South-west of the Sahara lie the Upper Guinean Highlands (1,948 m) and the Adamaoua Highlands (2,679 m). In Central Africa a vast tectonic depression formed the Congo Basin (3 million sq.km). Its centre is 300–500 m high, and the border ridges are between 500 and 1,000 m. The Lower Guinean Highlands (2,620 m) rise at its western border. South of the Luanda-Katanga Plateau lies the synclinal Kalahari Basin, a plain (average height 950 m) and to the west, along the coast, the Namib Desert, 1,500 km in length. South Africa comprises the Karroo Plateau, the Cape Mts. (2,326 m) and the Drakensberg Mountains, which are South Africa's highest at Thabana-Ntlenyana 3,482 m. The Ethiopian Highlands (average altitude 2,500 m) are the eastern continuation of the Saharan-Arabian Tableland (highest point: Ras Dashen, 4,620 m). The Assal Depression in the Afar Pan by the Red Sea is the lowest point in Africa, –173 m below sea level. The East African Plateau has the most varied forms: tectonic rifts (e.g. the Great Rift Valley), mountain ridges (Ruwenzori, Ngaliema, 5,119 m), volcanoes, craters (Ngorongoro, 3,648 m) and plateau. Africa's highest mountain stands here; the volcanic Kilimanjaro with its three conical peaks, Uhuru, 5,895 m being the highest.

Africa's **rivers** were formed more recently. The network of rivers and drainage is highly irregular. The average volume of water flow per year is 4,657 cubic km. Almost one third of Africa lacks any form of drainage, especially the Sahara. More than one third of Africa drains into the Atlantic Ocean. Africa's major river is the Congo (Zaïre), 4,835 km in length with a river basin of 3,822,000 sq.km, the mean discharge is 41,000 cub.m per second. The Niger reaches the Gulf of Guinea through the Niger delta; its length is 4,160 km, the river basin occupies 2,092,000 sq.km. Africa's longest river is the Nile (length: 6,671 km, river basin 2,881,000 sq.km, mean discharge 1,600 cubic m per second). It forms a vast delta (25,000 sq.km) as it flows into the Mediterranean Sea. The greatest river in South Africa is the Zambezi. Most of the great African **lakes** are of tectonic origin, the largest being Lake Victoria (68,800 sq.km) and the deepest Lake Tanganyika (1,470 m, its bottom lying 697 m below sea level).

In view of its position Africa is the warmest continent. The climatic differences between regions are conditioned by pressure systems on the mainland and the adjacent ocean. Four **climatic zones** can be distinguished: the equatorial zone (Congo Basin and the coast of the Gulf of Guinea) has a hot wet climate all year; the zone of equatorial monsoons affects one third of Africa (to 15° N.Lat. and 18° S.Lat.) with hot wet summers and warm dry winters; the zone of tropical trade-winds (Sahara and Kalahari deserts) to the north and the south of the continent suffers extreme drought; the subtropical (Mediterranean) zone has hot dry summers and temperate rainy winters. The maximum absolute temperature is found at Al-Azizīyah (Libya) 58 °C; the highest average annual temperature, 34,4 °C was recorded in Dalol (Ethiopia) and the lowest, –15 °C in the Atlas Mts. Maximum rainfall in Africa was measured at C. Debunja (Cameroon): 10,470 mm, while Aswân (Egypt) is the driest place (0.5 mm).

Mean January and July temperatures in °C (annual precipitation in mm): Alger 10.3 and 24.4 (746), Al-Qāhirah 13.8 and 28.4 (25), Al-Khurtúm 22.5 and 30.8 (168), Tombouctou 22.6 and 31.5 (230), Conakry 26.5 and 25.6 (4,349), Kumasi 25.2 and 24.2 (1,530), Douala 27.3 and 24.8 (4,439), Mesewa 25.5 and 34.5 (181), Mombasa 27.8 and 23.9 (1,197), Kisangani 25.5 and 24.2 (1,530), Lusaka 20.6 and 15.5 (837), Windhoek 23.5 and 14.0 (386), Antananarivo 21.3 and 14.7 (1359), Pretoria 21.0 and 10.3 (748), Cape Town 22.7 and 18.4 (644).

In terms of its **flora**, Africa is divided into two regions: the Holarctic realm in the north and the Sahara desert and the larger, the Paleotropical, south of the Sahara. Tropical evergreen rain forests in the wettest regions are bordered to the north, east and south by grass savannas (covering 35% of the land) and gallery woods in the river valleys, grass and scrub semi-deserts and deserts (xerophilous and succulent scrub). The north has Mediterranean evergreen scrub and dry forests. The flora of the Cape region is related to these of south-west Australia. The **fauna** of Africa is mostly found in the Ethiopian region. The savannas are inhabited by antelopes, elephants, giraffes, hippopotami, rhinoceroses, zebras, wildebeests, lions, leopards, hyenas, monkeys, crocodiles, ostriches, waterfowl (flamingos, pelicans, cranes, herons, etc), vultures and insects (termites, locusts); the forests by gorillas, chimpanzees, vervets, buffaloes, parrots, beetles and butterflies. Madagascar has fauna of the Tertiery era: lemurs, running-birds, iguanas, etc. Africa has a number of extensive National Parks and wildlife reservations where the animals and the environment are protected. The best-known are: Etosha Pan (69,153 sq.km), Kafue (22,400 sq.km), Salonga, Tsavo, Serengeti, Virunga, Kruger N.P., Kalahari-Gemsbok, Wankie, Ngorongoro, Selous, Southern N.P., Gorongoza etc.

Africa takes up 20.3% of the area of the world, and in 1985 **555 million people** lived on the continent, i.e. 11.5% of the world's population. With 18 persons per sq.km Africa is the least densely populated continent. The unevenness of settlement is most striking in a comparison between the density of population in the Nile Valley (over 500 persons per sq.km) and that in desert areas where there is less than 1 person per sq.km. Apart from certain islands, the greatest density of population is found in Rwanda, Burundi and Nigeria, and the lowest (1 person per sq.km) in Botswana, Mauritania, Namibia and the Western Sahara. From 1980–85 the average annual

map 26

LONGEST RIVERS

Name	Length in km	River Basin in sq.km
Nile – Kagera	6,671	2,881,000
Congo (Zaïre) – Lualaba	4,835	3,822,000
Niger	4,160	2,092,000
Zambeze (Zambezi)	2,660	1,450,000
Ubangi – Uele	2,280	770,000
Kasai (Kwa, Cassai)	2,200	875,000
Shebele	1,950	.
Al-Bahr al-Azraq /Blue Nile/ – Abay	1,900	324,500
Volta – Volta Noire	1,900	440,000
Orange	1,860	1,020,000
Okavango (Cubango)	1,800	785,000
Luvua – Luapula	1,800	.
Juba	1,650	200,000
Limpopo – Krokodil	1,600	440,000
Lomani	1,500	110,000
Benue (Benoué)	1,450	319,000
Chari – Ouham	1,450	880,000
Sénégal – Bafing	1,430	450,000
Cuando	1,400	.
Kwango (Cuango)	1,400	.
Aruwimi – Ituri	1,300	116,100

LARGEST LAKES

Name	Area in sq.km	Greatest Depth in m	Altitude in m
L. Victoria (Ukerewe)	68,800	125	1,134
L.Tanganyika	32,880	1,470	773
L. Nyasa (Malawi)	28,480	785	473
L. Chad	20,700	4-7	240
L. Turkana+ /L. Rudolf/	8,560	404	375
Chott Melrhir+	6,700	.	-30
Chott Djerid+	5,700	.	16
L. Albert	5,345	57	619
L. Mweru	4,920	18	917
L. Tana	3,630	72	1,830
L. Bangweulu	2,850	4	1,067
L. Kivu	2,650	496	1,455
L. Rukwa	2,640	4	793
L. Kyoga	2,600	5	1,033
B. al-Manzilah	2,600	.	2
L. Mai-Ndombe	2,320	15	340
L. Edward	2,150	117	914
Chott ech Chergui+	2,000	.	940
B. al-Burullus	1,930	.	2
L. Chilwa	1,240	.	600
L. Abaya	1,162	13	1,285
+salt lake			

LARGEST ISLANDS

Name	Area in sq.km	Name	Area in sq.km	Name	Area in sq.km
Madagascar	587,041	Mauritius	1,865	Jarbah (Î.d. Djerba)	1,050
Suqutrā (Socotra)	3,579	Fuerteventura	1,722	São Tiago	991
Réunion	2,510	Zanzibar I.	1,658	Pemba	984
Bioko	2,017	Gran Canaria	1,376	Dahlak Kebir I.	900
Tenerife	1,946	Njazidja (Gde. Comore)	1,148	São Tomé	836

HIGHEST MOUNTAINS

Name (Country)	Height in m	Name (Country)	Height in m	Name (Country)	Height in m
Kilimanjaro-Uhuru (Tanz.)	5,895	Mt. Elgon (Kenya-Ugan.)	4,321	Lesatima (Kenya)	3,994
Mt. Kenya (Kenya)	5,194	Batu (Eth.)	4,307	Amba Ferit (Eth.)	3,975
Kilimanjaro-Mawenzi (Tanz.)	5,149	Abuye Meda (Eth.)	4,305	Mt. Kinangop (Kenya)	3,906
Ngaliema (Margherita) (Ugan.-Zaïre)	5,119	Guna (Eth.)	4,231	Jbel Tignûsti (Mor.)	3,825
		Guge (Eth.)	4,200	Ari n'Ayachi (Mor.)	3,737
Ras Deshen (Eth.)	4,620	Abune Yosef (Eth.)	4,190	Gurag (Eth.)	3,719
Mt. Meru (Tanz.)	4,567	Jbel Tubqāl (Mor.)	4,165	Loolmalassin (Tanz.)	3,648
Buahit (Eth.)	4,510	Birhan (Eth.)	4,154	Thabana-Ntlenyana (Les.)	3,482
V. Karisimbi (Rwanda-Zaïre)	4,507	Muhavura (Ugan.)	4,113	Emi Koussi (Chad)	3,415
Talo (Eth.)	4,413	Irhil M'goun (Mor.)	4,071	Ngorongoro-Oldeani (Tanz.)	3,188

ACTIVE VOLCANOES

Name (Country)	Altitude in m	Latest eruption
Mt. Cameroun/Fako (Cameroon)	4,070	1982
Pico de Teide (Canary Is.)	3,718	1909
Nyiragongo (Zaïre)	3,470	1977
Nyamulagira (Zaïre)	3,056	1984
Ol Doinyo Lengai (Tanzania)	2,878	1960
Pico (Cape Verde Is.)	2,829	1951
Piton de la Foumaise (Réunion)	2,631	1983
La Caldera (Canary Is.)	2,423	1971

LARGEST NATIONAL PARKS

Name (Country)	Area in sq.km
Kafue (Zambia)	22,400
Salonga (Zaïre)	22,300
Tsavo (Kenya)	20,800
Kalahari-Gemsbok (Botsw., S.-A.)	18,550
Kruger (South Africa)	18,170
Southern N.P. (Sudan)	16,000
Serengeti (Tanzania)	14,500
Wankie (Zimbabwe)	13,353
Ruaha (Tanzania)	11,500

map 27

AFRICA

Country	Area in sq.km	Population year 1985	Density per sq.km	Capital
Algeria	2,381,740	21,718,000	9	Alger
Angola	1,246,700	8,754,000	7	Luanda
Benin	112,622	3,932,100	35	Porto-Novo
Botswana	600,372	1,084,900	1.8	Gaborone
Burkina Faso (Upper Volta)	274,200	6,942,000	25	Ouagadougou
Burundi	27,834	4,717,703	170	Bujumbura
Cameroon	475,442	9,873,000	21	Yaoundé
Canary Islands (prov. of Spain)	7,273	1,444,626	200	Madrid
Cape Verde	4,033	326,000	81	Praia
Central African Republic	622,984	2,607,800	4	Bangui
Chad	1,284,000	5,018,000	4	Ndjamena
Comoros	2,236	444,000	199	Njazidja (Moroni)
Congo	342,000	1,740,000	5	Brazzaville
Djibouti	23,000	430,000	19	Djibouti
Egypt	1,001,449	48,503,000	48	Al-Qāhirah
Equatorial Guinea	28,051	392,000	14	Malabo
Ethiopia	1,221,900	43,349,900	36	Addis Abeba
Gabon	267,667	1,151,000	4	Libreville
Gambia	11,295	695,886[1]	62	Banjul
Ghana	238,537	12,205,574[1]	51	Accra
Guinea	245,857	6,075,000	25	Conakry
Guinea-Bissau	36,125	890,000	25	Bissau
Ivory Coast	322,464	9,810,000	30	Abidjan
Kenya	582,646	20,333,275	35	Nairobi
Lesotho	30,355	1,527,500	50	Maseru
Liberia	111,369	2,189,030	20	Monrovia
Libya	1,759,540	3,637,488[1]	2	Tarābulus
Madagascar	587,041	9,985,000	17	Antananarivo
Madeira (autonomous reg. of Port.)	794	252,844	318	Lisboa
Malawi	118,484	7,058,800	60	Lilongwe
Mali	1,239,710	8,205,580	7	Bamako
Mauritania	1,032,455	1,850,000	1.8	Nouakchott
Mauritius and dependencies	2,045	1,020,600	499	Port Louis
Morocco	458,730	21,941,000	48	Rabat
Mozambique	792,697	13,961,000	18	Maputo
Namibia	824,295	1,550,000	1.9	Windhoek
Niger	1,266,995	6,115,000	4.8	Niamey
Nigeria	923,768	95,198,000	103	Abuja, Lagos
Réunion (Fr.)	2,510	546,000	218	Saint-Denis
Rwanda	26,338	6,274,000	238	Kigali
Saint Helena and deps. (U.K.)	314	6,565[2]	21	Jamestown
São Tomé and Principe	964	108,165	112	São Tomé
Senegal	196,722	6,445,000	33	Dakar
Seychelles and dependencies	398	65,245	164	Victoria
Sierra Leone	71,740	3,517,530	49	Freetown
Somalia	637,657	4,653,000	7	Muqdisho
South Africa	1,221,037	32,392,000	27	Pretoria, Cape Town
Spanish North Africa	33	129,313[3]	3,612	–
Sudan	2,505,813	21,550,000	9	Al-Khurtūm
Suqutrā/Socotra (Dem. Yemen)	3,626	15,000[3]	4.1	–
Swaziland	17,363	647,415	37	Mbabane
Tanzania	945,087	21,733,000	23	Dar es-Salaam
Togo	56,785	2,960,000	52	Lomé
Tunisia	163,610	7,080,000	43	Tūnis
Uganda	236,036	15,475,000	62	Kampala
Western Sahara	252,210	163,868[2]	0.6	El Aaiún
Zaire	2,345,409	30,362,750	13	Kinshasa
Zambia	752,614	6,665,000	8	Lusaka
Zimbabwe	390,580	8,350,000	20	Harare

[1] year 1984, [2] year 1982, [3] year 1981

population increase in Africa was 2.92%, the birth rate was 45.9, and the death rate 16.6 per 1,000. Relatively few persons live in towns, in 1980 the figure was only 32%. Africa has 16 cities with over one million inhabitants.

Africa's **economy** is typical of that of developing countries. With the exception of the Republic of South Africa, which is an advanced industrial and agricultural country, **agriculture** predominates in the economy of most African countries with the stress on the production of plantation crops. Plant production takes precedence over livestock breeding. Africa produces a major share in the world production of oil crops (groundnuts, palm kernels, palm oil), cocoa, sisal,

27a Tunisia and East Algeria
1 : 15 000 000

map 27

dates and spices. It also possesses great wealth in its forests, especially in the wet equatorial parts of the continent and has rich sources of water power, which are still underdeveloped. The enormous wealth of mineral resources has only been partly prospected. **Mining** is fairly widespread. Africa leads world production in diamonds, gold, platinum, and contributes an important share in uranium, copper, manganese, chromium, cobalt, vanadium, bauxite, antimony and phosphates. The only **industry** that is to be found practically in all African countries is the food industry. **Transport and foreign trade** are of immense importance for the economic development of the continent.

ALGERIA

El Djemhouria El Djazaïria Demokratia Echaabia – République Algérienne Démocratique et Populaire, area 2,381,740 sq.km, population 21,718,000 (1985), **democratic people's republic** (President Bendzhedid Shadlí since 1979).

Administrative units: 48 departments. **Capital:** Alger 1,721,607 inhab. (1983); **other towns** (1983, in 1,000 inhab.): Oran (Ouahran) 663, Constantine 449, Annaba 348, Blida 191, Sétif 187, Sidi bel Abbès 147, Tlemcen 146, Skikda 141, Béjaia 124, Batna 123, Ech Chéliff 119. – **Currency:** Algerian dinar = 100 centimes.
Economy: agricultural country with developing industry, especially mining. **Agriculture : crops** (1983, in 1,000 tonnes): wheat 810, barley, potatoes 610, grapes 350, oranges 230, tangerines 120, lemons, olives 120, olive oil 12, dates 210, figs, fruit, tomatoes 310, tobacco, sugar beet 93: **livestock** (1983, in 1,000 head): cattle 1,400, sheep 13,750, goats 2,780, camels 154, horses, mules 207, asses; poultry 20,000, eggs 21,000 tonnes; fish catch 70,000 tonnes; cork oak 15,000 tonnes, alfalfa. **Mining** (1983, in 1,000 tonnes, metal content): crude petroleum 31,788 (Hassi Messaoud, Edjeleh, Ohanet); natural gas 515,700 TJ (Hassi R'Mel), iron ore 1,966, zinc, lead, mercury 345 tonnes (Ras el Ma), silver, salt 150, phosphates 893, pyrites. Electricity 8,520 mn. kWh (1983). **Industry:** food processing (canning plants, oil processing plants, mills), construction of metallurgy (Annaba), new plants for machinery and chemical industries, petroleum processing. **Production** (1983, in 1,000 tonnes): meat 186, milk 540, wine 264, cement 4,776. – **Communications:** railways 3,900 km, roads 102,000 km. Merchant shipping 1,372,000 GRT. – **Exports:** petroleum, natural gas, wine, fruit.

ANGOLA

República Popular de Angola, area 1,246,700 sq.km, population 8,754,000 (1985), **republic** (President José Eduardo Dos Santos since 1979).

Administrative units: 16 districts. **Capital:** Luanda 1,200,000 inhab. (with agglom. 1982); **other towns** (1982, in 1,000 inhab.): Lobito, 135, Huambo 110, Benguela 60, Cabinda 50. – **Currency:** kwanza = 100 lwei.
Economy: agriculture (1983, in 1,000 tonnes): coffee 27, sisal 20, maize (corn) 275, millet, manioc, cotton, groundnuts, palm oil, sugarcane, bananas, pineapples, tobacco; **livestock** (1983, in 1,000 head): cattle 3,300, goats 950, sheep; fish catch 112,400 tonnes (1983); roundwood 9 mn. cub.m (1983). **Mining** (1983, in 1,000 tonnes): crude petroleum 8,304, diamonds 1,200,000 carats, salt 41. – **Communications:** railways 2,900 km, roads 72,300 km. – **Exports:** petroleum, diamonds, coffee, etc.

BENIN

République populaire du Benin, area 112,622 sq.km, population 3,932,000 (1985), **republic** (President Gen. Mathieu Kérékou since 1972).

Administrative units: 6 departments. **Capital:** Porto-Novo 131,989 inhab., Cotonou (seat of president and government) 215,000 inhab. (1980); **other towns** (in 1,000 inhab.): Parakou, 61, Abomey 50, Natitingou 32. – **Currency:** CFA franc = 100 centimes. – **Economy:** developing agricultural country. **Agriculture** (1983, in 1,000 tonnes): maize, manioc 600, coffee, bananas, palm kernels 75, palm oil 34, groundnuts 50, cotton; **livestock** (1983, in 1,000 head): cattle 880, sheep 1,080, goats 1,000; fish catch 21,100 tonnes. – **Communications:** railways 579 km, roads 7,200 km. – **Exports:** palm kernels and oil.

BOTSWANA

Republic of Botswana, area 600,372 sq.km, population 1,084,900 (1985), **republic, member of the Commonwealth** (President Dr Quett Ketumile Jonny Masire since 1980).

Administrative units: 10 districts. **Capital:** Gaborone 72,200 inhab. (1983); **other towns** (1982, in 1,000 inhab.): Francistown 32, Selebi-Pikwe 29, Serowe 24, Kanye 22. – **Currency:** pula = 100 thebe. – **Economy:** livestock rearing (1983, in 1,000 head): cattle 3,050, sheep 160, goats 670; cultivation of millet, sorghum and maize (corn). **Mining** (1983, in 1,000 tonnes, metal content): nickel 18,200 tonnes, copper 20.3, gold, diamonds 11 mn. carats, coal 395. – **Communications:** railways 716 km, roads 8,026 km. – **Exports:** diamonds, meat, nickel.

BURUNDI

République du Burundi – Republica y'u Burundi, area 27,834 sq.km, population 4,717,703 (1985), **republic** (President Col. Jean-Baptiste Bagaza since 1976).

Administrative units: 8 provinces. **Capital:** Bujumbura 160,000 inhab. (1982). **Density** 170 persons per sq.km. – **Currency:** Burundi franc = 100 centimes. – **Economy:** developing agricultural country with livestock rearing. **Agriculture** (1983, in 1,000 tonnes): coffee 30, maize (corn), sorghum, manioc 500, sweet potatoes 502, bananas 970, groundnuts, tea, cotton; **livestock** (1983, in 1,000 head): cattle 560, sheep 310, goats 760; fish catch 12,000 tonnes in Lake Tanganyika. – **Communications:** roads 5,144 km. – **Exports:** coffee, tea, cotton, hides etc.

map 28

CAMEROON

République Unie du Cameroun, area 475,442 sq.km, population 9,873,000 (1985), **republic** (President Paul Biya since 1982).
Administrative units: 10 provinces. **Capital:** Yaoundé 488,000 inhab. (1983); **other towns** (1983, in 1,000 inhab.): Douala 713 , Nkongsamba 97, Maroua 95, Garoua 88. – **Currency:** CFA franc = 100 centimes.
Economy: developing agricultural country. **Agriculture** (1983, in 1,000 tonnes): cocoa beans 90, coffee 115, bananas 58, groundnuts 100, cotton; **livestock** (1983, in 1,000 head): cattle 3,000, sheep 2,190, goats 2,400, pigs 1,200; fish catch 84,300 tonnes; roundwood 9.9 mn. cub.m, rubber 17,600 tonnes. **Mining:** crude petroleum 5.6 mn. tonnes, tin, gold, titanium. – **Communications:** railways 1,172 km, roads 63,781 km. – **Exports:** petroleum, coffee, cocoa, wood.

CAPE VERDE

República do Cabo Verde, area 4,033 sq.km, population 326,000 (1985) **republic** (President Aristides Pereira since 1975).
Capital: Praia 40,000 inhab. (1982). – **Currency:** Cape Verde escudo = 100 centavos. – **Economy:** maize (corn), sweet potatoes, manioc, sugarcane, groundnuts, bananas, coffee; fishing. Important naval station.

CENTRAL AFRICAN REPUBLIC

Area 622,984 sq.km, population 2,607,800 (1985), **republic** (President André Kolingba since 1986).
Administrative units: 14 prefectures. **Capital:** Bangui 387,143 inhab. (1981). – **Currency:** CFA franc = 100 centimes.
Economy: chiefly agriculture; **crops** (1983, in 1,000 tonnes): cotton lint 13, coffee 16, maize (corn), rice, millet, manioc 800, sweet potatoes, groundnuts, sesame; **livestock** (1983, in 1,000 head): cattle 1,500, goats 960; roundwood. **Mining:** diamonds 295,000 carats, gold. – **Communications:** roads 22,600 km. – **Exports:** diamonds, wood, coffee, cotton etc.

CHAD

République du Tchad, area 1,284,000 sq.km, population 5,018,000 (1985), **republic** (President Hissène Habré since 1982).
Administrative units: 14 prefectures. **Capital:** Ndjamena 303,000 inhab. (1980). – **Currency:** CFA franc = 100 centimes.
Economy: backward agricultural country. **Agriculture:** cotton lint, maize (corn), rice, millet, manioc, sweet potatoes, groundnuts, sugarcane, dates, sesame, tobacco; **livestock** (1983, in 1,000 head): cattle 3,600, sheep 2,300, goats 2,100, camels; roundwood; fish catch 110,000 tonnes (1983). – **Communications:** roads 40,000 km. – **Exports:** cotton, cattle, meat.

COMOROS

République fédérale et islamique des Comores, area 2,236 sq.km, population 444,000 (1985), **republic** (President Ahmed Abdallah Abderemane since 1978).
Capital: Njazidja (Moroni) 16,000 inhab. (1982). **Density** 199 persons per sq.km. **Currency:** CFA franc = 100 centimes. – **Production for export:** vanilla, ylang-ylang, cloves, sisal, coconuts, copra, cinnamon, essential oils.

CONGO

République populaire du Congo, area 342,000 sq.km, population 1,740,000 (1985), **republic** (President Colonel Denis Sassou-Nguesso since 1979).
Administrative units: 9 regions. **Capital:** Brazzaville 422,402 inhab. (1980, with agglom.); **other towns:** Pointe-Noire 185,105 inhab. – **Currency:** CFA franc = 100 centimes.
Economy: agricultural country. **Agriculture** (1983, in 1,000 tonnes): manioc 600, maize (corn), sweet potatoes, coffee, cocoa beans, palm oil 15, groundnuts 15, sugarcane, bananas; fish catch 31,900 tonnes; roundwood 2.2 mn. cub.m. **Mining** (1983, in 1,000 tonnes, metal content): crude petroleum 4,236, lead, zinc, gold, copper. – **Communications:** railways 802 km, roads 12,000 km, navigable waterways 5,000 km. – **Exports:** petroleum, wood, coffee, cocoa.

DJIBOUTI

République de Djibouti, area 23,000 sq.km, population 430,000 (1985), **republic** (President Hassan Gouled Aptidon since 1977).
Capital: Djibouti 120,000 (1983). – **Currency:** Djibouti franc = 100 centimes. – **Economy:** coffee grown for export; **livestock** (1983, in 1,000 head): goats 540, sheep, camels 52. – **Communications:** railways 90 km, roads 1,875 km.

EGYPT

Al-Jumhūrīya Misr al-'Arabīya, area 1,001,449 sq.km, population 48,503,000 (1985), **republic** (President Muhammad Hosni Mubarak since 1981).
Administrative units: 25 governorates. **Capital:** Al-Qāhirah (Cairo) 6,780,000 inhab. (1980) with agglom. 9,750,000 (1982);

map 28

towns (1980, in 1,000 inhab.): Kumasi 476, Tema 346, Sekondi-Takoradi 226, Tamale 196, Asamankese 135, Bolgatanga 110, Cape Coast 86. – **Currency:** cedi = 100 pesewas. **Economy:** based on agriculture specialized in products for export. Rich resources of raw materials. **Agriculture** (1983, in 1,000 tonnes): cocoa beans 160 (Ashanti region), maize (corn) 260, millet, rice, manioc 1,500, sugarcane, groundnuts, palm kernels 30, palm oil 25, coconuts 160, copra 7, coffee, oranges 35, lemons, pineapples, bananas, tomatoes 165; **livestock** (1983, in 1,000 head): cattle 800, sheep 2,000, goats 2,000, pigs 375; poultry 13,000; fish catch 228,000 tonnes (1983); roundwood 9.8 mn. cub.m (1983), natural rubber 3,000 tonnes. **Mining** (1983, in 1,000 tonnes, metal content): manganese 83, gold 8,602 kg, diamonds 369,000 carats, bauxite 70, salt. Electricity 2,589 mn. kWh (1983), of this 99% hydro-electric power stations (on the R. Volta at Akosombo). – **Communications:** railways 960 km, roads 47,190 km. Merchant shipping 186,000 GRT (1984). River transport on the R. Volta. – **Exports:** cocoa, gold, wood, diamonds, manganese.

GUINEA

République de Guinée, area 245,857 sq.km, population 6,075,000 (1985), republic (President Col. Lansana Conté since 1984).

Administrative units: 34 regions. **Capital:** Conakry 763,000 inhab. (1980): **other towns** (1980, in 1,000 inhab.): Labé 253, Kankan 229, Kindia 150. – **Currency:** Guinean franc = 100 centimes. **Economy:** agricultural products for export, mineral mining. **Agriculture** (1983, in 1,000 tonnes): rice 300, maize (corn), manioc 640, sisal, groundnuts 75, palm oil 45, coffee, bananas 110, pineapples, tobacco; **livestock** (1983, in 1,000 head): cattle 1,900, sheep 450, goats 440; roundwood 3.6 mn. cub.m (1983). **Mining** (1983, in 1,000 tonnes, metal content): bauxite 12,986 (second world producer, deposits Boké, Fria), diamonds 45,000 carats. Electricity 499 mn. kWh. **Industry:** production of aluminium, food processing. – **Communications:** railways 1,100 km, roads 30,000 km. – **Exports:** bauxite and aluminium 96%, coffee, groundnuts, diamonds, bananas, pineapples etc.

GUINEA-BISSAU

República da Guiné-Bissau, area 36,125 sq.km, population 890,000 (1985), republic (Head of State Chairman of the State Council Maj. João Bernardo Vieira since 1980).

Capital: Bissau 110,000 inhab. (1981). – **Currency:** Guinean peso = 100 centavos. – **Economy:** agricultural country. **Agriculture** (1983, in 1,000 tonnes): rice, groundnuts 30, palm kernels 5, palm oil, coconuts 25; roundwood 500,000 cub.m (1983).

IVORY COAST

République de Côte d'Ivoire, area 322,464 sq.km, population 9,810,000 (1985), republic (President Félix Houphouet-Boigny since 1960).

Administrative units: 34 departments. **Capitals:** Abidjan 1,600,000 inhab. (with agglom.; 1983) and Yamoussoukro 80,000 inhab. (1983); **other towns** (1983, in 1,000 inhab.): Bouaké 275, Korhogo 125, Man 110, Daloa 100, Grand Bassam 65. – **Currency:** CFA franc = 100 centimes. **Economy:** agricultural country, export products grown on plantations. **Agriculture** (1983, in 1,000 tonnes): millet, sorghum, rice 430, manioc 800, sugarcane 2,500, cotton lint 66, sesame, palm oil 133, coconuts 161, copra 23, groundnuts, coffee 225, cocoa beans 400 (leading world producer), bananas 150, pineapples 350; **livestock** (1983, in 1,000 head): cattle 780, sheep 1,380; fish catch 94,000 tonnes; roundwood 11.8 mn. cub.m, natural rubber 30,500 tonnes (1983). **Mining** (1983, in 1,000 tonnes): crude petroleum, 1,158. Electricity 1,932 mn. kWh (1983). **Processing** of agricultural products. – **Communications:** railways 665 km, roads 46,400 km. – **Exports:** cocoa, coffee, wood, bananas.

KENYA

Jamhuri ya Kenya, area 582,646 sq.km, population 20,333,275 (1985), republic, member of the Commonwealth (President Daniel Arap Moi since 1978).

Administrative units: 8 provinces. **Capital:** Nairobi 1,334,000 inhab. (with agglom.; 1983), **other towns** (1983, in 1,000 inhab.): Mombasa 504, Kisumu 189, Nakuru 120. Average annual rate of population increase 4.1%. – **Currency:** Kenyan shilling = 100 cents.
Economy: agricultural country with developing livestock production. **Agriculture** (1983, in 1,000 tonnes): maize (corn) 2,000, wheat, barley, rice, millet, manioc, sweet potatoes; on plantations: cotton, sisal 51, sugarcane, pyrethrum 11 (leading world producer), groundnuts, sesame, palm oil, copra, coffee 90, tea 112, pineapples 160, bananas 140; **livestock** (1983, in 1,000 head): cattle 11,500, sheep 6,500, goats 8,000, camels 620; poultry; fish catch 97,500 tonnes (1983);

add page 126

map 28

other towns (1976, in 1,000 inhab.): Al-Iskandarîyah (Alexandria) 2,415 (1978), Al-Jîzah 1,247, Shubrâ al Khaymah 394, Al-Mahallah al Kubrâ 293, Tantâ 285, Bûr Saʿîd (Port Said) 263, Al-Mansûrah 258, Asyût 214, Az-Zaqâzîq 203, As-Suways (Suez) 194, Damanhûr 189. – **Currency:** Egyptian pound = 100 piastres.
Economy: agricultural and industrial country; cultivated land only 2.8% in the Nile delta and valley. **Agriculture: crops** (1983, in 1,000 tonnes): wheat 1,996, maize (corn) 3,510, barley, rice 2,440, potatoes 1,150, sweet potatoes, sugarcane 9,000, cotton-seed 665, -lint 410; groundnuts, sesame, fruit: oranges 1,250, tangerines, lemons, grapes 310, bananas 140, dates 440 (leading world producer), figs-vegetables: tomatoes 2,500, onions 660, water-melons 1,200; **livestock** (1983, in 1,000 head); cattle 1,826, buffaloes 2,393, camels 80, asses 1,775, sheep 1,394, goats 1,498, poultry 28,000; fish catch 140,000 tonnes. **Mining** (1983, in 1,000 tonnes, metal content): crude petroleum 36,036 (Gulf of Suez region), natural gas 59,320 TJ, iron ore 2,064, phosphates 647, titanium, salt 918. Electricity 23 billion kWh (1983), of this 48% hydro-electric power stations; chief Aswân dam on the R. Nile. Most developed **industries:** textiles and food processing. **Production** (1983, in 1,000 tonnes): pig iron 196, crude steel 125, cement 4,080, nitrogenous fertilizers 406, cotton yarn 229, meat 507, milk 650, sugar 812; 44 billion cigarettes. – **Communications:** mainly along the Nile valley and Suez Canal zone; railways 4,385 km, roads 10,708 km, navigable waterways 3,100 km. Merchant shipping 779,000 GRT. **Suez Canal:** opened in 1869, length Bûr Saʿîd – As-Suways 161 km, width on level 70–125 m, depth 11–12 m, passage permitted to vessels up to 10.36 m draught. Civil aviation (1984): 35.3 mn. km flown and 2,786,000 passengers carried. – **Tourism:** 1,498,000 visitors (1983). – **Exports:** petroleum, cotton, fruit, rice.

EQUATORIAL GUINEA

República de Guinea Ecuatorial, area 28,051 sq.km, population 392,000 (1985), republic (President Lieut.-Col. Theodoro Obiango Nguema Mbasogo since 1979).

Administrative units: 2 provinces. **Capital:** Malabo 80,000 inhab. – **Currency:** ekuele = 100 centimos. **Agriculture:** manioc, sweet potatoes, palm oil, coffee, cocoa beans; roundwood. – **Exports:** coffee, cocoa, wood.

ETHIOPIA

Hybretesebawit Itjopja, area 1,221,900 sq.km, population 43,349,900 (1985), republic (Head of State Chairman of the Provisional Military Administration Council Lieut.-Col. Menghistu Haile Mariam since 1975).

Administrative units: 14 provinces. **Capital:** Addis Abeba 1,408,068 inhab. (1982); **other towns** (1982, in 1000 inhab.): Asmera 474, Dire Dawa 92, Gonder 86, Dese 83, Nazret 81. – **Currency:** birr = 100 cents. **Economy:** agricultural country with predominantly livestock production. **Agriculture** (1983, in 1,000 tonnes): wheat 950, barley 1,200, maize (corn) 1,600, millet, sorghum 1400, potatoes, sugarcane 1,600, cotton lint 27, flax, groundnuts, sesame 36, castor beans 12, coffee 204, bananas, legumes, tobacco; **livestock** (1983, in 1,000 head): cattle 26,300, sheep 23,400, goats 17,240, camels 1,010, horses 1,560, mules 1,460, asses 3,905; poultry 55,000; roundwood 29.8 mn. cub.m (1983). **Mining** (1983): gold 435 kg, platinum, salt 124,000 tonnes. **Production** (1983, in 1,000 tonnes): meat 540, milk 610. – **Communications:** railways 1,000 km, roads 23,158 km. – **Exports:** coffee, hides, skins, oil seeds, meat.

GABON

République Gabonaise, area 267,667 sq.km, population 1,151,000 (1985), republic (President Omar Bongo since 1967).

Administrative units: 9 provinces. **Capital:** Libreville 350,000 inhab. (with agglom., 1982); **other towns** (1982, in 1,000 inhab.): Port-Gentil 164, Franceville 75, Lambaréné 24. – **Currency:** CFA franc = 100 centimes. **Economy:** agricultural country with mining and wood processing industries. Forests cover 75% of the land area. **Crops:** rice, manioc, coffee, cocoa beans, bananas; roundwood 2.6 mn. cub.m (1983). **Mining** (1983, in 1,000 tonnes, metal content): crude petroleum 7,476, natural gas 6,000 TJ, manganese 947, uranium 1,042 tonnes, gold. – **Communications:** railways 410 km, roads 7,174 km. – **Exports:** petroleum (80%), wood, manganese, uranium, cocoa, coffee.

GAMBIA

Republic of Gambia, area 11,295 sq.km, population 695,886 (1984), republic, member of the Commonwealth (President Al Hadji Sir Dawda Kairaba Jawara since 1970).
Capital: Banjul 50,000 inhab. (1983). – **Currency:** dalasi = 100 bututs. – **Economy:** agriculture specialized mainly in growing groundnuts (106,000 tonnes), rice, millet, cotton, palm kernels and oil, cattle. – **Communications:** roads 3,083 km, goods transport on the R. Gambia. – **Exports:** groundnuts and groundnut oil.

GHANA

Republic of Ghana, area 238,537 sq.km, population 12,205,574 (1984), republic, member of the Commonwealth (Chairman of the Provisional National Defence Council Flight Lieutenant Jerry John Rawlings since 1982).
Administrative units: 10 regions. **Capital:** Accra 1,176,000 inhab. (1980, with agglomeration, 1,575,000); **other**

map 29

roundwood 29.3 mn. cub.m (1983). **Mining** gold, niobium, salt, soda. Electricity 2,166 mn. kWh (1983). **Industries:** processing of agricultural products, canning plants, processing of petroleum, fertilizers and textiles. **Production** (1983, in 1,000 tonnes): cement 1,280, sugar 355, milk 1,300. – **Communications:** railways 2,730 km, roads 53,500 km. – **Exports:** coffee, tea, petroleum products, sisal etc.

LESOTHO

Kingdom of Lesotho – 'Muso oa Lesotho, **area 30,355 sq.km, population 1,527,500** (1985), **kingdom, member of the Commonwealth** (King Moshoeshoe II since 1966).
Administrative units: 10 districts. **Capital:** Maseru 75,000 inhab. (1981). – **Currency:** maluti = 100 licente. – **Economy:** developing agriculture and livestock rearing. **Agriculture:** wheat, maize (corn), sorghum, **livestock** (1983, in 1,000 head): cattle 640, sheep 1,690, goats 1,000, wool 5,000 tonnes. **Mining** of diamonds. – **Exports:** wool, livestock, diamonds.

LIBERIA

Republic of Liberia, area 111,369 sq.km, population 2,189,030 (1985) **republic** (President Gen. Samuel Kanyon Doe since 1980).
Administrative units: 9 provinces. **Capital:** Monrovia 306,500 inhab. (1981). – **Currency:** Liberian dollar = 100 cents. **Economy:** agricultural country with a relatively developed mining industry. **Agriculture** (1983, in 1,000 tonnes): rice 250, manioc 300, palm kernels 8, palm oil 30, coffee 10, bananas 78, pineapples; roundwood 4.6 mn. cub.m (1983), natural rubber 76,000 tonnes. **Mining** (1983, in 1,000 tonnes): iron ore 9,671 (metal content), gold 479 kg, diamonds 462,000 carats. – **Communications:** railways 520 km, roads 10,219 km. Merchant shipping 62,025,000 GRT (1984, first place in the world). – **Exports:** iron ore, natural rubber, diamonds, wood, coffee.

LIBYA

Al-Jamahiriyah Al-Arabiya Al-Libya Al-Shabiya Al-Ishtirakiya, area 1,759,540 sq.km, population 3,637,488 (1984), **republic** (Secretary General – Gen. Muammar al-Qadhafi since 1969).
Administrative units: 10 provinces. **Capital:** Tarābulus (Tripoli) 989,000 inhab. (1982); **other towns** (1982, in 1,000 inhab.): Banghāzī 650, Misrātah 285, Zāwiyat al-Baydā 96, Tubruq 72. – **Currency:** Libyan dinar = 1000 dirhams.
Economy: developing agricultural country with major petroleum mining. Arable land 1.2% only on the coast and in the oases, unproductive land 91.1%. **Agriculture** (1983, in 1,000 tonnes): barley 195, olives 104, olive oil 16, dates 96, figs, agrums, tobacco, alfalfa; raising of livestock: sheep 4,800,000, goats, camels. **Mining** (1983, in 1,000 tonnes): crude petroleum 49,368, deposits Sarīr, Zaltan, Jālū etc.; pipelines to the coast; natural gas 384,500 TJ, salt. – **Communications:** roads 13,800 km. Merchant shipping 855,000 GRT (1984). – **Exports:** petroleum 93%.

MADAGASCAR

République démocratique de Madagascar – Repolika demokratika Malagasy, **area 587,041 sq.km, population 9,985,000** (1985), **republic,** (President Capt. Didier Ratsiraka since 1975).
Administrative units: 6 provinces. **Capital:** Antananarivo 800,000 inhab. (1982); **other towns** (1982, in 1,000 inhab.): Fianarantsoa 350, Antsirabe 300, Toamasina 200, Mahajanga 90. – **Currency:** Malagasy franc = 100 centimes.
Economy: developing agricultural country. **Agriculture** (1983, in 1,000 tonnes): rice 2,147, maize (corn), sweet potatoes 492, manioc 1,726, cotton, sisal 13, sugarcane 1,464, groundnuts, coconuts, oranges 56, bananas 297, pineapples, pepper 2.9, vanilla 3.3, cloves, coffee 81, tobacco; **livestock** (1983, in 1,000 head): cattle 10,322, pigs 1,300, sheep 630, goats 1,750, poultry 18,000; fish catch 54,500 tonnes; roundwood 6.3 mn. cub.m. **Mining** (1983, in 1,000 tonnes, metal content): chromium 12, gold, ilmenite, graphite 15.4, salt 30, mica. – **Communications:** railways 884 km, roads 40,000 km. – **Exports:** coffee, cloves, vanilla, sugar, chromium.

MALAWI

Republic of Malawi, area 118,484 sq.km, population 7,058,800 (1985), **member of the Commonwealth** (President Dr Hastings Kamuzu Banda since 1966).
Administrative units: 3 regions. **Capital:** Lilongwe 103,000 inhab. (1981); **other towns** (1981, in 1,000 inhab.): Blantyre 229, Zomba 25. – **Currency:** Malawi-kwacha = 100 tambals. – **Economy:** developing agricultural country. **Agriculture** (1983, in 1,000 tonnes): maize (corn) 1,500, rice, sorghum, manioc, sweet potatoes, cotton, tobacco 72, sugarcane 1,830, groundnuts 180, tung oil, tea 38, bananas; **livestock** (1983, in 1,000 head): cattle 900, goats 750; inland fish catch 58,400 tonnes. **Deposits** of coal, iron ore, gold, uranium, bauxite and asbestos. – **Communications:** railways 789 km, roads 16,500 km. – **Exports:** tobacco, tea, groundnuts, cotton.

MALI

République du Mali, area 1,239,710 sq.km, population 8,205,580 (1985), **republic** (President Gen. Moussa Traoré since 1968).
Administrative units: 6 regions. **Capital:** Bamako 570,000 inhab. (1981, with agglomeration); **other towns** (in 1,000

map 29

NAMIBIA

Suidwes-Afrika – South-West Africa, area 824,295 sq.km, population 1,550,000 (1985), trust territory of the United Nations administered by the Republic of South Africa. Administrative units: 5 bantustans. Capital: Windhoek 88,700 inhab. – Currency: South African rand = 100 cents. – Economy: livestock (1983, in 1,000 head): cattle 1,900, sheep 5,500 (4 mn. karakul skins), goats 2,200; fish catch 341,000 tonnes (1983). Mining (1983, in 1,000 tonnes, metal content): diamonds 963,000 carats, tin 800 tonnes, zinc 33.2, lead 33.8, copper 52.1, pyrites 202, silver 110 tonnes, uranium 3,719 tonnes, salt 137. – Communications: railways 2,600 km, roads 34,915 km.

NIGER

République du Niger, area 1,266,995 sq.km, population 6,115,000 (1985), republic (President of the Military Council Maj.-Gen. Seyni Kountche since 1974).
Administrative units: 7 departments. Capital: Niamey 399,100 inhab. (1983). – Currency: CFA franc = 100 centimes. – Economy: developing agricultural country with animal production predominating. Agriculture (1983, in 1,000 tonnes): millet 1,325, sorghum, rice, manioc, cotton, sugarcane, groundnuts 74, dates; livestock (1983, in 1,000 head): cattle 3,521, sheep 3,448, goats 7,478, horses 283, asses 501, camels 410. Mining (1983): uranium 4,265 tonnes, tin. – Communications: roads 8,547 km, river transport on the R. Niger. – Exports: uranium (over 75%), groundnuts, cattle.

NIGERIA

Federal Republic of Nigeria, area 923, 768 sq.km, population 95,198,000 (1985), federal republic, member of the Commonwealth (President Maj.-Gen. Ibrahim Babangida since 1985).
Administrative units: 19 states. Capital: Abuja 80,000 inhab. (1982) and Lagos 1,404,000 inhab. (1982, with agglom. 3.7 mn. inhab.); other towns (1982, in 1,000 inhab.): Ibadan 1,009, Ogbomosho 514, Kano 475, Oshogbo 336, Ilorin 335, Abeokuta 301, Port Harcourt 289, Ilesha 267, Zaria 267, Onitsha 262, Iwo 255, Ado-Ekiti 253, Kaduna 238, Mushin 234, Maiduguri 225. Density 103 persons per sq.km. – Currency: naira = 100 kobo. Economy: agricultural country with rapidly developing industry. Agriculture (1983, in 1,000 tonnes): maize (corn) 1,600, rice 1,000, millet 2,300, sorghum 2,660, manioc 9,950, sweet potatoes 260, cotton -seed 30, -lint 15; sugarcane 1,150, coconuts 90, palm kernels 360, palm oil 710, groundnuts 450, sesame 75, coffee, cocoa beans 150, tropical fruit 2,470, vegetables 3,600, tomatoes, tobacco 15; livestock (1983, in 1,000 head): cattle 12,300, sheep 12,850, goats 26,300, pigs 1,300, asses 700, poultry 150,000, eggs 235,000 tonnes; fish catch 515,200 tonnes (1983); roundwood 85.8 mn. cub.m, natural rubber 49,000 tonnes (1983). Mining (1983, in 1,000 tonnes): crude petroleum 61,150 (deposits in the Niger delta), natural gas 220,000 TJ, coal 40, tin 1,535 tonnes, columbite 182 tonnes (1982). Electricity 8,500 mn. kWh (1983), of this 60% hydro-electric power stations. Production (1983, in 1,000 tonnes): food processing of domestic agricultural production; beer 4 mn. hl, meat 826, milk 357; 10 billion cigarettes, cement 3,600, woven cotton fabrics 423 mn. sq.m. – Communications: railways 4,300 km, roads 115,000 km. Merchant shipping 442,000 GRT (1984), river transport. – Exports: petroleum 98%, cocoa, rubber, tin, palm kernels, groundnut oil.

RWANDA

République rwandaise – Republica y'u Rwanda, area 26,338 sq.km, population 6,274,000 (1985), republic (President Gen. Juvénal Habyalimana since 1973).
Administrative units: 10 prefectures. Capital: Kigali 155,000 inhab. (1981). – Currency: Rwanda franc = 100 centimes. – Economy: developing agricultural country. Agriculture (1983): coffee 28,000 tonnes, sorghum, potatoes, manioc, sweet potatoes, groundnuts, tea, tobacco; livestock: cattle 652,000 head, sheep and goats; roundwood 5.2 mn. cub.m (1983). – Exports: coffee, tin, tea, tungsten.

SÃO TOMÉ AND PRINCIPE

República democrática de São Tomé e Principe, area 964 sq.km, population 108,165 (1985), republic (President Dr Manuel Pinto da Costa since 1975).
Capital: São Tomé 17,000 inhab. (1979). – Currency: dobra = 100 centavos. – Economy: agriculture (1983): coffee, cocoa beans 8,000 tonnes, coconuts 42,000 tonnes, copra, palm oil, spice.

add page 130

map 29

inhab): Ségou 79, Mopti 65, Sikasso 57. – **Currency:** Mali franc = 100 centimes. – **Economy:** agricultural country with predominating livestock production. **Agriculture** (1983, in 1,000 tonnes): rice 122, maize (corn), millet, manioc, sweet potatoes, cotton -seed 65, -lint 43, groundnuts 70; **livestock** (1983, in 1,000 head): cattle 5,400, sheep 6,450, goats 7,500, horses 140, asses 425, camels 240, poultry 14,000; inland fish catch 33,000 tonnes. Mining (1983, in 1,000 tonnes): gold 404 kg, salt 6.– **Communications:** railways 645 km, roads 18,600 km, river transport on the R. Niger. – **Exports:** livestock, cotton, groundnuts, fish.

MAURITANIA

République Islamique de Mauritanie, area 1,032,455 sq.km, population 1,850,000 (1985), republic (Head of State Chairman of the Military Council Lieut.-Col. Maaouya Ould Sidi Ahmed Taya since 1984).

Administrative units: 12 regions and 1 capital district. **Capital:** Nouakchott 150,000 inhab. (1982). – **Currency:** ouguiya = 5 khoums. – **Economy:** agricultural country with predominating livestock production. **Agriculture:** growing of millet, maize (corn), rice, dates 11,000 tonnes (1983), gum arabic; **livestock** (1983, in 1,000 head): cattle 1,500, sheep 5,000, goats 3,000, camels 750; fish catch 53,800 tonnes (1983). **Mining:** iron ore 4,183,000 tonnes (1983, metal content), copper, ilmenite. – **Communications:** railways 652 km, roads 7,800 km. – **Exports:** iron ore 65%, fish, cattle, gum arabic.

MAURITIUS AND DEPENDENCIES

Area 2,045 sq.km, population 1,020,600 (1985), independent state, member of the Commonwealth (Prime Minister Aneerood Jugnauth since 1984).

Dependencies: Agaloga Is., Cargados-Carajos Shoals, Rodrigues Island (109 sq.km) is now part of Mauritius. **Administrative units:** 9 districts. **Capital:** Port Louis 147,386 inhab. (1981, with agglomeration 415,000 inhab.): other towns (in 1,000 inhab.): Beau-Bassin 87, Curepipe 57. **Density** 499 persons per sq.km. – **Currency:** Mauritius rupee = 100 cents.

Economy: agricultural country with monocultural cultivation of sugarcane – 5,500,000 tonnes in 1983; coconuts, copra, coffee, tea, bananas, vanilla, tobacco. Mining of salt. Food industry (sugar 567,000 tonnes in 1983), petroleum refinery.– **Communications:** roads 2,000 km. – **Exports:** sugar 60%, tea etc.

MOROCCO

al-Mamlaka al-Maghrebia, area 458,730 sq.km, population 21,941,000 (1985), kingdom (King Hassan II since 1961).

Administrative units: 31 provinces and 2 urban prefectures. **Capital:** Rabat 841,000 inhab. (1983, with agglomeration); other towns (1983, in 1,000 inhab.): Casablanca (Dar-el-Beida) 2,500 (with agglom.), Fès 562, Marrakech 548, Meknès 486, Oujda 470, Kenitra 450, Tétouan 371, Tanger 304, Safi 256. – **Currency:** dirham = 100 centimes.

Economy: agricultural country with a relatively developed mining industry. **Agriculture** (1983, in 1,000 tonnes): wheat 1,971, barley 1,228, maize (corn), rice, potatoes, cotton, sugar beet 2,400, groundnuts, olives 250, olive oil 25, oranges 691, tangerines 245, lemons, grapes 201, dates 66, figs, tomatoes 390, tobacco; **livestock** (1983, in 1,000 head): cattle 3,000, sheep 15,000, goats 6,270, asses 1,550, horses 315, camels 240, poultry 25,000; fish catch 439,000 tonnes; roundwood 1.7 mn. cub.m (1983). Mining (1983, in 1,000 tonnes, metal content): coal 816, natural gas, iron ore 153, manganese 37, copper 23, lead 102, zinc 7, cobalt 700 tonnes (1982), antimony 998 tonnes, silver 88 tonnes, phosphates 20,106 (deposits Khouribga and Youssoufia), pyrites, fluorite. Electricity 6,010 mn. kWh (1983). **Industry:** developed food processing (mills, oil presses, sugar refineries; fish, fruit and vegetable canning plants). Traditional textile industry; developing chemical and construction industries; processing of petroleum. **Production** (1983, in 1,000 tonnes): meat 297, milk 800, wine 83, cement 3,852. – **Communications:** railways 1,786 km, roads 25,700 km. Tourism 1,877,000 visitors (1983). – **Exports:** phosphates, citrus fruit, canned fish etc.

MOZAMBIQUE

República Popular de Moçambique, area 792,697 sq.km, population 13,961,000 (1985), people's republic (President Joaquim Alberto Chissano since 1986).

Administrative units: 11 districts. **Capital:** Maputo 785,500 inhab. (1982): other towns (1980, in 1,000 inhab.: Beira 350, Quelimane 184, Nampula 126 (1970). – **Currency:** Metical = 100 centavos.

Economy: developing agricultural country. **Agriculture** (1983, in 1,000 tonnes): maize (corn) 200, rice 30, sugarcane 1,000, cotton -seed 35, -lint 17, sisal 4, groundnuts 60, coconuts 400, copra 65, cashew nuts 70, tea 15, citrus fruit, bananas; **livestock** (1983, in 1,000 head): cattle 1,440, goats; roundwood 14.7 mn. cub.m (1983). Mining: coal 380,000 tonnes (1983), salt, beryllium, fluorite. Electricity 6,426 mn. kWh, of this 90% from hydroelectric power stations. – **Communications:** railways 3,843 km, roads 39,173 km. – **Exports:** cashew nuts, sugar, cotton, tea, wood.

map 30

SENEGAL

République du Sénégal, area 196,722 sq.km, population 6,445,000 (1985), **republic** (President Abdou Diouf since 1981).
Administrative units: 10 regions. **Capital:** Dakar 1,048,000 inhab. (with agglom. 1980); **other towns** (1979, in 1,000 inhab.): Thiès 127, Kaolack 116, Saint-Louis 97, Ziguinchor 79. – **Currency:** CFA franc = 100 centimes.
Economy: agricultural country, cultivates chiefly groundnuts. **Agriculture** (1983, in 1,000 tonnes): groundnuts 650, millet 352, rice 70, oranges, bananas; **livestock** (1983, in 1,000 head): cattle 2,250, sheep 2,100, goats 1,050, fish catch 212,900 tonnes; roundwood 3.9 mn. cub.m (1983). **Mining** (1983, in 1,000 tonnes): phosphates 1,397, salt 170. – **Communications:** railways 1,400 km, roads 14,500 km, river transport. – **Exports:** groundnut oil, phosphates.

SEYCHELLES AND DEPENDENCIES

Republic of Seychelles, area 398 sq.km, population 65,245 (1985), **republic, member of the Commonwealth** (President F. Albert René since 1977).
Capital: Victoria 23,000 inhab. (1982). – **Currency:** Seychelles rupee = 100 cents. – **Economy:** coconuts, copra, cinnamon, vanilla; cattle and pig breeding, fish catch. Mining of phosphates and sea salt.

SIERRA LEONE

Republic of Sierra Leone, area 71,740 sq.km, population 3,517,530 (1985), **republic, member of the Commonwealth** (President Joseph Momoh since 1985).
Administrative units: 3 provinces and capital district. **Capital:** Freetown 300,000 inhab. (1980). – **Currency:** leone = 100 cents. – **Economy:** developing agricultural country with important mineral mining. **Agriculture** (1983, in 1,000 tonnes): rice 609, maize (corn), millet, manioc, sweet potatoes, palm kernels 30, palm oil 45, groundnuts, piassaba, coffee 19, cocoa beans, citrus fruit 67; fish catch 53,000 tonnes; roundwood 8.1 mn. cub.m. **Mining** (1983, in 1,000 tonnes, metal content): iron ore 190, chromium, diamonds 345,000 carats, bauxite 600, rutile 47.7. – **Communications:** railways 597 km, roads 8,000 km. – **Exports:** diamonds, coffee, cocoa, rutile, bauxite, iron ore.

SOMALIA

Al-Jumhouriya As-Somaliya Al-Domocradia, area 637,657 sq.km, population 4,653,000 (1985), **republic** (President of the Supreme Revolutionary Council Marshal Mohammed Siyad Barre since 1969).
Administrative units: 8 regions. **Capital:** Muqdisho 500,000 inhab. (1981); **other towns** (1981, in 1,000 inhab): Hargeysa 90, Kismaayo 70, Berbera 65, Marka 60. – **Currency:** Somalian shilling = 100 centimes.
Economy: agricultural country. **Agriculture** (1983, in 1,000 tonnes): maize (corn), sorghum, cotton, sugarcane 480, groundnuts, sesame, bananas 80; fish catch 15,500 tonnes (1983); collection of gum arabic; **livestock** (1983, in 1,000 head): cattle 4,050, sheep 10,400, goats 16,900, camels 5,650 (leading world population). – **Communications:** roads 19,380 km. – **Exports:** cattle, meat, bananas.

SOUTH AFRICA

Republiek van Suid-Africa – Republic of South Africa, area 1,221,037 sq.km, population 32,392,000 (1985), **republic** (President Pieter Willem Botha since 1984).
Administrative units: 4 provinces, 4 bantustans. **Capital:** Pretoria: 739,043 inhab. (1980); Cape Town (legislative capital 213,830 inhab.; with agglom. 1,500,000); **other towns** (1980, in 1,000 inhab.): Johannesburg 1,726 (3,500 with agglomeration), Durban 961 (+Pinetown), Port Elizabeth 492, Vereeniging 448 (+Vanderbijlpark, Sasolburg), Germiston 222, Benoni 207, Bloemfontein 198, Pietermaritzburg 192, Springs 174. – **Currency:** rand = 100 cents.
Economy: highly developed industrial and agricultural country with enormous mineral wealth, economically the most important country of Africa. **Agriculture** (1983, in 1,000 tonnes): wheat 1,770, maize (corn) 3,910, sorghum 195, potatoes 900, cotton -seed 50, -lint 27; sugarcane 13,370, sunflower seeds 202, groundnuts 92, soya beans, oranges 483, lemons 48, grapefruits 108, bananas 115, pineapples 237, grapes 1,200, fruit, tobacco 38; **livestock** (1983, in 1,000 head): cattle 13,086, goats 5,950, sheep 31,750, pigs 1,450, horses, eggs 180,000 tonnes; fish catch 600,000 tonnes, whaling; roundwood 20.5 mn. cub.m. **Mining:** in a number of branches leading world output (1983, in 1,000 tonnes): coal 139,557, iron ore 10,459, manganese 1,154 (second world producer), chromium 703 (second world producer), copper 211, tin 2,668 tonnes, zinc 110, nickel 20.5, antimony 6,302 tonnes, lead 80, rutile 47, vanadium 8,074 tonnes (second world producer), zircon 125, gold 679,527 kg (leading world producer), silver 173 tonnes, platinum 75,000 kg (leading world producer), magnesite 21, uranium 9,600 tonnes (leading world producer), diamonds 10,311,400 carats, salt 727, phosphates 2,742, pyrites 1,475, sulphur, mica, asbestos 211. Electricity 108,961 mn. kWh (1982). **Principal industries:** iron metallurgy, machinery, shipbuilding, chemical, construction, textiles and foodstuffs. **Production:** (1983, in 1,000 tonnes): pig iron 5,208, coke 1,795, crude steel 7,068, copper 192, aluminium 163, nitrogenous fertilizers 397, phosphate fertilizers 420, synthetic rubber 27.5, cement 7,908, paper 896, cotton yarn 40.8, woven cotton fabrics 148 mn. sq.m., meat 1,096, butter 19, milk 2,600, beer 11.6 mn. hl, wine 9.2 mn. hl; 31.1 billion tobacco products. – **Communications:** railways 23,400 km, roads 229,372 km. Merchant shipping 712,000 GRT (1984). – **Exports:** diamonds, food products, metals, minerals, textiles, machines.

Equator

SOMALIA

Kismaayo

UGANDA
Kasese Kampala Eldoret Kisumu Isiolo Jamame
Mbarara Entebbe Jinja Nakuru Nyeri Embu Garissa
Biseruf Bukoba Lake Victoria **NAIROBI** Nanyuki
RWANDA Kibali Musoma Magadi L. Natron
BURUNDI Bujumbura Mwanza **KENYA**
Gitega Shinyanga L. Eyasi Arusha Tsavo Galana Malindi
Kigoma-Ujiji Tabora Singida Moshi Voi
Moba Karema Manyoni Kondoa Irangi **MOMBASA**
Mpanda Dodoma Korogwe Tanga Pemba I.
T A N Z A N I A Chake Chake Zanzibar
Kasama Isoka Manda Morogoro Zanzibar I.
Mansa Mbala L. Rukwa Iringa Kidatu Bagamoyo
Mbeya Mwaya Makumbako Kilosa **DAR ES-SALAAM**
L. Mweru Karonga Mafia I.
Kalulushi Chipata Mchinji Utete Kilwa Kivinje
Lichinga Lindi
Lundazi Lilongwe Nachingwea
Zumba L. Cabora Bassa Zomba Songea Mtwara
Songo Tete Blantyre Mocimboa da Praia C. Delgado Grande Comore

SEYCHELLES

Amirante Is.
Providence I.

Aldabra Is.
Cosmoledo Group
Assumption I.
Astove I.
Farquhar Group

COMOROS
Njazidja (Moroni)
Mwali Moheli
Anjouan Dzaoudzi
Îles Glorieuses (Fr.)
C. d'Ambre
Antseranana

MOZAMBIQUE
Pemba
Namapa Nosy-Be Ambanja
Nampula Nacala Sambava
Moçambique Antsohihy Antalaha
Angoche Maroantsetra
Mahajanga Mandritsara
Marovoay Fenerive
Maevatanana Toamasina
I. Juan de Nova (Fr.) Maintirano Ambatosoratra Ambatondrazaka
Belo Moramanga
ANTANANARIVO
Bassas da India (Fr.) Antsirabe Ambositra Morondava Fianarantsoa Mananjary
I. Europa (Fr.) Morombe Mangoky Ambohimahasoa Manakara
Ihosy Farafangana
Toliara Betroka Vangaindrano
Ampanihy Taolanaro
Ambovombe
C. Ste. Marie

M A D A G A S C A R

ZIMBABWE
Chinhoyi Bindura
HARARE (Salisbury) Mutare Manica
Gweru Chimoio Beira
Masvingo Nandi
Zvishavane
Beitbridge Sango Massangena
Messina Chicualacuala
TRANSVAAL
Olifants Guija
Komatipoort Xai-Xai
Mbabane **MAPUTO**
SWAZILAND
Lavumisa
Dundee Empangeni
Pietermaritzburg
DURBAN
Port Shepstone
Transkei
Town
Port Elizabeth

I N D I A N   O C E A N

M o z a m b i q u e   C h a n n e l

Mauritius inset:

A 1 55° 2 56° 3 57° Flat I. 4 Round I.

I N D I A N   O C E A N

Port Louis 20°
Beau Bassin Flacq
Quatre Bornes
Curepipe Mahebourg
MAURITIUS
Souillac

Saint-Denis **Réunion** (Fr.)
Le Port
St-Paul St-Benoit 21°
St-Louis St-Pierre

30a   Mauritius, Réunion
1 : 7 500 000

map 30

SUDAN

Jamhuryat es-Sudan Al Democratia, area 2,505,813 sq.km, population 21,550,000 (1985), **republic** (Chairman of the Supreme Council Ahmed Ali Mirghani since 1986).

Administrative units: 9 regions and 19 provinces. **Capital:** Al-Khurtūm (Khartoum) 557,000 inhab. (1983); **other towns** (1983, in 1,000 inhab.): Umm Durmān (Omdurman) 613, Al-Khurtūm Bahrī 341, Būr Südān (Port Sudan) 204, Kassalā 143, Wad Madanī 141, Al-Ubayyid 140. – **Currency:** Sudanese pound = 100 piastres.

Economy: developing agricultural country. **Agriculture** (1983, in 1,000 tonnes: millet 314, sorghum 1,819, wheat, rice, cotton -seed 379,-lint 201; sugarcane 4,000, groundnuts 900, sesame 235, dates 136, bananas 92, grapes 56, tomatoes 154; **livestock** (1983, in 1,000 head): cattle 19,550, sheep 19,500, goats 12,900, camels 2,730 (second world population), asses 688; roundwood 38.2 mn. cub.m, gum arabic 43,918 tonnes (90% of world production). **Mining:** iron ore, gold, chromium, manganese, salt. – **Communications:** railways 5,503 km, roads 23,042 km. – **Exports:** cotton, livestock, groundnuts, sesame, gum arabic.

SWAZILAND

Kingdom of Swaziland – Umbuso wake Ngwane, area 17,363 sq.km, population 647,415 (1985), **constitutional monarchy, member of the Commonwealth** (King Mswati III. since 1986).

Administrative units: 4 districts. **Capital:** Mbabane 29,875 inhab. (1976). – **Currency:** lilangeni = 100 cents. – **Economy:** developing agricultural country. **Agriculture** (1983, in 1,000 tonnes): maize (corn), rice, cotton, sugarcane 3,486, citrus fruit, bananas, tobacco, cattle and goat breeding. **Mining:** coal, tin, asbestos. – **Exports:** sugar, fruit, asbestos etc.

TANZANIA

United Republic of Tanzania, area 945,087 sq.km, population 21,733,000 (1985), **republic, union of Tanganyika and Zanzibar, member of the Commonwealth** (President Ali Hassan Mwinyi since 1985).

Administrative units: 22 regions. **Capitals:** Dar-es-Salaam 851,522 inhab. (1978); legislative capital Dodoma 158,577 inhab. (1978); **other towns** (1978, in 1,000 inhab.): Musoma 219, Zanzibar 111. – **Currency:** Tanzanian shilling = 100 cents.

Economy: agricultural country. **Agriculture** (1983, in 1,000 tonnes): maize (corn) 2,000, rice 400, millet, sorghum, manioc 6,800, sweet potatoes 307, potatoes, cotton -seed 109, -lint 57; sisal 82 (second world producer), sugarcane 1,320, coconuts 320, copra 29, palm kernels 5.4, cashew nuts 35, groundnuts, pyrethrum 1.0, coffee 48, tea 18, bananas 820, pineapples 50, tobacco 18, cloves 8,000 tonnes (leading world producer, Zanzibar and Pemba islands); **livestock** (1983, in 1,000 head): cattle 13,446, sheep 4,020, goats 6,031, asses; fish catch 272,500 tonnes; roundwood 39.8 mn. cub.m (1983). **Mining** (1983): gold, diamonds 250,000 carats, salt, mica – **Communications:** railways 3,550 km, roads 45,638 km. – **Exports:** coffee, cotton, sisal, diamonds, tea, cloves etc.

TOGO

République Togolaise, area 56,785 sq.km, population 2,960,000 (1985), **republic,** (President Gen. Gnassingbe Eyadema since 1967).

Administrative units: 5 regions. **Capital:** Lomé 240,000 inhab. (1980). – **Currency:** CFA franc = 100 centimes. – **Economy:** developing agricultural country. **Agriculture** (1983, in 1,000 tonnes): millet, maize (corn), manioc 400, cotton, coconuts, copra, palm oil 14, groundnuts, coffee 10, cocoa beans 10, bananas; raising of cattle, sheep, goats, pigs; fish catch 14,600 tonnes. **Mining** (in 1,000 tonnes): phosphates 2,081 (1983), deposits of iron ore and bauxite. – **Communications:** railways 516 km, roads 8,057 km. – **Exports:** phosphates, cocoa, coffee.

TUNISIA

Al-Djoumhouria Attunisia, area 163,610 sq.km, population 7,080,000 (1985), **republic** (President Habib Bourguiba since 1957).

Administrative units: 21 governorates. **Capital:** Tunis 596,654 inhab. (1984); **other towns** (1984, in 1,000 inhab.): Sfax 232, Ariana 99, Bizerte 95, Djerba 92, Gabès 92. – **Currency:** Tunisian dinar = 1,000 millimes.

Economy: agricultural country with developed mining industry. **Agriculture** (1983, in 1,000 tonnes): wheat 618, barley, potatoes, olives 600, olive oil 132, oranges 81, tangerines 34, lemons 22, dates 77, fruit, almonds, grapes 105, tomatoes 360, tobacco; **livestock** (1983, in 1,000 head): cattle 560, sheep 5,100, camels 175, asses; fish catch 67,100 tonnes; cork 5.9, alfalfa 59,000 tonnes. **Mining** (1983, in 1,000 tonnes): crude petroleum 5,578, natural gas 17,540 TJ, iron ore 169, lead 4.9, zinc 7.5, silver, salt 375, phosphates 5,924. – **Communications:** railways 2,032 km, roads 23,695 km. – **Exports:** petroleum, phosphates, olive oil, wine, fruit.

UGANDA

Republic of Uganda, area 236,036 sq.km, population 15,475,000 (1985), **republic, member of the Commonwealth** (President Yoweri Museweni since 1986).

Administrative units: 4 regions. **Capital:** Kampala 458,423 inhab.; **other towns** (1982, in 1,000 inhab.): Jinja 55, Bugembe 48. – **Currency:** Uganda shilling = 100 cents. – **Economy:** developing agricultural country. **Agriculture** (1983, in 1,000 tonnes): maize (corn) 450, millet 600, sorghum 470, manioc 1,650, sweet potatoes 760, cottonseed 95, groundnuts 100, sesame 38, tea 4, bananas 450; **livestock** (1983, in 1,000 head): cattle 5,100, sheep 1,080, goats; fish

map 31

catch 172,000 tonnes; roundwood 26.3 mn. cub.m. **Mining** (1983, tonnes metal content): tin 30, tungsten 14, salt 27,000. –
Communications: railways 1,300 km, roads 27,544 km. – **Exports:** coffee, cotton, tea.

BURKINA FASO (Upper Volta)

République de Burkina Faso, area 274,000 sq.km, population 6,942,000 (1985), republic
(President Capt. Thomas Sankara since 1983).
Administrative units: 11 departments. **Capital:** Ouagadougou 235,000 inhab. (1982). – **Currency:** CFA franc = 100 centimes. – **Economy:** developing agricultural country. **Agriculture** (1983, in 1,000 tonnes): maize (corn), millet 300, sorghum
600, rice 37, manioc, cotton -seed 50, -lint 29; sugarcane 330, groundnuts 77, sesame, tobacco; **livestock** (1983, in 1,000
head): cattle 2,950, sheep 2,000, goats 2,500.– **Communications:** railways 517 km, roads 18,000 km.

WESTERN SAHARA

Area 252,210 sq.km, population 163,868 (1982). The territory occupied by Morocco. Capital: El Aaiún 30,000 inhab.
(1980). – **Economy:** large supplies phosphates (mining 440,000 tonnes in 1978) and deposits of gold and uranium.

ZAÏRE

République du Zaïre, area 2,345,409 sq.km, population 30,362,750 (1985), republic (President
Gen. Mobutu Sese Seko since 1965).
Administrative units: 8 regions and capital district. **Capital:** Kinshasa 3,682,000 inhab. (1980); **other towns** (1985, in
1,000 inhab.): Kananga 938, Lubumbashi 765, Mbuji-Mayi 625, Kisangani 557, Bukavu 418, Kikwit 346, Mbandaka 294,
Matadi 216, Likasi 172 (1976). – **Currency:** zaïre = 100 makuta.
Economy: agricultural country with developed mining industry and metallurgy. **Agriculture** (1983, in 1,000 tonnes): maize
(corn) 668, rice 258, manioc 14,600, sweet potatoes 310, potatoes 206, cotton seed 50, sisal, sugarcane 740, palm oil 140,
groundnuts 370, coffee 50, tea 4, cocoa beans, pineapples 153, tobacco; **livestock** (1983, in 1,000 head): cattle 1,300,
sheep 760, goats 2,900, pigs 750; fish catch 102,000 tonnes; roundwood 31.3 mn. cub.m. natural rubber 24,000 tonnes.
Mining (1983, in 1,000 tonnes, metal content): crude petroleum 1,212, copper 535, zinc 75, tin 2.1, cobalt 11,300 tonnes
(leading world producer), tungsten 170 tonnes, cadmium, niobium, tantalum, gold 1,866 kg, silver 62 tonnes, diamonds
11,438,000 carats (leading world producer). Electricity 4,213 mn. kWh (1983). **Production** (1983, in 1,000 tonnes): copper
227, zinc 62.5, cement 400. – **Communications:** railways 5,254 km, roads 145,000 km, navigable waterways 16,400 km. –
Exports: copper, petroleum, coffee, diamonds, cobalt, palm oil, wood etc.

ZAMBIA

**Republic of Zambia, area 752,614 sq.km, population 6,665,000 (1985), republic, member of
the Commonwealth** (President Dr Kenneth David Kaunda since 1964).
Administrative units: 9 provinces. **Capital:** Lusaka 538,500 inhab. (1980); **other towns** (1980, in 1,000 inhab.): Kitwe-Ka-
lulushi 374, Ndola 282, Chingola-Chililabombwe 208, Mufulira 150. – **Currency:** kwacha = 100 ngwee.
Economy: chiefly mining and metallurgy of non-ferrous metals. **Agriculture** (1983): maize (corn) 935,000 tonnes, sugarcane 1 mn. tonnes, manioc, groundnuts, tobacco; **livestock** (1983, in 1,000 head): cattle 2,380, goats; poultry 18,000; fish
catch 67,200 tonnes; roundwood 9 mn. cub.m. **Mining** (1983, in 1,000 tonnes, metal content): coal 456, copper 576, lead
14.8, zinc 38, manganese, tin, cobalt 2,400 tonnes, gold 316 kg, silver 29 tonnes. Electricity 10,071 mn. kWh (1983). –
Communications: railways 2,189 km, roads 37,068 km. – **Exports:** copper 90%, zinc, cobalt, lead, maize etc.

ZIMBABWE

**Republic of Zimbabwe, area 390,580 sq.km, population 8,350,000 (1985), republic, member
of the Commonwealth** (President Canaan Banana since 1980).
Administrative units: 8 provinces. **Capital:** Harare (Salisbury) 656,000 inhab. (1982); **other towns** (1982, in 1,000
inhab.): Bulawayo 414, Chitungwiza 173, Gweru 79, Mutare 70, Kwekwe 58. – **Currency:** Zimbabwe dollar = 100 cents.
Economy: developed agriculture and mining industry. **Agriculture** (1983, in 1,000 tonnes): maize (corn) 1,023, wheat,
millet, cotton seed 101, sugarcane 3,700, groundnuts 32, tea, citrus fruit, bananas, tobacco 98; **livestock** (1983, in 1,000
head): cattle 5,350, sheep 455, goats 1,000; roundwood 6.7 mn. cub.m (1983). **Mining** (1983, in 1,000 tonnes, metal
content): coal 2,391, iron ore 554, chromium 144, copper, tin, nickel, tungsten, gold 14,090 kg, silver, antimony, magnesite,
emeralds, phosphates, pyrites, asbestos 153. Electricity 4,426 mn. kWh (1983). – **Communications:** railways 3,470 km,
roads 78,800 km. – **Exports:** tobacco, asbestos, gold, copper, chromium, sugar.

BRITISH TERRITORIES:
SAINT HELENA AND DEPENDENCIES – British colony and 5 dependencies. Saint Helena – **area 314 sq.km,
population 6,565** (1982). **Capital:** Jamestown 1,862 inhab. – **Currency:** English pound = 100 pence. – **Dependencies:**
Ascension, Tristan da Cunha and volcanic islands.

FRENCH TERRITORY:
RÉUNION – Area 2,510 sq.km, population 546,000 (1985). French overseas department. Capital: Saint-Denis 104,603
inhab. (1982). – **Currency:** CFA franc = 100 centimes. – **Economy:** sugar 223,700 tonnes, vanilla, oil of geranium, rum.

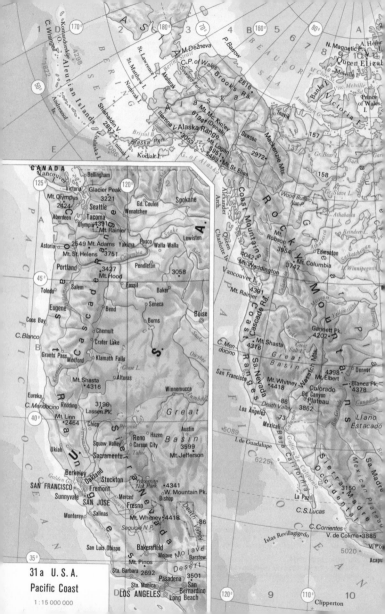

31a U.S.A.
Pacific Coast
1 : 15 000 000

map 31

NORTH AMERICA

The physical geography of the North American continent includes Central America, the islands of the Caribbean Sea and Greenland. It is the largest continent in the western hemisphere. The original term "the New World" (Mundus Novus) was replaced, in the first half of the 16th century, by the name America, after the Florentine Amerigo Vespucci, an Italian seafarer who took part in Columbus's expeditions in the late 15th century.

North America covers an **area of 24,360,000 sq.km**, i.e. 16.3% of the land area of the world; it has **401 mn. inhabitants** (1985), i.e. 8.3% of the world's population and a population density of 16.5 persons per sq.km. **Geographical position:** northernmost point: on the mainland – Cape Murchison on the Boothia Peninsula 71°50' N.Lat., of the entire continent – cape K. Morris Jesup 83°40' N.Lat. in Greenland; southernmost point: cape Punta Mariato on the Peninsula of Azuero in Panama 7°12' N.Lat.; easternmost point: on the mainland – Cape Charles 55°40' W.Long. in Labrador, in Greenland cape Nordostrundingen 11°39' W.Long.; westernmost point: on the mainland – Cape Prince of Wales on the Seward Peninsula in Alaska 168°05' W.Long. (here America comes within 75 km of Asia), of the entire continent – Cape Wrangell on the Aleutian island of Attu 172°27' E.Long. The American continent reaches its maximum length between Point Barrow (Alaska) and Punta Mariato (Panama) a total length of roughly 8,700 km; its width from the most westerly point of Alaska as far as Canso on the peninsula of Nova Scotia (Canada) measures 5,950 km; and the narrowest point is on the Isthmus of Panama, a mere 48 km.

Geological evolution gave North America highly varied contours, an uneven coastline and large numbers of islands (mostly of continental origin). North America has the longest coastline of all continents, reaching a length of 75,600 km. 1 km of shore corresponds to 320 sq.km on the continent. **Islands and peninsulas** makes up 25.4% of the area of the continent. The islands – 4,160,000 sq.km in area – are concentrated chiefly in the Arctic North. There lies Greenland, the largest island in the world (2,175,600 sq.km), and also the vast Canadian Arctic Archipelago (area: 1,405,000 sq.km) with the two largest islands Baffin I. (507,414 sq.km) and Victoria I. (217,274 sq.km). The second island region is that of the Caribbean Sea with the Greater (207,700 sq.km) and the Lesser Antilles (14,200 sq.km). The Aleutian Is. (37,850 sq.km) stretch northwest in the Pacific Ocean, together with the Alexander Archipelago (36,780 sq.km) and Queen Charlotte Is. (9,600 sq.km). The largest peninsula is Labrador (1,320,000 sq.km).

The surface of North America is divided in a north-south direction by the mountains of the Cordilleras with high plateaus between the ranges in the west of the continent, by the vast Great Plains and the Central Lowlands, the alluvial Mississippi Lowlands (1,000 km long and 80–100 km wide) in the interior of the continent, and by the eastern ranges (the Laurentin Plateau and the Appalachian Mts.), which line the coastal plain on the Atlantic Ocean and the Gulf of Mexico. The highest mountain of the continent is Mt. McKinley/Denali (6,194 m) in the Alaska Range in the Pacific Mountain System, which includes the Cascade Range (4,391 m) and the Sierra Nevada (Mt. Whitney, 4,418 m). The lowest point is Death Valley (–86 m) on the western edge of the Great Basin in California. The Rocky Mts. (Mt. Elbert, 4,398 m) enclose the Great Basin without outlet to the sea. The geologically younger Cordilleras in Central America have a number of volcanoes (V. Citlaltépetl 5,699 m), many of them active, and this is also a region of frequent earthquakes. The Laurentin Plateau, known as the Canadian Shield (comprising half of Canada) is geologically the oldest part of the continent; it is considerably worn down by glaciers, with a vast number of shallow valleys, rivers, streams and lakes. In the east of the continent the Paleozoic Appalachian Mts. reach the height of 2,037 m.

The river system, especially in the North of the continent, was greatly affected by Quaternary glaciation. The annual mean discharge is 7,130 cub.km. Most of the river basins drain into the Atlantic Ocean through the mouth of the third longest river in the world, the Mississippi-Missouri (length 6,212 km, draining an area of 3,250,000 sq.km with an average annual flow 19,800 cub.m per second) and the St. Lawrence (3,058m), which flows from the Great Lakes. Both of these are very important shipping routes. The Mackenzie, the longest river of Canada (4,240 m, drainage area 1,813,000 sq.km) drains into the Arctic Ocean, and in the West, the Colorado (with the famous Grand Canyon), the Columbia and the Fraser flow into the Pacific Ocean. The longest river in Alaska is the Yukon (3,185 km), which drains into the Bering Sea. The northern rivers have an ample supply of water from glaciers and snow-fall throughout the year, but they freeze up in winter. On the other hand, the rivers in the Central Basins of the South-West of the United States and Mexico often dry up in summer. The Great Lakes, the largest fresh water **lakes** in the world, covering an area of 246,515 sq.km, are of glacial and tectonic origin.

North America stretches across 3 **climatic zones** in the northern hemisphere. In the far North, on the Arctic islands and in Greenland there is the polar-Arctic-climate (mean annual temperature between 0°C and –20°C, precipitation c. 200 mm). The central part of the continent has an extreme climate (with great differences in temperature in summer and winter). A transitional zone of subtropical climate is found around the Gulf of Mexico (sufficient rainfall), in northern Mexico and southern California – U.S.A. (little rainfall). The climate of the Central American mainland and the islands in the Caribbean Sea is tropical, oceanic. In winter, blizzards blow from the North across the open continent, the temperature drops by about 20°C and in summer tornadoes and hurricanes strike the South-east of the continent and especially the islands. The highest temperature, 57°C, was measured in Death Valley and the lowest, at Fort Good Hope, was –78.2°C. Mean January and July temperatures in °C (and annual precipitation in mm): Barrow –26.4 and 4.5 (112), Dawson –29.4 and 15.6 (321), Cambridge Bay –30.7 and 9.6 (176), Úpernavik –21.8 and 4.9 (230), Prince Rupert 1.7 and 13.4 (2,417), Churchill –28.3 and 12.1 (405), Winnipeg –18.7 and 19.9 (535), St. John's –4.5 and 15.3 (1,348), Montréal –9.2 and 21.5 (1,061), New York 0.1 and 24.6 (1,076), Chicago –3.3 and 23.9 (843), Salt Lake City –2.6 and 24.7 (353), San Francisco 10.2 and 14.7 (528), Miami 19.2 and 27.4 (1,518), México 11.6 and 15.6 (765), Kingston 24.7 and 27.6 (802), Colón 26.2 and 26.7 (3,680).

There are two **natural vegetation** regions in North America, the Holarctic in the North and the neo-tropical in the South. From North to South we can find arctic deserts, tundra, North Canadian coniferous forest, a zone of Pacific forests, Laurentinian and South Atlantic mixed forest, grassland, steppe, shrub with cacti and thorn bushes, Central American coniferous forest and tropical swamp forest, savanna and tropical rain forest. There are also two zones of **animal life:** the neo-arctic (e.g. elk, "wapiti" stag, grizzly bear, racoon, beaver, puma, wild turkey, waterfowl, etc.) and the neo-tropical (e.g. jaguar, armadillo, tapir, porcupine, alligator, parrots, humming birds, etc.). Buffaloes exist only in reservations. Great attention is being paid to conservation; national parks, monuments and reservations have been established, the largest being Wood Buffalo N.P. in Canada (44,807 sq.km) and Yellowstone N.P. in the U.S.A.

map 32

LONGEST RIVERS

Name	Length in km	River Basin in sq.km
Mississippi-Missouri	6,212	3,250,000
Mackenzie-Athabasca	4,240	1,813,000
Yukon	3,185	848,400
St. Lawrence	3,058	1,260,000
Rio Grande/Bravo del Norte	3,023	580,000
Nelson-Saskatchewan	2,575	1,250,000
Arkansas	2,334	416,000
Colorado	2,334	590,000
Ohio-Allegheny	2,102	525,700
Columbia	1,954	668,000
Saskatchewan	1,940	336,700
Peace	1,923	303,000
Snake	1,671	382,300
Red	1,638	214,500
Churchill	1,609	410,000
Canadian	1,458	.
Tennessee	1,387	105,950
Fraser	1,368	232,800
Kuskokwim	1,287	126,900
Ottawa	1,271	.

LARGEST ISLANDS

Name	Area in sq.km
Greenland	2,175,600
Baffin I.	507,414
Victoria I.	217,274
Ellesmere I.	196,221
Cuba	110,922
Newfoundland	108,852
Hispaniola	77,218
Banks I.	70,023
Devon I.	55,243
Axel Heiberg I.	43,175
Melville I.	42,146
Southampton I.	41,211
Prince of Wales I.	33,336
Vancouver I.	31,282
Somerset I.	24,784
Bathurst I.	16,041
Prince Patrick I.	15,847
King William I.	13,110
Ellef Ringnes I.	11,294
Jamaica	11,424

LARGEST LAKES

Name	Area in sq.km	Greatest Depth in m	Altitude in m	Name	Area in sq.km	Greatest Depth in m	Altitude in m
L. Superior	82,414	393	183	Reindeer L.	6,651	.	337
L. Huron	59,596	226	176	Nettilling L.	5,542	.	30
L. Michigan	58,016	281	176	L. Winnipegosis	5,374	12	253
Great Bear Lake	31,328	137	157	L. Nipigon	4,848	123	261
Great Slave Lake	28,570	187	158	L. Manitoba	4,660	7	248
L. Erie	25,745	64	174	Great Salt Lake	4,365	16	1,283
L. Winnipeg	24,388	21	217	Lake of the Woods	4,349	21	323
L. Ontario	19,553	237	75	Dubawnt L.	3,833	.	236
Lago de Nicaragua	8,430	70	34	L. Melville	3,069	.	tidal
L.Athabasca	7,935	91	213	Wollaston L.	2,681	.	398

HIGHEST MOUNTAINS

Name (Country)	Height in m	Name (Country)	Height in m	Name (Country)	Height in m
Denali/Mt. McKinley (U.S.A.)	6,194	Mt. Bona (U.S.A.)	5,029	Mt. Shasta (U.S.A.)	4,316
Mt. Logan (Can.)	5,951	Mt. Sanford (U.S.A.)	4,940	Mt. Kennedy (Can.)	4,238
V. Citlaltépetl (Mex.)	5,699	Mt. Wood (Can.)	4,842	V. Tajumulco (Guat.)	4,220
Mt. St. Elias (Can.-U.S.A.)	5,489	Mt. Vancouver (Can.-U.S.A.)	4,785	Mt. Waddington (Can.)	4,042
Mt. Foraker (U.S.A.)	5,303	Toluca/Zinantecatl (Mex.)	4,577	Mt. Robson (Can.)	3,954
Ixtacihuatl (Mex.)	5,286	Mt. Whitney (U.S.A.)	4,418	Chirripó (Costa Rica)	3,837
Mt. Lucania (Can.)	5,227	Mt. Elbert (U.S.A.)	4,398	Mt. Columbia (Can.)	3,747
Mt. Blackburn (U.S.A.)	5,036	Mt. Rainier (U.S.A.)	4,391	Gunnbjörns Fjeld (Green.)	3,734

ACTIVE VOLCANOES

Name (Country)	Altitude in m	Latest eruption
V. Popocatépetl (Mex.)	5,452	1932
Mt. Wrangell (Alaska, U.S.A.)	4,268	1907
V. Acatenango (Guat.)	3,976	1972
V. de Colima (Mex.)	3,885	1983
V.Fuego (Guat.)	3,835	1980
V.Santiaguito (Guat.)	3,768	1983
V. Irazú (Costa Rica)	3,432	1967
Shishaldin V. (Alaska, U.S.A.)	2,857	1981
Mt. St. Helens (U.S.A.)	2,549	1982
V. El Chichón (Mex.)	2,225	1983

FAMOUS NATIONAL PARKS

Name (Country)	Area in sq.km
Wood Buffalo (Can.)	44,807
Wrangell-St. Elias (U.S.A., Alaska)	33,717
Gates of the Arctic (U.S.A., Alaska)	30,345
Denali/Mt.McKinley (U.S.A.,Alaska)	19,015
Katmai N.M. (U.S.A., Alaska)	14,886
Yellowstone (U.S.A.)	8,985
Jasper (Can.)	6,760
Everglades (U.S.A.)	5,660
Grand Canyon (U.S.A.)	4,930
Banff (Can.)	4,126

32 a New York   1 : 900 000

map 32

NORTH AMERICA

Country	Area in sq.km	Population year 1985	Density per sq.km	Capital
Anguilla (U.K.)	96	7,300	76	The Valley
Antigua and Barbuda	442	80,150	181	Saint John's
Bahamas	13,935	231,400	17	Nassau
Barbados	431	253,500	588	Bridgetown
Belize	22,965	166,000	7	Belmopan
Bermuda (U.K.)	53.5	78,000	1,458	Hamilton
Canada	9,976,139	25,378,800	2.5	Ottawa
Cayman Islands (U.K.)	260	19,850	76	Georgetown
Costa Rica	50,700	2,416,809[1]	48	San José
Cuba	114,524	10,098,900	88	La Habana
Dominica	751	76,000	101	Roseau
Dominican Republic	48,734	6,242,730	128	Santo Domingo
El Salvador	21,041	4,819,175	229	San Salvador
Greenland (Denmark)	2,175,600	54,000	0.02	Nuuk (Godthåb)
Grenada	344	112,000	326	Saint George's
Guadeloupe and Depend. (Fr.)	1,780	332,000	187	Basse – Terre
Guatemala	108,889	7,963,360	73	Guatemala
Haiti	27,750	5,185,000	187	Port-au-Prince
Honduras	112,088	4,372,490	39	Tegucigalpa
Jamaica	10,991	2,190,000	199	Kingston
Martinique (Fr.)	1,102	328,500	298	Fort-de-France
Mexico	1,972,546	78,524,158	40	(Ciudad de) México
Montserrat (U.K.)	98	13,000	133	Plymouth
Nicaragua	148,000	3,272,000	24	Managua
Panama (incl. Canal Zone)	77,326	2,180,490	28	Panamá
Puerto Rico (U.S.A.)	8,897	3,270,000[1]	368	San Juan
Saint Christopher and Nevis	242	47,000	179	Basseterre
Saint Lucia	616	134,000[1]	218	Castries
Saint Pierre et Miquelon (Fr.)	242	6,000	25	Saint-Pierre
Saint Vincent and Grenadines	389	105,000	270	Kingstown
Turks and Caicos Islands (U.K.)	430	8,100	19	Grand Turk
United States of America[+]	9,372,614	239,283,000	26	Washington
Virgin Islands (U.K.)	153	13,000	85	Road Town
Virgin Islands (U.S.A.)	344	108,000[1]	314	Charlotte Amalie

[+] with the area of Great Lakes 9,519,617 sq.km. [1] year 1984

Today's **racial and ethnic composition** of the inhabitants of North America (incl. Central America) is the consequence of an intermingling of races and nationalities that began after the discovery of the continent. The population can be divided into five groups: 1. the original inhabitants – Indians and Eskimos, 2. inhabitants of European origin (immigrants and their descendants), 3. inhabitants of African origin (Negroes and their descendants), 4. mixed races between Indians, Whites and Negroes, 5. a small number of immigrants from Asia. In 1985 the total **number of inhabitants was 401 million,** not quite 66% living in the U.S.A. and Canada (of this: 96,000 Eskimos, over 3/4 million Indians and more than 28 million Negroes and mixed races) and 34% in Mexico and the countries and islands of Central America (where Indians, Negroes and mixed races predominate). Population density per sq.km is highest, with 136 persons, on the islands of the Caribbean Sea (Barbados 588), 42 persons in Central America and lowest in North America, with 13 persons per sq.km. Between 1975 and 1985 **the population** of the continent **increased at the** high **rate of 1.8%** (Honduras 3.45%, the U.S.A. only 0.97%), resulting from a high birth rate of 26.8 per thousand (e.g. Honduras 43.9 per thousand in 1980–85) and a decreasing death rate of 8.5 per thousand (e.g. Haiti 14.2, Jamaica 5.6 per thousand). The annual migration inflow amounts to 600,000 persons. There has been a remarkable growth in the number of inhabitants of towns and conurbations. Urban populations are highest in North America 77.2% (Canada 78.5%, the United States 76.5% in 1983), lower in Central America 59.2% (Mexico 67%), and least on the islands in the Greater Antilles 50% (Cuba 65.5%, Haiti only 25%). North America had 12 cities with a population of over a million (without agglomeration) and 33 cities with more than 500,000 inhabitants in 1983.

Economy: The United States is economically the strongest and technologically the most advanced country in the western world. It produces about 35% of the entire industrial production and roughly 20% of the agricultural production of the world, excluding the socialist countries, and handles almost one fifth of world trade. Canada, too, is a highly advanced industrial and agricultural country with an important ore mining industry and very considerable agricultural output. The most developed country of Latin America is Mexico with its important mineral resources. Monoculture on plantations is the predominant form of agriculture in Central America.

CANADA

Area 9,976,139 sq.km, population 25,378,800 (1985), **independent federal state, member of the Commonwealth** (Prime Minister Martin Brian Mulroney since 1985, Governor-General Jeanne Sauvé since 1984).

Administrative units: 10 provinces and 2 territories (see table). **Capital:** Ottawa 295,163 inhab. (census 1981, with agglom. 737,600 inhab.); **other towns** (1981, in 1,000 inhab. and with agglom. 1983 in brackets): Montréal 980 (2,862),

map 33

Toronto 599 (3,067[+]), Calgary 593 (635), Winnipeg 565 (601), North York[+] 560, Edmonton 532 (699), Scarborough[+] 443, Vancouver 414 (1,311), Mississauga[+] 315, Hamilton 306 (548), Etobicoke[+] 299, Laval[+] 268, London 254 (287), Windsor 192 (245), Québec 166 (580), Regina 163 (168), York[+] 141, Saskatoon 154, Brampton[+] 149, Kitchener 140 (294), Burnaby 136, Saint Catharines 125 (304), Longueuil 124, Oshawa 118, Halifax 115 (281), Burlington 115, Thunder Bay 112, East York[+] 102, Richmond 96, Montréal-Nord[+] 95, Sudbury 92 (150), Nepean 85, Saint John's 84 (155), Sault Sainte Marie 83, Saint John 81 (114). **Population** (1981, in 1,000): British Canadians 9,674, French Canadians 6,439, Indians 332 (1984), Eskimos 28; Germans 1,142, Italians 748, Ukrainians 530, Dutch 408, Chinese 289, Scandinavian 283, Poles 254 and others. **Density** more than 2.5 persons per sq.km; average annual rate of population increase 1.1%, birth rate 15.1 per 1,000 and death rate 7.3 per 1,000 (1980–85). Immigration: 121,147 (1982). Urban population 75.7% (1981). Economically active inhabitants 12.68 mn. of which only 4.3% worked in advanced agriculture, 28.4% in industry, 6.1% in transport and 61.2% in services (1984). – **Currency:** Canadian dollar = 100 cents.

Province	Area in sq.km	Population (in 1,000, 1985)	Density per sq.km	Capital (population in 1,000, 1981)
Alberta	661,185	2,368.5	3.6	Edmonton (532.2)
British Columbia	948,596	2,883.0	3.0	Victoria (64.4)
Manitoba	650,086	1,065.2	1.6	Winnipeg (564.5)
New Brunswick	73,437	717.2	9.8	Fredericton (43.7)
Newfoundland	404,517	578.9	1.4	St. John's (83.8)
Nova Scotia	55,491	878.3	15.8	Halifax (114.6)
Ontario	1,068,582	9,023.9	8.4	Toronto (599.2)
Prince Edward Island	5,657	126.8	22.4	Charlottetown (15.3)
Québec	1,540,680	6,562.2	4.3	Québec (166.5)
Saskatchewan	651,902	1,016.4	1.6	Regina (162.6)
Northwest Territories	3,379,682	50.5	0.01	Yellowknife (9.5)
Yukon Territory	536,324	22.8	0.04	Whitehorse (14.8)
CANADA	9,976,139[+]	25,293.7	2.5	Ottawa (295.2)
[+] including interior water areas				

Economy: highly advanced industrial country. Canada's contribution to industrial production of non-socialist countries is roughly 3%, to the total turnover of foreign trade is 3.5% and it is the third largest in agricultural production. In 1983/84 Canada had the highest output of uranium (28.8% of world output), zinc (19.3%) and newsprint (32.9%), sulphur recovered as by-product (25.7%); it held second place in the production of nickel (24.7%), asbestos, platinum, cobalt, titanium, potash salt, gypsum; in the production of wood pulp, nickel; third place in the output of natural gas, tungsten, gold, production of aluminium, zinc, paper and paperboard, sawnwood, electric energy. – **Principal industries:** metallurgy, mining of fuels and ores, electricity, processing of fuels, engineering, food processing, wood-working, paper and textile industry.

Mining (1984, in 1,000 tonnes metal content): coal 32,064 (Alberta, Nova Scotia), brown coal 25,344 (Saskatchewan), crude petroleum 70,586 (Alberta, Saskatchewan, Brit. Columbia), natural gasoline 3,457, natural gas 2,969.2 PJ (Alberta, above all, Medicine Hat), iron ore 25,050 (Québec – Schefferville, Gagnon; Newfoundland – Labrador City Wabush), nickel 174.2 (Ontario – Sudbury, Falconbridge; Manitoba – Thompson, Lynn Lake), asbestos 838 (Québec – Thetford Mines, Asbestos; Ontario – Matheson), uranium 11,170 tonnes (Ontario – Elliot Lake; Saskatchewan – Key Lake, Uranium City), gold 83,450 kg (Ontario – Chemlo; Kirkland L., Porcupine, Red Lake; Québec – Val-d'Or, Malartic; Northwest Territories – Yellowknife; Yukon – region Klondike), silver 1,169 tonnes (British Columbia – Kimberley; Ontario – Timmins, Gowganda; Yukon – Faro), platinum 12,820 kg (Ontario – Sudbury; Manitoba – Thompson), cobalt 2,325 tonnes (Ontario – Cobalt, Lac Preissac), lead 307 (British Columbia – Kimberley, Slocan; Yukon – Faro, Mayo), zinc 1,207 (Ontario – Timmins; Québec – Mattagami, Amos; Manitoba – Flin Flon; British Columbia – Kimberley, Nelson, Remac; Yukon – Faro, Elsa; Northwest Ter. – Pine Point), copper 712 (Manitoba – Sherridon; Ontario – Manitouwadge, Copper Cliff; Québec – Noranda, Chibougamau; British Columbia – Highland Valley, Merritt), molybdenum 10,965 tonnes (British Columbia – Peachland, Revelstoke), tungsten 3,432 tonnes (Yukon – Tungsten), tin 216 tonnes, niobium 4,985 tonnes, columbite 3,086 tonnes (1982, Québec – Oka), salt 10,190 (largest Pugwash – Nova Scotia; Goderich, Sarnia – Ontario), potash salt 7,484 (Saskatchewan), gypsum 8,439, sulphur recovered as by-product 6,602 (Alberta 90%).

Industrial production – some branches belong to the largest in the world: production of paper and chemical wood pulp, newsprint, motor spirit and oils, electric energy, aluminium, nickel, zinc, sawnwood. In the South-east of Canada the engineering, metallurgy, textiles, chemical and food industries predominate. In the South-west of the country timber and paper industry, metallurgy of non-ferrous metals (especially aluminium), and engineering. Ontario is the most industrialized province – providing 60% of industrial production value.

Metallurgy (1984, in 1,000 tonnes): pig iron 9,704 and crude steel 14,568 (largest steel plants Hamilton), aluminium 1,295 (6.7% of world production; Arvida, Kitimat, Baie-Comeau, Tomago, Shawinigan), zinc 638 (10% of world production; Trail, Flin Flon, Timmins), lead 252 (Trail, Belldune Point); copper -smelted 440 (Noranda, Montréal, Flin Flon), -refined 504 (Montréal, Copper Cliff, Murdochville); cadmium 1,602 tonnes (Flin Flon, Trail). Processing of cobalt – Lynn Lake, Sudbury, Fort Saskatchewan; nickel 104 (15% of world production, Thompson, Bécancour, Sudbury); uranium – Port Hope in Ontario.

Engineering (1984): production of motor vehicles – passenger 1,033,000 units, – commercial 808,800 (Windsor, Oshawa, Toronto, Hamilton, St. Thomas) – aircraft (Toronto, Milton, Montréal, Vancouver); railway carriages and locomotives (Trenton, Montréal, London, Rivière-du-Loup, Winnipeg); vessels (Montréal, Sorel, Halifax, Victoria); electrotechnical industry (Toronto, Montréal, Ottawa, Trois-Rivières, Hamilton) – 705,000 radio and 444,000 television receivers (1980); machine tools, mining, textiles, agricultural machines (Toronto, Montréal, Vancouver, Winnipeg, Québec).

33 a Vancouver Area
1 : 10 000 000

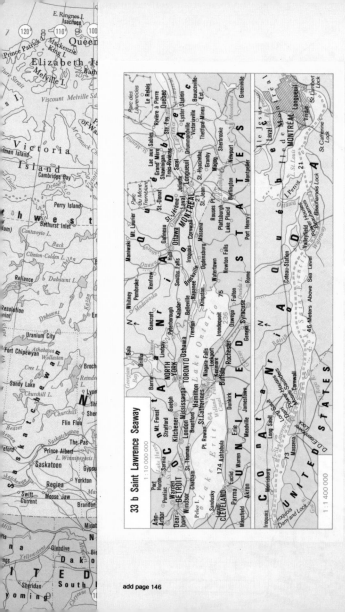

33 b Saint Lawrence Seaway

1 : 10 000 000

1 : 1 400 000

add page 146

map 33

Chemical industry – chief production centres: Sarnia, Welland, Trail, Ft. Saskatchewan, Calgary, Brandon, Red-water etc. Production (1984, in 1,000 tonnes): sulphur 6,620, sulphuric acid 4,043; fertilizers – nitrogenous 2,371, – phosphatic 655, – potash 7,154, organic chemicals 1,082, synthetic rubber 217, plastics 893. Capacity of petroleum refineries 108 mn. tonnes (largest Montréal, Sarnia, Québec, Edmonton, Vancouver, Regina, Calgary, Ft. McMurray, Winnipeg, Toronto, Halifax, Point Tupper, St. John etc.): production: motor spirit 23,965, jet fuels 3,403, kerosene 1,780, distilled fuel oils 20,115, residual fuel oils 8,261, gas (by cokeries) 45,453 TJ, liquefied petroleum gas 6,943, asphalt 2,664 (all 1984).

Wood and paper industry (1984, 1,000 tonnes): roundwood 141.5 mn. cub.m, sawnwood 48.1 mn. cub.m, news-print 9,013, mechanical wood pulp 8,800, chemical wood pulp 11,099, (second world producer), other paper and paperboard 4,807. Largest paper mills include Thunder Bay, Port Alberni, Kapuskasing, Campbell River, Hull, Corner Brook, St. John; wood processing plants: Vancouver, Prince George, Edmonton, Merritt, La Sarre and Ottawa. – **The textile industry** (Québec, Ontario – production 1981): cotton fabrics 289 mn. sq.m, woollen fabrics 29 mn. sq.m; synthetic fibres 65,900 tonnes.

The food industry is concentrated in large cities and ports. Production (1984, in 1,000 tonnes): meat 2,446, milk 8,200, cheese 229, butter 112, flour 1,710, sugar 1,135, beer 23.3 mn. hl, soft drinks 17 mn. hl, wine 55. **Production** of cement 8.6 mn. tonnes (Ontario, Québec), tyres 25 mn. units; 61.6 billion cigarettes.

Electricity (1983, +1984): installed capacity of electric power stations 89.8 mn.kW (of which 56.8% were hydro-electric power stations, 10.1% nuclear power stations), produced +437,990 mn. kWh (production of nuclear power stations +52,701 mn. kWh). Largest power stations: hydro-electric – La Grande 5,328 MW (Québec), Churchill Falls 5,225 MW (Labrador), Mica 2,610 MW, Bennett (Peace R.) and Revelstoke (Brit. Columbia), Manicouagane – Riv. aux Outardes, Beauharnois (Québec), Niagara-Queenston (Ontario) etc., nuclear – Bruce-Tiverton 2,984 MW and Pickering-Toronto 2,572 MW (Ontario) and others.

Agriculture: arable land 5.1%, meadows and pastures 2.6%, forests 35.4% of the land area. In 1983 658,000 tractors and 161,950 combine harvesters were in use. Only 446,000 people work in the advanced, highly mechanized system of agriculture. **Animal production** predominates (1984, in 1,000 head): cattle 12,284 (dairy cows⁺ 1,728, Alberta, Saskatchewan, Québec⁺, Ontario⁺), pigs 10,760 (Ontario, Québec), sheep 791 (Alberta, Ontario), horses 380, poultry 93 mn. (Ontario, Québec, British Columbia); (in 1,000 tonnes): eggs 328, honey 44, fresh hides 106, fish, frozen 236. Fish catch 1,337,300 tonnes. Hunting of fur animals. – **Vegetable production:** mostly cultivation of cereals and fodder (Edmonton – Regina – Winnipeg). **Crops** (1984, in 1,000 tonnes): wheat 21,200 (Saskatchewan 60%), barley 10,252 (Alberta 55%), oats 2,670 (Alberta 38%, third world producer), maize 7,024 (Ontario 70%), rye 664, potatoes 2,728, linseed 676 (second world producer), rapeseed 3,246 (second world producer), soya beans 934 (Ontario), pulses 230, vegetables 1,858 and fruit 717 (Ontario, British Columbia, Québec) sugar beet 932 (Alberta), tobacco 90.

Communications (1982): railways 72,678km mostly electrified, freight 196 billion tonnes/km; roads 928,258 km, of which 712,319 km were surfaced and 7,820 km of the Trans-Canada Highway: St John's – Victoria; motor vehicles in use 14.1 mn., of which 10.7 mn. passenger cars. Civil aviation: 324.7 mn. km flown and 19.4 mn. passengers carried (1984). Largest airports: Montréal, Ottawa and Vancouver. Naval transport: merchant shipping 3,449,000 GRT (1984, of which vessels 2.1 mn. GRT) including vessels for inland navigation with a gross tonnage of 4.8 mn., annual freight turnover in ports 186 mn. tonnes (1982). Almost 65% of merchant shipping operates on the 3,650km long "great inland waterway" from the St. Lawrence to Great Lakes. Largest ports: Vancouver, Port-Cartier, Montréal, Thunder Bay, Sept-Iles, St. John, Québec, Hamilton etc. Length of pipelines 36,500km (1983). Tourism 12.9 mn. visitors.

Foreign trade (1983) – **Exports** Canadian share in world export is 4.1%): transport equipment 31%, ores and other raw materials 15% (ores 3.2%, wood 4.5%), industrial products 15% (paper 5.6%), fuels 14.1% (petroleum and products 5.8%), cereals 6.6%; above all to the U.S.A. 72.6%, Japan 5.1%, the United Kingdom 2.7%, U.S.S.R. 2.1%, China, Fed. Rep. of Germany, the Netherlands, France, Italy, Belgium. – **Imports** (Canadian share in world import is 3.2%): machines 50.8% (transport equipment 25.7%), industrial products 12.3%, mineral fuels 6.8%, chemicals 6.6%, food and fruit 6%; above all from the U.S.A. 71.6%, Japan 5.9%, the United Kingdom 2.4%, Fed. Rep. of Germany, Mexico, Venezuela, France, Italy, Hong Kong etc.

UNITED STATES OF AMERICA

United States of America (U.S.A.), **area 9,372,614 sq.km, population 239,283,000** (1979), **census population** 1 April 1980 **226,545,825** (including armed forces overseas 227.66 mn.) **federal republic** (President Ronald Wilson Reagan since 1981).

Administrative units: 50 federal states and 1 federal district (the capital). To the continental U.S.A. belong overseas territories: 1. one self-governing federal state: the Commonwealth of Puerto Rico; 2 territories: American Samoa, Guam, Midway Is., Virgin Is.; 3. the United Nations Trust Territory of the Pacific Is.: the Commonwealth of the Northern Mariana Is., Republic of the Marshall Is., Republic of Palau, the Federated States of Micronesia.

Capital: Washington 623,000 inhab. (1984, with agglomeration 3.4 mn.); **other towns** (in 1,000 inhab., 1984, with agglom. in brackets): New York 7,165 (17,807), Los Angeles 3,097 (12,373), Chicago 2,992 (8,035), Houston 1,706 (3,566), Philadelphia 1,647 (5,755), Detroit 1,089 (4,577), Dallas 974 (3,348), San Diego 960 (2,064), Phoenix 853 (1,715), San Antonio 843 (1,138), Baltimore 764 (2,245), San Francisco 713 (5,685), Indianapolis 710 (1,195), San Jose 660, Memphis 648 (935), Milwaukee 621 (1,568), Jacksonville 578 (795), Boston 571 (4,027), Columbus 566 (1,279), New Orleans 559 (1,319), Cleveland 546 (2,788), Denver 505 (1,791), Seattle 488 (2,208), El Paso 464 (526), Nashville-Davidson 462 (890), Kansas City 460 (1,477), Oklahoma City 443 (963), St. Louis 429 (2,398), Atlanta 426 (2,380), Fort Worth 413 (2,372), Pittsburgh 402 (2,372), Austin 397 (645), Long Beach 380, Tulsa 374 (726), Miami 373 (2,799), Honolulu 373 (805), Cincinnati 370 (1,673), Portland 366 (1,341), Tuscon 365 (531), Minneapolis 358 (2,231), Oakland 353 (1,863), Albuquerque 351 (449), Toledo 344 (611), Buffalo 339 (1,205), Omaha 334

map 34

State (abbv.)	Area in sq.km	Population (in 1,000, 1984)	Density per sq.km	Capital (population in 1,000, 1984, +1982)
Alabama (Ala.)	133,667	4,021	30	Montgomery (185)
Alaska (Alas.)	1,518,775	521	0.3	Juneau (+21)
Arizona (Ariz.)	295,024	3,187	11	Phoenix (853)
Arkansas (Ark.)	137,539	2,359	17	Little Rock (170)
California (Calif.)	411,015	26,365	64	Sacramento (304)
Colorado (Colo.)	269,998	3,231	12	Denver (505)
Connecticut (Conn.)	12,973	3,174	245	Hartford (136)
Delaware (Del.)	5,328	622	117	Dover (+25)
District of Columbia (D.C.)	174	626	3,598	Washington (623)
Florida (Fla.)	151,670	11,366	75	Tallahassee (112)
Georgia (Ga.)	152,489	5,976	39	Atlanta (426)
Hawaii (Hi.)	16,705	1,054	63	Honolulu (373)
Idaho (Id.)	216,412	1,005	4.6	Boise (107)
Illinois (Ill.)	146,076	11,535	79	Springfield (102)
Indiana (Ind.)	93,994	5,499	59	Indianapolis (710)
Iowa (Ia.)	145,791	2,884	20	Des Moines (191)
Kansas (Kans.)	213,063	2,450	12	Topeka (119)
Kentucky (Ky.)	104,623	3,726	36	Frankfort (+27)
Louisiana (La.)	125,674	4,481	36	Baton Rouge (239)
Maine (Me.)	86,027	1,164	14	Augusta (+23)
Maryland (Md.)	27,394	4,392	160	Annapolis (+34)
Massachusetts (Mass.)	21,386	5,822	272	Boston (571)
Michigan (Mich.)	150,779	9,088	60	Lansing (128)
Minnesota (Minn.)	217,736	4,193	19	Saint Paul (266)
Mississippi (Miss.)	123,584	2,613	21	Jackson (209)
Missouri (Mo.)	180,486	5,029	28	Jefferson City (+34)
Montana (Mont.)	381,087	826	2.2	Helena (+26)
Nebraska (Nebr.)	200,018	1,606	8	Lincoln (180)
Nevada (Nev.)	286,298	936	3.3	Carson City (+35)
New Hampshire (N.H.)	24,097	998	41	Concord (+31)
New Jersey (N.J.)	20,295	7,562	373	Trenton (+93)
New Mexico (N.Mex.)	315,115	1,450	5	Santa Fe (52)
New York (N.Y.)	128,402	17,783	138	Albany (99)
North Carolina (N.C.)	136,197	6,255	46	Raleigh (169)
North Dakota (N.D.)	183,022	685	3.7	Bismarck (+46)
Ohio (Oh.)	106,765	10,744	101	Columbus (566)
Oklahoma (Okla.)	181,090	3,301	18	Oklahoma City (443)
Oregon (Oreg.)	251,181	2,687	11	Salem (+90)
Pennsylvania (Pa.)	117,412	11,853	101	Harrisburg (+53)
Rhode Island (R.I.)	3,144	968	308	Providence (154)
South Carolina (S.C.)	80,432	3,347	42	Columbia (99)
South Dakota (S.D.)	199,552	708	3.6	Pierre (+14)
Tennessee (Tenn.)	109,412	4,762	44	Nashville-Davidson (462)
Texas (Tex.)	692,407	16,370	24	Austin (397)
Utah (Ut.)	219,932	1,645	7	Salt Lake City (165)
Vermont (Vt.)	24,887	535	22	Montpelier (+9)
Virginia (Va.)	105,716	5,706	54	Richmond (219)
Washington (Wash.)	176,617	4,409	25	Olympia (+29)
West Virginia (W.Va.)	62,629	1,936	31	Charleston (+62)
Wisconsin (Wis.)	145,439	4,775	33	Madison (171)
Wyoming (Wyo.)	253,597	509	2	Cheyenne (+50)
UNITED STATES OF AMERICA (U.S.A.)	9,363,125‡	238,740	25.5	Washington (623)

‡9,519,617 including Great Lakes area

(607), Charlotte 331 (647), Newark 320 (1,882), Sacramento 304 (1,220), Louisville 290 (963), Virginia Beach 285, Wichita 283 (429), Birmingham 280 (895), Norfolk 280 (1,026), Tampa 275 (1,811) and further 121 cities with a population of more than 100,000. The share of the urban population was 76.2%.
Census population on 1 April 1980 was 226,545,825 inhabitants (excluding 995,546 inhab. overseas), of whom 188,340,790 were Whites, 26,488,218 Negroes and 11,716,817 other races (of whom 1,420,200 were Indians, 806,000 Chinese, 774,700 Filipino (on Hawaii 132,075), 701,000 Japanese (on Hawaii 239,734), in Alaska 78,480 were Indians, Aleutians and Eskimos; on Hawaii 118,251 were Hawaiians). The total population comprised 48.5% males and 51.5% females; 73.7% were urban and 26.3% were rural. The average annual rate of population increase was 0.88% (1980–85). The age composition was (1983): 0–14 years 22.1%, 15–64 years 66.3%, older than 65 years 11.6%. In 1983 the birth rate was 15.7 per 1,000, death rate 8.7 per 1,000, and infant mortality 10.6 per 1,000. The number of immigrants was 3.1 mn. in 1975–81, in 1981 it was 435,700 (15% from Europe, 36% from Asia, 12% from Mexico, 30% from America). There were 108.4 mn. economically active inhabitants in 1984, of which only 1.8% were in agriculture, 33.2% in industry and 65% in services. – **Currency:** US dollar = 100 cents.

34 a Panama Canal
1 : 1 000 000

Cross Section of Panama Canal (vertical exaggeration x 100)

map 34

Economy: developments in science, research and technology have created the most advanced industrial and agricultural country in the western world. The total volume of the gross domestic product reached 3,276,000 mn. dollars in 1983 (the gross domestic product per capita 13,968 dollars). The US share in the industrial production of all countries (excepting socialist) amounted to 35% and in agricultural production to 20%. The United States of America occupied the leading position (share in world production in 1984): – in mining: first place – mica (69%), bentonite (50%), molybdenum ore (49%), natural gasoline (37%), phosphates (33%), kaolin (31%), salt (22%); second place – sulphur (30%), natural gas (29%), coal (26%), talc (16%), uranium (15%), copper (13%); – in industrial production: first place – petroleum coke (78%), kraft paperboard (69%), chemical wood pulp (48%), magnesium (48%), jet fuel (46%), motor spirit (42%), aviation spirit (40%), paper (33%), tyres (28%), electric energy (27%), passenger cars (25%), beer (24%), lead (20%), cigarettes (20%), fuel oils (19%), copper-refined (16%), roundwood (15%); second place – aluminium (29%); – in agricultural production: first place – soya beans (56%), grapefruits (52%), corn (43%), sorghum (31%), margarine (30%), poultry meat (25%), beef meat (25%), cheese (19%), lemons (16%), tomatoes (14%); – second place: hops (21%), cotton-lint (16%), eggs (14%), milk (14%), tobacco (13%), pork meat (12%), wheat flour (10%), barley, peaches etc.

Industry: these industries hold a leading position in the U.S.A.: energy, mining of fuels and ores, metallurgy, engineering (especially transport and electrotechnical), nuclear industry, chemical industry (above all, petrochemistry and electrochemistry), production of plastics and artificial fibres.

Mining (1984, in 1,000 tonnes): coal and anthracite 750,262 (highest quality coking coal and anthracite – the Appalachians district, Pennsylvania, West Virginia, Kentucky, Illinois, Ohio), brown coal 57,262 (North and South Dakota, New Mexico), crude petroleum 438,127 (Texas 30%, Alaska 20%, Louisiana, California, Oklahoma) – verified deposits 3,775 mn. tonnes (1985), natural gasoline 10.7 mn. tonnes, natural gas 17,181 PJ (Texas 35%, Louisiana 33%, Oklahoma, New Mexico) – verified deposits 5,578 billion cub.m (1985), iron ore 33,640 (region around Lake Superior 80%: Minnesota, Wisconsin), copper ore 1,091 (Arizona 60%, Utah, New Mexico), lead ore 333 (Missouri, Idaho, Utah), zinc ore 278 (Tennessee, New York, Idaho, Colorado), molybdenum ore 47,021 tonnes (Colorado, Arizona, New Mexico), bauxite 856 (Arkansas, Alabama, Georgia), mercury 864 tonnes (California, Nevada, Idaho), gold 64,035 kg (South Dakota, Utah, Nevada, Arizona), silver 1,382 tonnes (Idaho, Arizona, Colorado. Montana), vanadium 1,467 tonnes (Colorado, Utah), tungsten 1,203 tonnes (California, Colorado), nickel ore 13.2, antimony ore, asbestos (California, Vermont), uranium 5,722 tonnes (New Mexico, Wyoming, Utah, Colorado), sulphur – native 4,193 (Texas, Louisiana, California), natural phosphates 49,197 (Florida, Idaho, Tennessee, Montana), kaolin 6,534, bentonite 2,862, mica 146 (North Carolina, Alabama, New Mexico), potassium salt 1,564 (New Mexico, California, Utah), salt 35,544 (Louisiana, Texas, Ohio, New York), asphalt 2,662 (Texas, Utah, Alabama), barytes 703, borate minerals 1,240, gypsum 13,000, pyrites 676 (Tennessee, Colorado), ilmenite 239 (1982, Florida, New Jersey, New York), talc 1,061.

Energy production (1984): capacity of all electric power stations 675 mn. kW, of which hydro-electric power plants 79 mn. kW (11.7%) and nuclear 68 mn. kW (10%). Electricity 2,472 billion kWh (1984), of which nuclear 294 billion kWh and hydro-electric 334 billion kWh (1983). Some of the largest thermal power plants: e.g. Monroe, Pittsburg (Cal.), Paradise, Johnsonville, Sammis, Stuart, Gavin, Houston etc.; largest hydro-electric power plants: e.g. the Grand Coulee 6,494 MW, John Day, Chief Joseph, Niagara Falls System, Raccoon Mt., Ludington, The Dalles, Hoover, St. Lawrence Power System, Castaic, Glen Canyon; largest nuclear power plants: Browns Ferry, McGuire, Trojan, Le Salle, Salem, Susquehanna, Peach Bottom, San Onofre, Zion. Production of gas (by cokeries) 260,371 TJ (1984). **Metallurgy:** production (1984, in 1,000 tonnes): pig iron 47,090 and crude steel 83,940 (13% of the world production, Pennsylvania, Indiana, Ohio, the Appalachians district – Pittsburgh, Youngstown, Chicago, Cleveland, Bethlehem, Sparrows Point), steel products 79,200 (especially Pittsburgh, Chicago, Youngstown, Steubenville, Trenton), aluminium 5,705 (Rockdale, Bellingham, Evansville, Massena), copper -smelted 1,014, -refined 1,516 (Anaconda, Morenci, Garfield, Carteret, El Paso), lead 978 (El Paso, East Helena, Herculaneum, Omaha), zinc 331 (Josephtown, Anaconda, Corpus Christi), cadmium 1,682 tonnes, magnesium 188 (Freeport, Albany, Henderson), uranium processing (Bluewater, Moab, Uravan, Shirley Basin).

Engineering – production (1984): motor vehicles – passenger 7.62 mn., – commercial 3.1 mn., road tractors 156,600 units (Detroit, Cleveland, Kenosha, San Francisco, Toledo, Kansas City), seeders 492,807 and combine harvesters 11,296 units, locomotives and railway carriages (Chicago, Erie, Greenville), aircraft (Los Angeles, Wichita, New York, Fort Worth, Columbus), vessels 286,000 GRT (1982, Baltimore, Boston, Norfolk, Pascagoula, San Diego, San Francisco), machinery equipment, machines and apparatus (Chicago, New York, Cleveland, Philadelphia, Boston, Los Angeles, Worcester, St. Louis, Detroit, Houston, radio 9.8 mn. and television receivers 13.4 mn. (95% colour), (Los Angeles, Rochester, New York etc.), refrigerators 7.5 mn., washing machines 5 mn. units. The rocket and astronautical industries are concentrated on the Pacific coast (San Diego, Los Angeles, San Jose, Seattle), in Texas (Fort Worth, Dallas, Houston), Florida (Orlando), on the Atlantic coast (New York, Philadelphia, Hartford, Boston) and around the Great Lakes (Chicago, Detroit, Buffalo, Cleveland, Cincinnati etc.

Chemical industry (1984, in 1,000 tonnes): sulphuric acid 36,217, nitrogenous fertilizers 9,682, plastics 15,505, synthetic rubber 2,219. Sulphur (as by-product) 5,214. Petroleum refineries have an annual capacity of 771 mn. tonnes (Houston, Beaumont, Port Arthur, Baton Rouge, Philadelphia, Toledo, Chicago, Tulsa, Los Angeles, San Francisco, New York and others). Leading world producer (in 1,000 tonnes): motor spirit 277,887, jet fuels 53,356 and fuel oils 184,989. Production of tyres 209.4 mn. units (Akron). **The timber and paper industries** (1984) are concentrated in the states of Washington, Oregon, California, Montana and in the South- and North-east of the U.S.A. Roundwood 435.3 mn. cub.m, sawnwood 77.4 mn. cub.m. **Production** (1984, in 1,000 tonnes): chemical wood pulp 39,037, mechanical wood pulp 5,023, newsprint 5,121, other paper 16,348, kraft paperboard 33,901. Production of cement 70.6 mn. tonnes (states of California, Texas, Pennsylvania, New York).

The textile and clothing industries are concentrated in the East of the U.S.A. from the southern state of Alabama to the north-eastern state of Maine. Production (1983): cotton -fibres 1,064 mn. tonnes, -fabrics 3,505 mn. m, woollen-fibres 58,800 tonnes, -fabrics 120 mn. sq.m, 60.7 mn. m, 42,800 tonnes, linen fabrics, silk fabrics, synthetic fibres 1.29 mn. tonnes. Footwear 344.3 mn. pairs , rubber footwear 76.2 mn. pairs. Rubber (reclaimed) 72.7 mn. tonnes.

Food industry (1984, in 1,000 tonnes): meat 25,627 (of which poultry 7,479), milk 61,436, cheese 2,042, butter 508, margarine 2,920, soya bean oil 4,931, wheat flour 13,584, sugar 8,434, canned fish 407, beer 228.9 mn. hl, alcoholic beverages 14.4 mn. hl, wine 25.73 mn. hl; 699 billion cigarettes, 3.7 billion cigars.

map 35

Agriculture: arable land covers 187,895,000 ha (i.e. 20.5% of the area of the country), permanent crops 2,034,000 ha. (0.2%), meadows and pastures 26.4%, forests 28.9%; irrigated land 19.8 mn. ha (1983, i.e. 10.6% of the arable land), 4.3 mn. inhabitants engaged in agriculture (1984, i.e. 1.8% of the total population) and 1.95 mn. persons work in advanced agricultural production (i.e. 1.8% of economically active inhabitants). In 1983 4.55 mn. tractors and 676,000 harvester-threshers were used on highly mechanized and specialized farms. The number of farms declined from 6.3 mn. in 1940 to 2,370,000 in 1983. – **Animal production** predominates in the region of the Great Lakes and in California (Wisconsin, Minnesota, New York, Pennsylvania, Ohio etc.), pasture cattle-farming on the prairies (Texas, Iowa, Nebraska, Montana).

Livestock (1984, in 1,000 head): cattle 114,040 (dairy cows 11,204), pigs 55,819 (Iowa, Illinois, Indiana, Minnesota), sheep 11,411 (Texas, California, Colorado, Utah, Wyoming), horses 10,300, poultry 394 mn. production (1984, in 1,000 tonnes): eggs 4,035, honey 95, fresh hides 1,073 (sheepskins 20.7). Fish catch 4.14 mn. tonnes (1983). **Vegetable production:** the world's largest corn-growing region, known as the "corn-belt", runs through the Mid-West (from the Great Lakes along the Canadian frontier to the Great Plains), the Mississippi Lowlands to the Appalachian Mts. Wheat, barley, soya beans, fodder plants, sugar beet, potatoes and vegetables are all grown there. **Crops** (1984, in 1,000 tonnes): maize (corn) 194,475 (Iowa, Illinois, Indiana, Nebraska, Minnesota), wheat 70,638 (Kansas, North Dakota, Oklahoma, Montana, Washington), oats 6,850 (Minnesota, North Dakota, Iowa), barley 12,988 (North Dakota, California, Montana, Idaho), rice 6,216 (Arkansas, Texas, California, Louisiana), sorghum 21,994 (Kansas, Texas, Nebraska, Montana), potatoes 16,404 (Idaho, Washington, Oregon, Maine, California), sweet potatoes 589, pulses 1,164, soya beans 50,643 (Illinois, Iowa, Montana, Indiana, Ohio), groundnuts 2,008, linseed 178, sunflower seed 1,699, cotton -seed 4,811, -lint 2,894 (Texas, California, Mississippi, Arizona), vegetables 28,073 (California, Texas, Ohio, Florida), tomatoes 8,165 (California, Ohio etc.), fruit 22,743 (California, Washington, New York, Michigan, Florida), apples 3,729, peaches 1,365; grapes 4,644 (California), raisins 280, sugarcane 25,427 (Hawaii, Louisiana, Florida), sugar beet 20,146 (California, Idaho, Colorado etc.), oranges (+ tangerines) 6,566 (+446) – lemons 787 – grapefruits 1,945 (California, Florida, Texas, Arizona); pineapples 544 (Hawaii), almonds 417 (37% of the world crops), walnuts 191, tobacco 791 (North Carolina, Kentucky, Virginia, South Carolina, Georgia); hops 25.5, strawberries 447.

Communications (1982): length of railways, decreasing, 265,542 km, carried 17.7 billion passenger-km and 1,340 billion tonnes-km freight; surfaced roads 6,364,955 km (of which 1,332,252 km highways and 687,430 km federal highways); passenger cars 130,053,000 and commercial vehicles (incl. buses) 38,554,000 (1984), 30% of all automobiles in the world. Petroleum pipelines 343,880 km, inter-state gas pipelines 437,500 km, other gas pipelines 1.6 mn. km (1983). Civil aviation (1984); leading world position: 15,831 airports (of which 4,805 public), civil aircraft 264,866, length of federal air-routes 489,619 km, flown 4,825 mn. km, passengers carried 331.4 mn., recorded 479 billion passenger-km and 10.1 billion tonnes-km. Largest airports: Chicago, New York, Atlanta, Los Angeles, Dallas, Denver, Santa Ana, San Francisco, Phoenix. Sea-going merchant vessels (1984) 752 (of 1,000 grosstonnes or over) with tonnage of 24.4 mn. GRT, of which 274 tankers of 16.16 mn. GRT, 24 bulk carriers 1.1 mn. GRT. US exports and imports carried on dry cargo and tanker vessels in the year 1983 totalled 630 mn. tonnes, of which 36.7 mn. tonnes or 5.8% were carried in US flag vessels. Largest ports: New Orleans, New York, Houston, Corpus Christi, Baton Rouge, Norfolk, Tampa, Baltimore, Los Angeles, Beaumont, Philadelphia; inland ports: Duluth, Pittsburgh, Chicago, St. Louis, Toledo, Cincinnati, Detroit. Tourism 21.7 mn. visitors (1983).

The foreign trade of the U.S.A. reached a total turnover of 470,416 mn. dollars in 1983 (i.e. 12.6% of the world turnover), of which exports amounted to 200,538 (11%) and imports to 269,878 (14%) mn. dollars. – **Exports:** machines, machinery equipment, transport vehicles (especially cars and aircraft), metal products and others 50.6%, agricultural products 14.6%, chemicals 14.5%, raw materials (ores, coal etc.) 4.2%, foodstuffs and tobacco products 5.6%. Exports mainly to Canada 18.6%, Japan 10.8%, United Kingdom 5.2%, Mexico 4.6%, Fed. Rep. of Germany 4.2%, Netherlands 3.8%, Saudi Arabia, France, Rep. of Korea etc. – **Imports:** machines, apparatus, industrial products 31.5%, crude petroleum and fuels 22.2%, consumer goods 15.9%, foodstuffs and tropical fruit 7.5%, passenger cars 9.3% etc. Imports came mostly from Canada 19.2%, Japan 16.2%, Mexico 6.3%, Fed. Rep. of Germany 4.9%, United Kingdom 4.8%, Rep. of Korea 2.9%, Hong Kong 2.5%, France 2.4%, Italy, Indonesia, Brazil, Venezuela etc.

PUERTO RICO

Commonwealth of Puerto Rico, area 8,897 sq.km, population 3,389,686 (1985), **self-governing federal state of the United States of America** (since 25 July 1952).

Capital: San Juan 434,849 inhabitants (census 1980, with agglom. 820,442 inhab.); **other towns** (1980, in 1,000 inhab.): Bayamón 196, Ponce 189, Carolina 166, Caguas 118, Mayagüez 96, Arecibo 87, Guaynabo 81. **Density** 368 persons per sq.km; average annual rate of population increase 1.6%, birth rate 19.8 per 1,000, death rate 6.5 per 1,000 (1980–85); urban population 67.1%. – **Currency:** US dollar = 100 cents.

Agriculture: arable land 15%, meadows and pastures 37.5%, forests 21%; crops (1983, in 1,000 tonnes): sugarcane 1,287, bananas 99, pineapples 36, citrus fruit 37, coffee 15, high quality tobacco 1.4; cattle 585,000, pigs 206,000, poultry 6.2 mn. head; milk 384, eggs 20; fish catch 2.54 mn. tonnes. **Production** (1983, in 1,000 tonnes): sugar 101, cement 855, petroleum refineries (largest: Guayanilla, Bayamón and Ponce), motor spirit 2,441, oils 3,870, chemicals, cigars, textiles, electric machinery and equipment, pharmaceuticals, spirits. Electricity (1983) 12.1 billion kWh (of which 96% thermal). – **Communications** (1982): roads 16,827 km, cars 1,164,000. Tourism 1.56 mn. visitors. – **Exports:** sugar, tobacco, textiles, chemicals, spirits.

BAHAMAS

The Commonwealth of the Bahamas, area 13,935 sq.km, population 231,400 (1985), **member of the Commonwealth** (Prime Minister Lynden Oscar Pindling since 1973).

Nearly 700 islands (largest Andros I. 4,145 sq.km). **Capital:** Nassau 135,437 inhab. (1985). **Population:** Negroes, mestizos 85%, Whites 15%. Average annual rate of population increase 1.9%. **Currency:** Bahamian dollar = 100 cents. **Economy:** chiefly tourism – 1.84 mn. visitors (1982); sugarcane 228,000 tonnes, rum, pineapples, sisal, roundwood, mining of salt 684,000 tonnes, fish catch, light industry. Electricity (1983) 905 mn. kWh. – **Exports:** crabs, salt, wood, rum.

map 35

BARBADOS

Area 431 sq.km, population 253,500 (1985), **sovereign state, member of the Commonwealth** (Prime Minister Errol Walton Barrow since 1986).
Capital: Bridgetown 7,552 inhab. (1980, with agglomeration 99,953). **Population:** Negroes 89%. Density 588 persons per sq.km. – **Currency:** Barbadosian dollar = 100 cents.
Economy (1983, in 1,000 tonnes): 45% of island area covered by sugarcane plantations, crops 805, vegetables 12.5; most important products: sugar 83, world-famous rum, electrical goods. Fish catch 3,480 tonnes. Tourism 385,000 visitors (1982). – **Exports:** sugar (45%), rum, electrical goods, chemicals, fish.

BELIZE

Area 22,965 sq.km, population 166,000 inhab. (1985), **autonomous state of the Commonwealth** (Prime Minister Manuel Amadeo Esqivel since 1985).
Capital: Belmopan 2,935 inhab. (1980), **largest town** and harbour Belize 39,771 inhab. **Currency:** Belize dollar = 100 cents. **Economy** (1983, in 1,000 tonnes): sugarcane 1,150, sugar 116, citrus fruit 70, bananas 18, maize 22, coconuts, fishing, hardwoods 118,000 cub.m. – **Exports:** sugar, canned fruit, wood, chicle, fish. Trading partner: U.S.A.

COSTA RICA

República de Costa Rica, area 50,700 sq.km, population 2,416,809 inhab. (census 1984), **republic** (President Oscar Arias Sánchez since 1986).
Administrative units: 7 provinces. **Capital:** San José 277,754 inhab. (1984, with agglom. 766,960); other towns (in 1,000 inhab.): Limón 55, Alajuela 43, Puntarenas 36, Heredia 30, Cartago 29. Average annual rate of population increase 2.6% (1980–85). – **Currency:** colón = 100 centimos.
Economy (1983, in 1,000 tonnes): high quality coffee 126, bananas 1,021, sugarcane 2,560, cocoa beans 5, rice 242, maize 95, cotton-seed 10, oranges 784, coconuts 27, palm oil 24, sugar 200, cattle 2.3 mn. head; poultry 6 mn. head; rare hardwoods 2.6 mn. cub.m; fish catch 10,900 tonnes. Gold 933kg. Cement 0.8 mn. tonnes. Electricity 2,700 mn. kWh (85% hydro energy). – **Communications** (1981): railways 1,285km, roads 28,525km. – **Exports** (1982): coffee 29%, bananas 24%, meat, medicaments, sugar, cocoa. Chief trade with: U.S.A. (40%), Fed Rep. of Germany, Guatemala, Venezuela, Mexico.

CUBA

República de Cuba, area 114,524 sq.km, population 10,098,900 inhab. (1985), **republic** (President Dr Fidel Castro Ruz since 1976).
Administrative units: 14 provinces. **Capital:** La Habana 1,924,886 inhab. (census 1981): other towns (in 1,000 inhab.): Santiago de Cuba 345, Camagüey 245, Holguín 186, Santa Clara 172, Guantánamo 167, Cienfuegos 103, Bayamo 101, Matanzas 99, Pinar del Río 95. **Population:** Creoles 72%, mulattoes 15%, Negroes 12%. Urban population 70%. 21.5% inhabitants employed in agriculture (1983). – **Currency:** Cuban peso 100 centavos.
Economy: monocultural agriculture, mineral mining and industry developing. **Agriculture** (1983): (crops in 1,000 tonnes): sugarcane 66,000 (7.5% of world crops), tobacco 37, citrus fruit 616, bananas 185, pineapples 16, coffee 26, rice 490, manioc 335, maize 96, vegetables 503, potatoes 222, sweet potatoes 332; eggs 115; **livestock** (1983, in 1,000 head): cattle 6,305, pigs 2,100, horses 820, sheep 370, poultry 24 mn.; fish catch 198,500 tonnes. – **Mining** (1983, in 1,000 tonnes, metal content): nickel 39.3 (6.3% of world output), manganese 28, chromium 8, copper 2.7, crude petroleum 742, marble 14, limestone 5,118, salt 180. **Industrial production** (1983, in 1,000 tonnes): sugar 7,480 (7.6% of world production), meat 317, milk 1,109; 16.8 billion cigarettes, 333 mn. cigars; woven cotton fabrics 170 mn. sq.m, silk fabrics 14 mn. sq.m, sulphuric acid 356. Electricity 11,551 mn. kWh. – **Communications** (1982): railways 14,872km, roads 33,200km. Merchant shipping 959,000 GRT. – **Exports** (1983): sugar (75% of turnover), nickel ores, fruit, tobacco and tobacco products, fish. Chief trading partners: U.S.S.R. (70%), Japan, German Dem. Rep., China, Bulgaria, Czechoslovakia.

DOMINICA

The Commonwealth of Dominica, area, 751 sq.km, population 76,000 (1985), **member of the Commonwealth** (President Clarence Augustus Seignoret since 1984).
Capital: Roseau 8,346 inhab. (1981). **Population:** Negroes 74%. **Currency:** Eastern Caribbean dollar = 100 cents.
Economy (1983, in 1,000 tonnes): bananas 37, cocoa beans 3.5, citrus fruit 13, coconuts 15. Forests 42% of the area. Fisch catch. – **Exports:** coconut oil, laurel oil, bananas, citrus fruit. Trade with: United Kingdom, U.S.A., Jamaica.

DOMINICAN REPUBLIC

República Dominicana, area 48,734 sq.km, population 6,242,730 (1985), **republic** (President Dr. Joaquín Balaguer since 1986).
Administrative units: 26 provinces and 1 national district. **Capital:** Santo Domingo 1,318,172 inhab. (census 1981, with agglomeration 1.6 mn. inhab.) – oldest town in America established by Europeans in 1496; other towns (in

map 36

1,000 inhab.); Santiago de los Caballeros 279, La Romana 92, San Pedro d. Mac. 79, San Francisco d. Mac. 65, San Cristóbal 59, Concepción d. l. Vega 52. **Population:** mulattoes 68%, Creoles 20% and Negroes 12%. Average annual rate of population increase 2.3% (1980–85). 54% of inhabitants engaged in agriculture (1983). – **Currency:** peso = 100 centavos. **Economy: Agriculture** (1983, in 1,000 tonnes): sugarcane 11,520, coffee 68, cocoa beans 45, tropical fruit 1,370 (of which citrus fruit 74, avocadoes and mangoes 320, bananas 320), tobacco 34, cattle 2 mn. head, poultry 9 mn. head; fish catch 13,170 tonnes. **Mining and industry** (1983, in 1,000 tonnes): nickel 20.2, gold 11,618 kg, salt 46; production of sugar 1,219; 3.6 billion cigarettes. Electricity: 3,400 mn. kWh. **Communications:** railways 1,076km, roads 17,227 km. – **Exports:** sugar (43%), coffee and cocoa (21%), tropical fruit. Chief trade with: U.S.A., Venezuela, Mexico.

EL SALVADOR

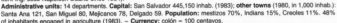

República de El Salvador, area 21,041 sq.km, population: 4,819,175 (1985), **republic** (President Ing. José Napoleon Duarte since 1984).
Administrative units: 14 departments. **Capital:** San Salvador 445,150 inhab. (1983); **other towns** (1980, in 1,000 inhab.): Santa Ana 121, San Miguel 80, Mejicanos 78, Delgado 59. **Population:** mestizos 70%, Indians 15%, Creoles 11%. 48% of inhabitants engaged in agriculture (1983). – **Currency:** colón = 100 centavos.
Economy (1983, in 1,000 tonnes): good quality coffee 155, maize (corn) 444, cotton -seed 60, -lint 41; sugarcane 2,984, citrus fruit 122, bananas 55; raising of cattle 0.95 mn. head, poultry 4.9 mn. head; fish catch 13,490 tonnes; roundwood 4.5 mn. cub.m, balsam gum (the world's principal source). **Production** (in 1,000 tonnes): sugar 234, cement 320, textiles, paper; gold 93kg. Electricity 1,610 mn. kWh. **Communications:** railways 602km, roads 12,235 km. – **Exports** (1982): coffee (29%), cotton, textile yarn, textiles, fish. Chief trade with: Guatemala, U.S.A., Fed. Rep. of Germany, Venezuela.

GRENADA

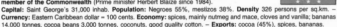

Area 344 sq.km (including part of Grenadine Is. with area 33 sq.km, **population 112,000** (1985), **member of the Commonwealth** (Prime minister Herbert Blaize since 1984).
Capital: Saint George's 31,000 inhab. **Population:** Negroes 55%, mestizos 38%. **Density** 326 persons per sq.km. – **Currency:** Eastern Caribbean dollar = 100 cents. **Economy:** spices, mainly nutmeg and mace, cloves and vanilla; bananas 14,000 tonnes, cocoa beans 3000 tonnes, coconuts, good quality cotton. – **Exports:** cocoa (45%), spices, bananas.

GUATEMALA

República de Guatemala, area 108,899 sq.km, population 7,963,360 (1985), **republic** (President Vinicio Cerezo Arévalo since 1986).

Administrative units: 22 departments. **Capital:** Guatemala 754,243 inhab. (1981); **other towns** (in 1,000 inhab.): Escuintla 77, Quezaltenango 73, Pto.Barrios 53, Retalhuleu 49. **Population:** Indians 55%, mestizos 30%. 53% of inhabitants engaged in agriculture (1983). – **Currency:** quetzal = 100 centavos.
Economy (1983, in 1,000 tonnes): coffee 153, bananas 675, sugarcane 6,624, cotton -seed 76, -lint 48; maize (corn) 1,046, chicle '900 tonnes; cattle 2.2 mn. head, pigs 806,000, sheep 657,000, poultry 14.8 mn.; rare hardwoods 6.8 mn. cub.m; mining (1983): crude petroleum 0.6 mn. tonnes, antimony; production of sugar 536,000 tonnes. Electricity 1,705 mn. kWh. – **Communications** (1981): railways 946km, roads 17,465km. – **Exports:** coffee (28%), cotton, bananas, sugar, chicle, essential oils. Chief trade with: U.S.A., El Salvador, Fed. Rep. of Germany, Japan.

HAITI

République d'Haiti, area 27,750 sq.km, population 5,185,000 (1985), **republic** (President Lieut.-Gen. Henri Namphy since 1986).
Administrative units: 9 departments. **Capital:** Port-au-Prince 684,284 inhab. (1982). **Population:** Negroes 60%, mulattoes 30% and Creoles 10%. 65% of inhabitants engaged in agriculture. – **Currency:** gourde = 100 centimos.
Economy (1983, in 1,000 tonnes): high quality coffee 35, sugarcane 3,000, bananas 230, mangoes 340, rice 113, maize (corn) 180; breeding of pigs 0.6 mn. head, cattle 1.3 mn., goats 1.1 mn., mining of bauxite 431,000 tonnes; roundwood 5.6 mn. cub.m. – **Exports:** coffee (30%), bauxite, sugar, fruit. Chief trade with: U.S.A. (65%), France, Canada.

HONDURAS

República de Honduras, area 112,088 sq.km, population 4,372,490 (1985), **republic** (President José Simon Azcona del Hoyo since 1986).
Administrative units: 18 departments. **Capital:** Tegucigalpa 508,000 inhab. (1983); **other towns** (in 1,000 inhab.): San Pedro Sula 398, El Progreso 105, La Ceiba 61, Choluteca 54, Puerto Cortés 40. Average annual rate of population increase 3.4% (1980–85). – **Currency:** lempira = 100 centavos.
Economy: Agriculture (1983, in 1,000 tonnes): bananas 1,186, sugarcane 3,195, coffee 87, maize (corn) 458, palm kernels, citrus fruit; cattle 2.7 mn. head, pigs 409,000, poultry 5.2 mn. head. **Mining** (1983, in 1,000 tonnes): lead 19.3, zinc 38, silver 78 tonnes, salt 32; production of sugar 213; roundwood 5.2 mn. cub.m. Electricity 1,150 mn. kWh. – **Communications** (1983): railways 1,268km, roads 9,718km. – **Exports:** bananas (35%), coffee (25%), wood, meat, ores. Chief trade with: U.S.A. (47%), Trinidad, Japan, Guatemala.

MEXICO:

States:		
1 Aguascalientes	9 Durango	18 Nuevo León	27 Tamaulipas
2 Baja California Norte	10 Guanajuato	19 Oaxaca	28 Tlaxcala
3 Baja California Sur	11 Guerrero	20 Puebla	29 Veracruz
4 Campeche	12 Hidalgo	21 Querétaro	30 Yucatán
5 Chiapas	13 Jalisco	22 Quintana Roo	31 Zacatecas
6 Chihuahua	14 México	23 San Luis Potosí	
7 Coahuila	15 Michoacán	24 Sinaloa	Distrito Federal
8 Colima	16 Morelos	25 Sonora	(México)
	17 Nayarit	26 Tabasco	

1 : 25 000 000

0   200   400   600 Km
0   100   200   300   400 Mi

36a Cuba
1 : 10 000 00

map 36

Economy (1983, in 1,000 tonnes: cotton -seed 119, -lint 80; coffee 48, sugarcane 2,911, maize (corn) 218, rice 171, oranges 55, pineapples 37, bananas 128; cattle 2.1 mn. head, poultry 5 mn. head. **Mining:** gold 1,444 kg, silver 2,000 kg. Sugar 249,000 tonnes, meat 88,000 tonnes. – **Communications:** railways 344 km, roads 24,748 km. – **Exports:** coffee (40%), cotton (23%), sugar, meat. Chief trade with Mexico, Fed. Rep. of Germany, U.S.S.R., Costa Rica, Japan.

PANAMA

República de Panamá, area 77,326 sq.km (incl. Canal Zone), **population 2,180,490** (1985), **republic** (President Eric Arturo del Valle since 1985).
Administrative units: 10 provinces. **Capital:** Panamá 388,600 inhab. (1980, with agglom. 645,000); other towns (in 1,000 inhab.): San Miguelito 158, Colón 60, David 51, La Chorrera 37. **Population:** mestizos 60%, Whites 15%, Indians 10%, Negroes, mulattoes. Average annual rate of population increase 2.2% (1980–85). – **Currency:** balboa = 100 centesimos.
Economy (1983, in 1,000 tonnes): bananas 1,100, maize (corn) 69, rice 198, oranges 65, coconuts 23, sugarcane 2,094; sugar 188; cattle 1.5 mn. head, poultry 6 mn. head; fish catch 166,100 tonnes. Roundwood 2.1 mn. cub.m – forests cover 53% of the land area. Electricity: 2,700 mn. kWh. – **Communications** (1984): railways 185 km, roads 8,862 km, petroleum pipeline 130 km. Merchant shipping 37,244,000 GRT (third place in world; tankers 7,920,000 and ore vessels 14,558,000 GRT). – **Exports:** bananas (25%), fish, sugar, petroleum products. Chief trade with: U.S.A. (42%), Venezuela, Mexico, Japan.
CANAL ZONE, area 746 sq.km, **population 38,750** (1982), **territory of Panama** rented to the U.S.A. till 2000. **The Panama Canal** was built in 1903–14, length 81.6 km, depth 12.5–13.7 m, 6 locks lifting ships to 26 m above sea-level. In 1984 11,230 ships passed through the canal with a cargo of 140.5 mn. tonnes (of which 78.3 mn. tonnes from the Atlantic to the Pacific Ocean and 62.2 mn. tonnes from the Pacific to the Atlantic Ocean). Railways 77 km.

ANTIGUA AND BARBUDA

Area 442 sq.km, population 80,150 (1985), **sovereign state, member of the Commonwealth** (Prime Minister Vere C. Bird since 1981).

Islands: Antigua (280 sq.km), Barbuda (160 sq.km) and Redonda (2 sq.km). **Capital:** St. John's 18,000 inhab. (1980). **Economy:** sugarcane, cotton. **Production:** sugar, rum, spirits. Tourism 64,400 visitors (1981).

SAINT CHRISTOPHER AND NEVIS

Area 261 sq.km, population 47,000 (1985), **member of the Commonwealth** (Prime Minister Dr. Kennedy Alphonse Simmonds since 1980).

Islands: St. Christopher 168 sq.km, Nevis 93 sq.km. **Capital:** Basseterre 15,726 inhab. **Population:** Negroes, mestizos. – **Currency:** Eastern Caribbean dollar = 100 cents.
Economy (1983, in 1,000 tonnes): sugarcane 315, cotton, coconuts 3, copra, sugar 30, salt. Tourism. – **Exports:** salt, cotton, copra.

SAINT LUCIA

Area 616 sq.km, population 134,000 (1984), **member of the Commonwealth** (Prime Minister John G. M. Compton since 1985).

Capital: Castries 47,000 inhab. (1982). **Population:** Negroes 65%, mestizos 20%, Indos. **Density** 190 persons per sq.km. – **Currency:** Eastern Caribbean dollar = 100 cents.
Economy (1983, in 1,000 tonnes): bananas 61, mangoes 45, coconuts 30, copra 5, cocoa beans, citrus fruit and citrus juices, ginger. Tourism 87,610 visitors. – **Exports:** bananas, copra, juices.

SAINT VINCENT AND GRENADINES

Area 389 sq.km, population 105,000 (1985), **member of the Commonwealth** (Prime Minister James Fitz Allen Mitchell since 1985).

Capital: Kingstown 24,764 inhab. (1982). **Population:** Negroes and mulattoes 75%, mestizos 15%. – **Currency:** Eastern Caribbean dollar = 100 cents.
Economy (1983, in 1,000 tonnes): world producer of arrowroot (used in pharmacy), bananas 33, coconuts 21, copra, nutmeg, ginger and other spices. – **Exports:** arrowroot, bananas, spices.

add page 158

map 36

JAMAICA

Area 10,991 sq.km, population 2,190,000 (1985) **member of the Commonwealth** (Prime Minister Edward Seaga since 1980).

Capital: Kingston 100,637 inhab. (1982, with agglom. 565,487); **other towns** (in 1,000 inhab.): Spanish Town 81, Portmore 67, Montego Bay 60. **Population:** Negroes and mulattoes 97%. Only 19% of inhabitants engaged in agriculture (1982). – **Currency:** Jamaica dollar = 100 cents.

Agriculture (1983, in tonnes): sugarcane 2,655, bananas 160, citrus fruit 79, coconuts 112, Jamaica pepper 3,790 tonnes; cattle 315,000 head, poultry 5 mn. head. **Mining** (1983, in 1,000 tonnes): bauxite 7,672 (10% of world production); **production:** aluminium 1.73 mn. tonnes, cement 240, sugar 198, world-famous rum 186,000 hl, light industry. Electricity: 2,350 mn. kWh. – **Communications:** railways 328 km, roads 4,737 km. Tourism 408,000 visitors. – **Exports** (1983): aluminium (47%), bauxite (18%), sugar, rum, bananas.

MEXICO

Estados Unidos Mexicanos, area 1,972,546 sq.km, population 78,524,158 (1985), **federal republic** (President Miguel de La Madrid Hurtado since 1982).

Administrative units: 31 federal states and 1 federal district. **Capital:** México 9,373,353 inhab. (census 1980; with agglom. 15.7 mn., 1983); **other towns** (1980, in 1,000 inhab.): Guadalajara 2,245, Monterrey 1,916, Netzahualcoyotl 1,341, Puebla 836, León 656, Ciudad Juárez 567, Culiacán 560, Mexicali 511, Tijuana 461, Mérida 425, Acapulco 409, Chihuahua 407, San Luis Potosí 407, Torreón 364, Aguascalientes 359, Toluca 357, Morelia 353, Hermosillo 340, Saltillo 322, Durango 321, Veracruz 305, Querétaro 293, Tampico 268, Villahermosa 251, Mazatlán 250, Irapuato 246, Matamoros 239, Cuernavaca 232, Celaya 219, Jalapa 213, Reynosa 211, Nuevo Laredo 203, Coatzacoalcos 186, Cd. Obregón 182 and further 24 cities with more than 100,000 inhabitants. **Population:** mestizos 55%, Indians 30%, Whites and Creoles 15%. **Density** 40 persons per sq.km (1985); average annual rate of population increase 2.7%, birth rate 34 per 1,000, death rate 7.1 per 1,000 (1980–85); urban population 66.5% (1982). Economically active 21.8 mn., 33.5% engaged in agriculture (1983). – **Currency:** Mexican peso = 100 centavos.

Economy: agricultural and industrial country with important mineral mining, among the most developed countries in Latin America. **Agriculture:** arable land covers 12.3% (of this: 5.3 mn. ha irrigated), meadows and pastures 38.7% and forests 25% of the land area (1983). **Crops** (1983, in 1,000 tonnes): cereals 15,740 (of this: wheat 3,697, rice 655, barley 533, maize (corn) 13,928, sorghum 6,367 (10% of world production), potatoes 910, beans 1427 (11% of world production), soya beans 880, groundnuts 51, sesame 41 (states Michoacán, Guerrero, Oaxaca), cotton -seed 350, -lint 220; coconuts 825, copra 145, olives 44, palm kernels 8.5, vegetables 2,560 (tomatoes 1,090), sugarcane 36,000, fruit 7,208 (oranges and tangerines 1,710, lemons 580, avocadoes 448, mangoes 665, pineapples 410, bananas 1,624, grapes 480), coffee 240 (states Veracruz, Chiapas, Oaxaca), cocoa beans 43, tobacco 66. **Livestock** (1983, in million head): cattle 33.9 (dairy cows 9.1), pigs 18.9, sheep 6.5, horses 5.7 (9% of world production), mules and asses 6.4, goats 10.4, poultry 219 (turkeys 14.2); eggs 660,220 tonnes, honey 70,000 tonnes, cowhides 101,000 tonnes; fish catch 1.1 mn. tonnes. Roundwood 19.8 mn. cub.m (1983), chicle 1.500 tonnes.

Mining (1983, in 1,000 tonnes, metal content): crude petroleum 138,577 (deposits 6,800 mn. tonnes, along the Gulf of Mexico: states Veracruz, Chiapas, Tabasco), natural gasoline 6,769, natural gas 1,048 PJ, silver 1,911 tonnes (first place, 14.1% of world output, states Hidalgo, Chihuahua), lead 167 and zinc 257 (Chihuahua, Nuevo Léon, Hidalgo): coal 7,830, iron ore 5,306 (states Durango, Colima), copper 206, manganese 133, molybdenum 5.9, gold 6,930 kg, antimony 2.5, mercury 221 tonnes, graphite 44.3, mica 1,560 tonnes, bismuth 606 tonnes, tungsten 71 tonnes, barytes 350, fluorite 605, sulphur 1,602, natural phosphates 210, salt 5,703. **Production** (1983, in 1,000 tonnes): pig iron 4,968, crude steel 6,727, lead 153, zinc 174 aluminium 40, copper 81; cars 284,100 units, tyres 8.7 mn. units, tractors 15,714 units, sulphuric acid 2,996, synthetic rubber 132, motor spirit 15,118, kerosene 1,828, jet fuels 1,288, fuel oils 30,960 (capacity of petroleum refineries 67.6 mn. tonnes), nitrogenous fertilizers 1,405, chemical wood pulp 405, paper 1,937, woven cotton fabrics 477 mn. sq.km, cement 17,363; 46.8 billion cigarettes, beer 24.1 mn. hl, soft drinks 52 mn. hl, wine 502,000 hl, meat 1,648, flour 2,435, sugar 2,920, oils of vegetable origin 769, milk 7,300, cheese 101, canned fish 69. Electricity (1983): capacity 21.9 mn. kWh, production 82,343 mn. kWh. – **Communications** (1983): railways 25,645 km, roads 216,100 km (of which 10,283 km Panamerican Highway), motor vehicles – passenger 5.2 mn. and commercial 1.9 mn. units. Merchant shipping 1,475,100 GRT. Civil aviation – 182 mn. km flown, 14.6 mn. passengers carried. Tourism 4.7 mn. visitors. – **Exports** (1983): crude petroleum and petroleum products (72%), chemicals, coffee, metals, natural gas, fruit, vegetables, fish and canned fish, sugar, cotton. Chief trading partners: U.S.A. (58%), Japan, Spain, France, Brazil, United Kingdom, Canada.

NICARAGUA

República de Nicaragua, area 148,000 sq.km, population 3,272,000 (1985), **republic** (Provisional President Daniel Ortega Saavedra since 1985).

Administrative units: 16 departments. **Capital:** Managua 627,000 inhab. (1981), **other towns** (in 1,000 inhab.): León 122, Granada 68, Masaya 65, Chinandega 54. **Population:** mestizos 70%, Whites, Indians 6%. Average annual rate of population increase 3.3% (1980–85). – **Currency:** córdoba = 100 centavos.

map 37

SOUTH AMERICA

The larger part of the South American continent lies in the Southern Hemisphere where it is isolated from the other continents, save North America to which it is linked by the narrow Isthmus of Panama (width 48 km). Christopher Columbus is generally recognized as one of the first explorers to have reached South America, and on his third expedition (1498–1500), he discovered Trinidad and the mouth of the Orinoco; in 1499 a Spanish expedition led by Alonso de Ojeda reached the mouth of the Amazonas (Amazon), and in 1500 the Portuguese P.A. Cabral reached the shores of Brazil.

South America is the fourth largest continent; it measures **17,843,000 sq.km**, has **269 mn. inhabitants** (1985) but with a density of only 15 persons per sq.km. **Geographical position:** northernmost point: Punta Gallinas 12°27′ N.Lat.; southernmost point – on the mainland: Cape Froward 53°54′ S.Lat., on the Peninsula de Brunswick, of the entire continent – Is. Diego Ramirez 56°32′ S.Lat. in Drake Passage; easternmost point: C.Branco 34°45′ W.Long.; westernmost point: Cape Punta Pariñas 81°22′ W.Long., incl. Galapagos Is. 92°01′ W. Long. The maximum length of the South American continent is 7,350 km, as far as Cape Horn 7,550 km, and its maximum width is 5,170 km.

The topography of South America has few distinguishing horizontal features. The coastline is 28,700 km long and islands make up but 1% of the area of the continent. The largest islands include Tierra del Fuego (71,500 sq.km) and the Falkland Is. (11,961 sq.km) in the South Atlantic Ocean, the Chilean Islands of Western Patagonia (18,000 sq.km) and the Galapagos Is. (7,844 sq.km) to the West of Ecuador in the Pacific Ocean, Ilha de Marajó (42,000 sq.km) and the Ilha Caviana (5,000 sq.km) in the mouth of the Amazonas and Trinidad in the Atlantic Ocean (4,827 km).

The vertical features of the continent are most striking in the West where the Andes rise to nearly 7,000 m, but otherwise low-lying land prevails. Lowlands not higher than 300 m make up more than 50% of the land area, and higher plateaux only 15%. The simple shape of the continent is due to its geological structure and geomorphological evolution. Above the geologically old depressions in the Pacific Ocean, from west of the Isthmus of Panama as far as the southern point of the continent, Tertiary and Quaternary folding raised the narrow strip of high mountain ranges of the South American Cordilleras, called the Andes, to a length of some 9,000 km. They are divided into 30 main ranges, of which the most important are: the north and north-western Andes reaching their highest point in P. Cristóbal Colón (5,775 m), the Ecuadorian Andes with the extinct crater of Chimborazo (6,297 m), the Peruvian Andes with the highest peaks Nevado de Huascarán (6,768 m) and Nudo Coropuna (6,425 m). In the Bolivian Cordillera Real, Nev. Ancohuma reaches the height of 6,550 m. The highest point of the continent, Aconcagua (6,959 m) rises in the Argentinian-Chilean Cordilleras, and the strongly glaciated Patagonian Cordilleras rise to 4,058 m on San Valentin. The core of the continent is formed by the vast, ancient Brazilian-Guyanian shield, which is composed of the oldest rocks and effusive plutonic rock, deeply eroded and denuded, which reach their highest point in the Brazilian peak of Pico de Neblina (3,014 m). Between these two main units, the Andes and the shield, stretch extensive lowlands: those of the Orinoco, the Amazonas and the Rio de La Plata where the basins of the great rivers form terraces and plains with slopes and plateaux – chapadas – at the watersheds. The lowest point is Salinas Chicas (–40 m) on the Valdés peninsula (Argentina). Volcanic activity in the Andes dates back to the end of the Tertiary period and it continues even now. There are some 40 inactive volcanoes and roughly 50 active ones (the highest: V. Guallatiri, 6,060 m, Lascar, 5,900 m and Cotopaxi, 5,897 m). The Chile-Peru Trench (8,066 m) off the west coast of the continent is the epicentre of powerful earthquakes.

The river network is one of the densest in the world. The annual mean discharge amounts to 7,904 cub.km. Almost 88% of the land drains into the Atlantic Ocean, where the Amazonas (Amazon), the longest river in the world, has its mouth (with the Ucayali-Apurímac: length 7,025 km, drainage area 7,050,000 sq.km, annual discharge 3,800 cub.km, maximum flow 225,000 cub.m per sec., minimum 115,000 cub.m per sec.). The Amazonas has 20 tributaries longer than 1,500 km. Other major rivers include the Paraná, Madeira, Orinoco, São Francisco, Paraguay and Magdalena. There are few **lakes**, the largest being L. de Maracaibo (14,343 sq.km), Lagoa dos Patos (10,145 sq.km), and L. Titicaca (6,850 sq.km). The Andes are characterized by valleys that have no outlet to the sea, extensive salt swamps – salars (Salar de Uyuni) and, in the South, lakes of glacial origin.

The main part of South America belongs to zones with tropical and subtropical **climates**, while the narrower South belongs to the temperate zone. Everywhere the climate changes with altitude, as do the natural and cultivated forms of vegetation. The highest annual mean temperature was measured at Maracaibo (Venezuela) 28.9°C, the lowest at Cristo Redentor in the Paso de Bermejo (Argentina) –1.8°C; absolute maximum temperature – Rivadavia 48.9°C (Argentina), minimum – Sarmiento (–33°C). Highest annual mean precipitation – Buenaventura 7,155 mm, lowest – Arica 0.8 mm. Mean January and July temperatures in °C (and annual rainfall in mm): Maracaibo 26.7 and 29.5 (577), Bogotá 14.2 and 13.9 (1,059), Quito 13.1 and 12.9 (1,246), Manaus 25.9 and 26.9 (2,001), Recife 27.1 and 24.2 (1,498), Lima 21.7 and 15.6 (41), Cuzco 13.6 and 10.3 (813), La Paz 11.6 and 8.7 (574), Arica 27.1 and 19.3 (0.8), Goiás 23.6 and 22.5 (1,646), Rio de Janeiro 25.4 and 20.2 (1,076), São Paulo 27.7 and 21.2 (1,361), Asunción 28.8 and 18.2 (1,344), Córdoba 32.1 and 18.6 (707), Buenos Aires 29.5 and 14.5 (1,008), Santiago 29.4 and 14.5 (351), Sarmiento 17.7 and 3.6 (142), Punta Arenas 10.8 and 2.0 (366).

The natural vegetation of the neotropical region: the largest evergreen rain forests in the world (Hylea), scrub steppe, savanna (llanos), Xerophilous Chaco woodlands, pampas, deserts with cacti, Andean desert (punas and paramos), Antarctic flora. The neotropical zone contains some **animal life**: pumas, jaguars, tapirs, mountain llamas, guanaco, vicuñas, alpaca, ant-eaters, sloths, armadillos, howler, chatter monkeys, etc. It has the richest bird life in the world, more than 3,500 species, including Harpie eagles, condors, toucans with brilliant plumage, humming-birds, parrots, as well as the largest snakes in the world – anacondas, rattle snakes, caymans – large numbers of insects and big fishes – piraibas, pirañas, multi-coloured aquarium fishes, etc.

The oldest **inhabitants** of South America are Indians. The inflow of White Europeans began in the 16th century and later Black Africans (and fewer Asians) arrived, which led to a marked intermingling of races: mestizos – Indian and White, mulattoes – Negro and White, and zamboes – Indian and Negro. In 1985 there were 269 mn. inhabitants, i.e. 5.6% of the world's population, of which 50.4% lived in Brazil, 11.4% in Argentina and 10.7% in Colombia. At almost 2.5% there is a high natural increase of population. Over 70% of the inhabitants live in towns (Uruguay 83.5%, Argentina 83%) and there has been a rapid expansion of the metropolises, usually the capital cities. There are 19 towns with over a million inhabitants (largest: São Paulo, Rio de Janeiro, Buenos Aires, Lima, Bogotá) and 18 towns with more than 500,000 inhabitants.

map 37

LONGEST RIVERS

Name	Length in km	River basin in sq.km
Amazonas (-Ucayali-Apurímac)	7,025	7,050,000
Paraná (-Grande)	4,380	4,250,000
Madeira (-Mamoré)	4,100	1,360,000
Purus	3,380	1,100,000
Juruá	3,285	
Tocantins (-Araguaia)	3,100	1,180,000
São Francisco	2,900	631,670
Japurá (-Caquetá)	2,820	
Orinoco	2,740	1,085,000
Tocantins	2,700	840,000
Araguaia	2,630	340,000
Paraguay	2,550	1,150,000
Uruguay (-Canoas)	2,200	420,000
Xingú	2,100	450,000
Ucayali (-Apurímac)	1,980	375,000
Tapajós	1,950	460,000
Parnaíba do Norte	1,720	

HIGHEST MOUNTAINS

Name (Country)	Height in m
Aconcagua (Arg.)	6,959
Ojos del Salado (Arg.-Chile)	6,880
Co. Bonete (Arg.)	6,872
Mte. Pissis (Arg.)	6,779
Co. Mercedario (Arg.)	6,770
Nev. de Huascarán (Peru)	6,768
V. Llullaillaco[+] (Chile-Arg.)	6,723
Nev. Cachi (Arg.)	6,720
Co. Yerupaja (Peru)	6,632
Nev. Ancohuma (Bol.)	6,550
Nev. Sajama (Bol.)	6,542
Nev. Illampú (Bol.)	6,485
Nudo Coropuna[+] (Peru)	6,425
Nev. Auzangate (Peru)	6,384
Chimborazo (Ecuador)	6,297
P. Cristóbal Colón (Col.)	5,775
[+] inactive volcano	

LARGEST LAKES

Name	Area sq.km	Altitude in m
Lago de Maracaibo	14,343	Sea level
Lagoa dos Patos	10,145	Sea level
Salar de Uyuni	10,000	3,660
Lago Titicaca	6,850	3,812
Lagoa Mirim	2,965	1
Lago de Poopó	2,530	3,690
Lago Buenos Aires	2,400	217
Lago Argentino	1,415	187

LARGEST ISLANDS

Name	Area in sq.km
Tierra del Fuego	71,500
Ilha de Marajó	42,000
Isla de Chiloé	8,394
Wellington	6,750
East Falkland	6,682
West Falkland	5,258
Trinidad	4,827
Isla Isabela	4,278

ACTIVE VOLCANOES

Name (Country)	Altitude in m	Latest eruption
V. Guallatiri (Chile)	6,060	1960
Lascar (Chile)	5,990	1968
Cotopaxi (Ecuador)	5,897	1975
Ubinas (Peru)	5,672	1969
Nev. del Ruiz (Col.)	5,380	1986
Sangay (Ecuador)	5,230	1981
Puracé (Col.)	4,756	1977
Reventador (Ecuador)	3,485	1976
V. Osorno (Chile)	2,661	1980

FAMOUS NATIONAL PARKS

Name (Country)	Area in sq.km
P. da Neblina (Braz.-Ven.)	35,600
Jaú (Braz., Amazonas)	27,720
Manu (Peru)	15,328
Nahuel Huapi (Argentina)	7,850
Def. del Chaco (Paraguay)	7,800
Galápagos (Ecuador)	6,912
Los Glaciares (Argentina)	6,430
Iguaçú (Braz.-Arg.)	2,530

SOUTH AMERICA

Country	Area in sq.km	Population year 1985	Density per sq.km	Capital
Argentina	2,780,092	30,563,830	11	Buenos Aires
Bolivia	1,098,581	6,429,226	6	Sucre and La Paz
Brazil	8,511,965	135,564,000	16	Brasília
Chile	757,402	12,074,480	16	Santiago
Colombia	1,138,914	28,840,000	26	Bogotá
Ecuador	283,561	9,377,980	33	Quito
Falkland Islands a. Depen. (U.K.)	16,439	2,200	0.1	Stanley
French Guiana (Fr.)	91,000	80,000	0.9	Cayenne
Guyana	214,969	790,400	3.7	Georgetown
Netherlands Antilles	993	260,000	262	Willemstad
Paraguay	406,752	3,681,460	9	Asunción
Peru	1,285,216	19,697,500	15	Lima
Surinam	163,265	389,000	2.4	Paramaribo
Trinidad and Tobago	5,128	1,185,000	231	Port of Spain
Uruguay	177,508	3,012,000	17	Montevideo
Venezuela	912,050	17,316,740	19	Caracas

map 38

South America has two distinct types of **economy:** one typical of the developing countries and the other typical of advanced, more industrialized countries, like Brazil, Argentina, Venezuela. The economies of countries with highly specialized industries fluctuate in accordance with world economics. Agriculture takes the form of monoculture on plantations: the most important crops are corn, manioc, sugarcane, soya beans, wheat, sunflower seed, coffee, bananas, oranges, while cattle breeding and sheep rearing are also important. The mining industry is highly developed and extremely important, but most of the products are exported as raw materials. Manufacturing is developing slowly as yet and plays only an insignificant part. The continent is densely covered in forests (53.4% of the total area) and it has the richest sources of water power in the world 617,600 MW (especially Brazil, 35%), but so far it has been put to limited use, for only in recent decades have major dams and hydro power-stations been built, mainly in Brazil. **Transport and foreign trade** are of exceptional importance to the economic development of South America.

ARGENTINA

República Argentina, area 2,780,092 sq.km, population 30,563,830 (1985), **federal republic** (President Dr. Raúl Alfonsín Foulkes since 1983).

Administrative units: 22 provinces, 1 federal district and 1 national territory. **Capital:** Buenos Aires 2,908,100 inhab. (1980, [+]metropolitan area Gran Buenos Aires 9,710,000 inhab.); **other towns** (1980 census, in 1,000 inhab.): Córdoba 989, Rosario 954, La Matanza[+] 947, Morón[+] 597, La Plata 560, Lomas de Zamora[+] 509, Gen. Sarmiento[+] 501, S.M.d. Tucumán[+] 466, Quilmes[+] 442, Gen. San Martín[+] 384, Mar del Plata 384, Santa Fe 375, Tres de Febrero[+] 340, Almirante Brown[+] 333, Avellaneda[+] 331, San Juan 291, Vicente López[+] 290, San Isidro[+] 287, Merlo[+] 283, Salta 266, Bahía Blanca 221, Corrientes 180, Resistencia 175, Paraná 160, Sgo. del Estero 148, Mendoza 118. **Population:** Argentinians (only 36,000 Indians). **Density** 11 persons per sq.km (1985); average annual rate of population increase 1.6%; urban population 83%. 12% of inhabitants employed in agriculture (1984). – **Currency:** Austral = 1,000 Pesos.
Economy: agricultural and industrial country. **Agriculture:** 13.2% of the land area covered by arable land, 52% meadows and pastures, 22% forests; irrigated land 1.62 mn. ha. **Crops** (1983, in 1,000 tonnes): wheat 11,700, maize (corn) 8,840, barley 171, oats 538, sorghum 8,250, rice 277, potatoes 2,013, sugarcane 15,794, soya beans 3,750, groundnuts 230, sunflower 2,300, flax (seed) 670 (28% of world crop – leading world producer), cotton -seed 202, -lint 111; olives 108, vegetables 1,561, fruit 6,471 (citrus fruit 1,454, grapes 3,555), tea 41, yerba maté tea 146, tobacco 74. **Livestock** (1983, in million head): cattle 53.7 (dairy cows 3.1), pigs 3.8, sheep 31, horses 3.1, poultry 48.1; fish catch 416,300 tonnes; production (1983, in 1,000 tonnes): meat 3,214, milk 5,730, eggs 306, tung oil 15, grease wool 104, cowhides 333, sheepskins 35.6. Roundwood: 10.4 mn. cub.m, quebracho 111,000 tonnes.
Mining (1983, in 1,000 tonnes, metal content): crude petroleum 25,220, natural gas 456.5 PJ, coal 518, iron ore 389.8, zinc 36.6, lead 32, silver 78 tonnes, gold 727 kg, uranium 180 tonnes, salt 1,095, beryllium, mica. Electricity: 42,998 mn. kWh (of this 5,054 nuclear). **Industry:** food processing predominates, light industry and metallurgy are important. **Production** (1983, in 1,000 tonnes): pig iron 972, crude steel 2,892, lead 39, zinc 27.6, aluminium 141, motor spirit 5,628, cement 5,868, sulphuric acid 264; fibres – cotton 83, paper 887, sunflower oil 468, flour 2,678, sugar 1,635, cheese 230, wine 25,1 mn. hl, 28.3 billion cigarettes.
Communications (1983): railways 36,185 km, roads 229,600 km (4,835 Panamerican Highway), passenger cars 3.6 mn. Merchant shipping 2,470,000 GRT. Civil aviation (1984): 70.8 mn. km flown and 5.1 mn. passengers carried. – **Exports** (1982): cereals (wheat, maize etc.) and animal (meat, hides, wool) products predominate, flour, foodstuffs (65% of turnover), machines, chemicals, leather, raw materials. Chief trading partners: U.S.A., U.S.S.R., Brazil, Japan, F.R. of Germany.

BOLIVIA

República de Bolivia, area 1,098,581 sq.km, population 6,429,226 (1985), **republic** (President Victor Paz Estenssoro since 1985).

Administrative units: 9 departments. **Capital:** La Paz 881,404 (seat of the government) and Sucre 79,941 inhab. **other towns** (1982, in 1,000 inhab.): Santa Cruz de la Sierra 377, Cochabamba 282, Oruro 132, Potosí 103. **Population:** Indians 65%, mestizos 30% and Creoles. 48% of inhabitants engaged in agriculture (1983); average annual rate of population increase 2.7%. – **Currency:** Boliviano.
Economy: principal branch – mineral **mining** (1983, in 1,000 tonnes, metal content): antimony 10.5 (prime world producer, Potosí), tin 25.3 (Oruro, Potosí), tungsten 2,410 tonnes (Atocha), crude petroleum 1,090, natural gas 88.5 PJ, zinc 48, lead 12.4, silver 158 tonnes, gold 1,545 kg. **Agriculture:** crops (1983, in 1,000 tonnes): maize 338, rice 61, manioc 180, potatoes 305, sugarcane 2,590, bananas 151, citrus fruit 132, coffee 18; sugar 249; **livestock** (1983, in million head): cattle 4.2, pigs 1.7, sheep 9.2, llamas and alpacas 1.9, poultry 10. Electricity 1,698 kWh (1983). – **Communications** (1983): railways 3,774 km, roads 40,969 km. – **Exports** (1982): tin (50%), base metal ores, natural gas etc. Chief trading partners: Argentina, U.S.A., Brazil, Japan, Peru.

BRAZIL

República Federativa do Brazil, area 8,511,965 sq.km, population 135,564,000 (1985), **federal republic** (President José Sarney de Araújo Costa since 1985).

Administrative units: 23 federal states, 3 federal territories, 1 federal district. **Capital:** Brasília 1,177,393 inhab.; **other towns** (1980 census, in 1,000 inhab.): São Paulo 8,494 (with agglomeration 12.8 mn.), Rio de Janeiro 5,093 (with agglom. 9.3 mn.), Belo Horizonte 1,782, Salvador 1,507, Fortaleza 1,309, Recife 1,205, Pôrto Alegre 1,126, Nova Iguaçu 1,095, Curitiba 1,026, Belém 934, Goiânia 718, Manaus 635, São Gonçalo 615, Duque de Caxias 576, Campinas 566, Santo

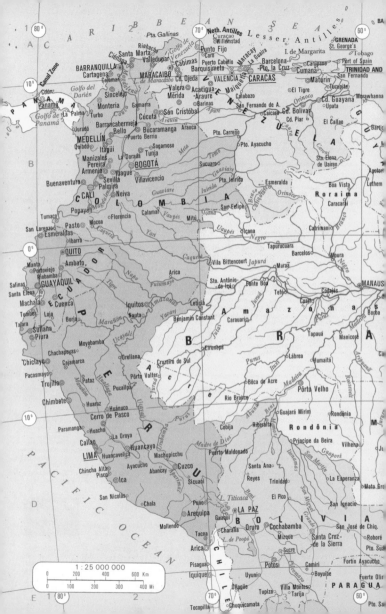

B R A Z I L

States:

1 Acre	17 Rio de Janeiro
2 Alagoas	18 Rio Grande do Norte
3 Amazonas	19 Rio Grande do Sul
4 Bahia	20 Santa Catarina
5 Ceará	21 São Paulo
6 Espírito Santo	22 Sergipe
7 Goiás	23 Rondônia
8 Maranhão	
9 Mato Grosso	Federal Territory:
10 Mato Grosso do Sul	24 Amapá
11 Minas Gerais	25 Fernando de Noronha
12 Pará	26 Roraima
13 Paraíba	
14 Paraná	
15 Pernambuco	Federal District:
16 Piauí	27 Distrito Federal

map 38

André 549, Osasco 474, São Luís 450, Santos 417, São Joao d.M. 399, Guarulhos 395, Niterói 386, São Bernardo d.C. 381, Natal 377, Maceió 376, Campos 349, Teresina 339, Jaboatão 331, João Pessoa 330, Londrina 302, Ribeirão Prêto 301, Juiz de Fora 300, Aracaju 293, Campo Grande 283, São José d.C. 268. – **Population:** Brazilians – Whites 62%, mestizos 28%, Negroes 8% and Indians 2%. **Density** 16 persons per sq.km (1985), average annual rate of population increase 2.3% birth rate 31 per 1,000, death rate 8.4 per 1,000 (1980–85); urban population 68%. Economically active inhabitants 43.5 mn., 36% engaged in agriculture (1983). – **Currency:** cruzado = 100 centavos.

Economy: agricultural and industrial country moving towards the group of countries with a highly developed economy. It has enormous mineral resources – the world's richest deposits of: iron ore, tin, manganese, bauxite, tungsten and precious stones. **Agricultural production** is among the greatest in the world; highly-productive monocultural plantations predominate. Arable land takes up 8.8% of the land area, meadows and pastures 19.2%, forests 67.4%. **Crops** (1983, in 1,000 tonnes): – leading world producer (% of world crops): coffee 1,705 (31%), bananas 6,690 (16%), manioc 22,096 (18%), sisal 188 (49%); – second largest producer in the world: oranges and tangerines 10,095 (22%), cocoa beans 350 (22.5%), soya beans 14,582 (19%); – third largest producer in the world: maize (corn) 20,165, beans 1,592 castor beans 172 (18.5%); other products: wheat 2,273, rice 7,960, potatoes 1,815, sweet potatoes 755, cotton -seed 1,025, -lint 552; coconuts 241, palm kernels 250, vegetables 4,537 (tomatoes 1,590), grapes 573, pineapples 841, tobacco 400, jute 61, natural rubber 33. **Livestock** (1983, in million head): cattle 94 (milk cows 14.7), pigs 34, sheep 17.6, horses 5.2, poultry 457; fish catch 846,000 tonnes. **Production** (1983, in 1,000 tonnes): meat 5,117, milk 10,810, eggs 835, cowhides 322. Roundwood: 220 mn. cub.m (1983).

Mining (1983, in 1,000 tonnes, metal content): iron ore 77,649 (second largest producer in the world, Minas Gerais, Pará), manganese 1,141 (Pará, Amapá), bauxite 7,200 (Pará, Minas Gerais), magnesite 486 (Ceará, Bahia), nickel 15,561 tonnes (Goiás), chromite 122 (Bahia, Minas Gerais, Goiás), tungsten 876 tonnes, tin 13.3 (Rondônia), coal 6,380, crude petroleum 23.2 mn. (1984, Bahia, Alagoas, Sergipe), natural gas 80.8 PJ, gold 53,684 kg (Minas Gerais), diamonds 570,000 carats, precious and semi-precious stones (Minas Gerais, Goiás), uranium 290 tons, zinc 73, mica 2, asbestos 159, niobium 16.8 (leading world producer), graphite 443 (Minas Gerais), phosphate rock 3,208, salt 3,259. **Industrial production** (1983, in 1,000 tonnes): pig iron 12,920, crude steel 14,660, fertilizers 1,590, synthetic rubber 221, 18.2 mn. tyres, cement 20,586, paper 3,320, aluminium 452, zinc 111; motor vehicles: passenger 718,300 and commercial 320,400 units; motor spirit 7,876, fuel oils 29,731; television receivers 1.9 mn. units; flour 4,539, sugar 9,460 (leading world producer), wine 261; 129 billion cigarettes. Electricity (1983): capacity 40.1 mn. kW (of which 85% hydro-electric power stations – e.g. Itaipú, Tucuruí, Paulo Afonso etc.), production 161,970 kWh.

Communications (1983): railways 32,136 km, roads 1,458,000 km (98,100 km hard-surfaced, 8,415 km Panamerican Highway); motor vehicles: – passenger 9.3 mn., – commercial 1.93 mn. Merchant shipping 5.8 mn. GRT. Civil aviation (1984): 225 mn. km flown and 12.9 mn. passengers carried. – **Exports** (1983): agricultural products 36% (coffee, fruit, sugar, cocoa etc.), industrial products 39.5%, iron ore, metals, motor vehicles, machines. Chief trading partners: U.S.A., Japan, Saudi Arabia, Iraq, Venezuela, F.R. of Germany, Netherlands, Argentina.

CHILE

República de Chile, area 756,945 sq.km, population 12,074,480 (1985), **republic** (President Gen. Augusto Pinochet since 1973).

Administrative units: 13 regions. **Capital:** Santiago 4,039,275 inhab.; **other towns** (1982, in 1,000 inhab.): Valparaíso 276, Viña del Mar 259, Concepción 266, Talcahuano 203, Antofagasta 183, Temuco 157, Rancagua 140, Arica 139, Talca 126, Chillán 121, San Bernardo 116, Iquique 110, Puente Alto 105, Valdivia 103. **Population:** Chileans (only 160,000 Indians). **Density** 16 persons per sq.km (1985), average annual rate of population increase 1.7%, urban population 82.4%. 16% of inhabitants engaged in agriculture. – **Currency:** Chilean peso = 100 centesimos.

Economy: developing agricultural and industrial country with important mineral mining. **Agriculture** – crops (1983, in 1,000 tonnes): wheat 810, maize (corn) 512, potatoes 684, sugar beet 1,460, vegetables 1,243, citrus fruit 140, grapes 1,000; **livestock** (1983, in million head): cattle 3.9, sheep 6.4, pigs 1.3, poultry 21.1; fish catch 4,060,000 tonnes; meat 382, milk 910, eggs 61. Roundwood 12.8 mn. cub.m. **Mining** (1983, in 1,000 tonnes, metal content): copper 1,256 (leading world producer – El Teniente, El Salvador and Chquicamata), coal 1,038, crude petroleum 1,772, natural gas 188 PJ, iron ore 3,602, saltpeter 578, iodine 2,605 tonnes (60% of world output), molybdenum 15.3, gold 17,759 kg, silver 468 tonnes, native sulphur 99, salt 715. **Production** (1983, in 1,000 tonnes): copper -smelted 893, -refined 695; pig iron 538, crude steel 611, cement 1,255, motor spirit 1,165, chemical wood pulp 637, paper 348; sugar 232, wine 575, fish meal 796, fish oil 145, flour 915; cigarettes 7,680 mn. Electricity 12,624 mn. kWh (of which 67% hydro--electric).

Communications (1983): railways 9,287 km, roads 80,060 km. Merchant shipping 487,000 GRT. Civil aviation: 22.5 mn. km flown and 652,000 passengers carried. – **Exports** (1983): copper (49%), raw materials, iron ore, fish, fish meal, roundwood. Chief trading partners: U.S.A., Fed. Rep. of Germany, Japan, Brazil, Argentina, France.

COLOMBIA

República de Colombia, area 1,138,914 sq.km, population 28,840,000 (1985), **republic** (President Virgilio Barco Vargas since 1986).

Administrative units: 23 departments, 4 intendancies, 5 commissaries and 1 Capital District. **Capital:** Bogotá 4,079,848 inhab. (with agglom. 4.58 mn.); **other towns** (1980 census, in 1,000 inhab.): Medellín 1,585, Cali 1,378, Barranquilla 859, Cartagena 435, Cúcuta 426, Bucaramanga 424, Ibagué 297, +Valledupar 263, Pereira 261, Manizales 253, Montería 236, Palmira 231, Pasto 214, Santa Marta 212, Buenaventura 185, +Cienága 181, Armenia 179, Bello 165, Neiva 161, +Villa-vicenco 144, +Tuluá 138, Tunja 135, Barrancabermeja 128, Popayán 115. **Population:** mestizos 50%, mulattoes 18%, Whites and Creoles 25%, Negroes, Indians 450,000. **Density** 26 persons per sq.km, average annual rate of population

map 39

increase 2.2%, birth rate 32.2 per 1,000, death rate 7.9 per 1,000 (1980–85); urban population 70%. 32% of inhabitants engaged in agriculture. – **Currency:** Columbian Peso = 100 centavos.
Economy: developing agricultural and industrial country with mineral mining. **Agriculture** – crops (1983, in 1,000 tonnes): chief products – coffee 798 (second world producer, 14.4% of world crops), bananas 1,280, plantains 2,247, surgarcane 28,000, rice 1,845, maize (corn) 867, sorghum 599, potatoes 2,132, manioc 2,188, soya beans 120, cotton -seed 132, -lint 64; coconuts 56, palm kernels 21.1, vegetables 1,469, citrus fruit 285, pineapples 110, cocoa beans 42, tobacco 47; **livestock** (1983, in million head): cattle 24.2, sheep 2.7, pigs 2.2, horses 1.8, poultry 34.5; fresh hides 74,470 tonnes; fish catch 71,410 tonnes. Forests cover 53% of the land area, roundwood 17 mn. cub.m.
Mining (1983, in 1,000 tonnes, metal content): gold 13,337 kg (dep. Antioquia), coal 5,880, crude petroleum 8,420, natural gas 232 PJ, iron ore 435, platinum 625 kg (1982), precious stones, salt 688, sulphur 30. **Production** (1983, in 1,000 tonnes): motor spirit 2,350, fuel oils 4,383, pig iron 270, crude steel 440, cement 3,480; palm oil 104, sugar 1,391, meat 865, milk 2,647, eggs 165; 21.7 billion cigarettes. Electricity 27,100 mn. kWh (68% hydro-electric). – **Communications** (1983): railways 3,485 km, roads 102,075 km (4,985 km Panamerican Highway), passenger cars 824,000. Merchant shipping 358,900 GRT. Civil aviation (1984): 60.8 mn. km flown and 5.8 mn. passengers carried. – **Exports** (1983): coffee (52%), bananas, cut flowers, petroleum, chemicals, sugar, cotton. Chief trading partners: U.S.A. (30%), Fed. Rep. of Germany, Venezuela, Japan, Italy, Brazil, Spain.

ECUADOR

República del Ecuador, area 283,561 sq.km, population 9,377,980 (1985), **republic** (President León Febres Cordero since 1984).
Administrative units: 20 provinces (inc. Arch. de Colón – Galapagos Is.). **Capital:** Quito 918,800 inhab. (1983); **other towns** (1983, +1981, in 1,000 inhab.): Guayaquil 1,249, Cuenca +144, Machala +114, Esmeraldas +110, Ambato +104, Manta +94. **Population:** mestizos 40%, Indians 40%, Creoles 10%. **Density** 33 persons per sq.km; average annual rate of population increase 3.1%. 38.2% of inhabitants engaged in agriculture. – **Currency:** sucre = 100 centavos.
Economy: agriculture predominates. **Agriculture:** crops (1983, in 1,000 tonnes): bananas 2,770, coffee 81, cocoa beans 58, citrus fruit 441, pineapples 102, sugarcane 5,620, rice 274, potatoes 314, coconuts 63; **livestock** (1983, in million head): cattle 3.3, pigs 3.7, sheep 2.3, poultry 42; fish catch 654,100 tonnes. Roundwood 7.8 mn. cub.m. **Mining** (1983): crude petroleum 11.8 mn. tonnes, gold 2,300 kg. **Production** (1983, in 1,000 tonnes): motor-spirit 985, -oils 2,420; milk 981, sugar 220, palm oil 43; cement 1,265. Electricity 4,289 mn. kWh. – **Communications:** railways 1,121 km, roads 37,980 km. – **Exports** (1982): petroleum (65%), bananas, coffee, cocoa, sugar, fish, balsawood. Chief trading partners: U.S.A. (40%), Fed. Rep. of Germany, Japan, Brazil, Rep. of Korea, Colombia.

GUYANA

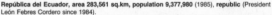

Co-operative Republic of Guyana, area 214,969 sq.km, population 790,400 (1985), **co-operative republic, member of the Commonwealth** (President Hugh Desmond Hoyte since 1985).
Capital: Georgetown 195,000 inhab. (1982 with agglomeration). **Population:** Indos 51%, Negroes 30%, mestizos 11%, Indians 5%. **Density** 3.7 persons per sq.km (1985). – **Currency:** Guyana dollar = 100 cents.
Economy: forests cover 83% of the land area. **Mining** (1983, in 1,000 tonnes): bauxite 1,791, gold 143 kg, diamonds 17,200 carats. **Agriculture:** (1983, in 1,000 tonnes): rice 246, sugarcane 3,628, coconuts 22; cattle 310,000 head; poultry 14.2 mn. head. **Production** (in 1,000 tonnes): sugar 256, aluminium 73, rum 75,000 hl. – **Exports** (1982): bauxite, sugar, aluminium, rice. Chief trade with United Kingdom, U.S.A., Trinidad – Tobago, Canada, Jamaica.

NETHERLANDS ANTILLES

De Nederlandse Antillen, area 993 sq.km, population 260,000 (1985) – 3 main islands: Curaçao, Aruba, Bonaire; 3 Leeward Islands: St. Maarten, St. Eustatius, Saba. **Autonomous state of the Netherlands** (Prime Minister Domenico Martina). Aruba, area 191 sq.km, population 66,502 (1983), separate state since 1. 1. 1986 (Prime Minister Henny Eman). **Capital:** Willemstad 94,133 inhab. Oranjestad 16,326 inhab. – **Currency:** guilder. – **Economy:** processing of petroleum imported from Venezuela; production (1981, in million tonnes): motor spirit 2.1, oils and naphtha 29.1 (capacity of refineries 39 mn. tonnes per year); electricity 2,310 mn. kWh. Tourism. – **Exports** (1981): petroleum products and chemicals (97%), chief trade with U.S.A., Venezuela, Netherlands, Nigeria.

PARAGUAY

República del Paraguay, area 406,752 sq.km, population 3,681,460 (1985), **republic** (President Gen. Alfredo Stroessner since 1954).
Administrative units: 20 departments. **Capital:** Asunción 455,517 inhab. (1982, with agglomeration 560,000 inhab.); **other towns** (in 1,000 inhab.): San Lorenzo 75, Fernando d.l.M. 67, Lambaré 62, Encarnación 50. **Population:** Indians (Guaraní) 65%, mestizos 30%; 48% of inhabitants engaged in agriculture. – **Currency:** guaraní = 100 centimos.
Economy: backward agricultural country. **Agriculture:** (1983, in 1,000 tonnes): manioc 2,150, maize 420, rice 75, soya beans 746, cotton -seed 171, -lint 81; castor beans 20, sugarcane 1,700, bananas 315, citrus fruit 360, pineapples 36, coffee 18, tobacco 17; extensive cattle breeding (in million head): cattle 5.6, pigs 1.4, poultry 14. **Production** (1983, in 1,000 tonnes): tung oil 13, orange oil 740 tonnes (70% of world production), cocos oil 16, sugar 95, meat 196; tannin 11, rare hardwoods 6.8 mn. cub.m. Electricity 848 mn. kWh. – **Communications** (1982): railways 634 km, roads 12,930 km. **Exports** (1982): cotton, soya beans, leather, meat, vegetable oils, wood, tannin, essential oils. Chief trading partners: Brazil, Argentina, Fed. Rep. of Germany, U.S.A., Netherlands.

39 a   River Plate Countries, Southern Brazil   1 : 15 000 000

ARGENTINA

Provinces:

1 Buenos Aires	14 Neuquén
2 Catamarca	15 Río Negro
3 Córdoba	16 Salta
4 Corrientes	17 San Juan
5 Chaco	18 San Luis
6 Chubut	19 Santa Cruz
7 Entre Rios	20 Santa Fe
8 Formosa	21 Santiago
9 Jujuy	del Estero
10 La Pampa	22 Tucumán
11 La Rioja	23 Federal Capital
12 Mendoza	24 Terr. Nac. de la
13 Misiones	Tierra del Fuego

map 39

PERU

República del Perú, area 1,285,216 sq.km, population 19,697,500 (1985), **republic** (President Alán García Pérez since 1985).

Administrative units: 24 departments and 1 constitutional province (Callao). **Capital:** Lima 3,968,972 inhab. (1981, with agglomeration 4.9 mn.); **other towns** (in 1,000 inhab.): Arequipa 447, Callao 441, Trujillo 355, Chiclayo 280, Chimbote 216, Piura 186, Cuzco 182, Iquitos 174, Huancayo 165, Ica 123, Sullana 109. **Population:** Indians 47% (Quechuas, Aymarás, Panos etc.), mestizos 32%, Whites 12%, Negroes and mulattoes. **Density** 15 persons per sq.km, average annual rate of population increase 2.7%, birth rate 37.3 per 1,000, death rate 10.7 per 1,000 (1980–85); urban population 68.8%. 36% of inhabitants engaged in agriculture. – **Currency:** inti = 100 centimos.
Economy: developing agricultural and industrial country with important mining of minerals. **Agriculture:** only 2.8% of the land is cultivated and of this 38% is irrigated. **Crops** (1983, in 1,000 tonnes): maize 585, rice 798, potatoes 1,290, manioc 361, pulses 89, vegetables 654, cotton -seed 165 and - lint 87, sugarcane 6,664, coffee 91, cocoa 14, citrus fruit 231, avocadoes and mangoes 103; **livestock** (1983, in million head): sheep 14.7, cattle 3.9, pigs 2.1, llamas, alpacas and vicuñas 2.2, horses 0.7, poultry 40; fresh hides 24,740 tonnes, grease wool 5,500 tonnes; fish catch 3.6 mn. tonnes. Forests cover 55% of the land, roundwood 7.8 mn. cub.m.
Mining (1983, in 1,000 tonnes, metal content): iron ore 4,220 (Ica, Arequipa), crude petroleum 8,462, natural gas 101 PJ, copper 336 (Cerro de Pasco, La Oroya), zinc 576 (Junín, 8.3% of world output), lead 213, silver 1,739 tonnes (12.8% of world output), tin 2.4, gold 4,821 kg, vanadium, bismuth 665 tonnes, antimony 713 tonnes, molybdenum 995 tonnes, tungsten 725 tonnes (dep. Áncash). **Production** (1983, in 1,000 tonnes): copper -smelted 296, -refined 191; lead 73, zinc 154, pig iron 113 and crude steel 289, motor spirit 1,517, oils 4,490, cement 2,165, sugar 535, meat 457, fish oil 190, milk 757, eggs 68. Electricity 10,408 mn. kWh (76% hydro-electric).
Communications (1982): railways 2,740 km, the Lima-La Oroya line reaches the highest world altitude 4,829 m at Galero: roads 66,210 km (Panamerican Highway 3,390 km), passenger cars 372,000. Merchant shipping 836,200 GRT. Civil aviation (1984): 24.4 mn. km flown, and 1.6 mn. passengers carried. – **Exports** (1982): metals (copper, zinc, lead etc.) – processed non-ferrous metals (39%), petroleum – petroleum products (27%),- silver, coffee, cotton. Chief trading partners: U.S.A., Japan, Brazil, Fed. Rep. of Germany, United Kingdom, Italy, Argentina, Spain.

SURINAM

Republiek van Suriname, area 163,265 sq.km, population 389,000 (1985), **republic** (Head of state Col. Desi Bouterse since 1982).
Capital: Paramaribo 67,718 inhab. (with agglomeration 164,879 inhab., census 1980). **Population:** Indos 35%, Creoles 32%, Indonesians (15%), Negroes, Indians. – **Currency:** Surinama guilder = 100 cents.
Economy: forests cover 95% of the land area. **Mining** of bauxite 2,793,000 tonnes (1983), gold 143 kg; production of aluminium 1.2 mn. tonnes; electricity 1,670 mn. kWh (83% hydro). **Agriculture:** (1983, in 1,000 tonnes): rice 278, bananas 42, coconuts 6.5, sugarcane 150; poultry 1 mn. head. – **Exports:** aluminium oxide, aluminium, bauxite, rice, fish. Chief trading partners: U.S.A., Netherlands, Japan, Trinidad and Tobago, Norway.

TRINIDAD AND TOBAGO

Republic of Trinidad and Tobago, area 5,128 sq.km, population 1,185,000 (1985), **republic, member of the Commonwealth** (President Sir Ellis Emanuel Clarke since 1976).
Capital: Port of Spain 65,904 inhab. (census 1980), San Fernando 33,395 inhab. **Population:** Negroes 41%, Indos 41%, mestizos 17%. **Density** 231 persons per sq.km. – **Currency:** Trinidad and Tobago dollar = 100 cents.
Economy (1983): agriculture with mining of petroleum 8.3 mn. tonnes, natural gas 190 PJ, asphalt 32,000 tonnes (Pitch Lake). **Agriculture:** crops (1983, in 1,000 tonnes): sugarcane 1,006, rice 17, cocoa beans 2.1, coffee 2.2, coconuts 58, copra 9, citrus fruit 18; cattle 76,000 head; poultry 8 mn. head. **Production** (1983): electricity 2,260 mn. kWh, sugar 77,000 tonnes, rum and spirits. **Communications:** roads 7,173 km. – **Exports** (1983): petroleum and petroleum products (83%), chemicals, sugar. Chief trading partners: U.S.A. (52%), United Kingdom, Canada, Japan, Jamaica.

URUGUAY

República Oriental del Uruguay, area 177,508 sq.km, population 3,012,000 (1985), **republic** (President Dr. Julio María Sanguinetti Coirolo since 1985).
Administrative units: 19 departments. **Capital:** Montevideo 1,329,899 inhab. (1981); **other towns** (in 1,000 inhab.): Paysandú 82, Salto 85, Mercedes 56, Las Piedras 54, Rivera 52. – **Population:** Whites (descendants of immigrant Spaniards) 90%, mestizos, Indians. **Density** 17 persons per sq.km; average annual rate of population increase 0.7%, urban population 83.5%. – **Currency:** nuevo peso = 100 centésimos.
Economy: agricultural country with extensive animal production. **Agriculture:** arable land 11%, meadows and pastures 82% of the land area. **Livestock** (1983, in million head): cattle 10.1, sheep 21.2, horses 0.53, pigs 0.44, poultry 6.2; grease wool 47,050 tonnes, hides 85,000 tonnes, fish catch 128,400 tonnes. **Crops** (1983, in 1,000 tonnes): wheat 450, rice 323, maize (corn) 104, sorghum 110, potatoes 118, sunflower 34, flax, sugar beet 394, sugarcane 551, citrus fruit 124, grapes 105. **Production** (1983, in 1,000 tonnes): petroleum oils 1,211, sugar 87, wine 85, meat 513, milk 896, production of shoes, clothing, cement 401. Electricity 7,343 mn. kWh. – **Communications** (1983): railways 3,018 km, roads 50,860 km, passenger cars 168,720. Merchant shipping 217,300 GRT. – **Exports** (1983): meat and meat products (26%), wool (18%), cereals, clothing, leather, fish. Chief trading partners: Brazil, Argentina, U.S.A., Nigeria, Fed. Rep. of Germany, Iran, Egypt, U.S.S.R., Mexico.

map 40

VENEZUELA

República de Venezuela, area 912,050 sq.km, population 17,316,740 (1985), **federal republic** (President Dr. Jaime Lusinchi since 1984).

Administrative units: 20 states, 2 federal territories, 1 federal district (the capital) and 1 federal dependency. **Capital:** Caracas 2,070,742 inhab. (1981, with agglom. 4.1 mn. inhab. in 1984); **other towns** (census 1981, in 1,000 inhab.): Maracaibo 920, Valencia 506, Barquisimeto 490, Maracay 348, Barcelona – Pto. l. Cruz 278, San Cristobal 275, Ciudad Guyana 220, Cabimas 175, Maturín 170, Cumaná 163. **Population:** mestizos 55%, Whites 38%, Indians 4%. **Density** 19 persons per sq.km; average annual rate of population increase 3.2%, birth rate 35 per 1,000, death rate 5.6 per 1,000 (1980–85); urban population 78.5%. 16% of inhabitants engaged in agriculture. – **Currency:** bolivar = 100 céntimos.
Economy: agricultural and industrial country with important mining of petroleum. **Agriculture:** arable land 6%, meadows and pastures 19%, forests 42% of the land area. **Crops** (1983, in 1,000 tonnes): rice 450, maize 488, sorghum 364, manioc 325, potatoes 238, sesame (seed) 57, cotton -seed 26, -lint 15; coconuts 161, sugarcane 4,816, bananas 934, oranges 384, pineapples 54, mangoes 111, coffee 59, cocoa beans 14. **Livestock** (1983, in million head): cattle 11.6, pigs 2.6, horses 0.5, poultry 42; fish catch 226,900 tonnes; fresh hides 45,875 tonnes. Roundwood 8 mn. cub.m.
Mining (1983, in 1,000 tonnes): crude petroleum 95,180 (in the Maracaibo Basin and lower reaches of the R. Orinoco) natural gas 1,415 PJ, good quality iron ore 5,928 (Cerro Bolívar, El Pao, Cd. Piar), gold 1,719 kg, diamonds 560,000 carats (of which 75% industrial), salt 361. **Production** (1983, in 1,000 tonnes): motor spirit 7,185, aviation spirit 2,650, oils and other petroleum products 27,745 (capacity of refineries 69,407), pig iron 202, crude steel 2,246, aluminium 335, car assembly 155,000 units; sugar 385, meat 748 and milk 1,518, eggs 138; cement 4,147; 20.2 billion cigarettes. Electricity 41,700 mn. kWh. – **Communications** (1983): railways 268 km, roads 65,780 km, motor vehicles – passenger 1.5 mn., – commercial 0.86 mn. Merchant shipping 973,000 GRT. Civil aviation (1984): 51.8 mn. km flown and 4.5 mn. passengers carried. – **Exports** (1975): petroleum and petroleum products (82%), iron ore, steel, natural gas, aluminium, diamonds, agricultural products. Chief trading partners: U.S.A., Canada, Italy, Japan, Brazil, Netherlands Antilles, Spain.

FALKLAND ISLANDS

Falkland Islands and Dependencies, area 16,439 sq.km, population 2,200 (1985), **British crown colony** to which Argentina lays claim as Islas Malvinas.
Administrative units: East and West Falkland (12,347 sq.km), **dependencies:** South Georgia 3,755 sq.km, South Sandwich Is. (337 sq.km). **Capital:** Stanley 1,050 inhab. (1980). – **Currency:** Falkland pound. – **Economy** (1983): sheep raising 669,000 head, cattle 8,000 head; grease wool 1,500 tonnes, skins, fish catch. – **Exports:** wool, skins.

FRENCH GUIANA

Guyane Française, area 91,000 sq.km, population 80,000 (1985), **French overseas department.**
Capital: Cayenne 38,135 inhab. (1982). – **Currency:** franc = 100 centimos. – **Economy:** forests cover almost 90% of the land area. **Production:** roundwood 51,000 cub.m; gold; crops: sugarcane, bananas, manioc, rice, rum, electricity 65 mn. kWh. – **Exports:** shellfish (74%), wood, essential oils. Trade predominantly to U.S.A., France, Japan.

AUSTRALIA AND OCEANIA

The smallest and least densely inhabited continent on the Earth is Australia with the island world of Oceania. It is very remote from the other continents: 13,000 km from South America and 350 km from Asia. It lies in the southern hemisphere surrounded by the waters of the Pacific and the Indian Oceans. The name derives from the Latin "australis", i.e. "southern" (Terra Australis Incognita). Australia was first discovered by the Dutch explorer W. Jansz, who in 1606 landed on the west coast of the Cape York Peninsula. In the forties of the 17th century Abel Tasman discovered Tasmania, New Zealand (1642), Tonga, Fiji and Bismarck Archipelago. The British seafarer Captain James Cook proved in 1769 that New Zealand consisted of islands, and in 1770 he discovered the eastern shores of Australia, which he named New South Wales. The British were not slow to colonize it. In 1788 the first convict colony was established and in the 19th century settlers came in the wake of the gold rush. The exploration of the inland areas was completed by the end of the century, and by 1884 the British had occupied Papua. On 1 January 1901 the individual British colonies on the Australian continent federated under the name of the Commonwealth of Australia. The colonization of New Zealand began in the first half of the 19th century despite resistance from the native Maoris.
The **area** of Australia is **7,686,848 sq.km** (8,910,000 sq.km including Oceania); it has **15,751,000 inhabitants** with Oceania 26 mn.). **Geographical position:** the northernmost point of the mainland is Cape York 10°41'S.Lat. (Mata Kawa I. 9°11' S.Lat.); southernmost point: South East Point 39°07' S.Lat. (South East Cape 43°39' S.Lat. – Tasmania); easternmost: Cape Byron 153°39' E.Long.; westernmost: Steep Point 113°09' E.Long. Width of the continent 3,200 km, length 4,100 km, length of the coastline 19,700 km. Oceania – the largest island area on Earth – extends in the central and south-western part of the Pacific Ocean: in the North, Kure I. (Midway Is.) 28°25' N.Lat., in the South, Campbell I. 52°30' S.Lat., in the East, Isla Sala y Gómez 105°28' W.Long. and in the West, Pulau Misool I. (Indonesia) 129°43' E.Long. Largest island: New Guinea (785,000 sq.km). Largest peninsula: Arnhem Land (243,000 sq.km).
The **geological structure** of Australia is very simple; **the surface** has three basic units. First, the Western Australian Hills (the oldest part) which cover one half of the continent, at an average height of 200–500 m rising to 1,524 m on Mt. Liebig in the Macdonnell Ranges; its deserts extend over an area of roughly 1.7 mn. sq.km. Second, the Central Australian Lowlands with the Great Artesian Basin and the Lake Eyre Basin, which has no outlet to the sea; the lowest point on the continent is Lake Eyre (–16 m) in the middle. Third, the Great Dividing Range, known as the Australian Cordilleras, which is the result of Hercynian folding in the East. It reaches its highest point at Mt. Kosciusko, 2,228 m, in the Australian Alps. The mountainous islands of New Zealand are varied in character. In the Southern Alps there are glaciers (Tasman Gl. 156 sq.km); the highest point is Mt. Cook (3,764 m). On North Island there is volcanic activity (Ruapehu, 2,796 m), hot springs and geysers. The islands of Oceania can be divided into two groups:

A New- Gulf of Papua
A **PAPUA NEW** G4 **GUINEA** Mt Victoria 4073 150°
Daru 140° Kerema Popondetta
Torres Strait Port Moresby u i n e a D'Entrecasteaux Is.
Thursday I. Alotau
C. York Louisiade Arch.
Weipa Tagula I.
Aurukun
Coen
Cooktown CORAL SEA ISLANDS
Laura
Normanton Cairns
Bartle Frere Innisfail TERRITORY
1611
Croydon Forsayth Greenvale Townsville
Kajabbi Charters Towers Bowen
Cloncurry Hughenden
Duchess 1277 Mackay
Winton Blair Athol
Longreach Emerald
Rockhampton
Yaraka Tambo Gladstone
L I A Theodore Bundaberg
Charleville Roma Maryborough Fraser I.
Quilpie Chinchilla Gympie
Cunnamulla Toowoomba Ipswich BRISBANE
Dirranbandi Warwick Gold Coast
Goondiwindi C. Byron
Bourke Glen Innes Lismore
N e w S o u t h Walgett Grafton
Broken Hill Armidale Coffs Harbour
Cobar 1615 Port Macquarie
W a l e s Tamworth
Roto 1585
Wentworth Orange Barrington Tops
Mildura West Wyalong Bathurst Maitland
Griffith Newcastle
Pingali Wagga Wagga Blue Mts. SYDNEY
Swan Hill Albury Wollongong
Horsham Echuca Australian Canberra
Bendigo Alps Mt. Kosciusko
V i c t o r i a 2228 Bombala
Hamilton Ballarat MELBOURNE Orbost
Geelong
Warrnambool South East Pt.

Bougainville (Pap. N.G.)
Choiseul S. Isabel
SOLOMON IS.
New Georgia Auki
Honiara Malaita
Guadalcanal
S. Cristóbal
Rennell I.

P A C I F I C

Îs. Chesterfield (N.Cal.)

New Caledonia (Fr.)

Tropic of Capricorn

O C E A N

40 a New Zealand
1 : 25 000 000

North C.
Opua
Takapuna Whangarei
Auckland
Manukau Hamilton
Whakatane East C.
Rotorua Gisborne
New Plymouth Ruapehu Napier
Wanganui 2796 Hastings
C. Farewell Palmerston North
Nelson Lower Hutt
Picton Wellington
Greymouth
Westport S o u t h
Hokitika Christchurch
Mt. Cook I s l a n d
Mt. Aspiring 3764 Timaru
3035 Kingston Oamaru
Invercargill Dunedin

N o r t h
I s l a n d

T A S M A N S E A

P A C I F I C O C E A N

L. Frome
Murray
Murrumbidgee

Tasmania
King I. Furneaux Group
Banks Str.
Devonport Burnie Launceston
Zeehan 1617
Queenstown
Hobart
South East Cape

Bass Strait

map 40

AUSTRALIA AND OCEANIA

LARGEST ISLANDS

Name	Area in sq.km
New Guinea	785,000
South I. (New Zealand)	150,461
North I. (New Zealand)	114,688
Tasmania	64,408
Birara (New Britain)	34,750
New Caledonia	16,058
Viti Levu	10,497
Hawaii	10,414
Tombara (New Ireland)	9,842
Bougainville	9,792
Guadalcanal	6,470
Vanua Levu	5,816

LARGEST RIVERS

Name	Length in km	River basin in sq.km
Murray-Darling	3,490	1,072,000
Darling (-Barwon)	2,720	710,000
Murrumbidgee	2,160	84,020
Fly	1,150	.
Lachlan	1,126	67,500
Cooper Creek (-Thomson)	960	.

LARGEST LAKES

Name	Area in sq.km	Altitude in m
L. Eyre	9,500	−16
L. Torrens	5,880	30
L. Gairdner	5,500	110
L. Frome	2,410	80
L. Barlee	1,450	370
L. McLeod	1,300	5
L. Cowan	1,035	380
L. Taupo	606	369

HIGHEST MOUNTAINS

Name (Country)	Altitude in m
Puncak Jaya (Irian-Indon.)	5,030
P. Mandala (Irian-Indon.)	4,760
P. Trikora (Irian-Indon.)	4,750
Mt. Wilhelm (Pap. N.Guinea)	4,509
Mauna Kea (Hawaii-U.S.A.)	4,205
Mt. Cook (N.Z.)	3,764
Mt. Tasman (N.Z.)	3,498
Mt. Sefton (N.Z.)	3,157
Mt. Orohena (Tahiti-Fr. Polynesia)	2,235
Mt. Kosciusko (Austr.)	2,228

ACTIVE VOLCANOES

Name (Country, Island)	Altitude in m	Latest eruption
Mauna Loa (Hawaii)	4,168	1984
Ruapehu (North I. N.Z.)	2,796	1982
Ulawun (Birara)	2,296	1984
Ngauruhoe (North I. N.Z.)	2,291	1975
Manam (Pap. N.Guinea)	1,830	1984
Kilauea (Hawaii)	1,222	1986

Country	Area in sq.km	Population year 1985	Density per sq.km	Capital
American Samoa (U.S.A.)	197	35,400	180	Pago Pago
Australia	7,686,848	15,751,000	2	Canberra
Cook Islands (N.Z.)	237	18,200[1]	77	Avarua
Fed. States of Micronesia (U.S.A.)	721	86,950	121	Kolonia
Fiji	18,272	696,000	38	Suva
French Polynesia (Fr.)	4,198	172,500	41	Papeete
Guam (U.S.A.)	549	115,756[1]	211	Agana
Hawaii-U.S.A.	16,706	1,054,000	63	Honolulu
Kiribati	868	64,000	74	Tarawa
Marshall Islands (U.S.A.)	205	33,600[1]	164	Uliga
Midway Islands (U.S.A.)	8	2,260[2]	283	
Nauru	21.4	8,000[1]	381	Yaren
New Caledonia and Depend. (Fr.)	19,058	153,000	8	Nouméa
New Zealand	268,675	3,254,000	12	Wellington
Niue Island (N.Z.)	263	3,800[1]	14	Alofi
Norfolk Island (Austral.)	36.3	2,250[2]	63	Kingston
Northern Mariana Islands (U.S.A.)	471	19,110[2]	41	Garapan
Palau (U.S.A.)	487	15,000[1]	31	Koror
Papua New Guinea	462,840	3,328,710	7	Port Moresby
Pitcairn Islands (U.K.)	37	61[2]	1.6	Adamstown
Samoa	2,842	163,400	58	Apia
Solomon Islands	29,785	270,600	9	Honiara
Tokelau Islands (N.Z.)	12.1	1,650[2]	136	Fale
Tonga	747	109,000	146	Nuku'alofa
Tuvalu	25.8	8,050[1]	312	Vaiaku
Vanuatu	14,763	142,000	10	Vila
Wake Island (U.S.A.)	8	1,640[2]	205	
Wallis and Futuna Islands (Fr.)	255	12,391[2]	49	Mata Utu

[1] year 1984, [2] year 1983

map 41

one of low, flat coral islands which arose on the atolls and submarine coral reefs and the other of hilly, volcanic or continental islands. The highest active volcano is Mauna Loa, 4,168 m. Inland New Guinea is mountainous – it contains the highest peak of the continent, Puncak Jaya (5,030 m) – and has swampy lowlands.

Australia lacks a developed **network of rivers**. 54% of the land has no outlet to the sea, 38% drains into the Indian Ocean and 8% into the Pacific Ocean. There is great fluctuation in water level, chiefly in the periodical and seasonal rivers. The mean annual discharge amounts to 610 cub.km. The biggest river is the Murray (-Darling) 3,490 km with a river basin of 1,072,000 sq.km, and a mean annual discharge of 1,900 cub.m per sec. New Zealand and New Guinea have numerous rivers with ample water throughout the year. The most remarkable of the numerous **lakes** is L. Manapouri in New Zealand with an area of 142 sq.km, depth 445 m, and whose bottom is 263 m below sea level.

Climate: Oceania (which, except for the most-southerly islands, has a mean annual temperature above 20°C and two fifths of the Australian continent lie within the tropical belt, and three fifths of Australia lie in the subtropical belt – as does the North of New Zealand, which has a generally mild oceanic climate. The warmest place in Australia is Marble Bar with a mean temperature of 34°C, in Oceania Canton I. 28.6°C; Cloncurry (Australia) has absolute maximum temperature at 52.8°C and Lake Tekapo minimum at –15.6°C (New Zealand), in Oceania Canton I. 36.7°C and Honolulu (Hawaiian Is.) 13.9°C. Maximum annual rainfall Ninati 6,350 mm (New Guinea), Tully 7,773 mm (Queensland) and world record is held by Waialeale 11,684 mm (Kauai in the Hawaiian Is.). Mean January and July temperatures in °C (and annual rainfall in mm) in selected places: Port Moresby 27.6 and 25.8 (1,038), Darwin 28.6 and 25.0 (1,491), Cairns 27.7 and 20.8 (2,253), Broome 29.7 and 21.1 (582), Cloncurry 31.1 and 17.8 (457), Brisbane 25.1 and 14.7 (1,135), Alice Springs 28.6 and 11.7 (252), Perth 23.3 and 13.0 (881), Sydney 21.9 and 11.7 (1,181), Auckland 19.2 and 10.6 (1,247), Dunedin 14.4 and 5.8 (937), Yap 27.1 and 27.6 (3,108), Kanton 28.4 and 28.7 (938), Honolulu 22.1 and 25.4 (697), Banaba 27.8 and 28.1 (1,874), Suva 26.3 and 22.9 (3,240), Papeete 25.7 and 24.1 (1,872).

The **fauna and flora** have a unique primordial character. Almost 75% of all plants are endemic. This includes eucalyptus forests, scrub-land, acacias with brightly coloured blossom, salt-scrub flora, and in the regions of heavy rainfall, there are tropical rain forests or subtropical forests with typical tree-sized ferns. New Zealand has evergreen broad-leaved forests and characteristic coniferous Kauri. In the drier regions to the East of South Island steppes are the predominant form. Oceania has large numbers of palm trees and forests rich in rare coloured timber varieties. The fauna supports a wide range of marsupials and monotremes, mainly kangaroos, koala bears, phalangers, gliders, wombats and the primitive platypus and the echidna. The largest Australian bird is the brown emu; there are 50 varieties of parrot, black swans, the kookaburra, the New Zealand kiwi, poisonous snakes, the rare Hatteris lizard. In New Guinea we find crocodiles, rare birds of paradise. Nature conservation has a long tradition: Australia's largest National Park is the Kosciusko N.P. (5,800 sq.km) and in New Zealand the Fiordland N.P. (11,200 sq.km).

The original **inhabitants** of Australia – the black Australians and the New Zealand Maoris – are today greatly reduced in number. On the other hand, in Oceania the original inhabitants form the main part of the population (the Papuas, pygmy tribes, Melanesians, Micronesians, Polynesians and others). The number of Australian Whites is growing (in mn.): 1900 – 3.8, 1950 – 8.3, 1985 – 15.7. The number of New Zealanders has more than trebled between 1900 and 1978, reaching 3.1 mn. 86.2% of the population of Australia and 83.8% of New Zealand reside in towns. The largest towns are Sydney, Melbourne, Brisbane, Adelaide, Perth, Honolulu, Auckland.

AUSTRALIA

The **Commonwealth of Australia, area 7,686,848 sq.km, population 15,751,000** (1985), **independent member of the British Commonwealth** (Prime Minister Robert Hawke since 1983, Governor-General Sir Ninian Martin Stephen appointed by the Queen in 1982).

Administrative units: 6 states (New South Wales, Victoria, Queensland, South Australia, Western Australia, Tasmania), 3 territories (Australian Capital Territory, Northern Territory, Coral Sea Islands Territory). **Capital:** Canberra 255,900 inhab. (1983, with agglomeration); **other towns** (1983, in 1,000 inhab. with agglom.): Sydney 3,333, Melbourne 2,865, Brisbane 1,138, Adelaide 970, Perth 969, Newcastle 414, Wollongong 235, Gold Coast 192, Hobart 174, Geelong 143. **Population:** 99% Whites of European descent of whom 92% British; Aborigines 144,665 (1981). **Density** 2 persons per sq.km (1985); average annual rate of population increase 1.35%, birth rate 16 per 1,000, death rate 7.6 per 1,000 (1980–85), urban population 85.7% (1981). Immigration: 102,860 (1982). – **Currency:** Australian dollar = 100 cents.
Economy: advanced industrial and agricultural country with rich deposits and important mining of minerals, food, metallurgical and chemical industries. **Mining** (1983, in 1,000 tonnes, metal content): coal 97,754 (N.S.Wales, Queensland), brown coal 34,686 (Victoria), iron ore 50,540 (Western Australia – Newman, Tom Price, Goldsworthy etc.), bauxite 22,865 (leading world producer, Weipa), lead 458 and zinc 678 (third world producer, Mt. Isa, Broken Hill), copper 235, tin 10.7, manganese 672, gold 25,825 kg, silver 1.02, tungsten 2.1, nickel 82.9, cobalt 2,833 tonnes, zirconium ore 317, rutile 221 and ilmenite 1,158 (leading world producer), crude petroleum 17,655, natural gas 463.3 PJ, salt 5,987, uranium 3,882 tonnes. **Production** (1983, in 1,000 tonnes): pig iron 4,990, crude steel 5,392, copper smelted 172 and refined 200, nickel 46, aluminium 404, lead 239, zinc 293; motor spirit 11,056, jet fuels 1,891 and oils 10,297 with refineries capacity 36 mn. tonnes; cement 5,351, tyres 5.8 mn. units, plastics 715, sulphuric acid 1,734, superphosphates 734, cars 363,000 units, cotton fibres 18.9 and woven fabrics 32 mn. sq.m, 35.4 billion cigarettes; foodstuffs: flour 1,085, meat 2,654, milk 5,685, butter 96,160, sugar 3,075; wine 340, beer 19.7 mn. hl. **Electricity** (1983): installed capacity of electric power stations 30.2 mn. kW; production 106,287 mn. kWh.
Agriculture is of major importance: sheep rearing, wool production and wheat cultivation. Arable land only 6.1% of the land area, meadows and pastures 58%, forests 14%. **Crops** (1983, in 1,000 tonnes): wheat 22,064, barley 4,937, rice 548, oats 2,270, sorghum 958, potatoes 858, pulses 245, sunflower 104, cotton -seed 164, -lint 101; vegetables 1,178, sugarcane 24,263, grapes 768, citrus fruit 478, pineapples 121, bananas 133, tobacco 13. **Livestock** (1983, in million head): cattle 22.5 (dairy cows 1.8), pigs 2.5, sheep 133.2 (second world producer), poultry 49; (in 1,000 tonnes): grease wool 702 (leading world producer) and scoured wool 424, hides 182, sheep skins 149.8, eggs 197, honey 22.4; fish catch 169; roundwood 16 mn. cub.m (1983).
Communications (1984): railways 40,860 km, roads 885,300 km; motor vehicles – passenger 6.64 mn. and commercial

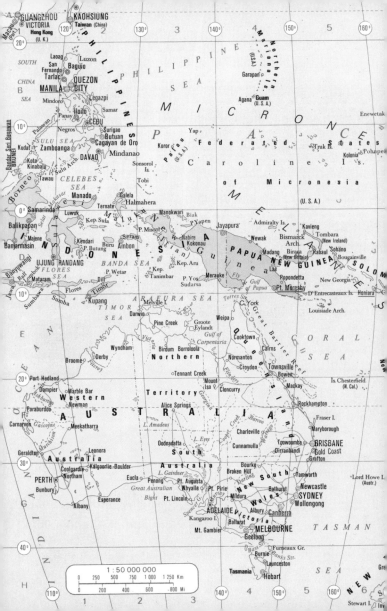

map 41

(1983 in 1,000 tonnes): coal 2,180, crude petroleum 631, natural gas 106 PJ, gold 249 kg. **Production** (1983, in 1,000 tonnes): aluminium 218.6, motor spirit 1,255, oils 962, superphosphates 330, paper 718, chemical wood pulp 471, meat 1,334, flour 242, sugar 116, milk 6,774, butter 295, cheese 115, cement 760. Electricity (1983): 25,527 mn. kWh (of which 77% is hydro-electric, 4% geothermal). **Communications** (1983): railways 4,418 km, passenger cars 1.4 mn., roads 92,648 km, aviation: 50 mn. km flown. – **Exports** (1983): meat (24%), wool (12%), dairy products (15%, butter-cheese 9.5%), aluminium (4.7%), machines, fish, newsprint, hides etc. Chief trading partners: Japan 16.7%, Australia 16.3%, U.S.A. 14.7%, United Kingdom 10%, Fed. Rep. of Germany, Iran, U.S.S.R., Indonesia, Singapore, Canada.

NEW ZEALAND TERRITORIES:

COOK ISLANDS, area 237 sq.km, population 18,200 (1984), annexed state with internal self-government; capital: Avarua (on Rarotonga) 850 inhab. **Economy:** citrus fruit, bananas, coconuts. **Exports:** tropical fruit, juices.
NIUE ISLAND, area 263 sq.km, population 3,800 (1984), annexed state with internal self-government; capital: Alofi. **Economy:** coconuts, copra, tropical fruit.
TOKELAU ISLANDS, area 12.1 sq.km, population 1,650 (1983), overseas territory, 3 atolls. Economy: coconuts, copra.

PAPUA NEW GUINEA

Area 462,840 sq.km, population 3,328,710 (1985), independent state, member of the Commonwealth (Prime Minister Michael Thomas Somare since 1984).

The territory of the state is formed by the eastern part of the island of New Guinea and 2,890 islands and islets; the largest are Birara (New Britain), Tombara, the northern part of Solomon Is. (the largest Bougainville), Admiralty Is. and Louisiade Arch. **Administrative units:** 19 provinces. **Capital:** Port Moresby 144,000 inhab. (1984); **other towns** (in 1,000 inhab.): Lae 62, Rabaul 48, Madang 21, Wewak 20. **Population:** Papuans and Melanesians. – **Currency:** kina = 100 toea.
Economy (1983): **mining:** copper 201,200 tonnes, gold 18,067 kg, silver 47 tonnes, platinum; **Agriculture:** crops (1983, in 1,000 tonnes): sweet potatoes 460, coconuts 750, copra 134, manioc 99, palm oil 84, vegetables 262, bananas 905, sugarcane 324, coffee 54; **livestock** (in 1,000 head): pigs 1,450, poultry 4,000; fishing. Forests cover 72% of the land area; tropical woods 6.8 mn. cub.m. Electricity: production 1,425 mn. kWh. **Communications:** roads 19,538 km, chief airport Port Moresby. – **Exports:** copper (51%), coffee (13%), wood, cocoa, palm – coconut oils. Trade with Australia, Japan.

SAMOA

Mālōtuto'atasi o Samoa, area 2,842 sq.km, population 163,400 (1985), kingdom (King Malietoa Tanumafili II since 1963), member of the Commonwealth.

Capital: Apia 33,170 inhab. (1981). **Currency:** tala. **Economy:** (1983, in 1,000 tonnes): coconuts 200, copra 23, cocoa, bananas 22, cattle, pigs, fishing. **Exports:** cocoa, copra.

add page 178

map 41

1.8 mn. Merchant shipping: 2.17 mn. GRT (of which 984,000 GRT are ore vessels); civil aviation: 196.3 mn. flown 13.2 mn. passengers carried. – **Exports** (1983): coal 15.4%, wool 8.4%, cereals 7.5%, meat 7.3%, iron ore 7.3%, non-ferrous metals 6.6%, alumina 5.5%, petroleum products, sugar. Chief trading partners: Japan 24%, U.S.A. 14.3%, United Kingdom 6.1%, Fed. Rep. of Germany, New Zealand, Saudi Arabia, Singapore, Rep. of Korea.

AUSTRALIAN OVERSEAS TERRITORIES:

CHRISTMAS ISLAND, area 135 sq.km, population 3,214 (1983), in the Indian Ocean on 10°25′ S.Lat. and 105°40′ E.Long.; **population:** Chinese 56% and Malays 29%. **Seat of administration:** Flying Fish Cove; **economy:** mining and export of phosphates 1,094,000 tonnes (1983): South Point.
COCOS ISLANDS, The Cocos (Keeling) Islands, area 14.2 sq.km, population 555 (1983); 27 coral islands in the Indian Ocean on 12°05′ S.Lat. and 96°53′E.Long. Islands became the part of Western Australia (since 1984). Seat of administration: Home Island; **economy:** coconuts 10,000 tonnes, oil and copra.
NORFOLK ISLAND, area 36.3 sq.km, population 2,250 (1983), in the Pacific Ocean on 29°04′ S. Lat. and 167°57′ E.Long.; **seat of administration:** Kingston; **economy:** vegetables, citrus fruit and especially tourism.

FIJI

Area 18,272 sq.km, population 696,000 (1985), independent state, member of the Commonwealth (Prime Minister Ratu Kamisese K. T. Mara since 1970, Governor-General Ratu Penaia Ganilau since 1983).
Administrative units: 4 divisions. 106 of the 844 islands and islets are inhabited; the largest, Viti Levu, 10,497 sq.km and Vanua Levu 5,534 sq.km. **Capital:** Suva 71,255 inhab. – **Currency:** Fiji dollar. **Economy** (1983, in 1,000 tonnes): sugarcane 2,260, sugar 276, coconuts 234, copra 24, rice 16, manioc 96, ginger; raising of cattle and poultry; fishing, mining of gold 960 kg (1981). – **Exports:** sugar, fish, coconut oil.

HAWAIIAN ISLANDS – U.S.A.

State of Hawaiian Islands, area 16,706 sq.km, population 1,054,000 (1985). Since 18 March 1959 50th **state of the U.S.A.** in the North Pacific Ocean.
The archipelago is formed by more than 20 islands, 7 of which are inhabited. The largest are Hawaii 10,414 sq.km, Maui 1,886 sq.km, Oahu 1,549 sq.km, Kauai 1,427 sq.km. **Capital:** Honolulu 365,048 inhab. (1980, with agglom. 762,565). **Economy:** farming – sugarcane, sugar, pineapples, vegetables, flowers, cattle raising, poultry, fishing; petroleum refinery at Honolulu. – **Communications** (1981): 7,231 km roads (526,000 cars), important air and naval crossroads. Tourism is of great importance 3.93 mn. visitors.

KIRIBATI

Republic of Kiribati, area 868 sq.km, population 64,000 (1985), republic, member of the Commonwealth (President Ieremia Tabai since 1979).
Includes 3 large groups of the Pacific coral islands: Kiribati Is. (Gilbert is.), Phoenix Is. 28 sq.km, Line Is. 595 sq.km (includes the world's largest atoll Kiritimati 359 sq.km) and Banaba (Ocean I.) 5.2 sq.km. **Capital:** Tarawa 17,188 inhab. **Population:** Micronesians. – **Currency:** Australian dollar. – **Economy:** (1983, in 1,000 tonnes): coconuts 77, copra 10, fish catch 24,050 tonnes. **Exports:** copra, fish. Trade with Australia.

NAURU

Republic of Nauru, Naoero, area 21.4 sq.km, population 8,000 (1984), republic, member of the Commonwealth (President Hammer De Roburt since 1972).
Coral island in the Pacific Ocean on 0°32′ S.Lat. and 166°55′ E.Long. **Capital:** Yaren 430 inhab. – **Currency:** Australian dollar = 100 cents. **Economy:** important mining of phosphates 1,684,000 tonnes for exports (1983).

NEW ZEALAND

Area 268,675 sq.km, population 3,254,400 (1985), independent state, member of the Commonwealth (Prime Minister David R. Lange since 1984, Governor-General Sir David Stuart Beattie since 1980).
Administrative units: 13 statistical areas, overseas territories. **Capital:** Wellington 135,094 inhab. (census 1981, with agglom. 343,982); **other towns** (1981, in 1,000 inhab., + with agglom.): Christchurch 290 (+323), Auckland 276 (+830), Dunedin 107 (+114), Hamilton 98 (+160), Invercargill 54. **Population:** New Zealanders and Maoris 282,600 (1982). **Density** 12 persons per sq.km; urban population 83.6%; 8.4% of inhabitants employed in agriculture. – **Currency:** New Zealand dollar = 100 cents.
Economy: advanced agricultural country with important animal production. Arable land covers only 1.8%, meadows and pastures 53% and forests 38% of the land area. **Agriculture:** crops (1983, in 1,000 tonnes): wheat 324, barley 346, maize (corn) 176, potatoes 250, peas 60, vegetables 405, fruit 374 (apples 194); **livestock** (1983, in 1,000 head): sheep 70,263 (6.2% of world population), cattle 7,630 (dairy cows 2,130), pigs 410, poultry 5,600; (in 1,000 tonnes): grease wool 371, hides and skins 177, eggs 57.2, fish catch 141.5, roundwood 10.3 mn. cub.m. **Mining**

map 42

SOLOMON ISLANDS

Area 29,785 sq.km, population 270,600 (1985), **independent state, member of the Commonwealth** (Prime Minister Peter Kenilorea since 1984, Governor-General Baddeley Devesi).
Administrative units: 4 divisions. **Capital:** Honiara (on Guadalcanal) 22,520 inhab. (1984). **Population:** Melanesians
94%, Polynesians. – **Currency:** Solomon dollar. – **Economy** (1983): forests cover 93% of the land area; roundwood
512,000 cub.m; gold 34 kg; crops (in 1,000 tonnes): coconuts 235, copra 31, sweet potatoes 48, rice, cocoa, palm oil 28;
raising of cattle, pigs, poultry; fish catch 47,200 tonnes. – **Exports:** copra, wood, fish, palm oil.

TONGA

Pule'anga Tonga – Kingdom of Tonga, area 747 sq.km, population 109,000 (1985), **kingdom,
member of the Commonwealth** (King Taufa'ahau Tupou IV since 1965).
The archipelago called Friendly Is. is formed by 169 islets; 3 chief groups: Tongatapu (257 sq.km), Ha'apai and Vava'u.
Capital: Nuku'alofa 20,564 inhab. **Currency:** pa'anga. **Economy:** coconuts, copra, citrus fruit, bananas; pigs, poultry.

TUVALU

The Tuvalu Islands, area 25.8 sq.km, population 8,050 (1984), **independent state, member of
the Commonwealth** (Prime Minister Dr. Tomasi Puapua since 1984).
The archipelago was formerly called Ellice Islands. **Capital:** Vaiaku (Funafuti I.) 826 inhab. **Population:** Polynesians. –
Currency: Australian dollar. – **Economy:** coconuts, copra, fishing; raising of pigs and poultry.

VANUATU

Ripablik blong Vanuatu, area 14,763 sq.km, population 142,000 (1985), **independent state**
(President Ati George Sokomanu since 1980).
The archipelago is formed by 40 islands; the largest are Espiritu Santo, Malekula, Efate, Eromanga. **Capital:** Vila (Efate I.)
14,880 inhab. (1980). **Currency:** vatu. – **Economy:** coconuts 280,000 tonnes, copra 37,000 tonnes, bananas, cocoa,
coffee; cattle 115,000 head, pigs; fishing. Deposits: manganese (Efate I.). – **Exports:** copra, fish, wood.

BRITISH TERRITORY:
PITCAIRN ISLANDS – area 37 sq.km, population 61 (1983). **Capital:** Adamstown. **Economy:** tropical fruit, vegetables.

FRENCH TERRITORIES:
FRENCH POLYNESIA – Polynésie Française, area 4,198 sq.km, population 172,500 (1985). **French overseas
territory** (High Commissioner: Alain Ohrel). **Administrative units:** 5 district: Îles du Vent 1,250 sq.km (the largest Tahiti
1,042 sq.km) and Îles sous le Vent 490 sq.km called Îles de la Société; Îles Tuamotu and Îles Gambier 948 sq.km,
Îles Marquises 1,345 sq.km, Îles Toubouai (Îs. Australes) 165 sq.km. **Capital:** Papeete 65,000 inhab.
Economy: deposits of phosphates (Makatea); crops (1983, in 1,000 tonnes): coconuts 90, copra 15, sugarcane 3, cotton,
coffee, tropical fruit; poultry, fish catch 2,680 tonnes. – **Exports:** copra, vanilla, citrus fruit. Tourism (111,000 visitors)
is of importance. The uninhabited island of **Clipperton** is under the authority of the Governor.
NEW CALEDONIA – Nouvelle-Calédonie, area 19,058 sq.km, population 153,000 (1985), **the Pacific overseas territory; dependencies:** Îles Loyauté (2,072 sq.km), Île des Pins, Îs. Huon, Îs. Bélep, Îs. Chesterfield, Î. Walpole. **Capital:**
Nouméa 60,112 inhab. (1983). **Population:** Melanesians (45%), French (36%), Polynesians. **Economy** (1983): important
mining of nickel 46,162 tonnes (third world producer), chromium 30,000 tonnes, cobalt; crops: coconuts, coffee, bananas;
raising of cattle, pigs. Tourism: 91,798 visitors. **Exports:** nickel and nickel ore (95%), cobalt, coffee, fruit.
WALLIS AND FUTUNA, area 255 sq.km, population 12,391 (1983), **overseas territory; seat of the administration:**
Mata Utu (Î. Uvéa) 590 inhab. **Economy:** coconuts 3,000 tonnes, copra, tropical fruit, livestock.

TERRITORIES OF THE UNITED STATES:
AMERICAN SAMOA and dependency, area 197 sq.km, population 35,400 (1985), **unincorporated territory of the
U.S.A. Capital:** Pago Pago 2,451 inhab. (on Tutuila), **seat of the Government:** Fagatogo 1,340 inhab. **Economy:**
coconuts, bananas, copra, cocoa; fishing tinned fish 90,100 tonnes. – **Exports:** tinned fish, copra.
FEDERATED STATES OF MICRONESIA, area 721 sq.km, population 86,950 (1985), includes atolls of the Caroline
Is. in Micronesia. Federated **4 states:** Kosrae, Pohnpei, Truk, Yap (President: Tosiwo Nakayama). **Capital:** Kolonia
(Pohnpei I.). **Economy:** coconuts, copra, fruit; fishing.
GUAM, area 549 sq.km, population 115,756 (1984), **unincorporated territory of the U.S.A. – Capital:** Agana 2,199 inhab.
Economy – crops: maize (corn), bananas, coconuts, citrus fruit, sugarcane; fishing; jet fuel. The air and naval base.
MARSHALL ISLANDS, area 205 sq.km, population 33,600 (1984), **republic** (President: Kabua), includes atolls of the
northeastern Micronesia. **Capital:** Uliga. **Economy:** coconuts, copra, tropical fruit; fishing.
MIDWAY ISLANDS, area 8 sq.km, population 2,260 (1983), **overseas territory of the U.S.A.** under naval administration.
NORTHERN MARIANA ISLANDS, area 471 sq.km, population 19,110 (1983), commonwealth, 14 islands – the largest
Saipan, Tinian. **Capital:** Garapan. **Economy:** crops: tropical fruit, coconuts, fishing. Important tourism.
PALAU, area 487 sq.km, population 15,000 (1985), **republic** (President: Lazarus Salii), includes coral islands of Palau Is.
Capital: Koror. **Economy:** corn, coconuts, copra, fruit; fishing.
WAKE ISLAND, area 8 sq.km, population 1,640 (1983), island under naval administration of the U.S.A., air base.

EXPLORATION ROUTES TO THE NORTH POLE REGIONS

Norwegian Expeditions:
- — — — Nansen 1893–1896 on board the "Fram"
- ······· on sledge
- — · — · — Amundsen 1903–1906
- — — — Amundsen 1926

American Expeditions:
- +++++ Peary 1908–1909
- ········ nuclear submarine Nautilus, August 3, 1958 - N. P.

Russian and Soviet Expeditions:
- — — — Vilickij 1914–1915
- +++++ Northern Sea Route 1932–1935 (Samojlovič, Šmidt, Ušakov)
- ······· Čkalov 1937
- — · — · — Gromov 1937
- — — — Papanin 1937–1938
- — — nuclear ice breaker Arktika, Aug. 17, 1977 - N. P.

Swedish Expedition:
- — — — Nordenskjöld 1878–1879

EXPLORATION ROUTES IN GREENLAND

Norwegian Expedition:
- +++++ Nansen 1888

German Expedition:
- — — — Wegener 1930

Danish Expeditions:
- — — — Rasmussen 1912
- ········· Koch 1913

EXPLORATION ROUTES TO [Antarctica?]

British Expeditions:
- — — — Cook 1772–1775
- — · — · — Weddell 1820–1824
- ········ Scott 1910–1912
- +++++ Fuchs 1957–1958

American Expedition:
- — · — · — Byrd 1929

SCIENTIFIC STATIONS IN ANTARCTICA

- ★ U.S.S.R.
- ■ U.S.A.
- ▲ Gt. Britain
- ⋈ Argentina
- Fr. ● France
- Ch. ● Chile

map 42

bird, though there are large numbers of animals in the sea. As far as **Man** is concerned the region is inhabited only by the staff of the scientific research stations. Great mineral wealth is assumed, but no mining is as yet in progress.

In 1773 Captain James Cook was the first to set eyes on South Georgia and the Sandwich Group during his voyage along the Antarctic Circle. The Russian explorers F. F. Bellingshausen and M. P. Lazarev discovered Peter Ist I. and saw Alexander I. in 1819–21; in 1819 the South Shetland Is. were discovered by W. Smith, but the coast of the Antarctic continent was not discovered until 27 February 1831 when John Biscoe reached the mountainous Enderby Land. J. C. Ross discovered Victoria Land, Ross I. and the Ross Ice Shelf in 1840–43. The first to stand on the continent was C. E. Borchgrevink (1894–95) near Cape Adare. Attempts to reach the South Pole date from the early 20th century; in October 1909 E. Shackleton reached Lat. 88°23' – 180 km from the Pole, but he was forced to turn back. The first to stand on the Pole was Roald Amundsen on 14 December 1911, and he was followed by R. F. Scott on 18 January 1912. Aerial surveys of Antarctica began in 1928; in the years 1928–30 H. Wilkes explored Palmer Land, on 20 November 1929 R. E. Byrd reached the Pole and he led a total of 5 expeditions until 1947. During expeditions in 1934–38 L. Ellsworth crossed Western Antarctica by plane. The first research stations were set up in 1947, and during the International Geophysical Year 1957–58 alone there were 55 such bases. On 14 December 1958 a Soviet expedition reached a place known as the Pole of Relative Inaccessibility, 82°06' S.Lat. and 54°58' E.Long. On 1 December 1959 a treaty was signed for peaceful cooperation in scientific investigation and research and the demilitarization of Antarctica; the treaty came into force on 23 June 1961. Some countries lay claim to territory in Antarctica in the given **sectors** (south of 60° S.Lat.).

AUSTRALIAN ANTARCTIC TERRITORY 45° to 136° E.Long. and 142° to 160° E.Long, an **area** roughly **6.4 mn. sq.km** with Mawson as the largest station; incl. Macquarie Is. 176 sq.km, Heard I. and McDonald I. 258 sq.km.
BRITISH ANTARCTIC TERRITORY 20° to 80° W.Long., since 1962 a colony roughly **388,500 sq.km in area**, incl. the South Orkney Is. 622 sq.km, South Shetland Is. 4,622 sq.km and Graham Land. Argentina has laid claims to a part of the British sector from 25° to 74° W.Long. and Chile to 53° to 90° W.Long. and have set up their own stations.
TERRES AUSTRALES ET ANTARCTIQUES FRANÇAISES, since 6 August 1955 French overseas territory, roughly **395,500 sq.km in area**. Adélie Coast, about 388,500 sq.km with the Dumont d'Urville station from 136° to 142° E.Long; islands in the Indian Ocean: Îles Kerguélen 6,232 sq.km with the Pt-aux-Français research station, Îs. Crozet 476 sq.km, Î. Amsterdam 66 sq.km and Î. St. Paul 7 sq.km.
NORWEGIAN DEPENDENCY 20° W.Long. to 45° E.Long., known as Queen Maud Land. The Dependencies in the Atlantic Ocean: Bouvetøya 59 sq.km, Peter Ist I. 249 sq.km.
NEW ZEALAND ROSS DEPENDENCY between 160° E.Long. and 150° W.Long., an **area of about 414,500 sq.km**, mostly ice shelf (330,000 sq.km) with the Scott Station.
PRINCE EDWARD ISLAND and MARION ISLAND, area 255 sq.km, occupied by South Africa since 1947.
The **SECTOR OF THE U.S.A.**, between 80° and 150° W.Long. has not been officially proclaimed. Of the four American bases in the Antarctic, McMurdo Station is the largest; it has an atomic power station. The Amundsen-Scott Station stands on the South Pole itself.
The **U.S.S.R.** has 6 permanent scientific research bases in Antarctica; the largest of these is Mirnyj.

add page 182

POLE REGIONS

[...]an and Soviet Expeditions:
[...]gshausen, Lazarev 1819-1821
[...]t expedition 1958–1959
[...] Zealand Expedition:
1957–1958
[...]egian Expedition:
[...]dsen 1910–1912

Brazil	F.R.G. ●	F.R.G.
Australia	Ind. ●	India
New Zealand	S. Afr. ●	South Africa
Japan	Pol. ●	Poland

map 42

ARCTIC REGIONS

The Arctic – the northern Arctic polar region – owes its name to the Ancient Greeks, for it lies below the northern constellation of the Great Bear, and the Greek for bear was "Arktos". The boundary of the Arctic region does not run only along the Arctic Circle (66°32' N.Lat.), making it 21.18 mn. sq.km in area; it is defined climatically by the 10°C July isotherm, which roughly coincides with the northern timber line and the range of tundra and taiga. This gives the Arctic an **area of 26.4 mn. sq.km**, of which 18.5 mn. sq.km are ocean and 7.9 mn. sq.km (30%) islands and continent. The point closest to the North Pole is Morris Jesup Cape on Greenland (83°40' N.Lat.). **The largest islands** are Greenland 2,175,600 sq.km and the Canadian Arctic islands 1,403,134 sq.km, of which Baffin I. 507,414 sq.km, Victoria I. 217,274 sq.km, Ellesmere I. 196,221 sq.km lie within the American Arctic, Novaja Zemľa 82,180 sq.km, Svalbard 62,050 sq.km and Zemľa Franca-Iosifa 16,100 sq.km are within the European Arctic, and Novosibirskije Ostrova 38,400 sq.km, Severnaja Zemľa 37,560 sq.km and Ostrov Vrangeľa 7,270 sq.km are in the Asian Arctic. **The Arctic Ocean** proper covers an area of 13,950,000 sq.km, with a maximum depth of 5,527 m; in the region of the North Pole it is covered with a thick layer of pack-ice and drift-ice, which extends southwards beyond 70° N.Lat. The depth of the ocean at the North Pole is 4,316 m.

Climate: The inner part of the Arctic Ocean is permanently covered with pack-ice (annual precipitation is 100–300 mm), and such is the intense cold that its effects spread far into the northernmost countries of the world. The warming effect of the ocean and its currents make it possible for the temperature to rise in the short summer on the North Pole to +1 to +3°C, while in the long winter it drops in January to about –35 to –40°C. Extreme winter temperatures spread to subarctic continental Sibiŕ (Siberia) (Ojm'akon –78°C), Canada (Fort Good Hope –78.2°C) and Greenland (–62°C). The ice shield covers 1,830,000 sq.km of Greenland and 155,000 sq.km of the Canadian Arctic islands. The land that is not icebound has permafrost with tundra **vegetation** (mosses, lichens, perennial plants, dwarf bushes) that passes into subarctic taiga. **Animal life** is limited in species and number (polar bears, polar foxes, hares, reindeer, caribou, waterfowl, etc.), and there are more species in the sea (cod, flatfish, walrus, seal, whale). Along the edge of the Arctic there are only sparse **settlements** of Eskimos, Lapps, Nenets, Yakufs, Chukchi, white immigrants and others, who make a living by fishing, trapping and reindeer farming and the extraction of minerals, which is on the increase. The northernmost settlement is Alert in Canada (82°30' N.Lat.) on Ellesmere I., 3,480 inhabitants live on Svalbard (1984, of these 2,228 Russians) and 502,000 tonnes of coal were mined (1983). Petroleum is being drilled in North Alaska, petroleum and natural gas are also found on the Arctic islands of Canada.

The Vikings, who settled in Iceland 870–930, were the first to explore the Arctic. Eric the Red discovered Greenland in 986, and around 1000 Leif Eriksson reached the American continent near Cape Dyer on Baffin I. Svalbard was discovered in 1194. The Russians explored northern Sibiŕ (Siberia) in the 17th century, and in 1648 S. Dezhnyov circumnavigated the eastern point of Asia. The North-East passage along the northern coast of Europe and especially Asia was first made by A. E. Nordenskjöld (1878–79), the North-West passage along the North American coast by R. McClure (1850–53) from the Bering Strait in the direction of the Atlantic Ocean, and in the opposite direction by Roald Amundsen (1903–06). The scientific exploration of the Arctic region began at the end of last century: F. Nansen and O. Sverdrup crossed the South of Greenland in 1888.

Robert E. Peary explored northern Greenland in 1892–1900 and he and M. Henson were the first people to stand on the North Pole (6 April 1909). Richard E. Byrd reached the Pole by air on 6 May 1926, two days later R. Amundsen, L. Ellsworth and U. Nobile did so in an airship; in 1937 the Russian polar explorers I. Papanin and O. Schmidt again used a plane; the Americans reached the Pole under the sea in their nuclear submarine Nautilus on 3 August 1958; Guido Monzino followed Peary's route with a dog team and reached the Pole on 19 May 1971. The Soviet atomic ice-breaker Arktika reached the Pole on 17 August 1977.

ANTARCTICA

Antarctica – the southern Antarctic polar region – derives its name from the Greek word for "opposite the Arctic", "opposite the North". The boundary of Antarctica is given by the Antarctic Circle (66°32' S.Lat.) as well as by the climatic 10°C January isotherm (the warmest), roughly concurrent with the southern timber line; within this boundary the **Antarctic measures 67.84 mn. sq.km** (incl. parts of South America). It comprises the Antarctic continent 14,108,000 sq.km in area, incl. the ice shelf, 13,175,000 sq.km without the ice shelf (i.e. 8.8% of land surface), with 75,570 sq.km of islands and the surrounding sea with the more distant subantarctic islands extending over an area of 13,198 sq.km. Antarctica lies at a distance of 4,000 km from Africa, 3,200 km from Australia and only 1,450 km from South America. The Ross Sea (off the Pacific Ocean) and the Weddell Sea (off the Atlantic Ocean) penetrate deep into the continent and divide it into the larger Eastern Antarctica on the side of the Atlantic and Indian Oceans and the smaller Western Antarctica of the Pacific side, where the large Antarctic Peninsula stretches in the direction of South America. The permanent ice-cap, of mean thickness 2,500 m, leaves only insignificant parts of the coast and the highest rocks free of ice. The average altitude of Antarctica is 2,280 m. The South Pole lies on the South Polar Plateau at a height of 2,800 m above sea level and the thickness of ice there reaches 2,810 m. The highest peak, the Vinson Massif in the Ellsworth Mts. in Western Antarctica is 5,140 m high, Mt. Kirkpatrick in the Transantarctic Mts. in Eastern Antarctica is 4,528 m and the highest active volcano is Mt. Ere-bus, 3,795 m, on Ross I.

The region of the South Pole has a severe, harsh polar **climate,** for the mean summer temperature (January) is –28°C, the July temperature (winter) is about –50°C, with precipitation not exceeding 80 mm in the prevailing calm; by contrast, the Antarctic coast (e.g. Wilkes Land) has the following mean temperatures: January –0.2°C, July –25°C, mean annual temperature –13.9°C, and 340 stormy days (highest number in the world). Absolute minimum temperature was recorded at the Vostok station (3,488 m high): –89.2°C. The lowest annual mean temperature is found at the Pole of Cold: –57.8°C. **Flora:** there exist only 3 species of flowering plants in Antarctica, about 60 varieties of moss and lichen, and microbes, algae, bacteria and fungi live below the surface of the weatherworn rocks. As regards its **fauna** there are two species of penguin as well as the skua, a predatory gull-like

INDEX

The index contains in alphabetical order all geographical names used in the maps. Apart from towns and cities all names are marked with appropriate abbreviations (for example, R. = river, I. = island, L. = lake, etc.). Following each name there is a number signifying the map number, and a letter and a number indicating the section of the map in which the place is located. The letters (marked in red on the maps) refer to sections of latitude, and the numbers (also marked in red) to sections of longitude. For example, "Mamoré, R., 37 D 3" means that the river Mamoré appears on map 37 in square D 3.

Rivers are indexed under the names given them by the country of their source. Thus the Danube comes under Donau and the Rijn under Rhein. For major geographical names, the squares given are those in which the name actually appears. For example, England, 9 B-D 3-5.

In some maps the names of administrative units, states and their subdivisions have been replaced by numbers, which are explained in the legend for the map. In the index this number is given in brackets after the name of the administrative unit.

When there is more than one place with the same name, the country where each is situated is given in brackets. For example, Victoria (Canada) 33 D 7; Victoria (Hong Kong), 19a B 3; Victoria (U.S.A.), 34 F 7. In the case of rivers, the sea, lake or river into which they flow is given, e.g. Negro (Amazonas), R., 37 C 3; Negro (Atlantic Ocean), R., 37 F 3.

ABBREVIATIONS USED IN THE INDEX

Admin. U. = Administrative Unit
Arch. = Archipelago
B. = Bay
C. = Cape
Can. = Canal
Chann. = Channel
Depr. = Depression
Des. = Desert
Fs. = Falls
G. = Gulf
Glac. = Glacier
H., Hs. = Hill, Hills
I., Is. = Island, Islands
L. = Lake

Mt., Mts. = Mountain, Mountains
Pen. = Peninsula
Pk. = Peak
Pl. = Plain
Plat. = Plateau
R. = River
Reg. = Region
Res. = Reserve, Reservoir
S. = Sea
St. = State
Str. = Strait
Sw. = Swamp
Val. = Valley
Vol. = Volcano

ABBREVIATIONS USED IN THE TEXT

m = metre
km = kilometre
sq.m = square metre
sq.km = square kilometre
ha = hectare
kg = kilogramme
ton = metric ton (tonne) = 1,000 kg

cub.m = cubic metre
l = litre
hl = hectolitre
mn. = million
agglom. = agglomeration
R.S.F.S.R. = Russian Soviet Federal Socialist Republic

A

Aachen, 12C2
Aakba, 5aB2
Aare, R., 11C4
Aba, 29D7
Ābādān, 21C5
Ābādeh, 21C6
Abadla, 28A2
Abaetetuba, 38C5
Abagnar Qi, 24B5
Abakaliki, 29D8
Abakan, 16D10,11
Abancay, 38D2
Abashiri, 25B7
Abay, R., 28C6
Abbeville, 11B3
Abéché, 28C5
Abengourou, 29D5
Abenra, 12B3
Abeokuta, 29D6
Aberdeen (U.K.), 10B3
Aberdeen (U.S.A., South Dakota), 34B7
Aberdeen (U.S.A., Washington), 34B2
Aberystwyth, 9C2
Abhā, 28C7
Abhar, 21C5
Abidjan, 29D4,5
Abilene, 34E7
Abilibi, R., 33C,D11
Abisko, 15A6
Abkhaz Autonomous Soviet Socialist Republic, (1) Admin. U., 18D5
Abomey, 29D6
Abong-Mbang, 29E9
Abqaiq, 21D5
Abrantes, 11G1,2
'Abrī, 28B6
Abruzzi (1), Admin. U., 13B3
Abū Hamad, 28C6
Abuja, 29C7
Abū Kabīr, 26aB3
Abū Kamāl, 20bB3
Abuná, R., 38D3
Abū Zabad, 28C5
Abū Zanīmah, 28B6
Abū-Zaby, 21E6
Acajutla, 36C3,4
Acapulco, 36C2,3
Acarigua-Araure, 38B3
Accra, 29D5,6
Achalciche, 18aA1
Achil Island, I., 7E2
Achtubinsk, 18C6
Achtyrka, 18B3,4
Ačinsk, 16D10,11
Acireale, 13C3
Acklins Island, I., 36B5
Aconcagua, Mt., 37F2,3
Acqui Terme, 13aB2
Acre, Admin. U., 38C2,3
Acton, 9a
Adamaoua, Mts., 26D6
Adam's Bridge, I., 20aB2
Adamstown, 41F13
Adan, 28C7
Adana, 21aB3
Adapazan, 21aA2
Adda, R., 13aA3
Ad Damazin, 28C6
Ad-Dāmir, 28C6
Ad-Dammān, 28B7,8
Ad-Dawhah, 21D6
Addis Abeba, 28D6
Ad-Dīwānīyah, 21C4,5

Ad-Duwaym, 28C6
Addy, 33aB4
Adelaide, 40D3
Adélie Coast, Reg., 42F22,23
Aden see Adan
Adige, R., 13A2
Adigrat, 28C6,7
Adiyaman, 21aB3
Admiralty Island, Is., 41D4
Ado-Ekiti, 29D7
Adour, R., 11D2
Adra, 11G3
Adrar, 28B2
Adré, 28C5
Adrī, 28B4
Adria, 13aA5,6
Adrian, 33aC4
Adriatic Sea, 5C6
Adwa, 28C6
Adygei Autonomous Region, (7) Admin. U., 18C5
Adzhar Autonomous Soviet Socialist Republic, (2) Admin. U., 18aA1
Adz'vavom, 17A9
Aegean Sea, 14D3
Aershan, 24B6
Afareaitu, 41dB1
Afghanistan, St., 22A2,3
Afikpo, 29D7
Africa, 3
Afyon, 21aB2
Agadez, 29A7
Agadir, 28A1,2
Agana, 41B4
Agartala, 22B5
Agawa, 34B4
Agboville, 29D4,5
Agdam, 18aB2
Agen, 11C3
Aginskoje, 24A5
Āgra, 22B3
Agri, R., 13B4
Agrigento, 13C3
Agrinion, 14D2
Agua Prieta, 36A2
Aguascalientes, 36B2
Aguascalientes (1), Admin. U., 36B2
Aguelhok, 29A6
Aguilas, 11G3
Agulhas Negras, Mt., 37E5
Agusan, R., 23C4
Agutaya, 23bB2
Ahaggar, Mts., 26B5
Ahar, 18aA2
Ahmadābād, 22B2
Ahmadnagar, 22C3
Ahvāz, 21C5
Ahvenanmaa, Is., 15C6,7
Aibihu, L., 24B2
Aigaioi Nisoi (1), Admin. U., 14D3
Ain (01), Admin. U., 11C4
Aïnazi, 17C2
Aïn Beïda, 27aA2
Aïn Sefra, 28A2,3
Aïr, Mts., 26C5
Aire, R., 7E7
Aisne (02), Admin. U., 11B3
Aisne, R., 11B4
Aix-en-Provence, 11D4
Aïzawl, 22B5
Aizu-wakamatsu, 25C6,7

Ajaccio, 11D5
Ajaguz, 24B2
Ajan, 16D15
Ajat, R., 17aC3
Ajdābiyah, 28A5
Ajkino, 17B7
Ajmer, 22B3
Ajo, 34E4
Ak-Dovurak, 24A3
Akesu, 24B2
Aketi, 28D5
Akhelóós, R., 14D2
Akhisar, 21aB1
Akimiski Island, I., 33C11
Akita, 25C6,7
Akjoujt, 28C1
'Akko, 20bB1
Akköy, 21aB1
Aklavik, 33B6
Akola, 22B3
Akordat, 28C6
Akpatok Island, I., 33B13
Ákra Maléa, C., 14D2
Ákra Sídheros, C., 14E3
Ákra Spátha, C., 14E2,3
Ákra Taínaron, C., 14D2
Akron, 35C4
Akrotíri, 19cB2
Akrotírion Akámas, C., 19cA1
Akrotirion Apostólou, C., 19cA3
Akrotírion Gátas, C., 19cB1,2
Akrotírion Kormakíti, C., 19cA1
Akrotirion Pidálion, C., 19cB3
Aksaray, 21aB2
Akşehir, 21aB2
Aktogaj, 24B1,2
Akt'ubinsk, 16D,E7
Akulurak, 33B3
Akure, 29D7
Akureyri, 15aB3
Akwanga, 29C8
Ala, 13aA4,5
Alabama, Admin. U., 35E3
Alabama, R., 35E3
Alagir, 18D5
Alagoas (2), Admin. U., 38C6
Alagoinhas, 38D6
Alagón, 11F3
Al-Ahmadī, 21D5
Alajuela, 36D4
Alakurtti, 17A4
Al-'Alamayn, 28A5
Al-'Amārah, 21C5
Al-Āmiriyah, 26aB1,2
Alamogordo, 34E5
Alamos, 36B2
Åland see Ahvenanmaa
Alanya, 21aB2
Alapajevsk, 17aB3
Al-'Aqabah, 20bC1
Al-'Arīsh, 21aC4
Alaska, Admin. U., 33B3-5
Alaska Peninsula, 33C3,4
Alaska Range, Mts., 31C5,6
Alatyr', 18B6
Alaverdi, 18aA1
Al-'Ayn, 21E7
Al-Azīzīyah, 26A6
Alba, 13aB2
Al-Bāb, 20bA2
Albacete, 11G3

Alba-Iulia, 14B2
Al-Bahr al-Abyad, R., 28C6
Al-Bahr al-Azraq see Abay
Al-Bahr al-Jabal, R., 28D6
Albania, St., 13B,C4,5
Albany (Australia), 40D1
Albany (U.S.A., Georgia), 35E4
Albany (U.S.A., New York), 35C6
Albany, R., 33C11
Al-Basrah, 21C5
Al-Bawītī, 28B5
Al-Baydá', 28A5
Albenga, 13aB2
Alberta, Admin. U., 33C8
Albi, 11D3
Alborg, 12A3
Alborz, Mts., 19F7
Al-Buhayrat al-Murrah al Kubrá, L., 26aB4
Albuquerque, 34D5
Al-Buraymí, 21E7
Albury, 40D4
Alcalá de Henares, 11F3
Alcamo, 13C2
Alcañiz, 11F3
Alcántara, 11G2
Alcázar de San Juan, 11G3
Alcira, 11G3
Alcoy, 11G3
Alcudia, 11G4
Aldabra Islands, Is. 30B5
Aldan, 16D14
Aldan, R., 16C15
Alderney, I., 6aA2
Aldershot, 9D4
Aleg, 29A2
Alegrete, 39aC2
Aleksandrija, 18C3
Aleksandrov, 17C5
Aleksandrov Gaj, 18B6
Aleksandrovsk, 17aB2
Aleksandrovskoje, 18D5
Aleksandrovsk-Sachalinskij, 16D16
Aleksejevka, 18B4
Aleksin, 18B4
Alençon, 11B3
Alenuihaha Channel, Str., 35aB,C3
Alert, 32A13,14
Alès, 11C4
Alessandria, 13A2
Ålesund, 15C3
Aletai, 24B2
Aleutian Islands, Is., 32D2-4
Alexander Archipelago, Is., 33C6
Alexander Bay, 30D2
Alexander I. Island, I., 42F8
Alexandria (Romania), 14C3
Alexandria (U.S.A.), 35E2
Alexandria see Al-Iskandarīyah
Alexandroúpolis, 14C3
Al-Fāshir, 28C5
Al-Fayyūm, 28B5,6
Alfonsine, 13aB6
Al-Fujayrah, 21D7
Al-Furāt see Firat
Algeciras, 11G2
Alger, 28A3
Algeria, St., 28B2,3
Alghero, 13B2
Al-Ghurdaqah, 28B6

Al-Hadīthah, 21 C 4
Al-Hammadah Al-Hamrá, Des., 26 B 5,6
Al-Hasakah, 20 b A 3
Al-Hillah, 21 C 4
Al-Hoceima, 11 H 2,3
Al-Hudaydah, 28 C 7
Al-Hufrah, 28 B 4
Al-Hufūf, 28 B 7
Aliakmón, R., 14 C 2
Ali-Bajramly, 18 a B 2
Alicante, 11 F 3
Alice, 34 F 7
Alice Springs, 40 C 3
Alida, 34 B 6
Alīgarh, 22 a B 1
Al-Iskandarīyah, 28 A 5,6
Al-Ismā'īliyah, 28 A 6
Al-Jaghbūb, 28 B 5
Al-Jawf (Libya), 28 B 5
Al-Jawf (Saudi Arabia), 28 B 6
Al-Jīzah, 28 A,B 6
Al- Jubayl, 28 B 7
Al-Junaynah, 28 C 5
Al-Karak, 20 b C 1,2
Al-Kāzimīyah, 21 C 4
Al-Khalīl, 20 b C 1
Al-Khandaq, 28 C 5,6
Al-Khārijah, 28 B 6
Al-Khasab, 21 D 7
Al-Khums, 28 A 4
Al-Khurtūm, 28 C 6
Al-Khurtūm Bahrī, 28 C 6
Alkmaar, 12 B 2
Al-Kufrah Oasis, Reg., 28 B 5
Al-Kuwayt, 21 D 5
Al-Lādhiqīyah, 20 b B 1,2
Allāhābād, 22 B 4
Allentown, 35 C 5
Alleppey, 20 a B 1,2
Aller, R., 12 B 3
Alliance, 34 C 6
Allier (03), Admin. U., 11 C 3
Allier, R., 11 C 3
Allison Harbour, 33 a A 1
Alloa, 10 B 3
Alma, 35 B 6
Alma-Ata, 16 E 9
Almada, 11 G 1
Almadén, 11 G 2
Al-Madīnah, 28 B 6,7
Al-Mahallah al-Kubrā, 26 a A,B 2,1
Al-Manāmah, 21 D 6
Al-Mansūrah, 26 a A,B 3
Al-Manzilah, 26 a A 3
Al-Marj, 28 A 4,5
Al-Maşīrah, I., 21 E 7
Al-Matarīyah, 26 a A 3
Al- Mawsil, 21 B 4
Almazón, 11 F 2
Almeirim, 38 C 4
Almería, 11 G 3
Al'metjevsk, 18 B 7
Al-Minyā, 28 B 6
Al-Mubarraz, 21 D 5,6
Al-Mudawwarah, 20 b C 1,2
Al-Muglad, 28 C 5
Al-Mukallā, 28 C 7
Al-Mukhā, 28 C 7
Alnwick, 9 B 4
Alofi, 41 E 8,9
Alor Setar, 23 C 1,2
Alotau, 40 B 3
Alpena, 35 B 4
Alpes de Haute-Provence (04), Admin. U., 11 D 4

Alpes (Hautes-) (05), Admin. U., 11 C 4
Alpes-Maritimes (06), Admin. U., 11 C 4
Alpine, 34 E 6
Alps, Mts., 19 E 2-4
Al-Qadārif, 28 C 6
Al-Qāhirah, 28 A 5,6
Al-Qā'im, 20 b B 3
Al-Qāmishlī, 20 b A 3
Al-Qantarah, 26 a B 4
Al-Qasr, 28 B 5
Al-Qatif, 21 D 5
Al-Qaysūmah, 21 D 5
Al-Qusayr, 28 B 6
Alta, 15 A 7
Altai, Mts., 19 E 10-12
Altaj, 24 B 3
Altamaha, R., 35 E 4
Altamira, 38 C 4
Altanbulag, 24 A 4
Alteelva, R., 15 A 8
Altena, 12 a B 4
Alto Cedro, 36 a B 6
Altoona, 35 C 5
Alto Paraguai, 38 D 4
Alturas, 34 C 2
Altus, 34 E 7
Al-Ubayyid, 28 C 5,6
Al-Uqsur, 28 B 6
Alušta, 16 a B 2
Alvdal, 15 C 4
Al-Wajh, 28 B 6
Alwar, 22 B 3
Alyangula, 40 B 3
Alyialoúsa, 19 c A 3
Alytus, 18 B 1
Amada Gaza, 29 D 9
Amadjuak Lake, L., 33 B 12
Amadora, 11 G 1
Amakusa-shotó, Is., 25 D 4
Amapá, 38 B 4
Amapá, Admin. U., 38 B 4
Amarillo, 34 D 6
Amasya, 21 a A 3
Amazonas, Admin. U., 38 C 3,4
Amazonas, R., 37 C 2
Ambála, 22 A 3
Ambanja, 30 C 5
Ambarčík, 16 C 17,18
Ambarnyj, 17 A 4
Ambato, 38 C 2
Ambatondrazaka, 30 C 5
Ambatosoratra, 30 C 5
Amberg, 12 C 3,4
Ambérieu, 11 C 4
Ambidédi, 29 B 3
Ambon, 23 D 4
Ambositra, 30 D 5
Ambovombe, 30 D 5
Ambriz, 30 B 2
Ambrose Channel, Chann., 32 a
Amderma, 16 B,C 8
Amdo, 24 C 3
American Highlands, Reg., 42 G 28,29
American Samoa, Admin. U., 41 c A,B 3,4
Amery, 33 C 10
Amery Ice Shelf, 42 F 29
Ameson, 35 B 4
Amfípolis, 14 C 2,3
Amga, R., 16 C 15
Amguid, 28 B 3
Amiens, 11 B 3
Amirante Islands, Is., 27 E 10
Amlekhganj, 22 a B 3
Ammān, 20 b C 1,2

Ammassalik, 33 B 16
Ammókhostos, 19 c A 2,3
Amnok-kang, R., 25 B 4
Amorgós, I., 14 D 3
Ampanihy, 30 D 5
Amrāvati, 22 B 3
Amritsar, 22 A 3
Amsterdam, 12 B 2
Am Timan, 28 C 4,5
Amudarja, R., 16 E,F 8
Amundsen Gulf, G., 33 A 7
Amundsen-Scott, Station, 42 H
Amundsen Sea, 42 G 11,12
Amur, R., 16 D 14
Anabar, R., 16 B 13
Anaconda, 34 B 4
Anacortes, 33 a B 2,3
Anadyr', 16 C 19
Anadyr', R., 16 C 19
Anadyrskij Zaliv, B., 16 C 20
'Anah, 20 b B 3
Anaheim, 34 E 3
Anahim Lake, 33 a A 2
Anambra (1), Admin. U., 29 D 7
Anamur, 21 a B 2
Anapa, 18 D 4
Anápolis, 38 D 4,5
Anār, 21 C 6,7
Anarjokka, R., 15 A 8
Anchorage, 33 B 4,5
Ancona, 13 B 3
Ancud, 39 C 1
Anda, 24 B 6
Andalsnes, 15 C 3
Andalucía (1), Admin. U., 11 G 2
Andaman Islands, 22 C 5
Andaman Sea, 22 C 5
Andeg, 17 A 8
Anderson, R., 33 B 7
Andes, Mts., 37 C-G 2,3
Andfjorden, Str., 15 A 6
Andhra Pradesh, Admin. U., 22 C 3,4
Andong, 25 C 4
Andorra, 11 F 4
Andorra, St., 11 F 4
Andover, 9 D 4
Andøya, I., 15 A 5,6
Andria, 13 B 4
Andropov, 17 C 5
Andros, I., 14 D 3
Andros Island, I., 35 G 5
Andros Town, 35 G 5
Andújar, 11 G 2
Anécho, 29 D 6
Angara, R., 16 D 11
Angarsk, 16 b B 1
Ånge, 15 C 5,6
Angeles, 23 b A 2
Angermanälven, R., 15 B,C 6
Angicos, 38 C 6
Anglesey, I., 7 E 5
Angmagssalik see Ammassalik
Angoche, 30 C 4,5
Angola, St., 30 C 2,3
Angoulême, 11 C 3
Angra do Heroísmo, 11 a A 3
Anguilla, Admin. U., I., 36 b A 2
Anhui (6), Admin. U., 24 C 5

Aniak, 33 B 4
Anjouan, I., 30 C 5
Anju, 25 C 4
Ankang, 24 C 4,5
Ankara, 21 a A 2
Anna, 18 B 5
Annaba, 28 A 3
An-Nabk, 20 b B 2
An-Nafūd, Des., 19 G 6
An-Najaf, 21 C 4
Annan, 10 C 3
Annan, R., 10 C 3
Annapolis, 35 D 5
Ann Arbor, 35 b
An-Nāsirīyah, 21 C 5
Annecy, 11 C 4
An-Nuhūd, 28 C 5
Anqing, 24 C 5
Anshan, 24 B 6
Anshun, 24 D 4
Ansongo, 29 B 6
Antalya, 21 a B 3
Antalaha, 30 C 6
Antalya, 21 a B 2
Antalya Körfezi, B., 21 a B 2
Antananarivo, 30 C 5
Antarctica, 42
Antarctic Peninsula, Pen., 42 F,G 6,7
Antequera, 11 G 2
Antigua, I., 36 b A 2
Antigua and Barbuda, St., 36 b A 2
Antofagasta, 39 A 1,2
Antonina, 39 a C 4
Antrim, 10 D 6
Antrim (1), Admin. U., 10 D 6
Antrim Mountains, Mts., 7 D 4,5
Antserana, 30 C 5,6
Antsirabe, 30 C,D 5
Antsohihy, 30 C 5
Antwerpen, 11 B 4
Anuradhapura, 20 a B 3
Anvers see Antwerpen
Anxi, 24 B 3
Anyang, 24 C 5
Aomori, 25 B 7
Aosta, 13 A 1
Aotou, 19 a A 4
Aoulef, 28 B 3
Apa, R., 39 A 3
Aparri, 23 b A 2
Apatity, 17 A 4
Ape, 17 C 3
Apeldoorn, 12 B 2
Apia, 41 c A 2
Apoteri, 38 B 4
Appalachian Mountains, Mts., 31 E,F 12,13
Appennines, Mts., 5 C,D 5,6
Appleby, 10 C 3
Appleton, 35 C 3
Apšeronsk, 18 D 4
Apucarana, 39 a B 3
Apure, R., 37 B 3
Apurímac, R., 37 D 2
Arabatskaja Strelka, Pen., 16 a A,B 2
Arabian Peninsula, Pen., 19 G,H 6,7
Arabian Sea, 3
Aracaju, 38 D 6
Aracatuba, 39 a B 3,4
Araçuaí, 38 D 5
Arad, 14 B 2
Arafura Sea, 23 D 5

Azerbaijan Soviet Socialist Republic, Admin. U., 18aA2
Azores, Is., 11a
Azov, 18C4
Azovskoje More, S., 16E5
Azu, 39B2,3
Az-Zagãziq, 26aB3
Az-Zarqã', 20bB2
Az-Zãwiyah, 28A4

B

Baba Burnu, C., 19F4,5
Babajevo, 17C5
Bãb-el-Mandeb, Chann., 26C9
Bãbol, 21B6
Babuškin, 17b
Babuyan Islands, Is., 23B4
Bacabal, 38C5
Bacãu, 14B3
Bacharden, 21B7
Bachčisaraj, 16aB1,2
Bachmač, 18B3
Back, R., 33B9
Bacolod, 23B4
Bács-Kiskun (1), Admin. U., 14B1
Badajoz, 11G2
Badalona, 11F4
Badanah, 21C3,4
Baden-Baden, 12C3
Baden-Württemberg (1), Admin. U., 12C3
Bad Ischl, 12D4
Badulla, 20aC3
Bærum, 15D4
Bafatá, 29B2
Baffin Island, I., 33A,B11-13
Baffin Sea, 33A12,13
Bafing, R., 29B3
Bafoulabé, 29B3
Bafoussam, 29D8
Bãfq, 21C7
Bafra, 21aA3
Baga, 29B9
Bagamoyo, 30B4
Bagansiapi-api, 19bC2
Bagdarin, 16bB3
Bãgé, 39aD3
Baghdãd, 21C4,5
Baghlãn, 22A2
Baguio, 23B4
Bahamas, Is., 35F5
Baharampur, 22a B3,4
Bahãwalpur, 22B3
Bahia, Admin. U., 38D5,6
Bahía Blanca, 39B2
Bahía Blanca, B., 39B2,3
Bahia Grande, B., 39D2
Bahir Dar, 28C6
Bahrain, St., 21D6
Bahr al-'Arab, R., 28D5
Bahr al-Milh, L., 20bB3
Bahr Aouk, R., 28C5
Bahr Azoum, R., 28C5
Bahr el Ghazal, R., 28C4
Bahret al-Assad, Res., 21B3
Baía de Setúbal, B., 11G1
Baia-Mare, 14B2
Baicheng, 24B6
Baidoa, 28D7
Baie-Comeau, 35B7
Baie de la Seine, B., 11B2

Baile Átha Cliath see Dublin
Bailuondo, 30C2
Bairin Youqi, 25B2
Baise, 24D4
Baiyunebo, 24B4
Baja, 14B1
Baja California, Pen., 31F,G9
Baja California Norte (2), Admin. U., 36B1
Baja California Sur (3), Admin. U., 36B1
Bajanchongor, 24B4
Bajangol, 16bB1
Bajan-Uul, 24B5
Bajkal, 16bB1,2
Bajkal'sk, 16bB1
Bajkonur, 16E8
Bajo Nuevó, Is., 36C5
Bajram-Ali, 21B8
Bakal, 17aC2
Bakel, 29B2
Baker, 34C3
Baker Island, I., 41D8
Baker Lake, L., 33B10
Bakersfield, 34D3
Bakhtarãn, 21C5
Baku, 16E6,7
Bala (Canada), 33b
Bala (U.K.), 9C3
Balabac Island, I., 23C3
Balabac Strait, 23C3
Ba'labakk, 20bB2
Balakleja, 18C4
Balakovo, 18B6
Balašov, 18B5
Balaton, L., 14B1
Balboa Heights, 34a
Balbriggan, 10E6,7
Balcarce, 39aE2
Balchaš, 16E9
Balčik, 14C4
Baleares (4), Admin. U., 11G4
Baleares Islas, Is., 11F,G4
Balearic Islands see Baleares Islas
Bali, I., 23D3
Balikesir, 21aB1
Balikpapan, 23D3
Balintang Channel, 23B3,4
Balinzuoqi, 25B2
Balkan Peninsula, Pen., 5C6,7
Ballarat, 40D4
Ballater, 10B3
Ballé, 29B3
Balleny Islands, Is., 42F20
Ballina, 10D5
Ballinasloe, 10E5
Ballycastle, 10D6
Ballymena, 10D6
Ballymena (4), Admin. U., 10D6
Ballymoney, 10D6
Ballymoney (5), Admin. U., 10D6
Ballyshannon, 10D5,6
Balonne, R., 40C4,5
Balsas, 38C5
Balsas, R. 36C2
Balta, 18C2
Baltic Sea, 15D,E6,7
Baltijsk, 17D1,2
Baltim, 26aA3
Baltimore, 35D5

Bam, 21D7
Bama, 29C9
Bamako, 29B4
Bamba, 29A5
Bambari, 28D5
Bamberg, 12C3
Bambuí, 39aB4
Bamenda, 29D8
Bãmïãn, 22A2
Bampür, 21D8
Banaba, I., 41D6,7
Banamba, 29B4
Banana, 30B2
Banãs, R., 22B3
Banbridge, 10D6
Banbridge (6), Admin. U., 10D6
Banbury, 9C4
Bancroft, 33b
Bãnda, 22aB2
Banda Aceh, 23C1
Banda Sea, 23D4,5
Bandama, R., 29D4
Bandar 'Abbãs, 21D7
Bandar-e Anzalï, 21B5
Bandar-e Khomeynï, 21C5,6
Bandar-e Lengeh, 21D6
Bandar-e Torkeman, 21B6
Bandar Seri Begawan, 23C3
Bandiagara, 29B5
Bandirma, 21aA1
Bandon, 10F5
Bandundu, 30B2
Bandung, 23D2
Banes, 36aB6
Banff (Canada), 33C8
Banff (U.K.), 10B3
Banfora, 29C4
Bangalore, 22C3
Bangassou, 28D5
Bangbu, 24C5
Banghãzï, 28A4,5
Bangka,, I., 23D2
Bangkalan, 23aA3
Bangkok see Krung Thep
Bangladesh, St., 22a B,C4
Bangor (U.K., Northern Ireland), 10D7
Bangor (U.K., Wales), 9C2,3
Bangor (U.S.A.), 35C7
Bangui, 28D4
Banhã, 26aB3
Bani, R., 29B4
Bani Suwayf, 28B6
Bãniyãs, 20bB1
Banja Luka, 13A4
Banjarmasin, 23D3
Banjul, 29B1
Bank, 18aB2
Bankas, 29B5
Banks Island, I., 33A7,8
Banks Strait, Str., 40E4
Bann, R., 7D4
Banská Bystrica, 12C5
Bantry, 10F5
Bantry Bay, B., 7F2,3
Banyo, 29D8,9
Banyuwangi, 23D3
Baoding, 24C5
Baoji, 24C4
Baotou, 24B4,5
Baoulé, R., 29C4
Bar, 13B4
Baracoa, 36aB6
Barakah, R., 28C6
Bãrãn, 22aB1
Baranoviči, 18B2

Baranya (2), Admin. U., 14B1
Barbacena, 38E5
Barbados, St., I., 36bB2
Barbar, 28C6
Barbuda, I., 36bA2
Barcellona, 13C3
Barcelona, 11F4
Barcelona-Puerto la Cruz, 38A3
Barcelos, 38C3
Barcoo, R., 40C4
Barddhamãn, 22aC3,4
Bardera, 28D7
Bardi, 13aB3
Bardiyah, 28A5
Bardsey Island, I., 9C2
Bardsnehorn, C., 15aB4
Bareilly, 22B3
Barents Sea, 16B4-7
Barfleur, 6aA3
Bari, 13B4
Barinas, 38B2,3
Barïsãl, 22aC4
Barito, R., 23D3
Barkley Sound, B., 33aB1,2
Bar-le-Duc, 11B4
Barletta, 13B4
Barmer, 22B3
Barnaul, 16D9,10
Barnes, 9a
Barneville-Carteret, 6aA3
Barnouic, Is., 6aA2
Barnsley, 9C4
Barnstaple, 9D2
Baro, 29C7
Baro, R., 28D6
Barqah, Reg., 28A5
Barquisimeto, 38A3
Barra, 38D5
Barra, I., 7C4
Barrado Garças, 38D4
Barra do-São Manuel, 38C4
Barragen de Alqueva, Res., 11G2
Barra Head, C., 7C4
Barrancabermeja, 38B2
Barranquilla, 38A2
Barraute, 35B5
Barreiras, 38D5
Barreiro, 11G1
Barretos, 39aB4
Barrie, 33b
Barrington Tops, Mt., 40D5
Barrow, 33A4
Barrow, R., 7E4
Barrow-in-Furness, 9B3
Barrow Strait, 33A10
Barry, 9D3
Barstow, 31aC,D2
Bartica, 38B4
Bartin, 21aA2
Bartle Frere, Mt., 40B4
Barumun, R., 19bD1,2
Baruun Urt, 24B5
Barwon, R., 40C4
Baryš, 18B6
Basel, 11C4
Bashi Channel, 24D6
Basilan Island, I., 23C4
Basildon, 9D5
Basilicata (2), Admin. U., 13B4
Basingstoke, 9D4
Baskir Autonomous Soviet Socialist Republic, Admin. U., 17aB,C1,2

Bassano, 34A4
Bassano del Grappa,
 13aA5
Bassari, 29C6
Bassas da India, I., 30D4
Bassein, 22C5
Basse Santa Su, 29B2
Basseterre, 36bA2
Basse Terre, 36bA2
Bassila, 29C6
Bass Strait, Str., 40D4
Bastia, 11D5
Bastogne, 11B4
Bata, 29E8
Batajsk, 18C4,5
Batang, 24C,D3
Batangas, 23B4
Batan Islands, Is., 23A4
Bâtdâmbâng, 22C6
Bath, 9D3
Bathurst (Australia), 40D4
Bathurst (Canada), 35B7
Bathurst Inlet, 33B9
Bathurst Island, I.,
 (Australia), 40B2
Bathurst Island, I.,
 (Canada), 33A9,10
Batié, 29C5
Batman, 21aB4
Batna, 28A3
Baton Rouge, 35E5
Batouri, 29D9
Battersea, 9a
Batticaloa, 20aC3
Battle Harbour, 33C14
Batu, Mt., 26D8
Baturni, 16E5,6
Batu Pahat, 19bD3
Baturaja, 23D2
Baubau, 23D4
Bauchi, 29C8
Bauchi (2), Admin. U.,
 29C8
Baukau, 23D4
Bauru, 38E5
Bawku, 29C5
Bayamo, 36aB5
Bayamón, 36bA1
Baybay, 23bB2,3
Bayburt, 21aA4
Bay City, 35F1
Bayern (2), Admin. U.,
 12C4
Bayeux, 11B2
Bay of Bengal, B., 22C4
Bay of Biscay, B.,
 11E,F2,3
Bay of Fundy, B., 33D13
Bayonne, 11D2
Bayreuth, 12C3
Bayrût, 20bB1
Baza, 11G3
Bazdâr, 21D8,9
Beachy Head, C., 7F8
Bear Island see
 Bjørnøya
Beás, R., 22A3
Beatrice, 35C1
Beau-Bassin, 30aB3
Beauceville-Est, 35B6
Beaufort Sea, 33A5,6
Beaufort West, 30E3
Beauharnois Lock, 33b
Beauly, R., 7C5
Beaumont, 35E2
Beaune, 11C4
Beauvais, 11B3
Beaver, 34B2
Beaver, R., 33C9
Beâwar, 22B3
Bebedouro, 39aB4

Béchar, 28A2
Beckley, 35D4
Bedford, 9C4
Bedfordshire (9), Admin.
 U., 9C4
Bedlington, 9B4
Beechey Point, 33A5
Be'er Sheva', 20bC1
Begna, R., 15C4
Behbehân, 21C6
Beian, 24B6
Beihai, 24D4
Beijing, 24C5
Beijing (28), Admin. U.,
 24B5
Beipiao, 25B3
Beira, 30C4
Beirut see Bayrût
Beitbridge, 30D3,4
Beja, 11G2
Beja (2), Admin. U., 11G2
Béja, 28A3
Bajaia, 28A3
Béjar, 11F2
Békés (3), Admin. U.,
 14B2
Békéscsaba, 14B2
Bela, 22B2
Belaja, R., 17aC2
Belaja Cerkov', 18C3
Belcher Islands, Is.,
 33C11,12
Bel'cy, 18C2
Beled Weyne, 28D7
Belém, 38C5
Belfast, 10D6,7
Belfast (7), Admin. U.,
 10D7
Belfast Lough, B., 7D5
Belfort, 11C4
Belgaum, 22C3
Belgium, St., 11B3,4
Belgorod, 18B4
Belgorod-Dnestrovskij,
 18C2,3
Belgrade see Beograd
Belitung, 23D2
Belize, 36C4
Belize, St., 36C4
Bella Coola, 33aA1,2
Bellary, 22C3
Bella Vista, 39aC2
Belle-Île, I., 11C2
Belleville, 35C5
Bellevue, 34B2
Bellingham, 34B2
Bellingshausen Sea,
 42F,G8-10
Bello, 38B2
Belluno, 13A2,3
Belmopan, 36C4
Belmullet, 10D5
Belo, 30C5
Belogorsk (R.S.F.S.R.),
 24A6
Belogorsk (Ukraine),
 16aB2
Belo Horizonte, 38D,E5
Beloje More, S., 16C5,6
Belomorsko-Baltijskij
 Kanal, Can., 17B4
Belopolje, 18B3
Belorečensk, 18D4,5
Beloreck, 17aC2
Bel'ov, 18B4
Beloz'orsk, 17B,C5
Belyj Jar, 16D10
Bembe, 30B2
Bemidji, 35B2
Benavente, 11F2

Benbecula, I., 7C4
Bend, 34C2
Bendaja, 29D3
Bendel (3), Admin. U.,
 29D7
Bender Beila, 28D7,8
Bendery, 18C2
Bendigo, 40D4
Benevento, 13B3
Bengkalis, 19bD2,3
Bengkulu, 23D2
Benguela, 30C2
Beni, R., 38D3
Béni Abbès, 28A2
Beni-Mellal, 28A2
Benin, St., 29C6
Benin City, 29D7
Benjamin Constant,
 38C2,3
Ben Lawers, Mt., 7C5
Ben Lomond, Mt., 7C5
Ben Macdhui, Mt., 7C5,6
Ben More (U.K., Mull), Mt.,
 7C4,5
Ben More (U.K., Nort West
 Highlands), Mt., 7B5
Ben Nevis, Mt., 7C5
Benoni, 30D3
Bénoué, R., 29C9
Benue see Bénoué
Benue (4), Admin. U.,
 29D8
Ben Wyvis, Mt., 7C5
Benxi, 24B6
Benzu, 5aB3
Beograd, 13A5
Berat, 13B4,5
Berbera, 28C7
Berbérati, 28D4
Berck-sur-Mer, 9D5
Berd'ansk, 18C4
Berdičev, 18C2
Beregovo, 18C1
Berens, R., 35A2
Berens River, 33C10
Berežany, 18C1
Berezina, R., 18B2
Bereznik, 17B6
Berezniki, 16D7,8
Berga, 11F4
Bergama, 21aB1
Bergamo, 13A2
Bergen, 15C3
Bergerac, 11C3
Berhampur, 22C4
Beringovskij, 16C19
Bering Sea, 33B,C2,3
Bering Strait, Str.,
 33S3
Berkatit, 16D14
Berkeley, 34D2
Berkner Island, I.,
 42G,H5,6
Berkshire (10), Admin. U.,
 9D4
Berlevåg, 15A9
Berlin, 12B4
Berlin (1), Admin. U.,
 12B4
Bermejo, R., 37E3,4
Bermondse, 9a
Bermuda, Admin. U., Is.,
 32F14
Bern, 11C4
Bernburg, 12C3
Beroun, 12C4
Ber'oza, 18B1,2
Ber'ozovka, 18C3
Ber'ozovo, 16C8
Berriane, 27aB1
Bertoua, 29D9

Berwick-upon-Tweed,
 10C3
Besançon, 11C4
Beslan, 18D5
Besni, 21aB3
Bessarabka, 18C2
Bétaré Oya, 29D9
Bethal Green. 9a
Bethel, 33B3
Bethlehem, 30D3
Bethune, 11B3
Béthune, R., 9E5
Betroka, 30D5
Betsiamites, 35B7
Betsiboka, R., 30C5
Bettles Field, 33B4
Bettola, 13aB3
Betwa, R., 22aB1
Beverley, 9C4
Bexhill, 9D5
Beykoz, 14C4
Beyla, 29C3
Beypazarı, 21aA2
Beyşehir, 21aB2
Beyşehir Gölü, L., 21aB2
Bežeck, 17C5
Béziers, 11D3
Bhâgalpur, 22B4
Bhaktapur, 22a B3
Bhatinda, 22A3
Bhâtpâra, 22aC4
Bhâvnagar, 22B3
Bhilai, 22B4
Bhopâl, 22B3
Bhubaneswar, 22B,C4
Bhuj, 22B2
Bhutan, St., 22aB4
Biak, 23D5
Biak, I., 23D5
Biała Podlaska, 12B,C6
Białogard, 12B5
Białystok, 12B6
Biarritz, 11D2
Bida, 29C7
Biddeford, 35C6,7
Bideford, 9D2
Biel, 11C4
Bielefeld, 12B3
Biella, 13A1,2
Bielsko-Biała, 12C5
Bié Plateau, Plat., 26F6
Big Delta, 33B5
Biggar, 34A5
Bighorn, R., 34B5
Bight of Benin, 29D6,7
Bight of Bonny, 29D,E7,8
Big Quill Lake, L., 34A6
Bihać, 13A3
Bihâr, 22B4
Bihâr, Admin. U., 22B4
Bijâpur, 22C3
Bijâr, 21B5
Bijeljina, 13A4
Bijie, 24D4
Bijsk, 16D10
Bikaner, 22B3
Bikin, 16E15
Bikini, I., 41B6
Bilâspur, 22B4
Bilbao, 11F3
Bilbays, 26aB3
Bilecik, 21aA1,2
Bilibino, 16C18,19
Billings, 34B5
Bilma, 28C4
Biloxi, 35E,F3
Biłgds Qism Awwal,
 26aA3
Biltine, 28C5
Bina-Etâwa, 22aB1
Bindura, 30C4

Binghamton, 35C5
Bingöl, 21aB4
Binjai, 19bC1
Bintulu, 23C3
Bioko, I., 26D5
Birao, 28C,D5
Birara, I., 41D4,5
Birätnagar, 22aB3
Birdsville, 40C3
Birdum, 40B3
Birecik, 21aB3
Birendranagar, 22aA2
Bir Hooker, 26aB2
Birjand, 21C7
Birkat Qārūn, L., 26aC2
Birkenhead, 9C3
Birlad, 14B3
Birmingham (U.K.), 9C4
Birmingham (U.S.A.),
  35E3
Bir Mogrein, 28B1
Birnin Kebbi, 29B7
Birni Nkonni, 29B7
Birobidžan, 16E15
Birr, 10E6
Birsk, 17aB2
Birtle, 34A6
Biržai, 17C2
Bishofshofen, 12D4
Bisha, 28C6
Bishop, 34D3
Biskra, 28A3
Bislig, 23bC3
Bismarck, 34B6
Bismarck Archipelago,
  Arch., 41D4,5
Bissau, 29B,C2
Bistrita, 14B3
Bistriţa, R., 14B3
Bitlis, 21aB4
Bitola, 13B5
Bitterfontein, 30E2
Biu, 29C4
Biwa-ko, L., 25C6
Bizerte, 28,A3,4
Björna, 15C6
Bjørnøya, I., 42C21
Blackburn, 9C3
Blackpool, 9C3
Black Sea, 5C7,8
Black Volta see
  Volta Noire
Blackwater, R., (Ireland),
  7E3
Blackwater, R., (U.K.),
  10D6
Blagodarnyj, 18C5
Blagoevgrad, 14C2
Blagoevgrad (1), Admin.
  U., 14C2
Blagoveščensk (U.S.S.R.,
  Chabarovsk), 16D14
Blagoveščensk (U.S.S.R.,
  Ufa), 17aB2
Blair Athol, 40C4
Blanca Peak, Mt., 31F10
Blanes, 11F4
Blanquillo, 39aD2
Blantyre, 30C4
Blasket Islands, Is., 7E2
Blida, 28A3
Blind River, 35B4
Blitta, 29C6
Bloemfontein, 30D3
Blois, 11C3
Bloomington, 35C2
Bluefields, 36C4
Blue Mountains, Mts.,
  40D4,5
Blue Nile see Abay
Bluff Knoll, Mt., 40D1

Blumenau, 39A3,4
Blyth, 9B4
Blythe, 34E3,4
Bo 29C,D3
Boac, 23bB2
Boa Vista, 38B3
Boa Vista, I., 28aB2
Bobo Dioulasso, 29C4,5
Bobrov, 18B5
Bobrujsk, 18B2
Bôca do Acre, 38C3
Bocaranga, 29D9
Bochum, 12aB3
Bodajbo, 16D13
Bodélé, Reg., 26C6
Boden, 15B7
Bodensee, L., 12D3
Bodmin, 9D2
Bodmin Moor, Reg., 7F5
Bodø, 15B5
Bodrum, 21aB1
Boende, 30B3
Boffa, 29C2
Bogandović, 17aB3
Bognor Regis, 9D4
Bogor, 23D2
Bogorodskoje, 17b
Bogotá, 38B2
Bogučar, 18C5
Bogué, 29A2
Bo Hai, B., 24C5,6
Bohemian Forest, Mts.,
  5C6
Bohol, I., 23C4
Boise, 34C3
Boise City, 34D6
Bojnürd, 21B7
Bojuru, 39aD3
Boké, 29C2
Boknafjorden, B., 15D3
Bokovskaja, 18C5
Bol, 28C4
Bolama, 29C2
Bole, 29C5
Bolgatanga, 29C5
Bolgrad, 18C2
Boli, 25A5
Bolívar, 39aE1
Bolivia, St., 38D3,4
Bollnäs, 15C5,6
Bologna, 13A2
Bologoje, 17C4
Bol'šaja Gluśica, 18B7
Bol'šoj Irgiz, R., 18B6
Bol'śoj Kavkaz, Mts.,
  19E5,6
Bol'šoj Uzen', R., 18B6
Bolton, 9C3
Bolu, 21aA2
Bolzano, 13A2
Boma, 30B2
Bombala, 40D4,5
Bombay, 22C3
Bomi Hills, 29D3
Bom Jesus da Lapa,
  38D5
Bomu, R., 28D5
Bonas Hill, H., 7A7
Bonda, 30B2
Bondo, 28D5
Bondoukou, 29C5
Bondowoso, 23aA3
Bong, 29D3
Bongor, 28C4
Bonn, 12C2
Bonny, 29D7
Bonthain, 23D3
Bonthe, 29D2
Bontoc, 23bA2
Boothia Peninsula
  33A10

Booué, 30B2
Boquerón, 36aC6
Bor (U.S.S.R.), 17C6
Bor (Yugoslavia), 13A5
Borama, 28C,D7
Borãs, 15D5
Borba, 38C4
Bordeaux, 11C2
Borders (55), Admin. U.,
  9B3
Bordeyri, 15aB2
Bordj Omar Driss, 28B3
Bordo (5), Admin. U.,
  29B9
Borgarnes, 15aB2
Borgholm, 15D6
Borgo Val di Taro, 13aB3
Borisoglebsk, 18B5
Borisov, 18B2
Borispol', 18B3
Borja, 38C2
Borlänge, 15C5
Bormida, R., 13A2
Borneo, I., 23C,D3
Bornholm, I., 15E5,6
Borongan, 23bB3
Borovići, 17C4
Borovloola, 40B3
Borsod-Abaúj-Zemplén
  (4), Admin U., 14A2
Bôrujerd, 21C5
Borz'a, 16D13
Bosanac, 28C7
Bosna, R., 13A4
Bosna i Hercegovina, (1),
  Admin.U., 13A4
Bossangoa, 28D4
Boston (U.K.), 9C4,5
Boston (U.S.A.), 35C6
Boteti, R., 30D3
Botev, Mt., 5C7
Botoşani, 14B3
Botswana, St., 30D3
Bottrop, 12aA2
Botucatu, 39aB4
Bouaké, 29D4
Bouar, 28D4
Bou Arfa, 28A2
Bouches-du-Rhône (13),
  Admin. U., 11D4
Bou Djébéha, 29A5
Boufarik, 27aA1
Bougainville, I., 40A5
Bougouni, 29C4
Boulder City, 34D3
Boulia, 40C3
Boulogne-sur-Mer, 11B3
Bouna, 29C5
Boundiali, 29C4
Bounty Islands, Is., 3
Bourail, 41aA1
Bouraké, 41aA1,2
Bourem, 29A5
Bourg-en-Bresse, 11C4
Bourges, 11C3
Bourg-Saint-Maurice,
  11C4
Bourke, 40D4
Bournemouth, 9D4
Bou Saâda, 27aA1
Boutilimit, 29A2
Bouvetøya, I., 3
Bow, R., 34A4
Bowen, 40B4
Bowie, 34E5
Bowling Green, 35D3
Boyle, 10E5
Boyne, R., 7E4
Boyuibe, 38E3
Bozeman, 34B4

Bozoum, 28D4
Bra, 13aB1
Brach, 28B4
Bräcke, 15C5
Brad, 14B2
Bradenton, 35F4
Bradford (U.K.), 9C4
Bradford (U.S.A.), 35C5
Braga, 11F1
Braga (3), Admin. U.,
  11F1
Bragança (4), Admin. U.,
  11F2
Bragança (Brazil), 38C5
Bragança (Portugal), 11F2
Brahmaputra see
  Yaluzangbujiang
Brăila, 14B3
Brainerd, 35B2
Bralorne, 33aB1,2
Branco, I., 28aA1
Branco, R., 38B3
Brandberg, Mt., 26G6
Brandenburg, 12B3,4
Brandon, 33D9
Brandon Mount, Mt.,
  7E2,3
Br'ansk, 18B3
Brantford, 35C4
Brasília, 38D5
Braşov, 14B3
Brass, 29D7
Bratislava, 12C5
Bratsk, 16D12
Bratskoje Vodochranilišče,
  Res., 16bA1
Braunschweig, 12B3
Brava, I., 28aB1
Bravo del Norte, R., 36B2
Bray, 10E6,7
Brazeau, 33C8
Brazil, St., 39C2-5
Brazilian Highlands, Hs.,
  37D4,5
Brazo Casiquiare, R.,
  36B3
Brazos, R., 34E6,7
Brazzaville, 30B2
Brda, R., 15E6
Breckland, Reg., 7E8
Břeclav, 12C5
Brecon, 9D3
Brecon Beacons, Mt., 7F6
Breda, 12C2
Bregenz, 12D3
Breidafjördur, B.,
  15aB1,2
Bremen, 12B3
Bremen (3), Admin. U.,
  12B3
Bremerhaven, 12B3
Bremerton, 33aC2,3
Brent, Res., 9a
Brent, R., 9a
Brenta, R., 13aA5
Brentwood, 9D5
Brescia, 13A2
Bressay, I., 10a
Brest (France), 11B1
Brest (U.S.S.R.), 16D4
Bretagne, Pen., Reg.,
  5C4
Brežnev, 17C8
Bria, 28D5
Briançon, 11C4
Bricquebec, 6aA3
Bridgeport, 35C6
Bridgetown (Australia),
  40D1
Bridgetown (Barbados),
  36bB2

Bridgwater, 9D3
Bridlington, 9B4,5
Bridlington Bay, B., 9B,C4,5
Brig, 11C4,5
Brighton, 9D4,5
Brikama, 29B1
Brindisi, 13B4
Brisbane, 40C5
Bristol, 9D3
Bristol Bay, 33C3,4
Bristol Channel, B., 7F5,6
British Columbia, Admin. U., 33C7
British Islands, Is., 19D1
Brive-la-Gaillarde, 11C3
Brno, 12C5
Broad Law, Mt., 7D6
Brochet, 33C9
Brockville, 33b
Brockway, 34B5
Brodick, 10C2
Brodokalmak, 17aB3
Brody, 18D3
Broken Hill, 40D4
Bronx, 32a
Brooklyn, 32a
Brooks Range, Mts., 31C5,6
Broome, 40B2
Bromsgrove, 9c3
Brownsville, 34F7
Brownsweg, 38B4
Brownwood, 34E7
Bruck an der Mur, 12D4
Brue, R., 9D3
Brugge, 11B3
Brunei, St., 23C3
Brunswick, 35E4
Brush, 34C6
Brussel see Bruxelles
Bruxelles, 11B4
Bryan, 35E1
Brzeg, 12C5
Bučač, 18C2
Bucak, 21aB2
Bucaramanga, 38B2
Buccles, 9C5
Buchan Ness, C., 7C7
Buchanan, 29D3
Buchara, 16F8
Bucharest see Bucureşti
Buckie, 10B3
Buckinghamshire (11), Admin. U., 9D4
Buckleboo, 40D3
Bucklin, 34D7
Bu Craa, 28B1
Bucureşti, 14B3
Budapest, 14B1
Bûdardalur, 15aB2
Budd Coast, Reg., 42F25
Budennovsk, 18D5
Búdir, 15aB2
Budrio, 13aB5
Buea, 29D8
Buenaventura, 38B2
Buenos Aires, 39B2,3
Buenos Aires, Admin. U., 39B2,3
Buerjin, 24B2
Buffalo, 35C5
Bug, R., 18B1
Bugrino, 17A7
Bugul'ma, 18B8
Buguruslan, 18B7
Buhayrat al-Burullus, L., 26aA2,3

Buhayrat al-Manzilah, L., 26aA4
Builth Wells, 9C3
Buinsk, 18B6
Buj, 17C6
Bujnaksk, 18D6
Bujumbura, 30B3,4
Bukama, 30B3
Bukavu, 30B3
Bukittinggi, 23D1,2
Bukoba, 30B4
Bulawayo, 30D3
Bulgan, 24B4
Bulgaria, St. 14C2,3
Bulo Burti, 28D7
Bulu Rantekombola, Mt., 19J13,14
Bumba, 28D5
Bunbury, 40D1
Buncrana, 10D6
Bundaberg, 40C5
Bünyan, 21aB2
Burao, 28D7
Buras, 35F3
Buraydah, 28B7
Burdur, 21aB1,2
Bure, R., 9C5
Bureja, R., 24A7
Bür Fuâd, 26aA4
Burgas, 14C3
Burgas (2), Admin. U., 14C3
Burgenland (1), Admin. U., 12D5
Burgos, 11F3
Burgsvik, 15D6
Burhânur, 22B3
Burketown, 40B3
Burkina Faso, St., 29B,C4-6
Burlington (U.S.A., Vermont), 35C6
Burlington (U.S.A., Washington), 33aB3
Burma, St., 22B5
Burnaby, 33aB2
Burnie, 40E4
Burnley, 9C3
Burns, 34C3
Bursa, 21aA1
Bür Safâjah, 28B6
Bür Sa'îd, 28A6
Bür Südân, 28B7
Bür Tawfîq, 26aB,C4
Burton upon-Trent, 9C4
Buru, I., 23D4
Burundi, St., 30B3,4
Bury, 9C3
Bury Saint Edmunds, 9C5
Büsehr, 21D6
Busira, R., 30A,B3
Busselton, 40D1
Busto Arsizio, 13A1,2
Buta, 28D5
Butehaqi, 24B6
Butte, 34B4
Butterworth, 23C1,2
Butt of Lewis, C., 7B4,5
Butuan, 23C4
Buturlinovka, 18B5
Büyük Ağrı Daği, Mt., 19F6
Büyükmenderes, R., 21aB1
Buzău, 14B3
Buzaûl, R., 14B3
Buzuluk, 18B7
Bydgoszcz, 12B5

Byelorussian Soviet Socialist Republic, Admin. U., 16D4,5
Bykovo, 18C6
Bylot Island, I., 33A11,12
Bytom, 12C5

C

Caazapá, 39A3
Cabanatuan, 23B4
Cabimas, 38A2
Cabinda, 30B2
Cabo Bojador, C., 28B1
Cabo Branco, C., 37C6
Cabo Catoche, 31G,H12
Cabo Corrientes, C., 31G9,10
Cabo da Roca, C., 5D3,4
Cabo de Creus, C., 11F4
Cabo de Finisterre, C., 11F1
Cabo de Gata, C., 11G3
Cabo de la Nao, C., 11G4
Cabo Delgado, C., 30C5
Cabo de São, Vicente, C., 11G1
Cabo Horn, C., 37H2,3
Cabo Maisi, C., 36aB6,7
Cabo Orange, C., 37B4,5
Cabo San Antonio, C., 36aA,B1
Cabo San Lucas, C., 36B1,2
Cabo Tres Puntas, C., 37G3,4
Cabot Strait, Str., 31E15
Čačak, 13B5
Cacequi, 39aD3
Cáceres (Brazil), 38D4
Cáceres (Spain), 11G2
Cachoeira de Paulo Afonso, Fs., 37C5,6
Cachoeira do Sul, 39aD3
Cachoeira de Itapemirim, 38E5
Cader Idris, Mt., 7E5,6
Cadiz, 34E3
Cádiz, 11G2
Caen, 11B2
Caernarvon, 9C2
Caernarvon Bay, B., 7E5
Caerphilly, 9D3
Cagan-Aman, 18C6
Cagayan, R., 23B4
Cagayan de Oro, 23C4
Čagda, 16D15
Cagliari, 13C2
Caguas, 36aA1
Caha Mountains, Mts., 7F3
Cahirciveen, 10F4
Cahors, 11C3
Caibarien, 36aA4
Caicara, 38B3
Cains, 40B4
Cairo see Al-Qâhirah
Cairo Montenotte, 13aB2
Cajamarca, 38C2
Čajkovskij, 17aB1,2
Calabar, 29D8
Calabozo, 38B3
Calabria (3), Admin. U., 13C4
Calafat, 14C2
Calais, 11B3
Calama, 39A2
Calamar (Colombia, Cartagena), 38A2
Calamar (Colombia, Neiva), 38B2

Calamian Group, Is., 23B3
Calapan, 23bB2
Câlâraşi, 14B3
Calatayud, 11F3
Calbayog, 23B4
Calcutta, 22B4
Caleta Larga, 36aB1
Calgary, 33C8
Calicut, 22C3
Caliente, 34D4
California, Admin. U., 34C,D2,3
Callao, 38D2
Caltanissetta, 13C3
Calvados (14), Admin. U., 11B2
Calvi, 11D5
Calvinia, 30E2,3
Calzada Larga, 34a
Cam, R., 9C4
Camagüey, 36aB4,5
Camaquã, 39aD3
Camaquã, R., 39aD3
Camarones, 39C2
Cambay, 22B3
Camberwell, 9a
Camborne, 9D2
Cambrai, 11B3
Cambrian Mountains, Mts., 7E6
Cambridge (U.K.), 9C5
Cambridge (U.S.A.), 35C6,7
Cambridge Bay, 33B9
Cambridgeshire (12), Admin. U., 9C4
Camden (U.S.A., Arkansas), 35E2
Camden (U.S.A., New York), 35D6
Cameroon, St., 29C-E8,9
Cametá, 38C4,5
Camiri, 38D3
Camocim, 38C5,6
Camooweal, 40B3
Camopi, 38B4
Campania (4), Admin. U., 13B3
Campbell Island, I., 3
Campbell River, 33aB2
Campbellton, 33D13
Campbeltown, 10C2
Campeche, 36C3
Campeche (4), Admin. U., 36C4
Campina Grande, 38C6
Campinas, 39A4
Campina Verde, 39aA3,4
Campobasso, 13B3
Campo Grande, 38E4
Campo Mourão, 39aB3
Campos, 38E5
Campos Belos, 38D5
Cam-Ranh, 22C6,7
Canada, St., 33C6-13
Canadian, R., 34D6
Canadian Shield see Laurentian Plateau
Çanakkale, 21A1
Çanakkale Boğâzı, Str., 21aB1
Canala, 41aA1,2
Canal de la Mona, 36C5,6
Canal du Midi, Can., 11D3
Canal Zone, Admin. U., 36C,D4,5
Cananéia, 39aB4
Canarias (5), see Islas Canarias

Clusone, 13aA3
Clwyd (47), Admin. U., 9C3
Clyde, 33A13
Clyde, R., 7D5,6
Clydebank, 10C2
Coahuila (7), Admin. U., 36B2
Coari, 38C3
Coast Land, Reg., 42G2,3
Coast Mountains, Mts., 31D7,8
Coast Ranges, Mts., 31E,F8,9
Coatbridge, 10C2,3
Coats Island, I., 33B11
Coatzacoalcos, 36C3
Cobalt, 33D11,12
Cobar, 40D4
Cobh, 10F5
Cobija, 38D3
Cocalinho, 38D4
Cochabamba, 38D3
Cochin, 20aC2
Cochrane, 33D11
Coco, R., 31H12
Cocos Islands, Is., 23E1
Codajás, 38C3
Codigoro, 13aB6
Codó, 38C5
Codogno, 13aA3
Cody, 34C5
Coen, 40A1
Coeur d'Alene, 34B3
Coffs Harbour, 40D5
Cognac, 11C2
Coimbatore, 22C3
Coimbra, 11F1
Cojbalsan, 24B5
Colatina, 38D5
Colby, 34D5
Colchester, 9D5
Coleraine, 10D6
Coleraine (10), Admin. U., 10D6
Colima, 36C2
Colima (8), Admin. U., 36C2
Coll, I., 7C4
Colmar, 11B3
Cologna Veneta, 13aA5
Cologne see Köln
Colômbia, 38E5
Colombia, St., 38B2,3
Colombo, 20aC2
Colón (Cuba), 36aA3
Colón (Panama), 36D5
Colonia Las Heras, 39aD2
Colonia del Sacramento, 39aD2
Colonsay, I., 7C4
Colorado, Admin. U., 34D5,6
Colorado (Atlantic Ocean), R., 37F3
Colorado (G. of Mexico), R., 34F7
Colorado (Pacific Ocean), R., 34E4
Colorado Plateau, Plat., 31F9,10
Colorado Springs, 34D6
Columbia, R., 33C8
Columbus (U.S.A., Georgia), 35E4
Columbus (U.S.A., Mississippi), 35E3
Columbus (U.S.A., Ohio), 35C,D4

Colville, R., 33B4
Colwyn Bay, 9C3
Comacchio, 13aB6
Combra (6), Admin. U., 11F1
Comilla, 22aC4
Como, 13A2
Comodoro Rivadavia, 39C2
Comoros, St., 30C5
Compiègne, 11B3
Conakry, 29C2
Conceição do Araguaia, 38C4,5
Concepción (Chile), 39B1
Concepción (Paraguay), 39A3
Concepción del Uruguay, 39aD2
Conchos, R., 34F5,6
Concord, 35C6
Concordia, 39aD2
Côn Dao, Is., 22D6
Conegliano, 13aA6
Congo, R., 30B2
Congo, St., 30A,B2
Congo Basin, Reg., 26D,E6,7
Coniston, 34B4
Connecticut, Admin. U., 35C6
Conselheiro Lafaiete, 39aB5
Consett, 10C4
Constanţa, 14B4
Constantine, 28A3
Contwoyto Lake, 33B8,9
Coober Pedy, 40C3
Cookhouse, 30E3
Cook Islands, Is., 41E9,10
Cookstown, 10D6
Cookstown (11), Admin. U., 10D6
Cook Strait, Str., 40aB2
Cooktown, 40B4
Coolgardie, 40D1,2
Coondapoor, 20aA1
Coopers Creek, R., 40C3,4
Coos Bay, 34C2
Čop, 12C6
Copenhagen see København
Copiapó, 39A2
Copparo, 13aB5
Copper, R., 33B5
Copper Harbor, 35B3
Coppermine, 33B8
Coquet, R., 9B4
Coquimbo, 39B2
Coral Harbour, 33B11
Coral Sea, 40B,C4,5
Coral Sea Islands Territory, Reg., 40B4,5
Corantijn, R., 38B4
Corbin, 35D4
Corby, 9C4
Corcaigh see Cork
Cordillera Cantábrica, Mts., 5C4
Cordillera Central, Mts., 37B2
Cordillera de Mérida, Mts., 37A,B2,3
Cordillera Occidental, Mts., 37B2
Cordillera-Oriental, Mts., 37B2
Córdoba (3), Admin. U., 39B2

Córdoba (Argentina), 39B2
Córdoba (Spain), 11G2
Cordova, 33B5
Corinto (Brazil), 39aA5
Corinto (Nicaragua), 36C4
Cork, 10F5
Cork, Admin. U., 10F5
Cork Harbour, B., 7F3,4
Çorlu, 21aA1
Cormoz, 17aB2
Corner Brook, 33D14
Corno Grande, Mt., 5C6
Cornomorskoje, 18C3
Cornth, 35D,E3
Cornwall (Bahamas), 35F5
Cornwall (Canada), 35B6
Cornwall (15), Admin. U., 9D2
Cornwallis Island, 33A10
Coro, 38A3
Coromandel, 39aA4
Coromandel Coast, 20aA,B3
Coronel Oviedo, 39A3
Coronel Suárez, 39aE1
Corpus Christi, 34F7
Corralillo, 36aA3
Corrèze (19), Admin. U., 11C3
Corrientes, 39A3
Corrientes (4), Admin. U., 39A3
Corse see Corsica
Corse (Haute-) (96), Admin. U., 11D5
Corse-du-Sud (20), Admin. U., 11D5
Corsica, I., 11D5
Corsicana, 35E1
Corte, 11D5
Çortkov, 18C2
Cortland, 35C5
Çoruh, R., 21aA4
Çorum, 21aA2
Corumbá, 38D4
Corvallis, 34C2
Corvo, I., 11aA1
Cosenza, 13C4
Cosmoledo Group, Is., 30B5
Costa Rica, St., 36C,D4
Cotabato, 23C4
Coteau-Station, 33b
Côte-d'Or (21), Admin. U., 11C4
Cotentin, Pen., 7G7
Côtes-du-Nord (22), Admin. U., 11B2
Cotonou, 29D6
Cotopaxi, Mt., 37B2
Cotswolds, Hs., 7E,F6,7
Cottbus, 12C7
Cottbus (2), Admin. U., 12C4
Cottondale, 35E3
Council Bluffs, 35C1,2
Courtenay, 33C,D7
Coutances, 6aA3
Coventry, 9C4
Covilhã, 11F2
Covington (U.S.A., Kentucky), 35D4
Covington (U.S.A., Virginia), 35D4,5
Cowes, 9D4
Coxim, 38D4
Cox's Bazar, 22B5
Coyhaique, 39C1

Cradock, 30E3
Craig, 34C5
Craigavon (12), Admin. U., 10D6
Craig Harbour, 33A11
Craiova, 14B2
Cranbrook, 34B3
Crater Lake, 34C2
Cratéus, 38C5,6
Crato, 38C6
Craven Arms, 9C3
Crawford, 34C6
Crawley, 9D4
Cree Lake, L., 33C9
Creil, 11B3
Crema, 13aA3
Cremona, 13A2
Crete see Kríti
Créteil, 11B3
Creuse (23), Admin. U., 11C3
Crewe, 9C3
Crianlarich, 10B2
Criciúma, 39aC3,4
Crikvenica, 13A3
Cristóbal, 34a
Crkvice, 5C6
Crna Gora (2), Admin. U., 13B4
Cross Fell, Mt., 7D6
Cross River (6), Admin. U., 29D8
Crotone, 13C4
Crow Agency, 34B5
Croydon, 40B4
Cruz Alta, 39aC3
Cruz del Eje, 39B2
Cruzeiro do Sul, 38C2
Csongrád (5), Admin. U., 14B2
Ču, 24B1
Ču, R., 24B1
Cuamba, 30C4
Cuando, R., 30C2,3
Cuango, R., 30C2
Cuanza, R., 30C2
Cuba, St., I., 36B4,5
Cubango, R., 30C2
Čuchloma, 17C6
Cúcuta, 38B2
Cuddalore, 22C3,4
Cuddapah, 22C3
Čudovo, 17C4
Čudskoje Ozero, L., 17C3
Cue, 40C1
Cuenca (Ecuador), 38C2
Cuenca (Spain), 11F3
Cuernavaca, 36C2,3
Čugujev, 18C4
Cuiabá, 38D4
Cuiabá, R., 38D4
Cuito, R., 30C2,3
Cuito Cuanavale, 30C2,3
Čukotskij Poluostrov, Pen., 19C20
Čukotskoje More, S., 16B,C20,21
Culebra, 34a
Culgoa, R., 40C4
Culiacán, 36C2
Culion, 23bB2
Cullera, 11G3
Cullin Hills, Mts., 7C4
Čul'man, 16D14
Čulym, R., 16D10
Cumaná, 38A3
Cumberland, R., 35D3
Cumberland Peninsula, Pen., 42B12

Filingué, 29B6
Findhorn, R., 10B3
Finike, 21aB2
Finistère (29), Admin. U., 11B2
Finke, 40C3
Finland, St., 15A-C7,8
Finlay, R., 33C7
Finn, R., 10D6
Firat, R., 21B3
Firenze, 13B2
Firenzuola, 13aB5
Firmat, 39aD1
Firozābād, 22aB1
Firth of Clyde, B., 7D5
Firth of Forth, B., 7C6
Firth of Lorn, B., 7C4,5
Firth of Tay, B., 7C6
Fish, R., 30D2
Fishguard, 9D2
Fitzhugh Sound, B., 33aA1
Fitzroy, R., 40B2
Fitzroy Crossing, 40B2
Fizuli, 18aB2
Flacq, 30aB3
Flagstaff, 34D4
Flamborough Head, C., 7D7,8
Flatey, 15aB2
Flathead Lake, L., 34B4
Flat Island, I., 30aA3
Flaxton, 34B6
Fleetwood, 9C3
Flekkefjord, 15D3
Flensburg, 12B3
Flinders, R., 40C4
Flin Flon, 33C9
Flint (Canada), 35C4
Flint (U.K.), 9C3
Flint, I., 41E10
Flint, R., 35E4
Flora, 15C3
Florence (Italy) see Firenze
Florence (U.S.A.), 35E5
Florencia, 38B2
Flores, 38C6
Flores (Atlantic Ocean), I., 11aA1
Flores (Indian Ocean), I., 23D4
Flores Sea, 23D3,4
Floriano, 38C5
Florianópolis, 39A4
Florida, 39aD2
Florida, Admin. U., 35E,F4
Florida Keys, Is., 35F,G4
Flórina, 14C2
Fly, R., 41D9
Fokku, 29C7
Foligno, 13B3
Folkestone, 9D5
Fond du Lac, 35C3
Fontainebleau, 11B3
Fonte Boa, 38C3
Forcados, 29D7
Forfar, 10B3
Forli, 13A2,3
Formby Point, C., 7E6
Formentera, I., 11G4
Formiga, 39aB4,5

Formosa see Taiwan
Formosa (Argentina), 39A3
Formosa (Brazil), 38D5
Formosa, Admin. U., 39A2,3
Fornovo di Taro, 13aB4
Forres, 10B3
Forrest, 40D2
Forsayth, 40B4
Fort Albany, 33C11
Fortaleza, 38C6
Fort Amador, 34a
Fort Augustus, 10B2
Fort Bragg, 34D2
Fort Chipewyan, 33C8
Fort Collins, 34C5
Fort Dodge, 35C2
Fort George, 33C12
Fort Good Hope, 33B7
Fortín Ayacucho, 38B4
Fort Lauderdale, 35F4,5
Fort Liard, 33B7
Fort Mac Murray, 33C8
Fort Myers, 35F4
Fort Nelson, 33C7
Fort Norman, 33B7
Fort Peck, 34B5
Fort Peck Lake, Res., 34B5,6
Fort Pierce, 35F4
Fort Providence, 33B8
Fort Randolph, 34a
Fort Resolution, 33B8
Fort Rupert, 33C12
Fort Saint John, 33C7
Fort Sandeman, 22A2
Fort Selkirk, 33B6
Fort-Ševčenko, 16E7
Fort Severn, 33C11
Fort Sherman, 34a
Fort Simpson, 33B7
Fort Smith (Canada), 33B8
Fort Smith (U.S.A.), 35D2
Fort Stockton, 34E6
Fort Vermilion, 33C8
Fort Wayne, 35C3
Fort William, 10B2
Fort Worth, 34E7
Fort Yukon, 33B5
Foshan, 24D5
Fossil, 31aB1,2
Fougères, 11B2
Foula, I., 10a
Foumban, 29D8
Foxe Basin, 33B11,12
Foxe Channel, 33B11,12
Foyle, R., 10D6
Foz do Iguaçu, 39aC3
Franca, 39aB4
France, St., 11B-D1-5
Franceville, 30B2
Francistown, 30D3
Frankfort, 35D4
Frankfurt, 12B4
Frankfurt (5), Admin. U., 12B4
Frankfurt am Main, 12C3
Franz, 35B4
Fraser, R., 33C7,8
Fraserburgh, 10B3
Fraser Island, I., 40C5
Fray Bentos, 39aD2
Fredericksburg, 35D5
Fredericton, 33D13
Frederikshåb see Pâmiut
Frederikshavn, 12A3

Fredrikstad, 15D4
Freeport, 35F5
Freetown, 29C2
Fregenal de la Sierra, 11G2
Freiburg, 12C2,3
Fremont (U.S.A., California), 31aC1
Fremont (U.S.A., Nebraska), 35C1
French Guiana, Admin. U., 38B4
French Polynesia, Admin. U., 41F10-12
Fresno, 34D3
Fria, 29C2
Fribourg, 11C4
Frijoles, 34a
Friuli-Venezia Giulia (6), Admin. U., 13A3
Frobisher Bay, 33B13
Frolovo, 18C5
Frosinone, 13B3
Fróya, I., 15C4
Frunze, 16E9
Frutal, 39aA4
Fuerte Olimpo, 39A3
Fuerteventura, I., 26bB3
Fuji, 25C6
Fujian (7), Admin. U., 24D5
Fuji-San, Vol., 19F15
Fukui, 25C6
Fukuoka, 25D4,5
Fukushima (Japan, Sapporo), 25B6,7
Fukushima (Japan, Tokyo), 25C7
Fukuyama, 25D5
Fulda, 12C3
Fulham, 9a
Fulton, 35D2
Fumaca, 38C5
Funing, 25D6
Funtua, 29C7
Furmanovo, 18C6,7
Furneaux Group, Is., 40D,E4
Fürth, 12C3
Fushun, 24B6
Fusong, 25B4
Futuna, I., 41E8
Fuxian, 25C3
Fuxin, 25B3
Fuyu, 25A3,4
Fuzhou (China, Fujian), 24D5,6
Fuzhou (China, Jiangxi), 24D5
Fyn, I., 12B3

G

Gabela, 30C2
Gabès, 28A4
Gabon, St., 30A,B2
Gaborone, 30D3
Gabrovo, 14C3
Gabon (3), Admin. U., 14C3
Gachsārān, 21C6
Gaďač, 18B3
Gadag, 20aA1,2
Gäddede, 15B5
Gadsden, 35E3

Gaeta, 13B3
Gafsa, 28A3
Gagarin, 17C4,5
Gagnoa, 29D4
Gagnon, 33C13
Gagra, 18D5
Gainesville, 35F4
Gainsborough, 9C4
Gaiping, 25B3
Gairloch, 10B2
Gajny, 17B8
Gajsin, 18C2
Galana, R., 30B4
Galapagos Islands see Archipiélago de Colón
Galashiels, 10C3
Galati, 14B3,4
Galela, 23C4
Galesburg, 35C2
Galič, 17C6
Galicia (11), Admin. U., 11F1,2
Galka'yo, 28D7
Galle, 20aC3
Gallipoli, 13B4
Gällivare, 15B7
Gallup, 34D5
Galty Mountains, Mts., 7E3,4
Galveston, 35F2
Galveston Bay, B., 35F2
Gálvez, 39aD1
Galway, 10E5
Galway Bay, B., 7E3
Gamarra, 38B2
Gambaga, 29C5
Gambela, 28D6
Gambell, 33B2
Gambia, St., 29B1,2
Gambie, R., 29B2
Gamboa, 34a
Gamboma, 30B2
Gand see Gent
Gandajika, 30B3
Gandak, R., 22B4
Gander, 33D14
Gandhinagar, 22B3
Gandia, 11G3,4
Ganga, R., 22B3
Ganges see Ganga
Gangtok, 22B4
Gannett Peak, Mt., 31E9,10
Gansu (8), Admin. U., 24B3
Ganta, 29D3
Ganzhou, 24D5
Ganzi, 24C4
Gao, 29A5
Gaoua, 29C5
Gaoual, 29C2
Gaoyou, 25D2
Gaoyouhu, L., 25D2
Gap, 11C4
Garafia, 26bB2
Garanhuns, 38C6
Garapan, 41B4
Gard (30), Admin. U., 11C4
Garden City, 34D6
Gardiner, 34B4,5
Gardo, 28D7
Gari, 17aB3
Garissa, 30B4,5
Garmsar, 21B6
Garonne (Haute-) (31), Admin. U., 11D3
Garonne, R., 11D3
Garoua, 29C9
Garry Lake, L., 33B10
Gartok, 24C2

Isla de San Andrés, I., 36C4,5
Isla Hoste, I., 39D1
Islāmābād, 22A3
Isla Magdalena, I., 39C1
Isla Navarino, I., 39D2
Island Anticosti, I., 33D13
Island of Newfoundland, I., 33D14
Isla Róbinson Crusoe, I., 37F2
Isla Sala y Gómez, I., 3
Isla San Ambrosio, I., 39A1
Isla San Félix, I., 37E1,2
Islas Canarias, Is., Admin. U., 28A,B1
Islas del Cisne, Is., 36C4
Islas Diego Ramírez, Is., 37H3
Islas Hanover, Is., 39D1
Islas Juan Fernández, Is., 37F1,23
Islas Los Testigos, Is., 36bB2
Islas Revillagigedo, Is., 36C1,2
Isla Tiburón, I., 36B1
Isla Wellington, I., 37G1,2
Islay, I., 7D4
Isle of Man, Admin. U., I., 7D5
Isle of Portland, I., 7F6
Isle of Wight (28), Admin. U., 9D4
Isle of Wight, I., 7F7
Isles of Scilly, Is., 7G4,5
Islington, 9a
Isnā, 28B6
Isoka, 30C4
Isola d' Elba, I., 13B2
Isola di Capri, I., 13B3
Isola di Pantelleria, I., 13C2,3
Isola di Ustica, I., 13C3
Isola Lipari, I., 13C3
Isola Stromboli, I., 13C3
Isole Egadi, Is., 13C2,3
Isole Eolie, Is., 13C3
Isparta, 21aB2
Íspir, 21aA4
Israel, St., 20bC1
Issoudun, 11C3
İstanbul, 21aA1
Isthmus of Panama, 37B1,2
Isthmus of Tehuantepec, 31H11
Istrije, Reg., 13A3
Itabuna, 38D6
Itacoatiara, 38C4
Itagüí, 38B2
Itaituba, 38C4
Itajaí, 39A4
Itajubá, 39aB4,5
Italy, St., 13A-C1-4
Itanagar, 22B5
Itapeva, 39aB4
Itapicuru, R., 38C5
Itapipoca, 38C6
Itaqui, 39aC2
Itararé, R., 39aB4
Itonamas, R., 38D3
Ittoqqortoormiit, 42C16,17
Ituiutaba, 39aA4
Ituri, R., 38C3
Ivaí, 39aB3
Ivalo, 15A8,9
Ivalojoki, R., 15A8

Ivangrad, 13B4,5
Ivano-Frankovsk, 18C1
Ivanovo, 17C6
Ivigtut, 33B15
Ivory Coast, Reg., 26D4
Ivory Coast, St., 29C,D4,5
Ivrea, 13aA1
Ivujivik, 33B12
Iwaki, 25C7
Iwo, 29D7
Iwôn, 25B4
İzad Khvāst, 21C6
Izberbaš, 18D6
Ižma, 17A8
Ižma, R., 17B8
Izmail, 18C2
Izmajlovo, 17b
İzmir, 21aB1
İzmir Körfezi, B., 14D3
İzmit, 21aA1
İznik Gölü, L., 14C4
Izuhara, 25D4
Iz'um, 18C4
Izu-shotō, Is., 25D6

J

Jabal al-'Uwaynāt, Mt., 26B7
Jabal ash-Shām, Mt., 19G7
Jabalpur, 22B3,4
Jablanica, 13B4
Jablonovo, 16bB3
Jablonovyj Chrebet, Mts., 19D12,13
Jaboatão, 38C6
Jaca, 11F3
Jacarèzinho, 39aB3
Jáchal, 39B2
Jackson (U.S.A., Michigan), 35C4
Jackson (U.S.A., Mississippi), 35E2
Jacksonville, 35E4
Jacobābād, 22B2
Jacuí, R., 39aD3
Jacuouara, 38C4
Jaén, 11G3
Jaffna, 20aB3
Jagdalpur, 22C4
Jaguarão, 39aD3
Jaguaríaíva, 39aB4
Jagüey Grande, 36aA3
Jahrom, 21D6
Jailolo, 23C4
Jaipur, 22B3
Jaisalmer, 22B3
Jajce, 13A4
Jakarta, 23D2
Jakobshavn see Ilulissat
Jakobstad, 15C7
Jakutsk, 16C14,15
Jalālābād, 22A2,3
Jalapa, 36B,C3
Jalingo, 29C8
Jalisco (13), Admin. U., 36C2
Jalón, R., 11F3
Jalta, 18D3
Jaluit, I., 41C7
Jamaica, 32a
Jamaica, St., 36C5
Jamaica Bay, B., 32a
Jamame, 30A5
Jamanxim, R., 38C4
Jambi, 23D2
Jambol, 14C3
Jambol (5), Admin. U., 14C3

James, R., 34C7
James Bay, B., 33C11,12
Jamestown (Saint Helena) 27F4
Jamestown (U.S.A., New York), 33b
Jamestown (U.S.A., North Dakota), 34B7
Jammu, 22A3
Jammu and Kashmir, Admin. U., 22A3
Jämnagar, 22B2,3
Jamshedpur, 22B4
Jana, R., 16C15
Janaul, 17aB1,2
Jandaq, 21C6
Jan Mayen, I., 42C18
Januária, 38D5
Japan, St., 25B-D5-7
Japanese Archipelago, Arch., 3
Japurá, R., 37C3
Jaransk, 17C7
Jarcevo, 18A3
Jarega, 17B8
Jarensk, 17B7
Jari, R., 38B4
Jaroslavl' 16D5,6
Jaroslaw, 12C6
Jarud Qi, 25B3
Jarvis Island, I., 41D9
Jāsk, 21D7
Jaškul', 18C6
Jasper, 33C8
Jatai, 38D4
Jaunpur, 22aB2
Java Sea, 23D2,3
Jawa, I., 23D2,3
Jayapura, 23D6
Jazireh-ye Khārk, I., 21D5,6
Jazykovo, 18B6
Jbel Tubqāl,, Mt., 26A4
Jebba, 29C7
Jędrzejów, 12C6
Jefferson City, 35D2
Jefremov, 18B4
Jega, 29B7
Jegorjevsk, 17C5
Jegorlyk, R., 18C5
Jejsk, 18C4
Jēkabpils, 17C3
Jelan', 18B5
Jelec, 18B4
Jelenia Góra, 12C4
Jelgava, 17C2
Jember, 23D3
Jemca, 17B6
Jemeck, 17B6
Jena, 12C3
Jenakijevo, 18C4
Jenisej, R., 16D11
Jenotajevka, 18C6
Jequié, 38D5
Jerbogačon, 16C12
Jeremie, 38D5
Jessore, 22aC4
Jevpatorija, 18C3
Jezioro Mamry, L., 12B6
Jezioro Śniardwy, L., 12B6
Jhānsi, 22B3

Jhelum, R., 22A3
Jiamusi, 24B7
Ji'an (China, Jiangxi), 24D5
Ji'an (China, Jilin), 25B4
Jiangsu (16), Admin. U., 24C6
Jiangxi (17), Admin. U., 24D5
Jiangzi, 24D2
Jianou, 24D5
Jianping, 25B2,3
Jiaoxian, 24C5,6
Jiaxing, 25D3
Jiayin, 24B6,7
Jiddah, 28B6
Jihlava, 12C4
Jihočeský kraj (2), Admin. U., 12C4
Jihomoravský kraj (6), Admin. U., 12C5
Jilin, 24B6
Jilin (18), Admin. U., 24B6
Jima, 28D6
Jinan, 24C5
Jingdezhen, 24D5
Jinghong, 24D3,4
Jingyuan, 24C4
Jinhua, 24D5,6
Jining (China, Neimenggu Zizhiqu), 24C5
Jining (China, Shandong), 24C5
Jinja, 30A4
Jinshajiang see Tongtianhe
Jinxi, 25B3
Jinxian, 25C3
Jinzhou, 24B6
Jitai, 24B2
Jiujiang, 24D5
Jiul, R., 14B2
Jiquan, 24C3
Jixi, 24B7
Joaçaba, 39aC3
João Pessoa, 38C6
João Pinheiro, 39aA4
Jodhpur, 22B3
Joensuu, 15C9
Joetsu, 25C6
Johannesburg, 30D3
Johnson-City, 35D4
Johnston Island, I., 41B9
Johnstown, 35C5
Johor (1), Admin. U., 19bC3
Johor Baharu, 23C2
Joinvile, 39A3,4
Jokkmokk, 15B6
Joliet, 35C3
Jolitte, 33b
Jolo, 23C4
Jolo Island, I., 23C4
Jones Sound, Str., 33A11,12
Jönköping, 15D5
Joplin, 35D2
Jordan, R., 20bB1
Jordan, St., 20bB,C2
Jörn, 15B7
Jos, 29C8
Joseph Bonaparte Gulf, G., 40B2
Joškar-Ola, 16D6
Jos Plateau, Plat., 26C,D5
Juárez, 39aE2
Juázeiro, 38C5
Juàzeiro do Norte, 38C5

Jubá, 28D6
Juba, R., 28D7
Júcar, R., 11G3
Júcaro, 36aB4
Juchitán, 36C3
Juchnov, 18B4
Juen Mina, 34a
Juiz de Fora, 38E5
Jujuy, Admin. U., 39A2
Julianehåb see Qaqortoq
Jundiaí, 39aB4
Juneau, 33C6
Junin, 39B2
Juquia, 39aB4
Jura (39), Admin. U., 11C4
Jura, I., 7C,D4,5
Jura, Mts., 5C5
Juradó, 38B2
Jurgamyš, 17aB3
Jurla, 17aB1
Jürmala, 17C2
Juruá, R., 37C3
Juruena, 38D4
Juruena, R., 37D4
Juškozero, 17B4
Jutaí, R., 38C3
Juxian, 25C2
Južna Morava, R., 13B5
Južno-Kuril'sk, 25B8
Južno-Sachalinsk, 16E16
Južno-Ural'sk, 17aC3
Južnyj Bug, R., 18C2
Jylland, Pen., 12A,B3
Jyväskylä, 15C8

K

Kaala-Gomen, 41aA1
Kabala, 29D7
Kabalo, 30B3
Kabardino-Balkar Autonomous Soviet Socialist Republic (4), Admin. U., 18D5
Kabba, 29D7
Kabelega Falls, Fs., 26D8
Kabinda, 30C3
Kabompo, R., 30C3
Kåbúl, 22A2
Kabwe, 30C3
Kača, 16aB1
Kachovskoje Vodochranilišče, Res., 18C3
Kačug, 16bB2
Kade, 29D5
Kadoma, 30C3,4
Kaduna, 29C7
Kaduna (9), Admin. U., 29C7
Kaduna, R., 29C7
Kadúr, 20aA1,2
Kadžerom, 17B9
Kaédi, 28C1
Kaesŏng, 25C4
Kåf, 20bC2
Kafan, 18B2
Kafanchan, 29C8
Kafr ash-Shaykh, 26aA2,3
Kafue, 30C3
Kafue, R., 30C3
Kaga Bandoro, 28D4,5
Kagan, 21B8,9
Kagoshima, 25D4,5
Kagul, 18C2
Kahemba, 30B2

Kahnúj, 21D7
Kahoolawe, I., 35aB3
Kaiama, 29C6,7
Kaifeng, 24C5
Kailu, 25B3
Kaimana, 23D5
Kainji Lake,Res., 29C7
Kaiserslautern, 12C2
Kaiwi Channel, 35aB3
Kaiyuan, 25B3
Kajaani, 15B8
Kajabbi, 40C3,4
Kåkå, 28C6
Kakinada, 22C4
Kalabaka, 14D2
Kalač, 18B5
Kalač-na-Donu, 18C5
Kaladar, 35C5
Kalahari Desert, Des., 26G6,7
Kalámai, 14D2
Kalimantan see Borneo
Kalamazoo, 35C3
Kalan, 21aB3
Kalančak, 16aA1
Kalapana, 35aC4
Kalát, 22B2
Kal'azin, 17C5
Kalecik, 21aA2
Kalemi, 30B3
Kalevala, 17A4
Kálfafell, 15aB,C3
Kalgoorlie-Boulder, 40D2
Kalianda, 23aA1
Kalibo, 23bB2
Kalima, 30B3
Kalinin, 16D5
Kaliningrad, 16D4
Kalininsk, 18B5
Kalispell, 34B4
Kalisz, 12C5
Kalixälven, R., 15B7
Kalmar, 15D5,6
Kalmyk Autonomous Socialist Republic, Admin. U., 18C5,6
Kaluga, 18B4
Kalundborg, 12B3
Kaluš, 18C1
Kama, R., 16D7
Kamaishi, 25C7
Kamaši, 21B9
Kambalda, 40D2
Kamčija, R., 14C3
Kamen, 12aA4
Kamen', Mt., 19C11
Kamenec-Podol'skij, 18C2
Kamenka, 18B5
Kamen'-Kaširskij, 18B1,2
Kamennomostskij, 18D4,5
Kamenskoje, 16C18
Kamensk-Šachtinskij, 18C5
Kamensk-Ural'skij, 17aB3
Kamina, 30B3
Kamloops, 33C7
Kampala, 30A4
Kampar, R., 23C,D2
Kâmpóng Saôm, 22C6
Kâmpôt, 22C6
Kampuchea, St., 22C6
Kamsar, 29C2
Kamskoje Vodochranilišče, Res., 17aB2
Kamyšin, 18B5,6
Kamyslov, 17aB3

Kamyzak, 18C6
Kanal Imeni Moskvy, Can., 17C5
Kananga, 30B3
Kanaš, 17C7
Kanawha, R., 35D4
Kanazawa, 25C6
Kânchipuram, 20aA2
Kandalakša, 16C5
Kandalakskij Zaliv, B., 17A4,5
Kandangan, 23D3
Kandavu, I., 41bB2
Kandavu Passage, Str., 41bB1,2
Kandi, 29C6
Kandy, 20aC3
Kaneohe, 35aB3
Kanevskoje Vodochranilišče, Res., 18B,C3
Kangān, 21D6
Kangar, 19bA2
Kangarē, 29C3,4
Kangaroo Island, I., 40D3
Kanggye, 25B4
Kangiqsualujjuaq, 33C13
Kangnŭng, 25C4
Kanin Nos, 17A6
Kankan, 29C3
Kano, 29B8
Kano (10), Admin. U., 29C8
Känpur, 22B4
Kansas, Admin. U., 34D6,7
Kansas, R., 35D1
Kansas City (U.S.A., Kansas), 35D1,2
Kansas City (U.S.A., Missouri), 35D2
Kansk, 16D11
Kansŏng, 25C4
Kantchari, 29B6
Kantemirovka, 18C4
Kanton Island, I., 41D8
Kanye, 30D3
Kaohsiung, 24D5,6
Kaolack, 29B1,2
Kaoma, 30C3
Kapaa, 35aA2
Kapanga, 30B3
Kap Arkona, C., 12B4
Kap Brewster, C., 42B,C16,17
Kap Farvel see Uummannarsuaq
Kapiri m'Poshi, 30C3
Kap Morris Jesup, C., 42D15-18
Kapoeta, 28D6
Kaposvár, 14B1
Kapsukas, 18B1
Kapuas, R., 23D2,3
Kapuskasing, 35B4
Kapustin Jar, 18C6
Karabaš, 17aB2,3
Karabük, 21aA2
Karačev, 18B3,4
Karachayevo-Cherkessk Autonomous Region (8), Admin. U., 18D5
Karāchi, 22B2
Karadeniz Boğazi, Str., 21aA1
Karaganda, 16E8,9
Karaidel'skij, 17aB2
Karaj, 21B6

Karakoram Range, Mts., 19F9,10
Karaköse, 21aB4
Karakumy, Des., 19F7,8
Karaman, 21aB2
Karamay, 24B2
Karasburg, 30D2
Karasjok, 15A8
Karasu, 14C4
Karawang, 23aA1
Karbalá', 21C4
Kardeljevo, 13B4
Kardhitsa, 14D2
Kärdla, 17C2
Kârdžali, 14C3
Kârdžali (6), Admin. U., 14C3
Karelian Autonomous Soviet Socialist Rep., Admin. U., 17A,B4
Karema, 30B4
Karesuando, 15A7
Kargopol', 17B5
Kariaí, 14C3
Kariba, 30C3
Kârikâl, 20aB2,3
Karis, 15C7
Karjepolje, 17A6
Karkheh, R., 21C5
Karkinitskij Zaliv, B., 18C3
Karl-Marx-Stadt, 12C4
Karl-Marx-Stadt (8), Admin. U., 12C4
Karlovac, 13A4
Karlovy Vary, 12C4
Karlshamn, 15D5
Karlskrona, 15D5,6
Karlsruhe, 12C3
Karlstad, 15D5
Karmah, 28C6
Karmøy, I., 15D3
Karnataka, Admin. U., 22C3
Karnobat, 14C3
Kärnten (2), Admin. U., 12D4
Karonga, 30B4
Kárpathos, 14E3
Kárpathos, I., 14E3
Karpinsk, 17aB2,3
Karpogory, 17B6,7
Kars, 21aA4
Karši, 21B9
Karskije Vorota, Chann., 16B,C7
Karskoje More, S., 16B8-10
Karstula, 15C7,8
Kartaly, 17aC3
Kärwär, 20aA1
Karymskoje, 16bB3
Kaş, 21aB1
Kasai see Cassai
Kasama, 30C4
Kasempa, 30C3
Kasenga, 30C3
Kasese, 30A4
Kāshān, 21C6
Kashi, 24C1
Kāshmar, 21B7
Kasimov, 18B5
Kašin, 17C5
Kašira, 18B4
Kaskö, 15C7
Kasongo, 30B3
Kaspijsk, 18D6
Kaspijskij, 18C6
Kassala, 28C6
Kassel, 12C3
Kastamonu, 21aA2

La Perla, 34 F6
La Perouse Strait, 25 A7
Lápithos, 19c A2
La Plata, 39 B3
Lappeenranta, 15 C8
Lappland, Reg., 5 A7
L'Aquila, 13 B3
Lär, 21 D6
Larache, 28 A2
Laramie, 34 C5
Laredo, 34 F7
Largeau, 28 C4
Largs, 10 C2
La Rioja, 39 A2
La Rioja (11), Admin. U.,
  (Argentina), 39 A2
La Rioja (12), Admin. U.,
  (Spain), 11 F3
Lárisa, 14 D2
Lårkåna, 22 B2
Lárnax, 19c B2
Larne, 10 D7
Larne (16), Admin. U.,
  10 D7
La Rochelle, 11 C2
La Roche-sur-Yon, 11 C2
Larsen Ice Shelf, 42 F,G6
Las Anod, 28 D7
Las Cascadas, 34a
Las Cruces, 34 E5
La Serena, 39 A1
La Serre, 35 B5
Las Flores, 39 B2,3
Lashio, 22 B5
Lashkar Gäh, 22 A2
Las Palmas, 28 B1
La Spezia, 13 B2
Las Piedras, 39a D2,3
Las Plumas, 39 C2
Lassen Peak, Vol., 31a B1
Las Truchas, 36 C2
Las Vegas, 34 D3
Latina, 13 B3
La Tuque, 35 B6
Latvian Soviet Socialist
  Republic, Admin. U.,
  16 D4
Lau Group, Is., 41b A,B3
Launceston (Tasmania),
  40 E4
Launceston (U.K.), 9 D2
La Unión, 36 C4
Laura, 40 B4
Laure, 35 E3
Laurentin Plateau, Plat.,
  31 C,D10-14
Lauria, 13 B,C3,4
Lausanne, 11 C4
Lautoka, 41b A1
Laval (Canada), 33 D12
Laval (France), 11 B2
Laverton, 40 C2
Lavras, 39a B5
Lavumisa, 30 D4
Lawra, 29 C5
Lawton, 34 E7
Lazio (7), Admin. U., 13 B3
Lea, R., 7 F7
Leader, 34 A5
Learmonth, 40 C1
Lebanon, St., 20b B1,2
Lebedin, 18 B3
Lebesby, 15 A8
Lębork, 12 B5
Lebu, 39 B1
Lecce, 13 B4
Lecco, 13a A3
Lech, R., 12 C3
Le Creusot, 11 C3,4
Le Croisic, 11 C2
Leďanaja, Mt., 42 B36

Leduc, 33 C8
Lee, R., 7 F3
Leeds, 9 C4
Leeuwarden, 12 B2
Leeward Islands, Is.,
  36b A,B2
Legazpi, 23 B4
Legnago, 13a A5
Legnano, 13a A2
Legnica, 12 C5
Leh, 22 A3
Le Havre, 11 B3
Leicester, 9 C4
Leicestershire (31),
  Admin. U., 9 C4
Leichlingen, 12a B3
Leiden, 12 B2
Leigh Creek, 40 D3
Leikanger, 15 C3
Leipzig, 12 C4
Leipzig (9), Admin. U.,
  12 C4
Leiria, 11 G1
Leiria (10), Admin. U.,
  11 G1
Leith Hill, H., 7 F7,8
Le Mans, 11 B3
Le Mars, 35 C1
Lemesós, 19c B2
Lena, R., 16 D12
Lendery, 17 B4
Leninabad, 21 A9
Leninakan, 18a A1
Leningrad, 16 C,D5
Leningradskaja, Station,
  42 F20,21
Lenino, 16a B2
Leninogorsk, 24 A2
Leninsk, 16 E8
Leninskoje, 17 C7
Lenkoran', 18a B2
Lenne, R., 12a B4
Lens, 11 B3
Lensk, 16 C13
Lenvik, 15 A6
Léo, 29 C5
Leoben, 12 D4
Leominster, 9 C3
León (Mexico), 36 B2
León (Nicaragua), 36 C4
León (Spain), 11 F2
Leonárison, 19c A3
Leonora, 40 C2
Lepel', 18 B2
Le Port, 30a B1
Le Puy, 11 C3
Léré, 29 C9
Le Relais, 33b
Lérida, 11 F4
Lerma, 11 F3
Lervick, 10a
Les Ecrins, Mt., 5 C5
Leskovac, 13a B3
Lesnoj, 17 C8
Lesosibirsk, 16 D11
Lesotho, St., 30 D,E3
Lesozavodsk, 25 A5
Les Sables-d'Olonne,
  11 C2
Lessay, 6a A3
Lesser Antilles, Is., 38 A3
Lešukonskoje, 17 B7
Lésvos, i., 14 D3
Leszno, 12 C5
Lethbridge, 33 D8
Lethem, 38 B4
Letiahau, R., 30 D3
Leticia, 38 C2,3
Letka, 17 C7
Le Tréport, 11 B3
Letterkenny, 10 D6

Leulumoega, 41c A1
Leuven, 11 B4
Levádhia, 14 D2
Levanger, 15 C4
Levaši, 18 D6
Levice, 12 C5
Levka, 19c A1
Levkás, I., 14 D2
Levkónoikon, 19c A2
Levkosia, 19c A2
Levuka, 41b A2
Lewes, 9 D5
Lewis, I., 7 B,C4
Lewisham, 9a
Lewiston (U.S.A., Idaho),
  34 B3
Lewiston (U.S.A., Maine),
  35 C6,7
Lexington-Fayette, 35 D4
Leyte, I., 23 B4
Leyton, 9a
L'gov, 18 B4
Lhasa, 24 D3
Lhokseumawe, 23 C1
Lianyungang, 24 C5,6
Liaocheng, 25 C2
Liaodongwan, B., 25 B3
Liaohe, R., 25 B3
Liaoning (19), Admin. U.,
  24 B6
Liaoyang, 25 B3
Liaoyuan, 25 B4
Liard, R., 33 B6,7
Libenge, 28 D4
Liberal, 34 D6
Liberec, 12 C4
Liberia, St., 29 D3
Libourne, 11 C2
Libreville, 30 A1,2
Libya, St., 28 B4,5
Libyan Desert, Des.,
  28 B6,7
Licata, 13 C3
Lichinga, 30 C4
Lichoslavl', 17 C5
Lida, 18 B2
Liechtenstein, St., 12 D3
Liège, 11 B4
Lieksa, 15 C9
Lienz, 12 D4
Liepāja, 16 D3,4
Liffey, R., 7 E4
Lifford, 10 D6
Liguria (8), Admin. U.,
  13 A2
Ligurian Sea, 13 B2
Lihue, 35a B2
Lijiang, 24 D3,4
Líkasi, 30 C3
Lille, 11 B3
Lillehammer, 15 C4
Lillooet, 33a B3
Lilongwe, 30 C4
Lim, R., 13 B4
Lima, 38 D2
Limavady, 10 D6
Limavady (17), Admin. U.,
  10 D6
Limay, R., 39 B2
Limbe, 29 D8
Limburg, 12 C3
Limeira, 39a B5
Limerick, 10 E5
Limerick, Admin. U., 10 E5
Limfjorden, Str., 12 A3
Límnos, I., 14 D3
Limoges, 11 C3
Limón, 36 D4
Limon, 34 D6
Limpopo, R., 30 D3

Linares (Chile), 39 B1
Linares (Mexico), 34 G7
Linares (Spain), 11 G3
Lincoln (U.K.), 9 C4
Lincoln (U.S.A.), 35 C1
Lincoln Sea, 42 D13,14
Lincolnshire (32),
  Admin. U., 9 C5
Lind, 34 B3
Lindesnes, C., 15 D3
Lindhos, 14 D3,4
Lindi, 34 B4
Lindi, R., 30 A3
Lindsay, 33b
Line Islands, Is.,
  41 C,D9,10
Linfen, 24 C5
Lingayen, 23 B3,4
Lingling, 24 D5
Linguère, 29 B2
Lingyuan, 25 B2
Linhai, 24 D6
Linhares, 38 D6
Linhe, 24 B4
Linjiang, 25 B4
Linköping, 15 D5,6
Linkou, 25 A4,5
Linqing, 25 C2
Lins, 39a B4
Linxi, 24 B5
Linxia, 24 C4
Linyi, 24 C5
Linz, 12 C4
Lipa, 23b B2
Lipeck, 18 B4
Lippe, R., 12a A2
Lisala, 28 D5
Lisboa, 11 G1
Lisboa (11), Admin. U.,
  11 G1
Lisbon see Lisboa
Lisburn, 10 D6,7
Lisburn (18), Admin. U.,
  10 D6
Lishui, 25 E2,3
Lismore, 40 C4
Listowel, 10 E5
Lithuanian Soviet Socialist
  Rep., Admin. U., 16 D4
Little Abaco Island, I.,
  35 F5
Little Colorado, R., 34 D4
Little Minch, Str., 7 C4
Little Missouri, R., 34 B6
Little Rock, 35 E2
Liuan, 25 D2
Liuzhou, 24 D4,5
Live Oak, 35 E4
Liverpool, 9 C3
Liverpool Bay, B., 9 C3
Livingstone see Maramba
Livny, 18 B4
Livorno, 13 B2
Lizard Point, C., 7 G5
Ljubljana, 13 A3
Ljungan, R., 15 C6
Ljusnan, R., 15 C5
Llandrindod Wells, 9 C3
Llanelli, 9 D2
Llanes, 11 F2
Llano Estacado, Plat.,
  31 F10
Llanos, Pl., 37 B2,3
Lleyn Peninsula, P., 7 E5
Lloydminster, 33 C8,9
Lobería, 39 B3
Lobito, 30 C2
Lobva, 17a B3
Locarno, 11 C5
Loch Awe, L., 7 C5
Lochboisdale, 10 B1

Madisonville, 35D3
Madiun, 23D3
Madras, 22C4
Madre de Dios, R., 38D2,3
Madrid, 11F3
Madrid (13), Admin. U., 11F3
Maduo, 24C3
Madura, I., 30B5
Madurai, 22C,D3
Maebashi, 25C6
Maevatanana, 30C5
Mafia Island, I., 30B5
Magadan, 16C,D16,17
Magadi, 30B4
Magdagasi, 16D14
Magdalena, R., 37B2
Magdeburg, 12B3
Magdeburg (10), Admin. U., 12B3
Magelang, 23D2,3
Magenta, 13aA2,3
Maghera, 10D6
Magherafelt, 10D6
Magherafelt (20), Admin. U., 10D6
Magnet, 40C1
Magnitogorsk, 16D7
Magog, 35B6
Magwe, 22B5
Mahajanga, 30C5
Mahakam, R., 23C,D3
Mahānadi, R., 22B4
Mahārāshtra, Admin. U., 22B3
Mahattat Harad, 28B7
Mahe, 20aB1
Mahébourg, 30aB3,4
Mahé Island, I., 27E10
Mahnomen, 34B7
Maho, 20aC3
Mahón, 11G5
Maidstone, 9D5
Maiduguri, 29C9
Main, R., 12C3
Maine, Admin. U., 35B7
Maine-et-Loire (49), Admin. U., 11C2
Mainland (Orkney Is.), I., 7B6
Mainland (Shetland Is.), I., 7A7
Maintirano, 30C5
Mainz, 12C3
Maio, I., 28aB2
Maipú, 39aE2
Maiquetía, 38A,B3
Maitland, 40D5
Maizuru, 25C6
Maja, R., 16D15
Majene, 23D4
Majkop, 18D5
Majskij, 18D5
Majuro, I., 41C7
Maka, 29B2
Makarjev, 17C6
Makarska, 13B4
Makassar see Ujung Pandang
Makat, 6C10
Makedhonia (5), Admin. U., 14C2
Makedonija (4), Admin. U., 13B5
Makejevka, 18C4
Makeni, 29C2,3
Makgadikgadi Pans, Pl., 30D3
Makkah, 28B6,7
Makokou, 30A2

Makoua, 30A2
Maksaticha, 17C5
Mākū, 21aB4
Makumbako, 30B4
Makurdi, 29D8
Malabar Coast, 20aA,B1,2
Malabo, 29E8
Malacca, 23C2
Málaga, 11G2
Malaita, I., 40A6
Malakāl, 28D6
Malang, 23D3
Malange, 30B2
Malanville, 29C6
Mālaren, L., 15D6
Malargüe, 39B2
Malatya, 21aB3
Malawi, St., 30C4
Malawi see Lake Nyasa
Malaya, Admin. U., 23C2
Malay Peninsula, 19
Malaysia, St., 23C2,3
Malazgirt, 21aB4
Malbork, 12B5
Malden Island, I., 41D10
Maldives, St., Is., 22D3
Maldonado, 39aE3
Malé, 22D3
Malen'ga, 17B5
Mali, St., 29A,B3-6
Malili, 23D4
Malindi, 30B5
Malin Head, C., 7D4
Mallaig, 10B2
Mallawi, 28B5,6
Mallorca, I., 11G4
Mallow, 10E5
Malmö, 15E5
Malmyž, 17C8
Malomra, R., 17C7
Malošujka, 17B5
Mālselv, 15A6
Malta, St., I., 13D3
Maluku, Arch., 23C,D4,5
Malung, 15C5
Malyj Uzen´, R., 18B,C6
Mamaja, 14B4
Mamberamo, R., 23D5
Mamburao, 23B2
Mamfe, 29D8
Mamoré, R., 37D3
Mamou, 29C2,3
Mampong, 29D5
Man, 29D4
Mana (French Guyana), 38B4
Mana (Hawaiian Is.), 35aA1,2
Manacor, 11G4
Manado, 23C4
Managhan, 10D6
Managua, 36C4
Manakara, 30D5
Mananjary, 30D5
Ma'nasi, 24B2
Manaus, 38C3,4
Manavgat, 21aB2
Manche (50), Admin. U., 11B2
Manchester (U.K.), 9C3
Manchester (U.S.A.), 35C6
Mand, R., 21D6
Manda, 30C4
Mandal, 15D3
Mandalay, 22B5
Mandalgov', 24B4
Mandritsara, 30C5
Manfredonia, 13B3,4
Mangaia, I., 41F10

Mangalia, 14C4
Mangalore, 22C3
Mango, I., 41bA3
Mangochi, 30C4
Mangoky, R., 30D5
Mangui, 24A6
Mangya, 24C3
Manhattan (U.S.A., Kansas), 35D1
Manhattan (U.S.A., New York), 32a
Maniamba, 30C4
Manica, 30C4
Manicoré, 38C3
Manihi, I., 41E11
Manihiki, I., 41E9,10
Manila, 23B4
Manila Bay, 23bB2
Manipur (2), Admin. U., 22B5
Manisa, 21aB1
Manitoba, Admin. U., 33C10
Manitoulin Island, I., 35B4
Manītsoq (Sukkertoppen), 33B14
Maniwaki, 35B5
Manizales, 38B2
Mankato, 35C2
Mankono, 29C4
Mankota, 34B5
Manna, 23D2
Mannar, 20aB2,3
Mannheim, 12C3
Manokwari, 23D5
Manono, 30B3
Manresa, 11F4
Mansa, 30C3
Mansel Island, I., 33B11,12
Mansfield (U.K.), 9C4
Mansfield (U.S.A.), 33b
Manta, 38C1,2
Mantova, 13A2
Manturovo, 17C6
Mantyluoto, 15C7
Manua Islands, Is., 41cB4
Manuelzinho, 38C4
Manukau, 40aA2
Manyč, R., 18C5
Manyoni, 30B4
Manzanares, 11G3
Manzanillo (Cuba), 36aB5
Manzanillo (Mexico), 36C2
Manzhouli, 24B5
Mao, 28C4
Maoming, 24D5
Mapuera, R., 38C4
Maputo, 30D4
Maraã, 38C3
Marabá, 38C5
Maracaibo, 38A2
Maracay, 38A3
Maradi, 29B7
Marae, 41dB1
Marāgheh, 21B5
Maramba, 30C3
Marand, 21B5
Maranhão, Admin. U., 38C5
Marañón, R., 37C2
Maraş, 21aB3
Marathon, 35B3
Marawi, 28C6
Marbella, 11G2
Marble Bar, 40C2
Marble Canyon, 34D4

Marburg an der Lahn, 12C3
March, 9C5
Marcha, R., 16C13
Marche (10), Admin. U., 13B3
Mar del Plata, 39B3
Mardin, 21aB4
Merengo, 33aC4
Marganec, 18C3,4
Margate, 9D5
Margerøya, I., 15A8
Mariana Islands, Is., 3
Mariánské Lázně, 12C4
Marias, R., 34B4
Mari Autonomous Soviet Socialist Republic, Admin. U., 17C7
Maribor, 13A3
Marica, R., 14C3
Maridī, 28D5
Marie Byrd Land, Reg., 42G12-14
Mariehamn, 15C6,7
Mariental, 30D2
Mariestad, 15D5
Marília, 38E4,5
Marinduque Island, I., 23bB2
Maringá, 39A3
Marka, 28D7
Markovo, 16C18,19
Marks, 18B6
Marl, 12aA3
Marmagao, 20aA1
Marmande, 11C3
Marne (51), Admin. U., 11B4
Marne, R., 11B3
Marne (Haute-) (52), Admin. U., 11B,C4
Maroantsetra, 30C5,6
Maromokotro, Mt., 26F9,10
Maroua, 29C9
Marovoay, 30C5
Marquette, 35B3
Marrakech, 28A2
Marree, 40C3
Marsabit, 28D6
Marsala, 13C3
Mars´aty, 17aA3
Marseille, 11D4
Marshall (Liberia), 29D3
Marshall (U.S.A.), 35D2
Marshall Islands, Admin. U., 41B,C7
Marsh Island, I., 35F2
Martaban, 22C5
Martapura, 23D3
Martí, 36aB5
Martil, 5aB3
Martin, 12C5
Martinique, Admin. U., I., 36bB2
Mary, 21B8
Maryborough, 40C5
Maryland, Admin. U., 35D5
Maryport, 10C3
Maryville, 35C2
Marzūq, 28B4
Masai Steppe, Pl., 26E8
Masan, 25C4
Masbate, 23bB2
Masbate Island, I., 23B4
Mascarene Islands, Is., 26F,G10,11
Maseru, 30D3
Masjed Soleymān, 21C5,6

Misiones (13), Admin. U., 39A3
Miskolc, 14A2
Mismär, 28C6
Misrätah, 28A4
Missinaibi, R., 35A4
Mississauga, 33b
Mississippi, Admin. U., 35E2,3
Mississippi, R., 35B2
Mississippi Lowlands, Pl., 31F11,12
Missoula, 34B4
Missouri, Admin. U., 35D2
Missouri, R., 34B5
Mitchell, 34C7
Mitchell, R., 40B4
Mit Ghamr, 26aB3
Mitilíni, 14D3
Mito, 25C7
Mittellandkanal, Can., 12B2,3
Mitú, 38B2
Mitwaba, 30B3
Miyake-jima, I., 25D6,7
Miyako, 25C7
Miyakonojô, 25D5
Miyazaki, 25D5
Mizdah, 28A4
Mizen Head, C., 7F2,3
Mizoram (7), Admin. U., 22B5
Mizque, 38D3
Mizuho, Station, 42G32
Mjésa, L., 15C4
Mława, 12B6
Mmabatho, 30D3
Moab, 34D5
Moala, I., 41bB2
Moanda, 30B2
Moba, 30B3
Moberly, 35D2
Mobile, 35E3
Mobile Bay, B., 35E,F3
Moçambique, 30C5
Mochudi, 30C4
Mocimboa da Praia, 30C5
Moclips, 34B2
Mocoa, 38B2
Mocuba, 30C4
Modaomen, R., 19aB1
Modena, 13A4
Moers, 12aB2
Moffat, 10C3
Mogil'ov, 18B3
Mogil'ov-Podol'skij, 18C2
Mogoča, 16D13
Mogzon, 16bB3
Mohács, 14B1
Mohammedia, 11H2
Mohéli, I., 30C5
Moirans, 11C4
Moisie, R., 33C13
Mojave, 34D3
Mojave Desert, Des., 31aC,D2
Mokolo, 29C9
Mokp'o, 25D4
Moktama Kwe, B., 22C5
Moldavian Soviet Socialist Republic, Admin. U., 18C2
Molde, 15C4
Moldoveanu, Mt., 5C7
Molepolole, 30D3
Molfetta, 13D4
Molise (11), Admin. U., 13B3
Mollendo, 38D2
Molodečno, 18B3

Molodežnaja, Station, 42G34,35
Molokai, I., 35aB3
Molopo, R., 30D3
Molucca Sea, 23C,D4
Mombasa, 30B4,5
Mombetsu, 25B7
Món, I., 12B4
Monaco, 11D4
Monaco, St., 11D4
Monaghan, 10D6
Monaghan, Admin. U., 10D,E6
Moncalieri, 13a A,B1
Mončegorsk, 17A4
Mönchengladbach, 12aB1,2
Monclova, 36B2
Moncton, 33D13
Mondovi, 13aB1
Monet, 35B5
Monforte de Lemos, 11F2
Mongo, 28C4
Mongolia, St., 24B3-5
Mongu, 30C3
Monmouth, 9D3
Mono, R., 29D6
Monroe (U.S.A., Louisiana), 35E2
Monroe (U.S.A., Washington) 33aC3
Monrovia, 29D3
Mons, 11B3
Monselice, 13aA5
Montana, Admin. U., 34B5
Montauban, 11C3
Montbard, 11C4
Montbéliard, 11C4
Mont Blanc, Mt., 5C5
Montélimar, 11C4
Monte Lirio, 34a
Montemorelos, 34F7
Montenegro, 39aC3
Montego Bay, 36C5
Monterey, 34D2
Montería, 38B2
Monterrey, 36B3
Montes Claros, 38D5
Montevideo, 39aD,E2
Mont Forel, Mt., 42B14,15
Montgomery, 35E3
Monticello, 34D5
Mont-Joli, 33D13
Mont Laurier, 33B5
Montlucon, 11C3
Montmartin-sur-Mer, 6aA3
Montpelier (U.S.A.), 35C6
Montpellier (France), 11C3
Montréal, 33D12
Montreux, 11C4
Montrose, 10B3
Montserrat, Admin. U., I., 36bA2
Monza, 13A2
Monzón, 11F4
Moorea, I., 41dB1
Moorhead, 34B7
Moosehead Lake, L., 33b
Moose Jaw, 33C9
Moosonee, 33C11
Mopti, 29B4,5

Mora, 15C5
Morädäbäd, 22B3,4
Moramanga, 30C5
Moratuwa, 20aC2,3
Morava, R., 12C5
Morawhanna, 38B3,4
Moray Firth, B., 7B,C6
Morbihan (56), Admin. U., 11C2
Mordovian Autonomous Soviet Socialist Rep., Admin. U., 18B5,6
Morecambe, 9B3
Morecambe Bay, B., 7D,E6
Morehead City, 35E5
More Laptevych, S., 16B13-15
Morelia, 36C2
Morella, 11F3,4
Morelos (16), Admin. U., 36C3
Mórfou, 19aA1
Morghäb, R., 21B8,9
Morioka, 25C7
Morlaix, 11B2
Morocco, St., 28A,B2
Morogoro, 30B4
Morombe, 30D5
Morón, 36aA4
Morón, 24B3,4
Morondava, 30D5
Moroni see Njazidja
Morotai, I., 23C4
Morozovsk, 18C5
Morpeth, 9B4
Morrinhos, 38D5
Morrisburg, 33b
Morristown, 35D4
Moršansk, 18B5
Mortara, 13aA2
Moscow, 34B3
Moscow see Moskva
Mosel see Moselle
Moselle (57), Admin. U., 11B4
Moselle, R., 11B4
Moses Lake, 34B3
Moshi, 30B4
Mosjöen, 15B5
Moskva, 16D5,6
Moskva, R., 17C5
Moss, 15D4
Mossel Bay, 30E3
Mossoró, 38C6
Most, 12C4
Mostar, 13B4
Mostardas, 39aD3
Motala, 15D5
Motherwell, 10C3
Motril, 11B3
Moudjéria, 29A2
Mouila, 30B2
Moulins, 11C3
Moulmein, 22C5
Moundou, 28D4
Mount Adams, Mt., 31aA1
Mountain Nile see Al-Bahr al-Jabal
Mountains Nimba, Mts., 26D4
Mount Amundsen, Mt., 42F,G26
Mount Aspiring, Mt., 40aB1
Mount Augustus, Mt., 40C1
Mount Columbia, Mt., 31D9,10
Mount Cook, Mt., 40aB1

Mount Cooke, Mt., 40D1
Mount Elbert, Mt., 31F9,10
Mount Elgon, Mt., 26D8
Mount Elkins, Mt., 42F31
Mount Erebus, Mt., •42G19,20
Mount Everest, Mt., 19G10,11
Mount Forest, 33b
Mount Gambier, 40D3,4
Mount Hawkes, Mt., 42H5-8
Mount Hood, Mt., 31aA1
Mount Isa, 40C3
Mount Jefferson, Mt., 31aC2
Mount Kenya, Vol., 26D8
Mount Kinabalu, Mt., 19 I 13
Mount Kirkpatrick, Mt., 42H20-24
Mount Kosciusko, Mt., 40D4,5
Mount Leinster, Mt., 7E4
Mount Liebig, Mt., 40C3
Mount Linn, Mt., 31aB1
Mount Lister, Mt., 42G21,22
Mount Logan, Mt., 31C6,7
Mount Markham, Mt., 42H21-23
Mount Mc Kinley, Mt., 31C5,6
Mount Meharry, Mt., 40C1
Mount Menzies, Mt., 42G30,31
Mount Meru, Vol., 26E8
Mount Minto, Mt., 42G19
Mount Mitchell, Mt., 31F12,13
Mount Olympus, Mt., 31aA1
Mount Ord, Mt., 40B2
Mount Pinos, Mt., 31aD2
Mount Pleasant, 35E2
Mount Rainier, Mt., 31aA1
Mount Ratz, Mt., 42A5,6
Mount Robson, Mt., 31D8,9
Mount Roraima, Mt., 37B3,4
Mount Saint Elias, Mt., 31C7
Mount Saint Helens, Vol., 31aA1
Mount's Bay, B., 9D,E2
Mount Shasta, Mt., 31aB1
Mount Sidley, Mt., 42G12,13
Mount Victoria, Mt., 40A4
Mount Waddington, Mt., 31D8,9
Mount Wells, Mt., 40B2
Mount Whitney, Mt., 31aC,,
Mount Woodroffe, Mt., 40C2,3
Moura (Brazil), 38C3
Moura (Portugal), 11G2
Mourdiah, 29B4
Mourne, R., 7D4
Mourne Mountains, Mts., 7D4,5
Moyale, 28D6
Moyamba, 29C2
Moyle (21), Admin. U., 10D6
Moyobamba, 38C2

Možajsk, 17C5
Mozambique, St., 30C,D4
Mozambique Channel,
 30C,D4,5
Mozdok, 18D5
Mozyr', 18B2
Mpanda, 30B4
Mpika, 30C4
M'Sila, 27aA1
Mtwara, 30C5
Muang Khammouan,
 22C6
Muar, 19bC,D3
Muarabungo, 23D2
Mubi, 29C9
Mucusso, 30C3
Mudanjiang, 24B6
Mudanjiang, R., 25B4
Mudanya, 21aA1
Mufulira, 30C3
Muğla, 21aB1
Muhammad Qawl, 28B6
Mui Bai-Bung, C., 22D6
Mujezerskij, 17B4
Mukačevo, 18C1
Mukden see Shenyang
Mulan, 15A4
Mulengzhen, 25B5
Mulhacén, Mt., 5D4
Mülheim, 12aA2,3
Mülhouse, 11C4
Mulinghe, R., 25A5
Mull, I., 7C4,5
Mullet Peninsula, Pen.,
 7D2
Mullewa, 40C1
Mullingar, 10E6
Mull of Galloway, C., 7D5
Mull of Kintyre, C., 7D5
Mulobezi, 30C3
Multān, 22A3
Mumra, 18C6
München, 12C3,4
Muncie, 35C3,4
Mungbere, 28D5
Munger, 22aB3
Munich see München
Münster, 12C2
Muonio, 15A7,8
Muqdisho, 28D7
Mur, R., 12D4
Muradiye, 21aB4
Muraşi, 17C7
Murat, R., 21aB4
Muratkovo, 17aB3
Murchison, R., 40C1
Murcia, 11G3
Murcia (14), Admin. U.,
 11G3
Mureşul, R., 14B3
Murgab, 24C1
Murgab see Morghāb
Murkong Selek, 22B5
Murmansk, 16C5
Murom, 17C6
Muroran, 25B7
Murray, R., 40D4
Murray Bridge, 40D3,4
Murrumbidgee, R., 40D4
Mururoa, I., 41F12
Murwāra, 22aC2
Muş, 21aB4
Musa, Mt., 5aB3
Musala, Mt., 5C7
Musan, 25B4
Mūs'a Qal'eh, 21C8
Musgrave Ranges, Mts.,
 40C3
Musi, R., 23D2
Muskegon, 35C3
Muskogee, 35D1

Musoma, 30B4
Musselburgh, 10C3
Mustafakemalpaşa,
 14C,D3,4
Mustvee, 17C3
Müt, 28B5
Mutare, 30C4
Mutnyj Materik, 17A8
Mutuali, 30C4
Muzaffarpur, 22aB3
Mwanza (Tanzania), 30B4
Mwanza (Zambia), 300B3
Mwaya, 30B4
Mweelrea, Mt., 7E2,3
Mweka, 30B3
Mwene-Ditu, 30B3
Myanaung, 22C5
Myeik, 22C5
Myeik Kyunzu, 22C,D5
Myingyan, 22B5
Myitkyinā, 22B5
Myla, 17A8
Mymensingh, 22aB4
Mys Arktičeskij, C.,
 16A10-12
Mys Čel'uskin, 16B12,13
Mys Čel'uskin, C.,
 19B12-14
Mys Dežneva, C.,
 19B,C20
Mys Fligeli, C., 42D25,26
Mys Kril'on, C., 25A7
Mys Lopatka, C.,
 19D17,18
Mys Navarin, C., 42B1
Mysore, 22C3
Mys Saryč, C., 18D3
Mys Šmidta, 16B20
Mys Želanija, 16B8
My-Tho, 22C6
Mytišči, 17C5
Mzuzu, 30C4

N

Naas, 10E6
Nabeul, 27aA3
Nabire, 23D5
Nabq, 21D2
Nābulus, 20bB1
Nacala, 30C5
Nachičevan, 16F6
Nachingwea, 30C4
Nachodka, 16E15
Nadon, 11H3
Nadvoicy, 17B4
Nadvornaja, 18C1
Nadym, 166C9
Næstved, 12B3
Naft-e Safid, 21C5,6
Naga, 23B4
Nāgāland (4), Admin. U.,
 22B5
Nagano, 25C6
Nagaoka, 25C6
Nāgapattinam, 22aB2,3
Nagar Pārkar, 22B3
Nagasaki, 25D4
Nagatino, 17b
Nāgercoil, 20aB2
Nagorno-Karabakh
 Autonomous Region (9),
 Admin. U., 18aA2
Nagorsk, 17C8
Nagoya, 25C6
Nágpur, 22B3
Nagqu, 24C3
Nagykanizsa, 14B1
Naha, 24D6

Nāhded, 22C3
Nahr al-Āsī, R., 20bA,B2
Nahr al-Khābūr, R.,
 20bA,B3
Na'īn, 21C6
Nairn, 10B3
Nairobi, 30B4
Najin, 25B5
Nakhichevan Autonomous
 Soviet Socialist
 Republic (5), Admin. U.,
 18aB2
Nakhon Ratchasima,
 22C6
Nakhon Sawan, 22C5,6
Nakhon Si Thammarat,
 22D5,6
Nakina, 33C11
Naknek, 33C4
Nakskov, 12B3
Nakuru, 30B4
Nal'čik, 18D5
Nālūt, 28A4
Namacunde, 30C2
Namangan, 16C4
Namapa, 30C4,5
Namche Bazar, 22aB3
Nam-Dinh, 22B6
Namib Desert, Des.,
 26F,G6
Namibe, 30C2
Namibia, Admin. U.,
 30C,D2
Namlea, 23D4
Nampa, 34C3
Namp'o, 25C3,4
Nampula, 30C4
Namsos, 15B4
Nam Tok, 22C5
Namuhu, L., 24C3
Namur, 11B4
Nanaimo, 33aB2,2
Nanchang, 24D5
Nanchong, 24C4
Nancy, 11B4
Nandi (Fiji), 41bA1
Nandi (Zimbabwe), 30D4
N'andoma, 17B6
Nanduri, 41bA2
Nanga-Eboko, 29D8,9
Nānga Parbat, Mt., 19F9
Nanjing, 24C5
Nanning, 24D4
Nanortalik, 33B15
Nanping, 24D5
Nansei-shotō, Is., 24D6
Nantes, 11C2
Nantong, 24C6
Nantou, 19aA2
Nanumea, I., 41D7
Nanyang, 24C5
Nanyanghu, L., 25C2
Nanyuki, 30A,B4
Nanyunhe, R., 25C2
Napanee, 33b
Napier, 40aA2
Naples see Napoli
Napo, R., 38C2
Napoli, 13B3
Nara (Japan), 25D6
Nara (Mali), 29B4
Narbonne, 11D3
Narew, R., 12B6
Narjan-Mar, 16C7
Narmada, R., 22B3
Narodnaja, Mt., 19C7,8
Narrogin, 40D1
Narssaq, 33B15
Narva, 17C3
Narva, R., 17C3
Narvik, 15A6

Naryn (Abakan), 24A3
Naryn (Alma-Ata), 24B1
Naryn, R., 24B1
Nashville-Davidson, 35D3
Näsik, 22B,C3
Nassau, 35F5
Nassau, I., 41E9
Nässjö, 15D5
Natal (Brazil), 38C6
Natal (Sumatera), 19bD1
Natal, Admin. U., 30D3,4
Natchez, 35E2
Nateva Bay, B., 41bA2,3
Natitingou, 29C6
Nauru, St., I., 41C6
Naŭski, 16D12
Nausori, 41bA2
Nauta, 38C2
Navan, 10E6
Navarra (15), Admin. U.,
 11F3
Naviti, I., 41bA1
Navľa, 18B3
Navoi, 21A9
Návplion, 14D2
Navrongo, 29C5
Navua, 41bA2
Nawābshāh, 22B2
Náxos, I., 14D3
Nayarit (17), Admin. U.,
 36B2
Nāy Band, 21D6
Nayoro, 25B7
Nazaré, 38D6
N'azepetrovsk, 17aB2
Nazerat, 20bB1
Nazilli, 21aB1
Nazret, 28D6
Nazwā, 21E7
N'Dalatando, 30B2
Ndendé, 30B2
Ndjamena, 28C4
Ndola, 30C3
Neah Bay, 33aB2
Néa Páfos, 19cB1
Neápolis, 14D2
Neath, 9D3
Nebit-Dag, 21B6
Nebolči, 17C4
Nebraska, Admin. U.,
 34C6,7
Neches, R., 35E2
Necochea, 39B2,3
Neene, 35C6
Nefta, 27aB2
Neftegorsk, 18B7
Neftekamsk, 17aB1,2
Neftekumsk, 18D5,6
Negeri Sembilan (5),
 Admin. U., 19bC3
Negombo, 20aC2
Negro (Amazonas), R.,
 37C3
Negro (Atlantic Ocean),
 R., 37F3
Negro (Uruguay), R.,
 39aD2,3
Negros, I., 23C4
Neijiang, 24D4
Nei Mongol Zizhiqu (2),
 Admin. U., 24B4-6
Neisse see Nysa Lużicka
Neiva, 38B2
Nejva, R., 17aB3
Nelidovo, 17C4
Nellore, 22C3,4
Nelson, 40aB2
Nelson, R., 33C10
Néma, 28C2
Neman, R., 18B2
Nemuro, 25B8

Nenagh, 10E5
Nenana, 33B5
Nene, R., 7E7
Nenjiang, 24B6
Nenjiang, R., 25A3
Nepal, St., 22aA,B2,3
Nepâlganj, 22aA2
Nephin, Mt., 7D3
Nerechta, 17C6
Neretva, R., 13B4
Nerja, 11G3
Ner'ungri, 16D14
Nes', 17A6
Neskaupstadur, 15aB4
Nesna, 15B5
Nestor Falls, 35B2
Néstos, R., 14C3
Netherlands, St.,
12B,C1,2
Netherlands Antilles,
Admin. U., 38A3
Nettiling Lake, L., 33B13
Neubrandenburg, 12B4
Neubrandenburg (11),
Admin. U., 12B4
Neuchâtel, 11C4
Neufchâtel-en-Bray, 9E5
Neumünster, 12B3
Neuquén, 39B2
Neuquén, Admin. U.,
39B,C1,2
Neuquén, R., 39B1,2
Neuruppin, 12B4
Neusiedler See, L., 12D5
Neuss, 12aB2
Neustrelitz, 12B4
Neuwied, 12C2
Neva, R., 17C4
Nevada, 35D2
Nevada, Admin. U., 34D3
Nevado Ancohuma, Mt.,
37D3
Nevado Auzangate, Mt.,
37D2,3
Nevado de Huascarán,
Mt., 37C2
Nevado del Huila, Mt.,
37B2
Nevel', 17C3,4
Nevers, 11C3
Nevinnomyssk, 18D5
Nevis, I., 36bA2
Nevjansk, 17aB3
Nevşehir, 21aB2
New Amsterdam, 38B4
Newark, 35C6
Newark Bay, B., 32a
Newark-upon-Trent, 9E4
New Bedford, 35C6,7
New Bern, 35D5
New Britain see Birara
New Brunswick, Admin.
U., 33D13
Newbury, 9D4
New Caledonia, I., 41a
Newcastle, 40D5
Newcastle under Lyme,
9C3
Newcastle upon Tyne,
9B4
Newcastle Waters, 40B3
Newcastle West, 10E5
New Delhi, 22B3
Newfoundland, Admin. U.,
33C,D13,14
New Georgia, I., 40A5
New Guinea, I., 41D3,4
Newhalem, 33aB3
New Hampshire, Admin.
U., 33D12
Newhaven, 9D5

New Haven, 35C6
New Hebrides see
Vanuatu
New Ireland see
Tombara
New Jersey, Admin. U.,
35D5,6
New Jilm, 35C1,2
New Kowloon, 19aB3
Newman, 40C1,2
Newmarket, 9C5
New Meadows, 34C3,4
New Mexico, Admin. U.,
34D,E5,6
New Orleans, 35F2,3
New Plymouth, 40aA2
Newport (U.K., Cardiff),
9D3
Newport (U.K.,
Portsmouth), 9D4
Newport (U.S.A.), 35C6
Newport News, 35D5
New Providence, I.,
35F5
Newquay, 9D2
New Rochelle, 32a
Newry, 10D6
Newry and Mourne (22),
Admin. U., 10D6
New South Wales, Admin.
U., 40D4,5
Newton Abbot, 9D3
Newton Falls, 33b
Newtonmore, 10B2,3
Newton Saint Boswells,
10C3
Newton Stewart, 10C2
Newtown, 9C3
Newtownabbey, 10D6,7
Newtownabbey (23),
Admin. U., 10D7
Newtownards, 10D7
New Westminster,
33aB2,3
New York, 35C6
New York, Admin. U.,
35C5,6
New Zealand, St., Is., 40a
Neyrîz, 21D6
Neyshâbûr, 21B7
Nežin, 18B3
Ngaliema, Mts., 26D7,8
Ngaoundéré, 29D9
Ngau, I., 41bA,B2
Nguigmi, 29B9
Nguru, 29B8
Nha-Trang, 22C6,7
Nhulunbuy, 40B3
Niafounké, 29B4
Niagara Falls, 35C5
Niagara Falls, Fs., 33b
Niagassola, 29B3
Niamey, 29B6
Nica, R., 17aB3
Nicaragua, St., 36C4
Nice, 11D4
Nicobar Islands, Is., 22D5
Nicolls Town, 35F5
Nicosia see Levkosia
Niederösterreich (3),
Admin. U., 12C4
Niedersachsen (6), Admin.
U., 12B3
Nièvre (58), Admin. U.,
11C3
Niğde, 21aB2
Niger (13), Admin. U.,
29C7
Niger, R., 29C3
Niger, St., 29A,B6-9
Nigeria, St., 29C7,8

Niigata, 25C6
Niihama, 25D5
Niihau, I., 35aB1,2
Nijmegen, 12C2
Nikel', 17A4
Nikolajev, 16E5
Nikolajevsk, 18B6
Nikolajevsk-na-Amure,
16D15,16
Nikol'sk, 17C7
Nikopol', 18C3
Nikšić, 13B4
Nile, R., 28C6
Nile Delta – Suez Canal,
26a
Nîmes, 11D4
Nimule, 28D6
Ningan, 25B4
Ningbo, 24D6
Ningwu, 24C5
Ningxia Huizu Zizhiqu (3),
Admin. U., 24C4
Niobrara, R., 34C6
Niono, 29B4
Nioro du Sahel, 29B3
Niort, 11C2
Nipigon, 33D11
Nipton, 34D3
Niquero, 36aB,C5
Niš, 13B5
Nissan, R., 12A4
Niteroi, 39A4
Nith, R., 7D5
Nitra, 12C5
Niue Island, I., 41E9
Nizâmâbâd, 22C3
Nižn'aja Peša, 17A7
Nižn'aja Tunguska, R.,
16C10,11
Nižn'aja Tura, 17aB2
Nižneangarsk, 16D12,13
Nižnegorskij, 18C3,4
Nižnejansk, 16B15,16
Nižnekamsk, 17C8
Nižnekamskoje Vodochra-
nilišče, Res., 17aB1,2
Nižneleninskoje, 24B7
Nižneudinsk, 16D11,12
Nižnevartovsk, 16C9,10
Nižnije Sergi, 17aB2
Nižnij Lomov, 18B5
Nižnij Tagil, 17aB2
Njazidja, 30C5
Nkawkaw, 29D5
Nkayi, 30B2
Nkongsamba, 29D8
Noatak, 33B3
Noatak, R., 33B4
Noboeka, 25D5
Nogales (Mexico), 36A1
Nogales (U.S.A.), 34E4
Nógrád (11), Admin. U.,
14B1
Nok Kundi, 21D8
Nolinsk, 17C7,8
Nome, 33B3
Nong'an, 25B4
Nong Khai, 22C6
Nootka, 33aB1
Nootka Sound, B., 33aB1
Noranda, 35B5
Nord, 42D17
Nord (59), Admin. U.,
11B3
Nordaustlandet, I.,
42C21-23
Nordfjord, B., 15C3
Nordfold, 15B5,6
Nordhausen, 12C3
Nordkapp, C., 15A8
Nordkinn, C., 15A8,9

Nordostrundingen, C.,
42D17-19
Nordreisa, 15A7
Nordrhein – Westfalen (4),
Admin. U., 12C2
Nore, R., 7E4
Norfolk (U.S.A.,
Nebraska), 34C7
Norfolk (U.S.A., Virginia),
35D5
Norfolk (33), Admin. U.,
9C5
Norfolk Island, I., 41F6,7
Noril'sk, 16C10,11
Normada, R., 19D9
Norman, 34D7
Normandie, Pen. and
Reg., 5C4,5
Normanton, 40B4
Norman Wells, 33B7
Norrköping, 15D6
Norrtälje, 15D6
Norseman, 40D2
Northallerton, 9B4
Northam, 40D1
North America, 3
Northampton, 9C4
Northamptonshire (34),
Admin. U., 9C4
North Battleford, 33C8,9
North Bay, 33D12
North Canadian, R.,
34D6,7
North Cape, C., 40aA2
North Carolina, Admin. U.,
35D4,5
North Channel, Str., 7D5
North Dakota, Admin. U.,
34B6,7
North Down (24), Admin.
U., 10D7
North Downs, Hs., 7F7,8
Northern Ireland, Admin.
U., 10D6,7
Northern Mariana Islands,
Admin. U., 41B4
Northern Territory, Admin.
U., 40B,C2,3
North Esk, R., 10B3
North European Plain, Pl.,
5B5-7
North Foreland, C., 7F8
North Frisian Islands, Is.,
12B3
North Island, I., 40aA2
North Little Rock, 35D,E2
North Magnetic Pole,
31B8-10
North Ossetian
Autonomous Soviet
Socialist Republic (6),
Admin. U., 18D5
North Platte, 34C6,7
North Platte, R., 34C6
North Pole, 42D
North Rona, I. 7B5
North Saskatchewan, R.,
33C8,9
North Sea, 5B5
North Tyne, R., 10C3
North Uist, I., 7C3,4
Northumberland (35),
Admin. U., 9B3
North Vancouver,
33aB2,3
North West Cape, C.,
40C1
North West Highlands,
Hs., 7B,C5
Northwest Territories,
Admin. U., 33C7-13

North York, 30 D 11,12
North York Moors, Mt., 7 D 7
North Yorkshire, (36), Admin. U., 9 B 4
Norton, 9 B 4
Norton Sound, Str., 42 B 2
Norway, St., 15 A-D 3-8
Norway House, 33 C 10
Norwegian Sea, 15 A,B 3-6
Norwich, 9 C 5
Noshiro, 25 B 6,7
Nosovaja, 17 A 8,9
Nossop, R., 30 D 3
Nosy-Be, 30 C 5
Noteč, R., 12 B 5
Nottaway, R., 33 C 12
Nottingham, 9 C 4
Nottinghamshire (37), Admin. U., 9 C 4
Nouadhibou, 28 B 1
Nouakchott, 28 C 1
Nouamrhar, 29 A 1
Nouméa, 41 a B 2
Nova, 11 F 1
Nova Iguaçu, 39 A 4
Novaja Kachovka, 18 C 3
Novaja Kazanka, 18 C 6
Novaja Laľa, 17 a B 2,3
Novaja Zemľa, Is., 16 B 7,8
Nova Olinda-do Norte, 38 C 4
Novara, 13 A 2
Nova Scotia, Admin. U., 33 D 13
Novgorod, 16 D 5
Novgorod-Severskij, 18 B 3
Novi Ligure, 13 a B 2
Novi Pazar, 13 B 5
Novi Sad, 13 A 4
Novoaleksandrovsk, 18 C 5
Novoaleksejevka, 16 a A 2
Novoanninskij, 18 B 5
Novoburejskij, 24 B 6,7
Novočeboksarsk, 17 C 7
Novočerkassk, 18 C 5
Novochop'orsk, 18 B 5
Novodvinsk, 17 B 6
Novograd-Volynskij, 18 B 2
Nôvo Hamburgo, 39 a C 3,4
Novokačalinsk, 25 A 5
Novokujbyševsk, 18 B 6,7
Novokuzneck, 16 D 10
Novolazarevskaja, Station, 42 G 34-36
Novomichajlovka, 25 B 5
Novomoskovsk (U.S.S.R., Dnepropetrovsk), 18 C 3,4
Novomoskovsk (U.S.S.R., Tula), 18 B 4
Novopolock, 17 C 3
Novorossijsk, 16 E 5,6
Novoržev, 17 C 3,4
Novošachtinsk, 18 C 4,5
Novosibirsk, 16 D 9,10
Novosibirskije Ostrova, Is., 16 B 15-18
Novosokoľniki, 17 C 3,4
Novoukrajinka, 18 C 3
Novouzensk, 18 B 6
Novozybkov, 18 B 3
Novyj Bor, 17 A 8
Novyj Bug, 18 C 3
Novyje Kuz'minki, 17 b
Novyj Port, 16 C 9
Nowy Sącz, 12 C 6
Nsawam, 29 D 5
Nsukka, 29 D 7

Nubian Desert, Des., 26 B 8
N'uchča, 17 B 7
Nudo Coropuna, Mt., 37 D 2
Nueces, R., 34 F 7
Nueltin Lake, L., 33 B 10
Nueva Gerona, 36 a B 2
Nueve de Julio, 39 a E 1
Nuevitas, 36 a B 5
Nuevo Chagres, 34 a
Nuevo Laredo, 36 B 2,3
Nuevo León (18), Admin. U., 36 B 2,3
Nujiang, R., 24 C 3
Nûk, 33 B 14
N'uksenica, 17 B 6
Nuku'alofa, 41 F 8
Nukus, 16 E 7,8
Nulato, 33 B 4
Nullarbor Plain, Pl., 40 D 2,3
Numan, 29 C 8,9
Numazu, 25 C,D 6
Nuneaton, 9 C 4
Nunivak Island, I., 33 C 3
Nuoro, 13 B 2
N'urba, 16 C 13
Nurlat, 18 B 7
Nurmes, 15 C 9
Nürnberg, 13 C 3
Nusaybin, 21 a B 4
Nushki, 22 B 2
Nyala, 28 C 5
Nyborg, 12 B 3
Nyeri, 30 B 4
Nyíregyháza, 14 A,B 2
Nykøbing Falster, 12 B 3,4
Nyköping, 15 D 6
Nysa, 12 C 5
Nysa Łużicka, R., 12 C 4
Nytva, 17 a B 1,2
Nzérékoré, 29 D 3
Nzi, R., 29 D 4

O

Oahu, 41 B 10
Oahu, I., 41 B 10
Oakland, 34 D 2
Oak Ridge, 35 D 4
Oamaru, 40 a B 2
Oates Coast, Reg., 42 F,G 20,21
Oaxaca, 36 C 3
Oaxaca (19), Admin. U., 36 C 3
Ob', R., 16 D 10
Oba, 35 B 4
Oban, 10 B 2
Obbia, 28 D 7
Oberhausen, 12 a B 2
Oberösterreich (4), Admin. U., 12 C 4
Óbidos, 38 C 4
Obihiro, 25 B 7
Objačevo, 17 B 7,8
Obluče, 24 B 7
Obninsk, 18 A 4
Obojan', 18 B 4
Obskaja Guba, B., 16 B,C 9
Obuasi, 29 D 5
Očakovo, 17 b
Ocala, 35 F 4
Očamčira, 18 D 5
Ocean Falls, 33 C 7
Oceanside, 34 E 3
Ocha, 16 D 16
Ochansk, 17 a B 1,2

Ochil Hills, Mts., 7 C 6
Ochotsk, 16 D 16
Odda, 15 C 3
Oddur, 28 D 7
Ödemiş, 21 a B 1
Odense, 12 B 3
Oder see Odra
Odessa (U.S.A), 34 E 6
Odessa (U.S.S.R.), 16 E 5
Odienné, 29 C 4
Odra, R., 12 C 5
Ofanto, R., 13 B 3,4
Offa, 29 C 7
Offaly, Admin. U., 10 E 6
Offenbach, 12 C 3
Ogasawara Guntō, Is., 4
Ogbomosho, 29 C 7
Ogden, 34 C 4
Ogdensburg, 35 C 5
Oglio, R., 13 a A 4
Ogoja, 29 D 8
Ogoki, R., 35 A 3
Ogoki, R., 35 A 3
Ogooué, R., 30 B 2
Ohata, 25 B 7
Ohio, Admin. U., 35 C 4
Ohře, R., 35 D 4
Ohře, R., 12 C 4
Ohrid, 13 B 5
Oiapoque, 38 B 4
Oich, R., L., 7 C 5
Oil City, 35 C 5
Oise (60), Admin. U., 11 B 3
Oise, R., 11 B 3
Oita, 25 D 5
Ojinaga, 36 B 2
Ojm'akon, 16 C 15,16
Ojos del Salado, Mt., 37 E 3
Oka (Angara), R., 16 b B 1
Oka (Volga), R., 16 D 5
Okahandja, 30 D 2
Okavango, R., 30 C 3
Okayama, 25 D 5
Okehampton, 9 D 2,3
Okene, 29 D 7
Okha, 22 B 2
Oki-guntō, Is., 25 C 5
Okinawa-jima, I., 24 D 6
Okitipupa, 29 D 7
Oklahoma, Admin. U., 34 D 7
Oklahoma City, 34 D 7
Oksino, 17 A 8
Oksovskij, 17 B 5
Okfabr'skij (U.S.S.R., Kujbyšev), 18 B 7
Okfabr'skij (U.S.S.R., Minsk), 18 B 2
Okfabr'skij (U.S.S.R., Vologda), 17 B 6
Okfabr'skoje, 16 a B 1,2
Oktember'an, 18 a A 1
Okulovka, 17 C 4
Okun'ov Nos, 17 A 8
Okushiri-tō, I., 25 B 6
Ólafsvík, 15 a B 1,2
Óland, I., 15 D 6
Olavarria, 39 B 2
Olbia, 13 B 2
Oldenburg, 12 B 2,3
Oldham, 9 C 3,4
Olean, 35 F 4
Olenegorsk, 17 A 4
Olen'ok, 16 C 12,13
Olen'ok, R., 16 B,C 13,14
Oleśnica, 12 C 5
Oľga, 25 B 6

Ölgij, 24 B 2,3
Olifants (Atlantic Ocean), R., 30 D 2
Olifants (Indian Ocean), R., 30 D 4
Ólimbos (Cyprus), Mt., 19 c B 1
Ólimbos (Greece), Mt., 5 D 7
Olinda, 38 C 6
Oliveira, 39 a B 4,5
Ollagüe, 39 A 2
Oľokma, R., 16 D 13,14
Oľokminsk, 16 C 14
Olomouc, 12 C 5
Olonec, 17 B 4
Olongapo, 23 B 3,4
Oľovannaja, 16 b B 4
Olsztyn, 12 B 6
Oltu, 21 a A 4
Oltul, R., 14 B 3
Olympia, 34 B 2
Omagh, 10 D 6
Omagh (25), Admin. U., 10 D 6
Omaha, 35 C 1
Omak, 33 a B 4
Oman, St., 21 D-F 6,7
Omaruru, 30 D 2
Omatako see Omuramba
Omo, R., 28 D 6
Omolon, R., 16 C 17,18
Omolon, R., 16 C 17,18
Omsk, 16 D 9
Omuramba, R., 30 C,D 2
Ómuta, 25 D 5
Omutninsk, 17 C 8
Ondangua, 30 C 2
Ondjiva, 30 C 2
Ondo, 29 D 7
Ondo (15), Admin. U., 29 D 7
Öndörchaan, 24 B 4,5
Onega, 17 B 5
Onega, R., 17 B 5
Oneida Lake, L., 33 b
Onežskaja Guba, B., 17 B 5
Onežskoje Ozero, L., 16 C 5,6
Ongjin, 25 C 3,4
Onitsha, 29 D 7
Onon, R., 16 D 13
Onslow, 40 C 1
Onsong, 25 B 4,5
Ontario, Admin. U., 33 C 10,11
Oodnadatta, 40 C 3
Oostende, 11 B 3
Opanake, 20 a C 3
Oparino, 17 C 7
Opatija, 13 A 3
Opava, 12 C 5
Opelika, 35 E 3
Opheim, 34 B 5
Opobo, 29 D 7
Opočka, 17 C 3
Opole, 12 C 5
Opua, 40 a A 2
Oradea, 14 B 2
Oran, 28 A 2
Orange (Australia), 40 D 4
Orange (France), 11 C 4
Orange, R., 30 E 3
Orange Free State, Admin. U., 30 D 3
Orbetello, 13 B 2
Orbost, 40 D 4
Orcadas, Is., 42 F 5
Orchon, R., 24 B 4
Ord, R., 40 B 2
Ordu, 21 a A 3

Misiones (13), Admin. U., 39A3
Miskolc, 14A2
Mismär, 28C6
Misrätah, 28A4
Missinaibi, R., 35A4
Mississauga, 33b
Mississippi, Admin. U., 35E2,3
Mississippi, R., 35B2
Mississippi Lowlands, Pl., 31F11,12
Missoula, 34B4
Missouri, Admin. U., 35D2
Missouri, R., 34B5
Mitchell, 34C7
Mitchell, R., 40B4
Mit Ghamr, 26aB3
Mitilíni, 14D3
Mito, 25C7
Mittellandkanal, Can., 12B2,3
Mitú, 38B2
Mitwaba, 30B3
Miyake-jima, I., 25D6,7
Miyako, 25C7
Miyakonojō, 25D5
Miyazaki, 25D5
Mizdah, 28A4
Mizen Head, C., 7F2,3
Mizoram (7), Admin. U., 22B5
Mizque, 38D3
Mizuho, Station, 42G32
Mjøsa, L., 15C4
Mława, 12B6
Mmabatho, 30D3
Moab, 34D5
Moala, I., 41bB2
Moanda, 30B2
Moba, 30B3
Moberly, 35D2
Mobile, 35E3
Mobile Bay, B., 35E,F3
Moçambique, 30C5
Mochudi, 30C4
Mocímboa da Praia, 30C5
Moclips, 34B1
Mocoa, 38B2
Mocuba, 30C4
Modaomen, B., 19aB1
Modena, 13A4
Moers, 12aB2
Moffat, 10C3
Mogil'ov, 18B3
Mogil'ov-Podol'skij, 18C2
Mogoča, 16D13
Mogzon, 16bB3
Mohács, 14B1
Mohammedia, 11H2
Mohéli, I., 30C5
Moirans, 11C4
Moisie, R., 33C13
Mojave, 34D3
Mojave Desert, Des., 31aC,D2
Mokolo, 29C9
Mokp'o, 25D4
Moktama Kwe, B., 22C5
Moldavian Soviet Socialist Republic, Admin. U., 18C2
Molde, 15C2
Moldoveanu, Mt., 5C7
Molepolole, 30D3
Molfetta, 13B4
Molise (11), Admin. U., 13B3
Mollendo, 38D2
Molodečno, 18B2

Molodežnaja, Station, 42G34,35
Molokai, I., 35aB3
Molopo, R., 30D3
Molucca Sea, 23C,D4
Mombasa, 30B4,5
Mombetsu, 25B7
Món, I., 12B4
Monaco, 11D4
Monaco, St., 11D4
Monaghan, 10D6
Monaghan, Admin. U., 10D,E6
Moncalieri, 13aA,B1
Mončegorsk, 17A4
Mönchengladbach, 12aB1,2
Monclova, 36B2
Moncton, 33D13
Mondovi, 13aB1
Monet, 35B5
Monforte de Lemos, 11F2
Mongo, 28C4
Mongolia, St., 24B3-5
Mongu, 30C3
Monmouth, 9D3
Mono, R., 29D6
Monroe (U.S.A., Louisiana), 35E2
Monroe (U.S.A., Washington) 33aC3
Monrovia, 29D3
Mons, 11B3
Monselice, 13aA5
Montana, Admin. U., 34B5
Montauban, 11C3
Montbard, 11C4
Montbéliard, 11C4
Mont Blanc, Mt., 5C5
Monte Lirio, 34a
Montemorelos, 34F7
Montenegro, 39aC3
Montego Bay, 36C5
Monterey, 34D2
Montería, 38B2
Monterrey, 36B3
Montes Claros, 38D5
Montevideo, 39aD,E2
Mont Forel, Mt., 42B14,15
Montgomery, 35E3
Monticello, 34D5
Mont-Joli, 33D13
Mont Laurier, 35B5
Montlucon, 11C3
Montmartin-sur-Mer, 6aA3
Montpelier (U.S.A.), 35C6
Montpellier (France), 11D3
Montréal, 33D12
Montreux, 11C4
Montrose, 10B3
Montserrat, Admin. U., I., 36bA2
Monza, 13A2
Monzón, 11F4
Moorea, I., 41dB1
Moorhead, 34B7
Moosehead Lake, L., 33b
Moose Jaw, 33C9
Moosonee, 33C11
Mopti, 29B4,5

Mora, 15C5
Morādābād, 22B3,4
Moramanga, 30C5
Moratuwa, 20aC2,3
Morava, R., 12C5
Morawhanna, 38B3,4
Moray Firth, B., 7B,C6
Morbihan (56), Admin. U., 11C2
Mordovian Autonomous Soviet Socialist Rep., Admin. U., 18B5,6
Morecambe, 9B3
Morecambe Bay, B., 7D,E6
Morehead City, 35E5
More Laptevych, S., 16B13-15
Morelia, 36C2
Morella, 11F3,4
Morelos (16), Admin. U., 36C3
Mórfou, 19cA1
Morghāb, R., 21B8,9
Morioka, 25C7
Morlaix, 11B2
Morocco, St., 28A,B2
Morogoro, 30B4
Morombe, 30D5
Morón, 36aA4
Mörön, 24B3,4
Morondava, 30D5
Moroni see Njazidja
Morotai, I., 23C4
Morozovsk, 18C5
Morpeth, 9B4
Morrinhos, 38D5
Morrisburg, 33b
Morristown, 35D4
Moršansk, 18B5
Mortara, 13aA2
Moscow, 34B3
Moscow see Moskva
Mosel see Moselle
Moselle (57), Admin. U., 11B4
Moselle, R., 11B4
Moses Lake, 34B3
Moshi, 30B4
Mosjøen, 15B5
Moskva, 16D5,6
Moskva, R., 17C5
Moss, 15D4
Mossel Bay, 30E3
Mossoró, 38C6
Most, 12C4
Mostar, 13B4
Mostardas, 39aD3
Motala, 15D5
Motherwell, 10C3
Motril, 11G3
Moudjéria, 29A2
Mouila, 30B2
Moulins, 11C3
Moulmein, 22C5
Moundou, 28D4
Mount Adams, Mt., 31aA1
Mountain Nile see Al-Bahr al-Jabal
Mountains Nimba, Mts., 26D4
Mount Amundsen, Mt., 42F,G26
Mount Aspiring, Mt., 40aB1
Mount Augustus, Mt., 40C1
Mount Columbia, Mt., 31D9,10
Mount Cook, Mt., 40aB1

Mount Cooke, Mt., 40D1
Mount Elbert, Mt., 31F9,10
Mount Elgon, Mt., 26D8
Mount Elkins, Mt., 42F31
Mount Erebus, Mt., •42G19,20
Mount Everest, Mt., 19G10,11
Mount Forest, 33b
Mount Gambier, 40D3,4
Mount Hawkes, Mt., 42H5-8
Mount Hood, Mt., 31aA1
Mount Isa, 40C3
Mount Jefferson, Mt., 31aC2
Mount Kenya, Vol., 26D8
Mount Kinabalu, Mt., 19I13
Mount Kirkpatrick, Mt., 42H20-24
Mount Kosciusko, Mt., 40D4,5
Mount Leinster, Mt., 7E4
Mount Liebig, Mt., 40C3
Mount Linn, Mt., 31aB1
Mount Lister, Mt., 42G21,22
Mount Logan, Mt., 31C6,7
Mount Markham, Mt., 42H21-23
Mount Mc Kinley, Mt., 31C5,6
Mount Meharry, Mt., 40C1
Mount Menzies, Mt., 42G30,31
Mount Meru, Vol., 26E8
Mount Minto, Mt., 42G19
Mount Mitchell, Mt., 31F12,13
Mount Olympus, Mt., 31aA1
Mount Ord, Mt., 40B2
Mount Pinos, Mt., 31aD2
Mount Pleasant, 35E2
Mount Rainier, Mt., 31aC.
Mount Ratz, Mt., 42A5,6
Mount Robson, Mt., 31D8,9
Mount Roraima, Mt., 37B3,4
Mount Saint Elias, Mt., 31C7
Mount Saint Helens, Vol., 31aA1
Mount's Bay, B., 9D,E2
Mount Shasta, Mt., 31aB1
Mount Sidley, Mt., 42G12,13
Mount Victoria, Mt., 40A4
Mount Waddington, Mt., 31D8,9
Mount Wells, Mt., 40B2
Mount Whitney, Mt., 31aC.
Mount Woodroffe, Mt., 40C2,3
Moura (Brazil), 38C3
Moura (Portugal), 11G2
Mourdiah, 29B4
Mourné, R., 7D4
Mourne Mountains, Mts., 7D4,5
Moyale, 28D6
Moyamba, 29C2
Moyle (21), Admin. U., 10D6
Moyobamba, 38C2

Možajsk, 17C5
Mozambique, St., 30C,D4
Mozambique Channel, 30C,D4,5
Mozdok, 18D5
Mozyr', 18B2
Mpanda, 30B4
Mpika, 30C4
M'Sila, 27aA1
Mtwara, 30C5
Muang Khammouan, 22C6
Muar, 19bC,D3
Muarabungo, 23D2
Mubi, 29C9
Mucusso, 30C3
Mudanjiang, 24B6
Mudanjiang, R., 25B4
Mudanya, 21aA1
Mufulira, 30C3
Muğla, 21aB1
Muhammad Qawl, 28B6
Mui Bai-Bung, C., 22D6
Mujezerskij, 17B4
Mukačevo, 18C1
Mukden see Shenyang
Mulan, 15A4
Mulengzhen, 25B5
Mulhacén, Mt., 5D4
Mülheim, 12aA2,3
Mülhouse, 11C4
Mulinghe, R., 25A5
Mull, I., 7C4,5
Mullet Peninsula, Pen., 7D2
Mullewa, 40C1
Mullingar, 10E6
Mull of Galloway, C., 7D5
Mull of Kintyre, C., 7D5
Mulobezi, 30C3
Multán, 22A3
Mumra, 18D6
München, 12C3,4
Muncie, 35C3,4
Mungbere, 28D5
Munger, 22aB3
Munich see München
Münster, 12C2
Muonio, 15A7,8
Muqdisho, 28D7
Mur, R., 12D4
Muradiye, 21aB4
Muraşi, 17C7
Murat, R., 21aB4
Muratkovo, 17aB3
Murchison, R., 40C1
Murcia, 11G3
Murcia (14), Admin. U., 11G3
Mureşul, R., 14B3
Murgab, 24C1
Murgab see Morghāb
Murkong Selek, 22B5
Murmansk, 16C5
Murom, 17C6
Muroran, 25B7
Murray, R., 40D4
Murray Bridge, 40D3,4
Murrumbidgee, R., 40D4
Mururoa, I., 41F12
Murwāra, 22aC2
Muş, 21aB4
Musa, Mt., 5aB3
Musala, Mt., 5C7
Musan, 25B4
Mūs'a Qal'eh, 21C8
Musgrave Ranges, Mts., 40C3
Musi, R., 23D2
Muskegon, 35C3
Muskogee, 35D1

Musoma, 30B4
Musselburgh, 10C3
Mustafakemalpaşa, 14C,D3,4
Mustvee, 17C3
Müt, 28B5
Mutare, 30C4
Mutnyj Materik, 17A8
Mutton Bay, 33C14
Mutuali, 30C4
Muzaffarpur, 22aB3
Mwanza (Tanzania), 30B4
Mwanza (Zambia), 300B3
Mwaya, 30B4
Mweelrea, Mt., 7E2,3
Mweka, 30B3
Mwene-Ditu, 30B3
Myanaung, 22C5
Myeik, 22C5
Myeik Kyunzu, 22C,D5
Myingyan, 22B5
Myitkyinä, 22B5
Myla, 17A8
Mymensingh, 22aB4
Mys Arktičeskij, C., 16A10-12
Mys Čel'uskin, 16B12,13
Mys Čel'uskin, C., 19B12-14
Mys Dežneva, C., 19B,C20
Mys Fligeli, C., 42D5,26
Mys Kriljon, C., 25A7
Mys Lopatka, C., 19D17,18
Mys Navarin, C., 42B1
Mysore, 22C3
Mys Saryč, C., 18D3
Mys Šmidta, 16B20
Mys Želanija, 16B8
My-Tho, 22C6
Mytišči, 17C5
Mzuzu, 30C4

N

Naas, 10E6
Nabeul, 27aA3
Nabire, 23D5
Nabq, 21D2
Nābulus, 20bB1
Nacala, 30C5
Nachičevan, 16F6
Nachingwea, 30C4
Nachodka, 16E15
Nadon, 11H3
Nadvoicy, 17B4
Nadvornaja, 18C1
Nadym, 166C9
Næstved, 12B3
Naft-e Safid, 21C5,6
Naga, 23B4
Nāgāland (4), Admin. U., 22B5
Nagano, 25C6
Nagaoka, 25C6
Nāgappattinam, 22aB2,3
Nagar Pārkar, 22B3
Nagasaki, 25C4
Nagatino, 17b
Nāgercoil, 20aB2
Nagorno-Karabakh Autonomous Region (9), Admin. U., 18aB2
Nagorsk, 17C8
Nagoya, 25C6
Nágpur, 22B3
Nagqu, 24C3
Nagykanizsa, 14B1
Naha, 24D6

Nähded, 22C3
Nahr al-Āsī, R., 20bA,B2
Nahr al-Khābūr, R., 20bA,B3
Na'īn, 21C6
Nairn, 10B3
Nairobi, 30B4
Najin, 25B5
Nakhichevan Autonomous Soviet Socialist Republic (5), Admin. U., 18aB2
Nakhon Ratchasima, 22C6
Nakhon Sawan, 22C5,6
Nakhon Si Thammarat, 22D5,6
Nakina, 33C11
Naknek, 33C4
Nakskov, 12B3
Nakuru, 30B4
Nal'čik, 18D5
Nālūt, 28A4
Namacunde, 30C2
Namangan, 16E9
Namapa, 30C4,5
Namche Bazar, 22aB3
Nam-Dinh, 22B6
Namib Desert, Des., 26F,G6
Namibe, 30C2
Namibia, Admin. U., 30C,D2
Namlea, 23D4
Nampa, 34C3
Namp'o, 25C3,4
Nampula, 30C4
Namsos, 15B4
Nam Tok, 22C5
Namuhu, L., 24C3
Namur, 11B4
Nanaimo, 33aB2
Nanchang, 24D5
Nanchong, 24C4
Nancy, 11B4
Nanded, 30B2
Ndjamena, 28C4
Ndola, 30C3
Neah Bay, 33aB2
Néa Páfos, 19cB1
Neápolis, 14D2
Neath, 9D3
Nebit-Dag, 21B6
Nebolči, 17C4
Nebraska, Admin. U., 34C6,7
Neches, R., 35E2
Necochea, 39B2,3
Neene, 35C6
Nefta, 27aB2
Neftegorsk, 18B7
Neftekamsk, 17aB1,2
Neftekumsk, 18D5,6
Negeri Sembilan (5), Admin. U., 19bC3
Negombo, 20aC2
Negro (Amazonas), R., 37C3
Negro (Atlantic Ocean), R., 37F3
Negro (Uruguay), R., 39aD2,3
Negros, I., 23C4
Neijiang, 24D4
Nei Mongol Zizhiqu (2), Admin. U., 24B4-6
Neisse see Nysa Lužicka
Neiva, 38B2
Nejva, R., 17aB3
Nelidovo, 17C4
Nellore, 22C3,4
Nelson, 40aB2
Nelson, R., 33C10
Néma, 28C2
Neman, R., 18B2
Nemuro, 25B8

Naryn (Abakan), 24A3
Naryn (Alma-Ata), 24B1
Naryn, R., 24B1
Nashville-Davidson, 35D3
Nāsik, 22B,C3
Nassau, 35F5
Nassau, I., 41E9
Nässjö, 15D5
Natal (Brazil), 38C6
Natal (Sumatera), 19bD1
Natal, Admin. U., 30D3,4
Natchez, 35E2
Nateva Bay, B., 41bA2,3
Natitingou, 29C6
Nauru, St., I., 41C6
Nauški, 16D12
Nausori, 41bA2
Nauta, 38C2
Navan, 10E6
Navarra (15), Admin. U., 11F3
Naviti, I., 41bA1
Navfa, 18B3
Navoi, 21A9
Návplion, 14D2
Navrongo, 29C5
Navua, 41bB2
Nawābshāh, 22B2
Náxos, I., 14D3
Nayarit (17), Admin. U., 36B2
Nāy Band, 21D6
Nayoro, 25B7
Nazaré, 38D6
N'azepetrovsk, 17aB2
Nazerat, 20bB1
Nazilli, 21aB1
Nazret, 28D6
Nazwä, 21E7
N'Dalatando, 30B2

page 212

Pinang (9), Admin. U., 19bB2
Pınarbaşı, 21aB3
Pinar del Río, 36aA1,2
Píndhos, Óros, Mts., 5C,D7
Pine Bluff, 35E2
Pine Creek, 40B3
Pinega, 17B6
Pinega, R., 17B7
Pine Point, 33B8
Pinghu, 19aA3
Pingliang, 24C4
P'ingtung, 25aB2
Pingxiang, 24D4
Piniós, R., 14D2
Pinsk, 18B2
Pin'ug, 17B7
Pioche, 34D4
Piombino, 13B2
Piotrków Trybunalski, 12C5
Pipestone, 34C7
Pipestone, R., 35A2
Pipinas, 39aE2
Piquiri, R., 99aB3
Piracicaba, 39aB4
Pirapora, 38D5
Pir'atin, 18B5
Pirgos, 14D2
Piripiri, 38C5
Pirot, 13B5
Pisa, 13B2
Pisagua, 38D2
Pisco, 38D2
Písek, 12C4
Pisogne, 13aA4
Pistoia, 13A,B2
Pisuerga, R., 11F2,3
Pita, 29C2
Pitcairn Island, I., 41F12
Pitea, 15B7
Piteälven, R., 15B6,7
Pitești, 14B3
Pitlochry, 10B3
Pittsburgh, 35C4,5
Pittsfield, 35C6
Piura, 38C1,2
Plain of France, Pl., 5C4,5
Plain of Hungary, Pl., 5C6,7
Plain of Po, Pl., 13a
Plainview, 34E6
Planalto do Mato Grosso, Plat., 37D4
Plasencia, 11F2
Plast, 17aC3
Plateau (17), Admin. U., 29C8
Plateau of Iran, Plat., 19F7
Plateau of Shotts, Plat., 5D5
Plato Usť Urt, Plat., 19E7
Platte, R., 34C7
Platte Island, I., 27E10
Plattsburgh, 35C6
Plauen, 12C4
Plavsk, 18B4
Pleseck, 17B6
Pleven, 14C3
Pleven (12), Admin. U., 14C3
Ploče see Kardeljevo
Płock, 12B5
Ploiești, 14B3
Plovdiv, 14C3
Plovdiv (13), Admin. U., 14C3
Plymouth (Lesser Antilles), 36bA2

Plymouth (U.K.), 9D2,3
Plynlimon, Mt., 7E5,6
Plzeň, 12C4
Pô, 29C5
Po, R., 13A1
Pobé, 29D6
Pocatello, 34C4
Poços de Caldas, 39aB4
Podkamennaja Tunguska, R., 16C,D11,12
Podoľsk, 17C5
Podor, 29A2
Podporožje, 17B4
Pogradec, 13B5
Pograničnyj, 25B5
P'ohang, 25C4
Pohnpei, I., 41C5,6
Point Barrow, C., 31B4,5
Pointe-à-Pitre, 36bA2
Pointe des Almadies, C., 26C2,3
Pointe du Raz, C., 11C1
Pointe-Noire, 30B2
Point Hope, 33B3
Poitiers, 11C3
Pokhara, 22aA2,3
Pok Liu Chao, I., 19aB3
Pokrovsk-Uraľskij, 17aA2
Poland, St., 12B4-6
Poľarnyj, 17A4
Polatlı, 21aB2
Pole of Inaccessibility, 42G,H30-33
Polesje, Reg., 5B7
Polevskoj, 17aB3
Pólis, 19cA1
Polock, 17C3
Pologi, 18C4
Poltava, 18C3
Polunočnoje, 6A10,11
Poluostrov Jamal, Pen., 16B8,9
Poluostrov Kamčatka, Pen. 16C,D17,18
Poluostrov Kanin, Pen., 17A6,7
Poluostrov Tajmyr, Pen., 16B10-12
Polynésia, Arch., 41A-F8-11
Pomeranian Bay see Zatoka Pomorska
Pomorie, 14C3
Pomozdino, 17B8
Pompano Beach, 35F4,5
Ponca City, 34D7
Ponce, 36bA2
Pondicherry, 22C3,4
Pondicherry (11), Admin. U., 22C3
Pond Inlet, 33A12
Ponérihouen, 41aA1
Ponferrada, 11F2
Ponoj, R., 17A5
Ponorogo, 23aA,B2
Ponta Delgada, 11aB3,4
Ponta Grossa, 39A4
Ponta Porã, 38E4
Pontevedra, 11F1
Pontiac, 33b
Pontianak, 23D2
Pontivy, 11B2
Pontoise, 11B3
Pontremoli, 13aB3,4
Pontypool, 9D3
Pontypridd, 9D3
Poole, 9D3,4
Popayan, 38B2
Poplar, 9a
Poplar Bluff, 35D2

Popondetta, 41D4
Poprad, 12C6
Porangatu, 28D4,5
Porbandar, 22B2
Porcupine, R., 33B5
Pordenone, 13A3
Pori, 15C7
Porpoise Bay, B., 42F24
Porsangen, B., 15A8
Portadown, 10D6
Portage-la-Frairie, 34A7
Port Alberni, 33aB2
Portalegre, 11G2
Portalegre (12), Admin. U., 11G2
Port Alfred, 30E3
Port-Alice, 33aA1
Port Angeles, 33aB,C2
Port Arthur, 35F2
Port Augusta, 40D3
Port-au-Prince, 36C5
Port Austin, 33C4
Port Blair, 22C5
Port Burwell, 33B13
Port Canaveral, 35F4,5
Port-Cartier, 33C13
Port Elizabeth, 30E3
Port Ellen, 10C1,2
Port-Gentil, 30B1
Port Harcourt, 29D7
Port Hardy, 33C7
Porthcawl, 9D3
Port Henry, 33b
Porthmadog, 9C2,3
Port Huron, 35C4
Port-Ilič, 18aB2
Portimão, 11G1
Portland (Australia), 40D3,4
Portland (U.S.A., Maine), 35C6,7
Portland (U.S.A., Oregon), 34B2
Port Laoise, 10E6
Port Lincoln, 40D3
Port Loko, 29C2
Port Louis, 30aB3
Port Macquarie, 40D5
Port Moresby, 41D4
Port Nelson, 33C10
Port Nolloth, 30D2
Porto, 11F1
Porto (13), Admin. U., 11F1
Pôrto Alegre, 39A3,4
Porto Amboim, 30C2
Porto Armuelles, 36D4
Pôrto Artur, 38D4
Porto Barrios, 36C4
Porto Cortés, 36D4
Porto de San José, 36C3
Porto Esperança, 38D,E4
Portoferraio, 13B2
Port of Spain, 38E4
Portogruaro, 13aA6
Pôrto Inglês, 28aB2
Portomaggiore, 13aB5
Pôrto Nacional, 38D5
Porto-Novo, 29D6
Porto Tolle, 13aB6
Porto Torres, 13B2
Pôrto União, 39aC3
Pôrto Valter, 38C2
Porto-Vecchio, 11D5
Pôrto Velho, 38C3
Portoviejo, 38C1,2

Port Pirie, 40D3
Port Radium see Echo Bay
Portree, 10B1
Port Renfrew, 33aB2
Port Rowan, 35C4
Port Said see Bûr Sa'îd
Port Shepstone, 30E4
Portsmouth (U.K.), 9D4
Portsmouth (U.S.A., Ohio), 35D4
Portsmouth (U.S.A., Virginia), 35D5
Port Sudan see Bûr Südān
Port Talbot, 9D3
Port Townsend, 33aB3
Portugal, St., 11F,G1,2
Posadas, 39A3
Pošechonje-Volodarsk, 17C5
Posjet, 25B5
Poso, 23D4
Postojna, 13A3
Potenza, 13B3
Potgietersrus, 30D3
Poti, 18D5
Potiskum, 29C8
Po Toi Group., Is., 19aB3
Potomac, R., 35D5
Potosí, 38D3
Potrerillos, 39A2
Potsdam, 12B4
Potsdam (12), Admin. U., 12B4
Pouso Alegre (Cáceres), 38D4
Pouso Alegre (Rio de Janeiro), 39aB4
Povoação, 11aB4
Povorino, 18B5
Povungnituk, 33B12
Powder, R., 34B5
Powell River, 33aB2
Power Houses Beaharnois, 33b
Power Houses Moses-Saunders, 33b
Powys (52), Admin. U., 9C3
Poyanghu, L., 24D5
Poza Rica de Hidalgo, 36B3
Poznań, 12B5
Pozoblanco, 11G2
Prague see Praha
Praha, 12C4
Prahovo, 13A5
Praia, 28aB2
Praia da Vitória, 11aA3
Prato, 13B2
Praya, 23aB4
Přerov, 12C5
Prescott, 34E4
Presidente Epitácio, 38E4
Presidente Prudente, 39aB3
Prešov, 12C6
Presque Isle, 35B7
Presqu'île de Taiarapu, C., 41dB2
Preston, 9C3
Pretoria, 30D3
Pribeľskij, 17aC2
Prieska, 30D3
Prijedor, 13A4

page 217

Rafsanjān, 21C6,7
Raga, 28D5
Ragusa, 13C3
Rahīmyār Khān, 22B3
Raiatea, I., 41E10
Rainy Lake, L., 35B2
Raipur, 22B4
Raisin, R., 33b
Rājahmundry, 22C4
Rajapalaiyam, 20aB2
Rājasthān, Admin. U., 22B3
Rājkot, 22B3
Rājshāhi, 22aB4
Rakahanga, I., 41D,E9
Rakvere, 17C3
Raleigh, 35D5
Rambi, I., 41bA3
Rāmhormoz, 21C5,6
Ramon', 18B4
Rāmpur, 22aA1
Ramsey, 9B2
Ramsgate, 9D5
Rana, 15B5
Rancagua, 39B1
Rānchī, 22B4
Randers, 12A3
Ranger, 34E7
Rangoon, 22C5
Rangpur, 22aB4
Rantauprapat, 23C1,2
Ranua, 15B8
Rapa, I., 41F11
Rapallo, 13aB3
Rapid City, 34C6
Rāpti, R., 22aB2
Rarotonga, I., 41F9
Ra's ad Daqm, 21F7
Ras Addar, C., 21aB3
Ra's al-Hadd, C., 21E8
Ra's al-Khaymah, 21D6,7
Ra's al-Unūf, 28A4
Ra's an-Naqb, 20bC1,2
Rās Asir, C., 26C10
Ras Ben Sekka, C., 28A3,4
Ras Dashen, Mt., 26C8
Ras Gharib, 28B6
Rās Hafūn, C., 26C10
Rashīd, 26aA2
Rasht, 21B5
Raso, I., 28aA1
Rás Sabartīl, C., 5aB1,2
Rathlin Island, I., 7D4
Ratingen, 12aB2
Ratlām, 22B3
Ratnapura, 20aC3
Rauma, 15C7
Raurkela, 22B4
Rava-Russkaja, 18B1
Ravenna, 13A3
Ravensthorpe, 40D2
Rāvi, R., 22A3
Rāwalpindi, 22A3
Rawāndūz, 21aB4
Rawlinna, 40D2
Rawson, 39C2
R'azan', 16D5,6
Razdol'noje, 16aB1
Razgrad, 14C3
Razgrad (14), Admin. U., 14C3
R'ažsk, 18B5
Reading (U.K.), 9D4
Reading (U.S.A.), 35C5
Reboly, 17B4
Rebun-jima, I., 25A6,7
Rečica, 18B3
Recife, 38C6
Recklinghausen, 12aA3
Reconquista, 39aC2
Redcar, 9B4

Red Deer, 33C8
Red Deer, R., 33C8
Redding, 34C2
Redditch, 9C4
Redeyef, 27aB2
Red Lake, L., 35B2
Redon, 11C2
Red (Mississippi), R., 34E6
Red (Winnipeg, L.) R., 34A7
Red Sea, 28B,C6,7
Redstone, 33aA2
Reed City, 35C3
Regaia, 5aB2
Regensburg, 12C4
Reggane, 28B3
Reggio di Calabria, 13C3,4
Reggio-nell'Emilia, 13A2
Regina, 33C9
Rehoboth, 30D2
Reigate, 9D4,5
Reims, 11B3,4
Reindeer Lake, L., 33C9
Reinosa, 11F2
Reliance, 33B9
Rembang, 23aA2
Remscheid, 12aB3
Renfrew, 33b
Reni, 14B4
Renmore, 33b
Rennell Island, I., 40B5,6
Rennes, 11B2
Reno, 34D3
Reno, R., 13aB5
Reo, 23D4
Represa de Furnas, Res., 38E5
Represa Itaipu, Res., 39aB,C3
Represa Tucuruí, Res., 38C4,5
Republic, 34B3
Republican, R., 34C6,7
Republic of Korea, St., 25C4
Requena, 11G3
Réservoir Cabonga, Res., 35B5
Réservoir Gouin, Res., 33D12
Réservoir Lagdo, Res., 29C9
Réservoir Mbakaou, Res., 29D9
Reshui, 24C3,4
Resistencia, 39A2,3
Reşiţa, 14B2
Resolute, 33A10
Resolution Island, I., 33B13
Restinga, 5aB3
Réthimnon, 14E3
Réunion, Admin. U., I., 30aB1,2
Reus, 11F4
Reut, R., 18C2
Revda, 17aB2,3
Revelstoke, 33C8
Rewa, 22aB2
Rexford, 34B3,4
Rey, 21B6
Rey Bouba, 29C9
Reyes, 38D3
Reykjavik, 15aB2
Reynosa, 36B3
Rež, R., 17aB3
Rēzekne, 17C3
Rhein, R., 12D3

Rheinland-Pfalz (8), Admin. U., 12C2
Rhin (Bas-) (67), Admin. U., 11B4
Rhin (Haut-) (68), Admin. U., 11C4
Rhode Island, (R.I.), Admin. U., 35C6
Rhodope Mountains, Mts., 5C7
Rhondda, 9D3
Rhône (69), Admin. U., 11C4
Rhône, R., 11C4
Rhourd-el-Baguel, 28A3
Rhum, I., 7C4
Rhyl, 9C3
Ribadeo, 11F2
Ribble, R., 7E6
Ribe, 12B3
Ribeira Grande, 28aA1
Ribeirão Prêto, 38E5
Riberalta, 38D3
Richmond, 35D5
Ridgeway, 34D5
Riesa, 12C4
Rieti, 13B3
Rifstangi, C., 15aA3,4
Riga, 16D4
Riihimäki, 15C7,8
Rijeka, 13A3
Rijn see Rhein
Rikaze, 24D2
Rikers Island, I., 32a
Rimini, 13A3
Rîmnicu-Vîlcea, 14B3
Rincon, 34E5
Ringerike, 15C4
Ringvassøya, I., 15A6
Rio Balsas, 36C3
Riobamba, 38C2
Rio Branco, 38C3
Río Cuarto, 39B2
Rio de la Plata, B., 37F4
Rio de Janeiro, 39A4
Rio de Janeiro (17), Admin. U., 39A4
Rio do Sul, 39aC4
Río Gallegos, 39D2
Río Grande, 39B3
Río Grande, 39D2
Rio Grande, R., 34E5
Rio Grande de Santiago, R., 36B2
Rio Grande do Norte (18), Admin. U., 38C6
Rio Grande do Sul, Admin. U., 39A3
Ríohacha, 38A2
Rio Negro, 39aC3,4
Río Negro, Admin. U., 39B,C1,2
Rioni, R., 18D5
Ripon, 9B4
Rishiri-tō, I., 25A7
Riva, 13aA4
Rivadavia, 37E3
Rivera, 39aD2
Rivers (18), Admin. U., 29D7
Riverside, 34D4
Rivière à Pierre, 33b
Rivière des Prairies, R., 33b
Rivière-du-Loup, 35B7
Rize, 21aA4
Rizokárpason, 19cA3
Rižskij Zaliv, B., 17C2
Road Town, 36bA1

Roanne, 11C4
Roanoke, 35D4,5
Roanoke, R., 35D5
Robertsport, 29D3
Roboré, 38D4
Rocas Formigas, I., 11aB4
Rocha, 39aD3
Rochdale, 9C3,4
Rochefort, 11C2
Roches Douvres, Is., 6aA2
Rochester (U.S.A., Minnesota), 35C2
Rochester (U.S.A., New York), 35C5
Rock Bay, 33aB1,2
Rockford, 35C2,3
Rockhampton, 40C5
Rock Hill, 35E4
Rockingham, 40D1
Rock Island, 35C2,3
Rock Springs, 34C5
Rocky Mountains, Mts., 31D-F8-10
Rødby, 12B3
Rodez, 11C3
Ródhos, 14D3,4
Ródhos, I., 14D3,4
Rodrigues, I., 26F11
Roebourne, 40C1
Rohtak, 22B3
Roja, 17C2
Rojas, 39aD1
Rokan, R., 19bD2
Rokel, R., 29C2
Roma (Australia), 40C4
Roma (Italy), 13B3
Romagnano Sesia, 13aA2
Roman, 14B3
Romania, St., 14B2,3
Romanovka, 16bB3
Romans, 11C4
Romblon, 23bB2
Rome (U.S.A., Georgia), 35E3,4
Rome (U.S.A., New York), 33b
Rome see Roma
Romny, 18B3
Ronda, 11G2
Rondônia, 38D3
Rondônia, Admin. U., 38D3
Rondonópolis, 38D4
Rønne, 15E5
Ronne Ice Shelf, 42G6
Roosevelt, R., 38C3
Roosevelt Island, I., 42G17-19
Roper, R., 40B3
Roque, 34a
Roraima, Admin. U., 38B3
Røros, 15C4
Rosalia, 33aC4
Rosario (Argentina), 39B2
Rosario (Azores), 11aA1
Rosario (Mexico), 34F5
Roscommon, 10E5
Roscommon, Admin. U., 10E5
Roscrea, 10E6
Roseau, 36bB2
Roseburg, 34C2
Rosenheim, 12D3,4
Rosignol, 38B4
Roşiori-de-Vede, 14B3
Roskilde, 12B4
Rosl'atino, 17C6

Toledo (U.S.A., Oregon), 34C2
Tolga, 27aB2
Toliara, 30D5
Toljatti, 18B6
Tolna (16), Admin. U., 14B1
Tolob, 10a
Toluca, 36C2,3
Tomakomai, 25B7
Tomaszów Mazowiecki, 12C6
Tombara, I., 41D5
Tombouctou, 29A5
Tombua, 30C2
Tomini, 23C4
Tomo, R., 38B3
Tom Price, 40C1
Tomsk, 16D10
Tone, R., 25C7
Tonekábon, 21B6
Tonga, St., Is., 41E,F8
Tongareva see Penrhyn
Tongatapu Group, Is., 41F8
T'ongch'ŏn, 25C4
Tongchuan, 24C4
Tonghua, 25D2
Tongjosŏn-man, B., 25C4
Tongliao, 24B6
Tongling, 25D2
Tongtianhe, R., 24C3
Tongue, 10A2
Tongyu, 25B3
Tongxian, 25C2
Tônlé Sab, L., 22C6
Tonsberg, 15D4
Toora-Chem, 24A3
Toowoomba, 40C5
Topeka, 35D1
Topolobampo, 36B2
Torbat-e Heydárieh, 21B7,8
Torino, 13A1
Torlino, 17aB3
Tormes, R., 11F2
Torneälven, R., 15B7
Torneträsk, L., 15A6,7
Toronto, 33D11,12
Toropec, 17F4
Toros Dağlari, Mts., 19F5
Torquay, 9D3
Torre del Greco, 13B3
Torrelavega, 11F2
Torreón, 36B2
Tôrres, 39A3
Torres Novas, 11G1
Torres Strait, Str., 40A,B4
Torsby, 15C5
Tortoli, 13C2
Tortona, 13aB2
Tortosa, 11F4
Toruń, 12B5
Tory Island, I., 10D5
Toržok, 17C4
Toscana (16), Admin. U., 13B2
Tosno, 17C4
Tostado, 39A2
Tosya, 21aA2
Tot'ma, 17C6
Totoya, I., 41bB3
Tottori, 25C5
Touba (Ivory Coast), 29C4
Touba (Senegal), 29B2
Tougan, 29B5
Touggourt, 28A3
Toukoto, 29B3

Toul, 11B4
Toulépleu, 29D3
Toulon, 11D4
Toulouse, 11D3
Toungoo, 22C5
Tourcoing, 11B3
Tours, 11C3
Townbridge, 9D3
Townsville, 40B4
Toyama, 25C6
Toyohashi, 25D6
Toyota, 25C6
Tozeur, 28A3
Trabzon, 21aA3
Tracade, 35B7
Tracadie, 35B7
Trail, 33D8
Tralee, 10E5
Tramore, 15E6
Trang, 22D5
Transantarctic Mountains, Mts., 42G,H
Trans-Carpathian Region (11), Admin. U., 18C3
Transkei, Admin. U., 30E3,4
Transvaal, Admin. U., 30D3,4
Trapani, 13C3
Traverse City, 35C3,4
Trby, 35C6
Trebbia, R., 13aB3
Treinta y Tres, 39aD3
Trelew, 39C2
Trelleborg, 15E5
Tremadoc Bay, B., 7E5
Tremp, 11F4
Trenčin, 12C5
Trent, R., 7E7
Trentino-Alto Adige (17), Admin. U., 13A2
Trento, 13A2
Trenton (Canada), 33b
Trenton (U.S.A.), 35C,D6
Tres Arroyos, 39aE1
Três Lagoas, 38E4
Treviso, 13A2
Trichúr, 20aB2
Trier, 12C2
Trieste, 13A3
Trikala, 14D2
Trikomon, 19cA2
Trim, 10E6
Trincomalee, 20aB3
Trinidad (Bolivia), 38D3
Trinidad (Cuba), 36aB3,4
Trinidad (Uruguay), 39aD2
Trinidad (U.S.A.), 34D5,6
Trinidad, I., 37A3,4
Trinidad and Tobago, St., 38A3,4
Trinity, R., 34E7
Tripoli see Tarábulus
Tripura (5), Admin. U., 22B5
Tristan da Cunha Group, Is., 3
Trivandrum, 22D3
Trnava, 12C5
Trogir, 13B4
Troick, 17aC3
Troicko-Pečorsk, 17B9
Trois-Rivières, 33D12
Trollhättan, 15D5
Trombetas, R., 38B4
Tromsø, 15A6

Trondheim, 15C4
Trondheimsfjorden, B., 15C4
Troon, 10C2
Troy, 35E3
Troyes, 11B4
Trujillo, 38C2
Trujillo, 11G2
Truk Islands, Is., 41C5
Truro (Canada), 39D13
Truro (U.K.), 9D2
Tsao, 30D3
Tsavo, 30B3
Tshane, 30D3
Tshela, 30B2
Tshikapa, 30B3
Tsu, 25D6
Tsuen Wan, 19aB3
Tsugaru-kaikyō, Str., 25B6,7
Tsumeb, 30C2
Tsuruga, 25C6
Tsuruoka, 25C6
Tsushima, Is., 25D4
Tsushima-kaikyō, Str., 25D4,5
Tual, 23D5
Tuam, 10E5
Tuapse, 18D4
Tuasivi, 41cA1
Tuban, 23aA3
Tubarão, 39aC4
Tübingen, 12C3
Tubruq, 28A5
Tubuai, I., 41F10,11
Tubuai, I., 41F10,11
Tucson, 34E4
Tucumán (22), Admin. U., 39A2
Tucumcari, 34D6
Tucupita, 38B3
Tucuruí, 38C4,5
Tudela, 11F3
Tudmur, 20bB2
Tuen Mun, 19aB2
Tugela Falls, Fs., 26G7,8
Tuguegarao, 23B4
Tuktoyaktuk, 33B6
Tula, 16D5
Tulare, 34D3
Tulcea, 14B4
Tulčin, 18C2
Tullahoma, 35D3
Tullamore, 10E6
Tulle, 11C3
Tuloma, R., 17A4
Tulsa, 35D1
Tulufan, 24B2
Tulun, 16Bb1
Tulungagung, 23aB2
Tumaco, 38C1
Tumannyj, 17A5
Tumbes, 38C1
Tumen, 16D8
Tumenjiang, R., 25B4,5
Tummo, 28B4
Tunas de Zara, 36aB3,4
Tunbridge, 9D5
Tunbridge Wells, 9D5
Tundža, R., 14C3
Tunis, 28A3,4
Tunisia, St., 28A3,4
Tunja, 38B2
Tunxi, 25E2
Tuotuo Heyan, 24C3
Tupelo, 35E3
Tupiza, 38E3
Tura, 16C12
Tura, R., 17aB3

Turanskaja Nizmennosť, Pl., 19E,F7,8
Turbat, 22B2
Turbo, 38B2
Turda, 14B2
Turgutlu, 14D3
Turia, R., 11G3
Terib'orka, 15A10
Turin see Torino
Turinsk, 17aB3
Turka (RSFSR), 16bB2
Turka (U.S.S.R.), 18C1
Turkey, St., 21aA,B1-4
Turkmen Soviet Socialist Republic, Admin. U., 16F7,8
Turks and Caicos Islands, Admin. U., 32G13,14
Turku, 15C7
Turnu-Măgurele, 14C3
Turtle Lake, 35B2
Turuchansk, 16C10,11
Tuscaloosa, 35E3
Tušino, 17b
Tuticorin, 20aB2
Tutrakan, 14B,C3
Tuttlingen, 12D3
Tutuila, I., 41cB3
Tuvalu, St., Is., 41D,E7
Tuxtla, 36C3
Túy, 11F1
Tuz Gölü, L., 21aB2
Tuzla, 13A4
Tyler, 35E1
Tymovskoje, 16D16
Tynda, 16D14
Tyne, R., 7D6,7
Tyne and Wear (5), Admin. U., 9B4
Tynemouth, 9B4
Tyrnyauz, 18D5
Tyrrhenian Sea, 13B,C2,3
Tywi, R., 7F5
Tywyn, 9C2
Tweed, R., 7D6
Twin Falls, 34C3,4

U

Uad Atui, R., 28B1
Uaupés, R., 38B3
Ubagan, R., 17aC3
Ubangi, R., 28D5
Úbeda, 11G3
Uberaba, 38D5
Uberlândia, 38D5
Ubinas, Mt., 37D2
Ubon Ratchathani, 22C6
Ubundi, 30B3
Ucayali, R., 37C2
Uchta, 16C7
Udaipur, 22B3
Uda, R., 16bB3
Uddevalla, 15D4
Uddjaur, L., 15B6
Udine, 13A3
Udmurt Autonomous Soviet Socialist Republic, Admin. U., 17C8
Udon Thani, 22C6
Uele, R., 28D5
Uelen, 16c20,21
Uelzen, 12B3
Ufa, 16D7
Ufa, R., 17aB2
Uganda, St., 30B4
Uglič, 17C5

Verchnij Baskunčak, 18C6
Verchnij Ufalej, 17aB3
Verchojansk, 16C15
Verchojanskij Chrebet, Mts., 19B,C14,15
Verchoturje, 17aB3
Verchovazje, 17B6
Verden, 12B3
Verdun (Canada), 33b
Verdun (France), 11B4
Vereeniging, 30D3
Vereščagino, 16C10,11
Verin, 11F2
Vermont, Admin. U., 35C6
Vernon, 34E7
Véroia, 14C2
Verona, 13A2
Versailles, 11B3
Veselovskoje Vodochranilišče, Res., 18C5
Vesjegonsk, 17C5
Vesoul, 11C4
Vesterålen, Is., 15A5,6
Vestfjorden, 15A5,6
Vestmannaeyjar, 15aC2
Vestspitsbergen, I., 42C21,22
Vesuvio, Vol., 5C6
Veszprém, 14B1
Veszprém (18), Admin. U., 14B1
Vetluga, 17C7
Vetluga, R., 17C7
Vetlužskij, 17C7
Viana do Castelo, 11F1
Viana do Castelo (16), Admin. U., 11F1
Viangchan, 22C6
Viareggio, 13B2
Viborg, 12A3
Vicenza, 13A2
Vich, 11F4
Vichigasta, 39A2
Vichy, 11C3
Vicklow Mountains, Mts., 7E4
Vicksburg, 35E2
Victor Harbour, 40D3
Victoria (Austr.), Admin. U., 40D4
Victoria (Canada), 33D7
Victoria (Hong Kong), 19aB3
Victoria (Seychelles), 27E10
Victoria (U.S.A.), 34F7
Victoria, R., 40B3
Victoria Beach, 34A7
Victoria de Las Tunas, 36aB4,5
Victoria Falls, 30C3
Victoria Island, I., 33A,B8,9
Victoria Land, Reg., 42G20,21
Victoria Nile, R., 28D6
Victoria River Downs, 40B3
Victoria Strait, Str., 33A,B9,10
Victoriaville, 33b
Vičuga, 17C6
Vidin, 14C2
Vidin (27), Admin. U., 14C2
Viedma, 39C2
Vienna see Wien
Vienne, 11C4

Vienne (86), Admin. U., 11C3
Vienne (Hautes-) (87), Admin. U., 11C3
Vienne, R., 11C3
Vientiane see Viangchan
Viersen, 12aB1
Vierzon, 11C3
Vietnam, St., 22B,C6
Vigan, 23bA2
Vigevano, 13aA2,3
Vigo, 11F1
Vijayawāda, 22C3,4
Vijosë, R., 13B4,5
Vík, 15aC3
Víkna, I., 15B4
Vila, 41E6
Vila da Ribeira Brava, 28aA1,2
Vila do Porto, 11aB4
Vila Nova de Gaia, 11F1
Vila Real, 11F2
Vila Real (17), Admin. U., 11F2
Vila Real de Santo António, 11G2
Vila Velha, 38E5
Vilejka, 18B2
Vilhelmina, 15B6
Vilhena, 38D3
Vilija, R., 18B2
Viljandi, 17C3
Villa Bittencourt, 38C3
Viljach, 12D4
Villa Dolores, 39B2
Villaguay, 39aD2
Villahermosa, 36C3
Villa María, 39B2
Villa Montés, 38E3
Villarrica, 39A3
Villarrobledo, 11G3
Villavicendo, 38B2
Villena, 11G3
Villeurbanne, 11C4
Vilnius, 16D4
Viľuj, R., 16C13
Viľujsk, 16C14
Vimmerby, 15D5,6
Viña del Mar, 39B1,2
Vinaroz, 11F4
Vincennes, 35D3
Vindelälven, R., 16B6
Vinh, 22C6
Vinh-Long, 22C,D6
Vinkovci, 13A4
Vinnica, 16E4
Vinson Massif, Mt., 42G,H8,9
Virac, 23bB2
Viranşehir, 21aB3
Virginia, 35B2
Virginia, Admin. U., 35D4,5
Virginia Beach, 35D5,6
Virgin Islands, Admin. U., Is., 36bA1
Virovitica, 13A4
Visby, 15D6
Viscount Melville Sound, Str., 33A8-10
Višera, R., 17aA,B2
Viseu, 11F2
Viseu (18), Admin. U., 11F1
Vişeu de Sus, 14B3
Vishākhapatnam, 22C4
Vitebsk, 17C4
Viterbo, 13B3
Viti Levu, I., 41bA2

Vitim, R., 16D13
Vitoria, 11F3
Vitória, 38E5,6
Vitória da Conquista, 38D5
Vittangi, 15B7
Vivero, 11F2
Vizianagaram, 22C4
Vizinga, 17B7
Vladimir, 17C6
Vladimirskij Tupik, 17C4
Vladimir-Volynskij, 18B1
Vladivostok, 16E15
Vlissingen, 12C1
Vloré, 13B4
Vltava, R., 12C4
Vochma, 17C7
Vodla, R., 17B5
Voe, 10a
Voghera, 13aB3
Voh, 41aA1
Voi, 30B4
Voinjama, 29C3
Vojkovo, 16aB1
Vojvodina (6b), Admin. U., 13A4
Voj-Vož, 17B8
Volcán Citlaltépetl, Vol., 31H11
Volcán de Colima, Vol., 31H10
Volcán Guallatiri, Vol., 37D2,3
Volcan Karisimbi, Vol., 26E7,8
Volcán Lanin, Vol., 37F2
Volcán Lascar, Vol., 37E3
Volcán Llullaillaco, Vol., 37E3
Volcano Maipó, Vol., 37F2
Volcano Osorno, Vol., 37G2
Volcán Popocatépetl, Vol., 31H10,11
Volcánsk, 18B4
Volcán Tajumulco, Vol., 31H11,12
Volchov, 17C4
Volchov, R., 17C4
Volga, R., 16D5
Volgo-Baltijskij Kanal, Can., 17B5
Volgodonsk, 18C5
Volgograd, 16E4
Volgogradskoje Vodochranilišče, Res., 18C6
Volkovysk, 18B1
Volnovacha, 18C4
Vologda, 16D5,6
Volonga, 17A7
Vólos, 14D2
Volovo, 18B4
Volsk, 18B6
Volta, R., 29D6
Volta Blanche, R., 29B5
Volta Noire, R., 29C4
Volta Redonda, 39aB4,5
Volta Rouge, R., 29C5
Volžskij, 18C5,6
Vopnafjörður, 15aB4
Vorarlberg (8), Admin. U., 12D3
Voriai Sporádhes, Is., 14D2,3
Vorkuta, 16C8
Voronež, 16D5,6

Vorošilovgrad, 18C4
Vórterkaka Nunatak, Mt., 42G33,34
Vosges (88), Admin. U., 11B,C4
Voss, 15C3
Vostočno-Sibirskoje More, S., 16B16-19
Vostok, Station, 42G26
Vostok Island, I., 41E10
Votkinsk, 17aB1
Votkinskoje Vodochranilišče, Res., 17aB2
Vožajol', 17B8
Vožega, 17B6
Vožgora, 17B7
Voznesensk, 18C3
Vraca, 14C2
Vraca (28), Admin. U., 14C2
Vranje, 13B5
Vrbas, R., 13A4
Vršac, 13A5
Vryburg, 30D3
Vulkan Ključevskaja Sopka, Vol., 19D18
Vung-Tau, 22C6
Vunindawa, 41bA2
Vuoksa, R., 17B3
Vuotso, 15A8
Vya, 34C3
Vyborg, 16C4,5
Vyčegda, R., 17B8
Vychino, 17B5
Východočeský kraj (5), Admin. U., 12C5
Východoslovenský kraj (10), Admin. U., 12C6
Vyksa, 17C6
Vym, R., 17B8
Vyšnij Voločok, 17C4
Vytegra, 17B5

W

Wa, 29C5
Wabash, R., 35D3
Waco, 34E7
Waddān, 28B4
Waddeneilanden, Is., 12B2
Waddenzee, S., 12B2
Wadebridge, 9D2
Wādī an-Natrūn, Depr., 26aB2
Wādī Halfa, 28B6
Wad Madani, 28C6
Wager Bay, 33B10
Wagga Wagga, 40D4
Waha, 28B4
Wahai, 23D4,5
Wahpeton, 34B7
Waialua, 35aB2
Waikato, R., 40aA2
Wailuku, 35aB3,4
Waingapu, 23D4
Wainwright, 33A4
Wajima, 25C6
Wajir, 30D7
Wakayama, 25D6
Wakefield, 9C4
Wake Island, Admin. U., I., 41B6
Wakkanai, 25A7
Wakre, 23D5
Wałbrzych, 12C5
Walcott, 34C5
Wales, 33B3

page 229